Contents

PART 1 Foundations of Learning and Motivation 1

PART 2   Motivational Strategies 73

PART 3   *Behavioral Strategies*...*107*

List of Figures

List of Tables

Preface

Many textbooks are available on how to become a more successful learner. As instructors of a "learning to learn" course, we have been concerned that many students who take such a course to improve their learning and study skills fail to change their behavior during or after the course. We strongly believe that simply telling students how to learn and providing some practice does not necessarily change attitudes, beliefs, or behavior. Changing ineffective learning and study habits is a difficult process, as is losing weight or stopping smoking. This textbook is the result of an instructional program we developed and evaluated with a wide range of college students. We have used the self-regulation approach presented in this text with students in high schools, community colleges, and four-year colleges. The primary purpose of the textbook is to help students change aspects of their motivation and learning strategies.

We place the responsibility for determining what behaviors or beliefs need to be changed on the students, not the instructor. The process of change begins by observing and reflecting on one's own behavior and then determining what needs to be changed and learning how to change. The features of this textbook are designed to identify the components of academic learning that contribute to high achievement, help students learn and practice effective learning and study strategies, and then complete self-regulation studies whereby they are taught a process for improving their academic behavior.

FEATURES OF THE TEXT

We attempt to accomplish our goals by incorporating the following features in the text. First, we identify six components that students need to regulate or manage to become successful learners—motivation, methods of learning, time management, physical and social environment, and monitoring performance. These components serve as the basis for organizing and integrating the content throughout the text. Further, this focus allows for the integration of both motivation and learning strategies. As students learn new learning strategies, they must develop the motivation to use them.

Second, the text begins with an overview of important research and theory to help students understand the reasons why they are asked to use different study and learning strategies in the text. Most study skill textbooks are atheoretical; that is, little, if any, research or theory is presented to students. We believe that learning how to learn is a specific academic specialization based on scientific knowledge, and students should learn this knowledge. Furthermore, we find that students are more motivated to learn when the course is conducted like a "real" academic course and not as a remedial experience.

Third, various Exercises are included in each chapter to help students observe and evaluate their own learning and study skills. In addition, more detailed Follow-Up Activities at the end of each chapter allow students to apply the content to their own academic learning. The primary purpose of these experiences is to encourage self-observation and evaluation.

Fourth, we include Follow-Up Activities that identify a topic for a self-regulation study. The appendices provide information as to how to conduct a self-regulation study (Appendix B) and include two studies conducted by students (Appendix C) in a "learning to learn" course. Note the instructor's evaluation at the end of each self-regulation study. The appendices should be read before students begin their own study.

Fifth, the Student Reflection sections allow students to read about the experiences of other students as they attempt to change their behavior and become more successful students.

Sixth, at the end of each chapter, a review of the specific procedures for using a learning strategy is provided. This section is particularly useful for students when they need a quick review of how to implement a given strategy.

Seventh, the Key Points at the end of each chapter highlight the important ideas presented in each chapter.

Eighth, a Glossary is included, with important terms in bold in the text.

OVERVIEW OF THE CHAPTERS

Unit I of the text includes three chapters. Chapter 1—"Academic Self-Regulation"—identifies the academic components that students need to control to attain their academic goals. In addition, the chapter introduces a four-step process used to change behavior—self-observation and evaluation, goal setting and strategic planning, strategy implementation and monitoring, and strategic-outcome monitoring. This process is used as the basis for conducting a self-regulation study and is explained in depth in Appendix B.

Chapter 2—"Understanding Motivation"—helps students understand how motivation can influence learning behavior. Important exercises are included to help the reader evaluate his or her own motivation.

Chapter 3—"Understanding Learning and Memory"—introduces the information-processing system and explains why students remember and forget information. This chapter emphasizes that the way students learn often determines what they remember.

Unit II of the text focuses on motivational strategies. Chapter 4—"Goal Setting"—instructs students how to write and implement specific goals. This chapter emphasizes that students cannot be motivated unless they have goals to attain in different areas of their life.

Chapter 5—"Self-Regulation of Emotions"—focuses on how to change negative emotions to more positive emotions, managing self-talk and reducing anxiety.

Unit III of the text deals with various behavioral strategies related to academic success. Chapter 6—"Time Management"—explains how students can better manage their time rather than having time manage them. Specific strategies to combat procrastination are presented.

Chapter 7—"Self-Regulation of the Physical and Social Environment"—focuses on improving attention and concentration and structuring productive study environments. In addition, the chapter provides information on how to seek help from instructors and conduct effective group study sessions.

Unit IV of the text introduces important learning and study strategies: "Learning from Course Materials" (Chapter 8), "Learning from Class" (Chapter 9), "Preparing for Exams" (Chapter 10), and "Taking Exams" (Chapter 11). Excerpts are used from textbooks and lectures to help students practice the skills in Chapters 8 and 9. Chapter 10 helps students develop a study plan for each exam, and Chapter 11 provides information about specific strategies for taking objective and essay tests.

WHAT'S NEW IN THE SIXTH EDITION?

There are a few trends in higher education that we acknowledge in the sixth edition. First, more and more non-traditional students are entering colleges and universities. According to the National Center for Education Statistics (NCES), there are a variety of definitions of non-traditional students but in general, it refers to students who start college at 25 years or older. In addition, non-traditional students may work full-time, have dependents, be single parents, attend college part-time, or be first-generation students, among other characteristics. In addressing our readers, we recognize that many of them are non-traditional students. Second, distance education enrollments are consistently increasing (Seaman, Allen, & Seaman, 2018). We discuss how to implement the learning strategies in media-rich environments such as via online flipped instruction. Third, technology plays an increasing role in our lives. In the sixth edition, we continue our emphasis on the positive and negative role of technology in learning situations. There are several free or low-cost mobile applications (apps) available to support learning. We encourage students to locate ones that they like, recognizing that new apps are launched constantly. On the other hand, recent research has focused on the impact of technology and media multitasking—or really, task switching—on our learning and productivity. We discuss the cost of technology-related task switching in multiple chapters.

In the sixth edition, we introduce the following:

- The role of metacognition in self-regulation (Chapter 1)
- The difference between outcome and process goals (Chapter 4)
- Strategies for creating healthy and strategic relationships with instructors (Chapter 7)
- The difference between multitasking and task switching (Chapter 7)
- Strategies for processing information from e-textbooks and videos (Chapter 8)
- Strategies for taking effective notes on PowerPoint slides (Chapter 9)
- Differentiating credible from not credible sources (Appendix A)
- Presenting research with academic integrity (Appendix A)
- Strategies for writing a research paper (Appendix A)
- Strategies for preparing for and delivering effective presentations (Appendix A)

We elaborate and extend the discussion of the following:

- The impact of screen usage on college students' emotional and mental health (Chapter 5)
- Use of technology to manage time (Chapter 6)
- The reasons for test anxiety (Chapter 11)

Based on current research, we update the discussion of the following:

- Criticism of the concept of learning styles (Chapter 3)

The current edition includes a companion website. It includes helpful information for teaching the material, such as sample essay test questions, and provides exercises and experiences for students in addition to those in the text. Our internet-based experiences connect students to valuable resources about topics related to areas of self-regulation. We also encourage students to conduct internet research to go more in depth with the theories and concepts discussed in the chapters. Finally, it includes information on how students can maintain a portfolio to demonstrate their acquisition of learning and study skills and guidelines for helping students complete a self-regulation study of their own academic behavior.

It is suggested that Unit I of the text be covered first to provide a framework for both the content and exercises in the remaining chapters. The remaining chapters can be covered in any order. One of the difficulties in teaching a "learning to learn" course is that one would like to cover many topics during the first two weeks, because everything is important. Unfortunately, all the chapters and topics cannot be taught in the first few weeks. This textbook allows the instructor to sequence the chapters as he or she sees fit.

Finally, we would appreciate reactions from students and instructors concerning the text. Please email the first author at helena.seli@rossier.usc.edu. We welcome your praise and criticism.

Acknowledgments

We would like to acknowledge the following individuals who provided valuable input on this edition of the book: our teaching assistants who contributed a great deal regarding how to teach students to become more successful students; our editor Heather Jarrow, senior editorial assistant Rebecca Collazo, and project manager Lisa Keating, who provided helpful assistance throughout the project; Professors Heidi Andrade, Kent Cameron, Stephanie Marsh, Stan Metzenberg, and Sandra J. Waters for their thoughtful reviews of the textbook; and Dr. Christine Mendoza who created the companion website.

—**Helena Seli**
—**Myron H. Dembo**

Credits

Figure 1.1. Zimmerman, B. J., Bonner, S., & Kovich, R. (1996). *Developing Self-Regulated Learners: Beyond Achievement to Self-Efficacy.* Washington, DC: American Psychological Association. Copyright © 1996 by the American Psychological Association. Adapted with permission.

Figure 2.1. From Covington, M. V., & Roberts, B. (1994). Self-worth and college achievement: Motivational and personality correlates. In R. Pintrich, D. R. Brown, & C. E. Weinstein (Eds.), *Student Motivation, Cognition, and Learning: Essays in Honor of Wilbert J. McKeachie* (pp. 157–187). Hillsdale, NJ: Erlbaum. Reprinted with permission from Erlbaum.

Table 2.1. Ames, C., & Archer, J. (1988). Achievement goals in the classroom: Students' learning strategies and motivation processes. *Journal of Educational Psychology, 80,* 260–267. Copyright © 1988 by the American Psychological Association. Adapted with permission.

Figure 2.2. Pintrich, P. R. (1994). Based on Student motivation in the college classroom. In K. W. Prichard & R. M. Sawyer (Eds.), *Handbook of College Teaching: Theory and Applications* (pp. 23–43). Westport, CT: Greenwood. Adapted with permission.

Figure 2.3. From Hirabayashi, K. (2015). *Motivational Indices and Constructs* [Class handout]. Los Angeles, CA: Rossier School of Education, University of Southern California. Adapted with permission from author.

Figure 3.2. From Bower, G. H., Clark, M. C., Lesgold, A., & Winzenz, D. (1969). Hierarchical retrieval schemes in recall of categorized word lists. *Journal of Memory and Language (Journal of Verbal Learning and Verbal Behavior), 8,* 323–343. Reprinted with permission from Elsevier.

Figure 4.3. From Smith, H. W. (1994). *The 10 Natural Laws of Successful Time and Life Management.* Copyright © 1994 by Hyrum Smith. Reprinted with permission of Grand Central Publishing. All rights reserved.

Figure 6.1. From Covey, S. R. (1990). *The 7 Habits of Highly Effective People.* New York: Simon & Schuster. Adapted with permission from Simon & Schuster.

Table 5.1. Nett, U. E., Goetz, T., & Daniels, L. M. (2010). What to do when feeling bored? Students' strategies for coping with boredom. *Learning and Individual Differences, 20,* 626–638. Reprinted with permission from Elsevier Publishing.

Table 8.1. From Kiewra, K. A., & Dubois, N. F. (1998). *Learning to Learn.* Boston, MA: Allyn & Bacon. Adapted with permission.

Table 10.1. From Van Blerkom, D. L. (2012). *College Study Skills: Becoming a Strategic Learner* (7th ed.). Boston, MA: Wadsworth. Adapted with permission from Wadsworth.

Part 1

Foundations of Learning and Motivation

The purpose of this unit is to explain how you can become a more successful learner by taking charge and regulating your own learning. To accomplish this goal, you need to understand how you learn and the factors that determine your motivation to learn. Learning and motivation are interrelated processes. Simply learning a new skill does not mean that you will use it unless you are motivated to do so. Therefore, our objectives are to present some new learning strategies and to convince you that there are payoffs for using them. These payoffs include the possibility of higher grades, more time to participate in enjoyable activities, and the confidence to become a successful learner in any course. The three chapters in this unit provide a framework for understanding why you need to use different strategies to manage the factors influencing your academic achievement. The remaining units teach you how and when to use these strategies.

Chapter 1 presents a model for **academic self-regulation**, identifying six components that you control—motivation, methods of learning, use of time, physical and social environment, and monitoring performance (Zimmerman & Risemberg, 1997). These components are organized by categories—motivational, behavioral, and learning and study strategies. Finally, a four-step process is described to help you change aspects of your academic career.

Chapters 2 and 3 provide an overview of learning and motivation from a **cognitive** and **social cognitive** perspective. Cognitive psychologists believe that

Academic Self-Regulation: The strategies students use to control the factors influencing their learning.

Cognitive: Explanations of learning and motivation that focus on the role of the learner's mental processes.

Social Cognitive: Explanations of learning and motivation that explain learning and motivation as an interaction between cognitive, behavioral, and contextual factors.

behavior is always based on cognition—an act of knowing or thinking about the situation in which the behavior occurs. As a result, they believe that learning can be explained by how knowledge is processed and organized. This means that the way one learns is an important factor in how much is remembered.

The social cognitive view of learning and motivation focuses on how an individual's internal state (i.e., his or her goals, beliefs, perceptions, and emotions), as well as external, contextual circumstances, influence behavior.

1 Academic Self-Regulation

As readers of this book, you are a diverse group with varied backgrounds and goals. Some of you are beginning your education at a college or university, whereas others have selected a community college. Some of you may have taken college courses last term, whereas others are returning to school after an absence. Some of you are full-time students, whereas others may have significant other responsibilities such as a job and caring for dependents. You may even be taking all your courses online. Some of you are taking a learning and study skills course because it is required, whereas others are enrolled in the course as an elective. Some of you are looking forward to taking the course, whereas others may doubt its usefulness. Wherever you are on your journey as a student, we have one goal: to help all those who read this book become more successful learners. Once you learn how to learn, you can apply these skills to any academic or work setting in which you participate.

Who is a successful learner? Most of us know, read about, or have observed successful and expert individuals in some field or profession (e.g., a musician, athlete, plumber, teacher, or artist). These individuals have special knowledge and skills in a particular field. Similarly, successful learners also possess special knowledge and skills that differentiate them from less successful learners.

Successful students are not simply individuals who know more than others. They also have more effective and efficient learning strategies for accessing and using their knowledge, can motivate themselves, and can monitor and change their behaviors when learning does not occur.

Just as individuals cannot learn to become expert musicians, dancers, or golfers without practice, learning to be a successful learner requires more than simply reading and listening to class lectures. For this reason, you will be asked throughout this book to respond to questions and exercises, and to actually practice some new ways of learning. The key to success is practicing the learning strategies taught here so they become automatic. As you practice, you will be able to learn more material in less time than prior to using these new strategies. Thus, you will learn to study "smarter," not necessarily harder.

Most of you have expertise in some activity or hobby. You have spent considerable effort and persistence in acquiring knowledge and developing your skills, and probably feel competent and motivated to excel. Much of the same self-discipline and self-motivation you apply to your present area(s) of expertise will be needed in your pursuit of academic excellence. After studying this chapter, you will be able to:

- identify specific behaviors that influence the level of academic success;
- use a process to self-regulate your academic behavior.

WHAT IS ACADEMIC SELF-REGULATION?

At one time, it was thought that intelligence was the main factor in determining academic success. After years of research in learning and motivation, educators have found that students can learn how to become more successful learners by using appropriate strategies to manage their motivation, behavior, and learning.

The word self-regulation is a key term in understanding successful learners. Self-regulation involves self-reflective, motivational, and behavioral processes (Zimmerman, 2015). Self-regulated learners control the factors influencing their learning. They establish optimum conditions for learning and remove obstacles that interfere with their learning. Educators use a variety of terms to describe these students (e.g., self-regulated, self-directed, strategic, and active). No matter what term is used, the important factor is that these students find a way to learn. It does not matter if the instructor is a poor lecturer, the textbook is confusing, the test is difficult, the room is noisy, or if multiple exams are scheduled for the same week, successful learners find a way to excel.

Let's look at an example of how one student managed his academic learning:

It was Thursday night and Robert was completing his final preparation for the following day's history exam. On the previous Sunday evening, he developed a plan for how he would prepare for the exam during the week. He identified what he had to learn, how he would study, and when he would accomplish each task. He began his study on Monday, attempting to gain a general understanding of the main ideas and to recall the most important facts. He paraphrased each section of the readings, underlined the important information, and monitored his own progress during study by developing possible questions that might be asked on the exam. While studying Wednesday night, he realized that he had difficulty comparing and contrasting some of the battles discussed in class. Therefore, he decided to develop a chart listing the different battles on top and different characteristics down the side. When he filled in the information on the chart, he found he was better able to answer the questions that might be asked regarding the material.

Around 10 p.m., Thursday, Robert's roommate came home from the library with some friends and began discussing a concert they planned to attend over the weekend. They were finished studying for the night. Robert decided to go to the study lounge down the hall to complete his last hour of studying. He told his friends that he would return for pizza around 11 p.m. As he returned to his study, he noticed some information in his notes that he did not understand. He texted his friend for clarification about the notes.

After another 20 minutes of studying, Robert got tired and started thinking of the double cheese and mushroom pizza he would be eating in a short time. He decided that he needed about 30 minutes to finish his studying for the evening. Therefore, he decided to take a five-minute break and go for a walk. He came back and finished his study for the evening.

What actions did Robert take to ensure optimum learning? First, he established a goal and action plan for how he was going to prepare for the examination. The plan started four days before the exam. Second, he used a variety of learning strategies, such as underlining, developing and answering questions, and making a chart to better compare and contrast the relevant information. In other words, when he found that he was not learning, he did something about it by changing his learning strategy. Third, he monitored his understanding of the material as he studied. He changed learning strategies and asked for help when he failed to understand his notes. Fourth, when his friends returned from the library, he decided that he would not be able to study in his room, so he left for the lounge. Finally, when he began to get tired and became less motivated to complete his studying, he took a break and was then able to return to his work. All of Robert's decisions played a major role in his ability to do well on the history exam the following day.

Given the same situation, think about how another student with less knowledge about learning and study strategies, and fewer self-regulation skills might have behaved in the same situation. The example just presented came from a student's journal. The situation occurred exactly as stated, only "the name was changed to protect the innocent." Robert did not come to college as an A student. As a matter of fact, he struggled during the first few weeks of the first term. When he began to learn how to learn and to take responsibility for his own learning, his academic performance improved dramatically.

As you develop the personal qualities to manage your learning, you will find that you can apply the same skills to situations outside the classroom, even at work. It does not matter what course, seminar, lecture, or job you experience, once you manage the factors influencing your learning, you can be more successful in any task.

One of the second author's students came to his office to discuss the amount of work she had to do in the learning course. She tended to turn in assignments late and, in general, appeared to have difficulty managing her time and motivation. During the conversation, she stated that she only wanted a C in the course. The first author stated that he had no problem giving her a C, but that many students who set this standard often underestimate their achievement and earn a D. He decided to pursue the issue further by asking the student the following question: "Are you also willing to find an average job and get an average salary?" "Oh no!" she stated, "I want a rewarding career and plan on making a great deal of money!"

Many individuals fail to realize that the self-regulation strategies used to become more successful learners often generalize to their personal and work lives. Who is more likely to be promoted in a job, an employee who can work independently and set and attain goals, or an employee who sets low performance goals and needs constant supervision in his or her daily work? Educators who emphasize the importance of self-regulation take the position that students can do a great deal to promote their own learning through the use of different learning and motivational strategies. In other words, these learners view academic learning as something they proactively do for themselves rather than as something that happens to them (Zimmerman, 2015).

Think about Zimmerman's quotation and what it means to you as someone who is attempting to become a more successful learner. What are some of the changes you think you may have to make?

We have taught thousands of undergraduates and have come to the conclusion that we as instructors cannot make students learn if they do not want to. We can help them and guide them, but we cannot make them learn. It is a joy to work with students who take an active role in their own learning. However, some students say they want to learn but do not want to do the things that are necessary to manage their own learning. How many times have you observed parents or other caregivers and teachers prodding or almost begging students to learn? In many cases, these students really want to be successful, but they do not fully understand their responsibilities in the learning process.

WHAT IS THE DIFFERENCE BETWEEN HIGH SCHOOL AND COLLEGE?

The most common observations of new college students are that, compared with high school, professors cover content at a much faster rate, that classes meet only two or three times a week as opposed to every day, and that there are fewer exams and fewer grades. One of the other differences in the transition from high school to college classrooms is the change from a teacher-directed to a student-directed environment. In high school, many teachers tend to guide students' learning by telling them what, when, and how to learn. For example, when assignments are given, high school teachers frequently help students manage the tasks necessary to complete the assignment, such as requiring outlines or drafts of papers. They may also use an electronic system that alerts students about all the due dates. In college, students are on their own. They can ask questions and obtain more information about an assignment, but rarely does a college instructor monitor students' progress or carefully remind them about all the due dates. In college, students are expected to manage their own learning (Bembenutty, 2011).

Another difference between high school and college is that high school teachers often spend considerable time attempting to motivate students to learn, whereas college instructors generally expect students to be self-motivated. Although students are told about the demands of college, many freshmen experience culture shock when they enter learning environments that differ from their past experiences. The following are comments written in a journal by a student in her first term in college.

> My professor was completing his last lecture on the first unit of the course and asked if we had any questions. We had to read chapters in three different textbooks, and I had about 40 pages of notes. I simply asked: "Could you tell us what are some of the important ideas you might cover on the exam?" He looked at me and said: "That's for you to determine!" Well, I felt like crawling under my desk. In high school, most of my teachers would summarize the key ideas that would direct our studying behavior. Here, I quickly learned that I have to do this work on my own!

WHY ARE SOME STUDENTS LESS SUCCESSFUL LEARNERS?

When discussing the reasons for low achievement, we are not including students who have serious learning disabilities, are learning in a non-native language, or who have experienced an inadequate education because of factors beyond their control. Instead, we are referring to students who should be achieving higher than their present performance. In many cases, more than one explanation may be appropriate for a given student.

THEY HOLD FAULTY BELIEFS ABOUT THEIR ABILITY, LEARNING, AND MOTIVATION

Some students believe that ability or intelligence is fixed. That is, they believe people are born with a certain amount of ability, and there is not much that can be done about it. This misperception often causes some students to accept their low achievement or to become satisfied with a B or C average, thinking that only the brightest students obtain an A. In reality, psychologists have found that self-discipline is more important in predicting academic performance than intelligence (Duckworth & Seligman, 2005).

It is unfortunate that many students go through school thinking they are not good learners and that little can be done to improve their achievement. This faulty belief often remains with individuals throughout their lives and limits their goals and aspirations. The problem is not that these students are incapable of being successful learners; they simply have not been taught how to study and learn effectively.

THEY ARE UNAWARE OF THEIR INEFFECTIVE LEARNING BEHAVIOR

Many students believe that if they simply spend a good deal of time studying, they will be successful. Successful learners do work hard, but they realize that how they study is more important than how much time they spend studying. For example, many college students report that they spend considerable time reading a book many times before an examination. Some students are not aware that the practice of underlining (highlighting) words and phrases in textbooks and simply rereading is generally an ineffective learning strategy because it consists of relatively passive activities involving little thinking. It is possible to spend considerable time underlining or rereading a chapter and still not remember many of the important ideas presented. Reading and remembering are two different tasks. Unless students are actively involved in outlining, organizing, questioning themselves, and summarizing the material while they read, much of the time is wasted (Cortina et al., 1995).

THEY FAIL TO SUSTAIN EFFECTIVE LEARNING AND MOTIVATIONAL STRATEGIES

Students usually take more exams and quizzes in high school. Therefore, if they score well on most of the evaluations but low on one or two, they can still maintain a high grade. In college, the situation is different. Fewer evaluations are given throughout the term. For example, a course may require a paper, two exams, and a final; each evaluation may involve 20 percent to 30 percent of the final grade. Students who want high grades cannot afford to let down during the semester.

Many students demonstrate the knowledge of how to learn and do well at times, but fail to attend class regularly, do not keep up with their assignments, and, in general, get behind in their work. Although these students have the potential for doing well, they cannot sustain their motivation and effort throughout the term. The end result is lower academic performance.

THEY ARE NOT READY TO CHANGE THEIR LEARNING AND STUDY BEHAVIOR

Some students are not convinced they need to change. After all, they got through high school and were able to get into college. These students often raise questions, publicly or privately: "Why do I need to change?" "I graduated from high school," or "I was accepted to this college." It is not until the first midterm exams that some students realize that many of the learning and study skills used in high school are insufficient for academic success in college. The earlier students become aware of this fact, the quicker they can begin to make the necessary changes.

Although many students realize they need to improve, they tend to stick with familiar strategies, even though they are not achieving the best results. They simply are not motivated to change. Some students believe that it takes too much effort and time to learn new methods of learning. Learning to play a new song on the guitar or a new dance routine takes effort. Yet, because individuals enjoy the activity and gain special satisfaction from excelling in an area, they do not consider it work. When students use their effort and time more wisely and use more effective methods of learning, they find that the amount of effort and time does pay off in terms of higher grades, greater knowledge and confidence, and more time for fun.

WHAT ARE THE SIX COMPONENTS OF ACADEMIC SELF-REGULATION?

The following are six major components of academic self-regulation. Learning the self-regulatory skills related to each of these components can help you exert control over your own learning and promote your own academic achievement (adapted from Zimmerman & Risemberg, 1997):

- Motivation
- Methods of learning
- Use of time
- Physical environment
- Social environment
- Monitoring performance

MOTIVATION

"Each semester, I write down goals that I want to attain."

"When I feel down, I talk to myself to motivate me to keep on task."

Although there are many different ways to define motivation, the approach taken in this book views motivation as the internal processes that give behavior its energy and direction. These internal processes include your goals, beliefs, perceptions, and expectations. For example, your persistence on a task is often related to how competent you believe you are to complete the task. Also, your beliefs about the causes of your successes and failures on present tasks influence your motivation and behavior on future tasks. For example, students who attribute failure to lack of ability behave differently from students who attribute failure to lack of effort.

In Chapter 2, you will learn that when you change your beliefs and perceptions, you change your motivation. During a presentation on self-motivation at a high school, a student asked one of the authors: "You mean that if you are bored, you can do something about it?" It was obvious that the student had not thought about the extent to which she had the ability to control her own motivation.

Think about the pilot of a 747 who wakes up in the morning knowing that she must fly a few hundred people from Los Angeles to New York, or the surgeon who must perform a delicate heart operation. The public is fortunate that these individuals know how to motivate themselves even when they do not feel like doing something. It would be alarming to hear a pilot say: "I don't feel like flying today," or a surgeon say: "Not another operation, I'm not in the mood."

One of the major differences between successful and less successful individuals in any field or specialization is that successful individuals know how to motivate themselves even when they do not feel like performing a task, whereas less successful individuals have difficulty controlling their motivation. As a result, less successful individuals are less likely to complete a task, or more likely to quit or complete a task at a lower level of proficiency. Although successful learners may not feel like completing required tasks, they learn how to motivate themselves to completion to maintain progress toward achieving their goals. Another issue is whether one has a problem in motivation or persistence. A student may be motivated to engage in a task but may have difficulty persisting because he or she easily becomes distracted while engaging in the task.

Think about your own behavior. Identify a situation in which follow-through, not motivation, was a problem. That is to say, you really wanted to complete a task, but you had difficulty persisting because you were easily distracted. Also, think about a situation in which you were successful in controlling your behavior in a potentially distracting situation. Which self-regulatory strategies did you use to maintain your persistence in a task?

To be a successful learner in college, students must be able to concentrate and deal with the many potential personal and environmental distractions that may interfere with learning and studying. Students use many different processes to control aspects of their behaviors. The following are examples of self-regulatory processes:

- "When I am in the library and distracted by a conversation, I move to another table."
- "When I start worrying on an exam, I immediately begin convincing myself that I can do well if I start my preparation early."
- "When I start thinking that I don't have the ability to achieve, I remind myself that more effort is needed."

A number of important motivational self-regulatory techniques can be used to develop and maintain motivation. The first is goal setting. Educational research indicates that high achievers report using goal setting more frequently and more consistently than low achievers (Zimmerman, 2011). When individuals establish and attempt to attain personal goals, they are more attentive to instruction, expend greater effort, and increase their confidence when they see themselves making progress. It is difficult to be motivated to achieve without having specific goals.

Self-Talk: The inner speech we use to make evaluative statements about our behavior.

A second motivational self-regulation technique is self-verbalization, or **self-talk**. This procedure takes many forms. For example, verbal reinforcement or praise can be used following the desired behavior. You simply tell yourself things like: "Great! I did it!" or "I'm doing a great job concentrating on my readings!" In fact, as you will read in Chapter 5, it might even be better if you do this in the second person ("Great! You did it!"). Reinforce yourself either covertly (to yourself) or aloud. At first, you may think it sounds strange or silly to use self-verbalization. Once you get familiar with it, you will find that it works. Don't underestimate the power of language in self-control of motivation. World-class athletes have been trained to use verbal reinforcement for years.

More elaborate self-talk training programs are available to help individuals control anxiety, mood, and other emotional responses (e.g., Ottens, 1991). These programs are based on the belief that what one says to oneself is an important factor in determining attitudes, feelings, emotions, and behaviors. This speech or self-talk is the running dialogue inside our heads. Some of our speech motivates us to try new tasks and persist in difficult situations; other self-talk is unproductive and inhibits our motivation to succeed. The goal of these programs is to change negative self-talk to positive self-talk. Chapter 5 describes this process in more detail.

Another motivational self-regulation technique is arranging or imagining rewards or punishments for success or failure at an academic task. Students who control their motivation by giving themselves rewards and punishments outperform students who do not use this control technique (Zimmerman, 2015). What self-control strategies have you used in the past to control your motivation? The following are examples reported by our students: "If I study for 50 minutes, I'll go get a latte"; or "If I work on my term paper for an evening, I'll treat myself to a pizza."

In summary, to control your motivation, you need to set goals; develop positive beliefs about your ability to perform academic tasks; and maintain these beliefs while faced with the many disturbances, distractions, occasional failure experiences, and periodic interpersonal conflicts in your life. You will have difficulty managing your behavior if you do not have confidence in your ability to succeed. In turn, you develop confidence in your ability by learning how to use different learning and study strategies that lead to academic success.

METHODS OF LEARNING

"While reading my sociology textbook, I write important questions to answer after reading each main heading."

"I use a timeline to recall the dates of major battles in my history course."

Another term for methods of learning is learning strategies. **Learning strategies are the methods students use to acquire information.** Higher achieving students use more learning strategies than do lower achieving students (Zimmerman & Martinez-Pons, 1988).

> **Learning Strategies:** Techniques or methods that students use to acquire information.

Underlining, summarizing, and outlining are examples of learning strategies. You will learn in Chapter 3 that different learning strategies serve different purposes.

Think about the large array of tools a plumber brings to each job. If he arrived at jobs with only a few wrenches or pliers, he would not be able to complete many jobs. Just as there are different tools for different jobs, there are different learning strategies for different academic tasks. Successful learners also need a large number of "tools" to make schoolwork easier and to increase the probability of their success. For example, knowing how to use maps or representations to organize information and how to generate and answer questions from notes and textbooks are important learning tools. Many students who have difficulty learning in school attribute their problem to a lack of ability when the problem actually may be that they have never been properly taught how to learn. Some students use one or two major learning strategies for all tasks in all courses. These students often do not have the necessary tools to learn the complex material they encounter in the courses they are required to take. For example, on exams, many instructors ask questions relating to topics that they did not directly discuss in lectures. Students must be able to organize and analyze notes so they are prepared to answer questions such as: "How does the government affect the allocation of resources through tax policy?" or "Why does the temperature of the water influence the velocity of sound?"

The plumbing example can be used to provide a practical example of understanding the relation between learning and motivation. The second author is going to admit something: He doesn't have confidence in his ability to do many household chores. Therefore, he procrastinates, fails to purchase the tools that could help him complete tasks, and doesn't pay much attention when friends try to explain how he can be a successful handyman. When his wife tells him that a water faucet is leaking and asks him to fix it, he often tells her to wait a few days—perhaps the leaking will stop! Even if he had the tools, he still might not attempt to complete the job himself.

You cannot become a successful learner merely by acquiring new learning and study skills. You also must deal with your motivation (i.e., beliefs and perceptions) regarding a task. Even if you know how to use an effective strategy, you may not be motivated to use it. Some educators (e.g., Hattie & Donoghue, 2015; Weinstein et al., 2011) describe these two important components of learning as the skill (i.e., learning strategies) and will (i.e., the motivation to use strategies).

Use of Time

"I keep a weekly calendar of my activities."

"I start studying at least one week before exams."

Educators have found a relation between time management and academic achievement. Students with better time-management skills tend to have a higher grade-point average (GPA) than students with poorer time-management skills. In fact, Britton and Tesser (1991) found that time-management skills measured in the freshman year were more predictive of GPAs in the senior year than were Scholastic Achievement Test (SAT) scores. Similarly, West and Sadoski (2011) found that time-management skills along with self-testing skills were better predictors of first semester medical school grades than the Medical College Admission Test (MCAT) scores.

Why does time management appear to be so important in determining academic success? One explanation is that use of time impacts self-regulation. If a student has difficulty dealing with time, he or she ends up doing what is most urgent when deciding which task to do first. If a paper is the next task that needs to be done, one works on the paper; if an exam is the next challenge, one studies for the exam. Little time is spent on any long-term planning to consider the importance of different tasks and how they can best be completed (Zimmerman et al., 1996).

How many times have you heard individuals state: "I don't have time." The problem for most individuals is not that there is not enough time to accomplish what needs to be done, but that they do not know how to manage the amount of time that is available each day. When students analyze their use of time, they find a great deal of it is wasted.

Physical and Social Environment

"I turn off my cell phone so I can concentrate on what I am doing."

"I go to the library to study before exams."

"When I find that I don't understand any material, I immediately make an appointment with my instructor."

"I organize a study group before an examination."

Another important aspect of self-regulation is the ability of learners to restructure their physical and social environments to meet their needs. Zimmerman and Martinez-Pons (1986) found that high achievers reported greater use of environmental restructuring and were more likely to seek help from others than were low-achieving students. For the most part, environmental restructuring refers to locating places to study that are quiet or not distracting. Although this task may not appear difficult to attain, it poses many problems for students who either select inappropriate environments initially or cannot control the distractions once they occur.

Self-regulation of the social environment relates to an individual's ability to determine when he or she needs to work alone or with others, or when it is time to seek help from instructors, tutors, peers, or non-social resources (such as reference books). Knowing how and when to work with others is an important skill often not taught in school. We will discuss this more in Chapter 7.

Educational research indicates that high-achieving students are more likely than low-achieving students to seek help from instructors, just the opposite of what one might expect (Newman & Schwager, 1992). Newman (1991) stated: "Seeking help from a knowledgeable other person can be more beneficial than giving up prematurely, more appropriate than waiting passively, and more efficient than persisting unsuccessfully on one's own" (p. 154).

It would seem logical that everyone would want to use all available resources and seek assistance from teachers and peers. Unfortunately, this is not the case. Some students do not seek help because they do not want to appear "dumb" or incompetent in the eyes of their peers or fail to seek help because of the extra effort it may entail. For example, in a class discussion, one of the students mentioned that she did not do well on a biology exam because she did not understand the instructor's expectations of the response to the essay questions. The second author suggested that she meet with the instructor to discuss his expectations. She agreed that this would be a good strategy. However, the following week she stated that too many students were waiting to talk to the instructor, so she got frustrated and left. The second author's response was that meeting with her instructor was a task that she had to accomplish. It was her responsibility to call for an appointment, wait to meet him after class, or at the beginning or end of the school day. If her success in the course depended on learning how to prepare and take his exams, then her job was to get to the instructor, one way or another.

Here is another example of the need to seek assistance. A student approached the first author at the end of the second lecture in the term and stated: "You're not going to count my quiz today? I haven't had an opportunity to buy my textbook?" The first author stated that the quiz would count and that he had numerous opportunities to locate the required five pages of reading for the quiz. He could have read the material at the reserve section of the library, where numerous copies of the reading had been placed. He could have borrowed the reading from another student in the class or asked the first author if he had a copy to loan him. In other words, it was his responsibility to get the material.

Both of these interactions with students provide excellent examples of the importance of managing one's learning. In both situations, the students failed to understand their responsibility in the learning process. Think about situations in your past where you would have benefited from managing some aspect of your physical or social environment. In addition to seeking help from your instructor and peers, your campus or online school is likely to have resources such as a writing and study skills center. Many centers offer both on-campus and online coaching and tutoring.

MONITORING PERFORMANCE

"I evaluate the results of each of my exams to determine how I can better prepare for future exams."

"If I find that I don't understand what I'm reading, I slow down and reread the material."

If you are a typical student, you likely get rid of evidence of poor performance on an exam by stashing it into the depths of your backpack or cramming it into a drawer. We can't blame you as we want to do the same when a manuscript is returned to us with critical comments from peer review. But there are valuable lessons in reviewing your work that can help improve your performance. The final factor of self-regulation is monitoring your performance. It is important that you do so both during as well as after performing.

As individuals, we not only regulate our performance but also monitor and evaluate it. Psychologists call monitoring your performance while performing "metacognition" (Brown, 1978; Flavell, 1976; Zimmerman, 2015). The term literally means "thinking about thinking" and refers to one's awareness of self as a learner. In addition to setting a goal for the study session, organizing the materials and determining the appropriate study strategies, a metacognitively aware student might analyze the usefulness of learning strategies while she studies and changes them if she fails to understand, stops and rereads when she gets confused, and periodically reviews them to reinforce understanding important relationships. If you would like to score yourself as a metacognitively aware learner, you can access the Metacognitive Awareness Inventory (MAI, Schraw & Dennison, 1994) via the web. **Metacognition** is a skill that will never become obsolete. As the world changes rapidly with advances in technology, metacognitively aware individuals will be successful in coping with new challenges.

Metacognition: Awareness and understanding of one's own thought processes.

The other aspect of monitoring performance occurs after performance, such as locating that exam you never wanted to see again. Look for repeated errors such as incorrect answers based on lecture versus textbook items or losing points for grammar versus content mistakes. By determining why you lost points, you can strategize how to improve your preparation. You might want to delay your error review by a few days, though, so you can do it with a calmer and more focused mind.

World-class athletes are good examples of individuals who monitor their performance. For example, competitive skiers often imagine themselves going through each slalom gate before making an actual run and concentrate on remaining relaxed during their run (Garfield, 1984). After each run, they observe and assess their performance (both from their perceptions and on videotape) to determine what modifications are needed to reach greater accuracy on the next run. They often use subvocal speech or self-talk to guide their behaviors and maintain attention to avoid distractions that may interfere with their performance.

When you learn how to monitor and control your own performance, that is, become metacognitively aware, you become your own coach or mentor. You can practice skills on your own, critique your own performance, and make the necessary changes to meet your goals at a high level of success.

WHAT DOES ACADEMIC SELF-REGULATION LOOK LIKE?

The following example is how one student, Josh, exhibited self-regulatory behavior in each of the components just discussed: Josh's goal was to join the debate team during the second term of his freshman year. He believed he could attain his goal by expending effort (motivation) in preparing for the tryouts. He first decided to study the topics that would dominate the debate season by reading magazine and newspaper articles (methods of learning). He then decided to practice his arguments with another friend (social environment) who also was interested in joining the team. They decided to reserve space at the speech clinic two evenings each week (time management) and use the available recording equipment (physical environment) to videotape their presentations and spend time critiquing themselves (monitoring performance).

Would Josh and his friend be successful if they failed to manage one or more factors influencing learning? Perhaps so, but we really do not know. For example, could they have been as successful practicing their arguments in their dorm rooms or whenever they found some time to meet, or without the recording machine? Could Josh have been as successful preparing by himself?

Although it is possible to self-regulate behavior in all six of the areas discussed, not all students do so. A reasonable goal is to manage as much of one's behavior and thoughts as possible. In the example discussed, Josh and his friend believed they would be better prepared to make the debate team following their plan of action. If you were in the same situation, you may have approached the task differently.

Remember the example we provided earlier in the chapter about Robert's study behavior for his history exam? Return to the description of his learning and studying behavior (p. 4) and identify how he managed each of the following factors: motivation; methods of learning; use of time; physical environment; social environment; and monitoring performance.

Throughout this book, you will be asked to set goals and develop a plan of action to attain them. During this process, you will learn how to manage different aspects of your academic learning that will affect your level of success. In each chapter, we provide examples of students' perceptions or beliefs about the learning strategies discussed in this textbook. These perceptions or student reflections, as we call them, are from students who have taken our course in learning strategies. As you read each reflection, think about your own perceptions, beliefs, or behavior related to the topic or issue. The following reflection illustrates how learning to manage one's academic behavior can also influence other aspects of one's life.

Student Reflections

I first thought that self-regulation was confined to academic learning. Now I see that it is also a great tool for life in general. As I learn more about self-regulation and practice the related skills, I find that I'm much more organized. Most important, I'm getting my work done instead of putting it off and procrastinating, as I have always done. As the class has progressed, it has affected my daily life. I'm starting to see that my life outside of school is starting to run more smoothly as well.

I was always an incredibly unorganized person. I would throw all my stuff (from mail, school work, even clothes) everywhere. I always was looking for things, losing things, and making a mess. Now I'm much more organized. I put things back when I'm finished with them, I keep my mail and outside school material in certain areas where I can find things, and my roommate is especially pleased, because I keep the room clean now. I'm also more prepared for whatever I have to do. I stick to schedules and plan for the events in my life. Basically, my life is more enjoyable! I'm happy now because of my continuing success at school, and this success has translated to my day-to-day life.

EXERCISE 1.1: SELF-OBSERVATION: ASSESSING YOUR SELF-REGULATORY SKILLS

Directions: Rate the extent to which you generally regulate or manage the factors influencing your learning by checking Always, Sometimes, or Never in the corresponding box, and be prepared to offer a short explanation of your ratings. What areas are your strengths and weakness? Explain why you rated each dimension as you did.

	Always	Sometimes	Never
Motivation (e.g., "I can self-motivate when I need to.")			
Use of Time (e.g., "I plan how I use my time.")			
Methods of Learning (e.g., "I use different study methods for different types of assignments and tests.")			
Physical Environment (e.g., "I modify or change my study environment so I can concentrate.")			
Social Environment (e.g., "I seek help when I need it.")			
Monitoring Performance (e.g., "I monitor and evaluate my performance to determine my progress toward meeting personal and academic goals.")			

Comments:

_____

_____

_____

_____

_____

HOW CAN I CHANGE MY BEHAVIOR?

Zimmerman et al. (1996) suggested a process that students can use to develop the self-regulatory skills necessary for academic success (see Figure 1.1). This process will help you develop control over the six components of motivation and behavior identified in the previous section. The first step in the process is self-observation and evaluation.

> Self-observation and evaluation occur when students judge their personal effectiveness, often from observations and recordings of prior performances and outcomes.

One problem is that some students study and prepare for examinations in the same way that they did in high school. They have yet to realize the differences in the two academic environments. In high school, teachers take most of the responsibility for their students' level of comprehension. High school teachers actively monitor the degree to which content is understood: They constantly quiz students, ask questions as they present new material, and place key ideas on the board. In contrast, college instructors expect students to do their own monitoring of their understanding. Therefore, problems arise early during the first college term if students do not know how to monitor their own understanding. An important part of becoming a more successful student is developing the ability to monitor one's knowledge and recognize when something is not understood. Think about expert performers in a variety of fields. In sports, elite athletes begin observing their performances by viewing videotapes. After a short period of time, they are able to modify their performances from the feelings and feedback they obtain by viewing their own physical movements; dance studios place handrails next to mirrors to enable students to self-observe as they practice their routines; musicians learn to listen to their playing to critique their own performances (Glaser, 1996).

Behavior cannot be regulated or managed unless you are aware of it. Therefore, you will be asked throughout this book to observe and evaluate your current learning and study methods to determine those that are ineffective so they can be replaced by better methods. Most important, you need to become aware of when and how these new learning and study methods improve your learning.

Each semester, we ask students to assess their use of time for a week. They usually are surprised to learn how much time they waste. They appear more motivated to change their time management after they have monitored and observed their use of time. Self-observation is an important first step in motivating students to consider changing their learning and study behaviors.

> Goal setting and strategic planning occur when students analyze the learning task, set specific goals, and plan or refine the strategy to attain the goal.

(Zimmerman et al., 1996, p. 11)

This second step, goal setting and strategic planning, is important in all academic tasks, including writing a paper. When given the task of writing a paper, you should start by analyzing your strengths

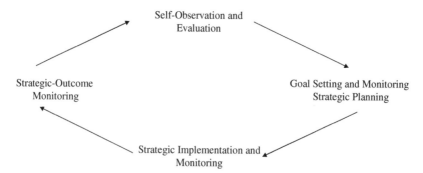

FIGURE 1.1   A Process for Self-Regulation of Academic Behavior (adapted from Zimmerman et al., 1996)

and weaknesses. Next, analyze the assignment to determine the nature of the paper and what needs to be done. Then, you should establish a goal for completion, with a number of intermediate or subgoals (e.g., locating necessary references and proofreading) for completing different sections of the paper. Finally, you should develop a strategy for completing each of the intermediate goals. We discuss this process in more detail in Chapter 4.

The same procedure can be used in test preparation. After analyzing previous tests as well as your present knowledge of the content (using self-observation and evaluation), you should determine what course material will be examined, establish goals for preparing for the exam, determine how you will study (i.e., what strategies will be used), and, finally, plan a time-management program consistent with your goals.

After you better understand your current behavior (through self-observation and evaluation), you will be in a better position to determine what needs to be accomplished (goals) and to develop a strategy to do it. Much of the content in this book focuses on this step in the cycle.

> Strategy-implementation and monitoring occur when students try to execute a strategy in structured contexts and to monitor their accuracy in implementing it.

The third step in the cycle focuses on the effectiveness of your learning strategy. Is the strategy working? Are you attaining each of your goals in completing your paper? Are you learning the necessary content for your exam? If your strategy is working, keep going. If not, you will want to make adjustments.

When you learn anything new, there is a tendency to revert back to familiar methods (even though they may be less successful). This happens to athletes, dancers, and students. Therefore, performers and learners need to monitor their behaviors closely to determine whether they are applying new strategies appropriately. The result of this monitoring may indicate a need to adjust the learning strategy to improve progress toward the attainment of your goal. You may even decide that it is time to seek help.

Remember the metacognitively aware student described earlier? When she realizes that she does not understand a portion of the text, she rereads the difficult section, slows the reading pace through difficult or unfamiliar material, and reviews course material that was not understood. It is important that students learn how to modify their study behavior to improve their understanding.

All students need to learn "fix-up" strategies to remedy learning problems. That is, they need to learn what to do after they find that they do not understand certain content. Often, different methods or strategies for learning must be undertaken (e.g., asking and answering questions) instead of continuing with the same ineffective strategy (e.g., underlining the content in a textbook).

> Strategic-outcome monitoring occurs when students focus their attention on links between learning outcomes and strategic processes to determine effectiveness.

(Zimmerman et al., 1996, p. 11)

The final stage in the cycle involves expanding your monitoring to include performance outcomes. At this stage, the following questions are answered: "Did the learning plan or strategy help me attain my goal?" "Did I have to make changes in my learning and study methods?" For example, you may have developed a strategy for studying for an objective test for the first examination of the term. You used the same strategy for a second examination, an essay test. Was the study strategy effective for both tests?

The cycle keeps going as self-observation is used to evaluate your exam performance by determining what questions you missed and the location of the information (i.e., notes or readings). A self-regulated learner is constantly monitoring learning outcomes to determine whether different strategies are needed to attain goals and maintain a high level of academic success.

When researchers study expert performance in such fields as music, sports, medicine, chess, and reading, they find a common element in their learning. Initially, experts depend on instruction from others, and, with time, they increasingly rely on their self-observation and self-judgments about their behavior. The ability to self-regulate enables experts to profit a great deal from practice and study by themselves without assistance from their coaches and teachers (Glaser, 1996).

Zimmerman et al. (1996) believe that one of the major advantages of using the self-regulatory process is that it does not only improve one's learning, but also enhances one's perception of self-confidence and control over the learning process. By learning to self-observe your current learning and study behavior, and by determining for yourself what methods are effective and ineffective, you can begin replacing ineffective methods with better ones and can become more aware of the improved effectiveness of these new strategies. This process helps you to become a more self-regulated learner.

The first exercise in the Follow-Up Activities section of this book, beginning with Chapter 2, identifies a topic and questions related to each of the four processes just discussed to change or modify your behavior. These questions provide the structure for conducting your own self-regulation study.

Appendix B provides detailed procedures for how to conduct such a study. You will learn how to identify a problem, observe your behavior, and develop a plan to improve and evaluate your academic learning. Read Appendix B as soon as possible. Appendix B provides two examples of such studies. You will find an evaluation of each self-study at the end of each report. Your instructor can provide specific directions about conducting such a study.

You may want to conduct a self-regulatory study to improve your time management, study environment, test preparation, motivation, or any other study-related skill. Read ahead in the textbook if you wish to conduct a study on a topic that will be discussed later in the term.

HOW DOES SELF-REGULATION OCCUR IN AN ACADEMIC CONTEXT?

Figure 1.2 is useful for understanding the organization of the remaining chapters in this book. Although all the components of self-regulation interact, it is easier in a textbook to present content in a linear fashion. Therefore, we have grouped the components into three different units. The self-regulation cycle can help you gain competence in each of the areas identified.

There are four key skills that must be mastered to perform successfully in any academic setting: learning from course materials, learning in class, preparing for exams, and taking exams. Writing, another important skill, is discussed under learning how to respond to essay exams.

The main factor influencing the effectiveness of your learning these skills is your ability to manage the various elements of your behavior. We group goal setting and management of emotion and effort under motivational strategies, and time management and management of physical and social environment under behavioral strategies. It is important to note that behavioral and motivational self-control are interrelated. The academic performance box in Figure 1.2 represents the performance dimension aspect of self-regulation.

The process we described here places a great deal of responsibility on you, the learner. We wish there were an easy way to become a more successful learner. Unfortunately, we do not know any other way. Educational research clearly indicates that students who take charge of their own learning are more likely to achieve at a higher level than students who fail to take this responsibility (Zimmerman & Schunk, 2008).

All students need to have effective academic beliefs, study skills, and habits, but self-regulatory skills are especially important in the context of online learning. Chances are that you will take a fully or partially online class at some point in your academic career. More than one in four students take some of their courses online (Seaman, Allen & Seaman, 2018) and the trend of online learning is on the rise. Because the online learning environment is often less structured than the traditional classroom, online courses require students to take complete responsibility for their own learning. Self-regulation, therefore, is critical in online learning.

Whether you are taking courses in the traditional or online learning environment, you will acquire important strategies to assist you in managing your learning behavior in each chapter of this

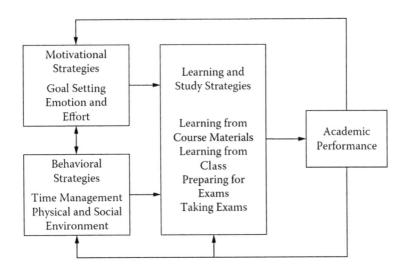

FIGURE 1.2   Academic Self-Regulation

book. For each strategy discussed, you will learn why it is important, when it can be used, and how it can be implemented. The key to success in this course is practicing the different strategies so they become automatic. As you practice, you will be able to learn more material in less time than you did prior to using these new strategies. In other words, you will learn to study smarter, not harder.

You are not alone on your journey to become a more successful student. Your instructor and peers will provide support and encouragement. You will be asked to complete various individual and group exercises and assignments as you read this book. You will find that working collaboratively with peers and giving and receiving feedback will be a valuable experience throughout the course.

Finally, you will only be taught strategies that thousands of students have found useful in learning academic material. After learning and practicing a strategy, only you will decide whether it is worth the effort and time to use it regularly in school. If the strategy proves useful, you will use it. Likewise, if you do not find the strategy helpful, you will modify it or disregard it. Try each new strategy before you reach any conclusions. Do not make the mistake of rejecting something new before you have the opportunity to see how it works.

Chapter Review

KEY POINTS

1 Successful learners use specific beliefs and processes to motivate and control their own behavior.

2 Some students fail to recognize the differences between high school and college learning during the first weeks in college.

3 Students can self-regulate six key components of academic learning that can influence their achievement level: motivation, methods of learning (i.e., learning strategies), use of time, physical environment, social environment, and monitoring performance.

4 The self-regulation cycle involves four interrelated processes: self-observation and evaluation, goal setting and strategic planning, strategy-implementation monitoring, and strategic-outcome monitoring.

5 An important part of becoming a more successful student is metacognitive awareness: developing the ability to monitor knowledge and understand one's own thought processes, recognize when something is not understood, and do something about it.

FOLLOW-UP ACTIVITIES

1. Evaluate Your Self-Regulatory Skills

Read the following two descriptions of community college students and use the criteria presented below to describe the extent to which each of the two students can be classified as self-regulated learners.

Components of Self-Regulation

1 Motivation
2 Use of time
3 Methods of learning
4 Control of one's physical environment
5 Control of one's social environment
6 Monitoring performance

Maria   On Sunday night, Maria reviews her work for the coming week and writes some short-term goals that she would like to accomplish. She then opens her weekly calendar and determines how much time is needed to complete her tasks. Maria works ten hours a week and realizes that she needs more time to prepare for her midterm in biology the following Monday. She makes plans to study for the exam on Monday, Wednesday, and Sunday. She realizes that her family is planning to attend her niece's birthday party next Sunday afternoon, but she needs the time to prepare for the exam. She calls her aunt to tell her that she can't attend the party on Sunday.

On Monday, Maria contacts two students in her biology class and asks them if they would be interested in forming a study group to review some possible questions that she thinks may be on the exam. She tells her two friends to create possible exam questions beforehand, so that they will be prepared for the study session. She also calls the library where she can reserve a study room for her group. After the study session on Monday, Maria and her friends determine that they have many unanswered questions about the blood circulation of the human heart. They write down these questions and decide that one of them would go to the instructor's office hours to get the questions answered and then email the instructor's response to the rest of the group.

After her study session on Sunday afternoon, Maria reviews all the material that will be on the exam the next day and makes a list of content material she feels that she doesn't fully understand. She reviews the course syllabus, notes, and textbook and decides that she needs to review two chapters in her textbook and a few lecture notes on Sunday evening before she is ready for the exam on Monday.

Jan is a freshman at a local college and wants to enter a journalism program. She recently purchased a car and feels that she has many expenses that need to be paid. As a result, she agrees to work 25 hours a week at the local electronics store. Jan sometimes works evenings, so her best time for study is early in the morning and late in the afternoon. She usually attempts to complete her reading assignments early in the morning. However, she is often tired and finds it difficult to concentrate. Since she doesn't have a computer at home, she uses a computer in the library to complete her writing assignments. However, she often finds it difficult to get to the library during her free time. As a result, she attempts to complete her assignments at her boyfriend's house. She spends time talking with her boyfriend and often finds that the time goes by very fast and she needs to go to work before her assignment is completed.

Jan would like to complete her work without asking for assistance, even though her instructor has office hours. She doesn't want her instructor to think she is not capable; therefore, she would rather ask her friends for help than meet with her instructor. When Jan studies for exams, she rereads her textbook and notes, even though she admits that sometimes she doesn't understand some of the notes she takes. Jan often complains that her English instructor speaks too fast and taking notes is very difficult in her class.

2. Analyze Your Beliefs about Learning and Motivation

Read each of the following statements and place the corresponding letter or letters whether you agree (A), disagree (D), or are not sure (NS) about the accuracy of each statement. After identifying your beliefs, think about how they influence your motivation and learning. Discuss your ratings with other students in your class.

1. "I can't do well in a course if I'm not interested in the content."
2. "I will not learn much if I am bored in class."
3. "Competition is a great motivator."
4. "Human intelligence is fixed by the time a student begins school."
5. "Sometimes there is not enough time in the day to do everything that needs to be done."
6. "If I simply listen in class and read my assignments, I should do well in college."
7. "The most important aspect of studying is finding enough time."
8. "The key to success in college is having good instructors."
9. "Procrastination is a personality trait that can't be changed."

3. Analyze the Meaning of Two Statements

An educational researcher has stated that self-regulated individuals believe that "learning is not something that happens to students; it is something that happens by students" (Zimmerman, 1989, p. 22). What do you think this statement means? What implications does it have for improving one's learning?

How does the following statement relate to your own learning experiences?

Part of being a good student is learning to be aware of the state of one's own mind and the degree of one's own understanding. The good student may be one who often says that he does not understand, simply because he keeps a constant check on his understanding. The poor student, who does not, so to speak, watch himself trying to understand does not know most of the time whether he understands or not. Thus, the problem is not to get students to ask us what they don't know; the problem is to make them aware of the difference between what they know and what they don't.

(Holt, 1982, p. 17)

4. Analyze Course Demands

You learned in this chapter that a successful student takes charge of his or her own learning. Therefore, it is important to understand the demands of each of the courses you are taking this term. In this way, you can set goals and develop a plan for achieving them. Use the summary sheet provided to analyze the syllabus, textbooks, and professor in each course. Write comments in abbreviated form so you can discuss them in class:

- Review each syllabus and identify major assignments and demands during the semester (e.g., papers, projects, weekly papers).
- Analyze each textbook to determine what learning aids are included (i.e., glossary, questions, summaries, objectives, or test questions) that help you comprehend the material. Also, identify any other characteristics of the books that make them easy or hard to read (e.g., bold headings, graphics, small type).
- Analyze the instructor's teaching style to determine whether it will make it easy or hard to take good notes. What do you like most and least about his or her style? How does she or he let you know what is important? What note-taking problems do you encounter? Identify any of the following characteristics about your instructor: speaks rapidly, speaks slowly, speaks loudly, speaks softly, does or does not use board or overheads, is well organized or is disorganized, and so forth.

What are your general impressions of the instructor and course demands? Identify your interest level and expectancy for success in each course. Identify any concerns you may have about doing well in a course and the steps you can take to deal with your concerns.

Courses	Syllabus	Textbooks	Professor
General Comments			
1.			
2.			
3.			
4.			
5.			

---

2 Understanding Motivation

As you consider the various components of academic self-regulation, you may find that you have no difficulty managing your motivation. You may exhibit a great deal of effort on tasks, persist even under difficult situations, and maintain positive beliefs about your academic abilities. If this is the case, this chapter will simply help you understand why you are motivated to succeed and how to maintain your level of motivation. However, if you have some difficulty managing your motivation, this chapter provides important background information to help you change.

MOTIVATIONAL PROBLEMS

Many of our students frequently state in class or in written assignments: "I have no motivation" or "I need to get motivated." Unfortunately, we find that many students do not understand the meaning of these statements. Actually, everyone is motivated. Educational researchers, such as Covington and Roberts (1994), have found that many different motivational patterns can be identified in any group of students. These motivational patterns are based on our relationship with success and failure.

All individuals can be characterized by two opposing motives: a motive to seek success and a motive to avoid failure. That is, some of us are motivated to achieve success and anticipate the feeling of pride and accomplishment related to our success while others are motivated to ensure that they do not fail and experience the shame and humiliation related to failure. But do we only desire success or seek to avoid failure? Obviously not. Most of us experience a combination of motives and can be categorized into one of four different motivational profiles as represented in Figure 2.1.

Let's look at these four types of students: the success-oriented students, failure avoiders, failure acceptors, and overstrivers.

- *Successful Sheila/Success-Oriented Student*: This student, high in motivation for success and low in fear of failure, is likely to be highly engaged in academic activities and not anxious about her performance. The success-oriented student uses effective learning strategies, sets goals, and self-regulates her learning.
- *Defensive Dimitri/Failure Avoider*: For this type of student, the desire to avoid failure outweighs the anticipation of success. He puts his energy into preventing anyone from interpreting his poor performance as evidence of lack of ability. He uses a number of failure-avoiding strategies, such as studying at the last minute so that if he fails, he has a ready excuse. He relies on memorization as the easiest way to get an adequate grade and puts in a great deal of time the last day or so as a way of making up for weeks of neglect and disinterest in coursework. Underneath the seeming apathy, though, he remains concerned about the implications of failure and defensively maneuvers to avoid looking not capable.
- *Anxious Anna/Overstriver*: This student is high in both motives. She seeks success but greatly fears failure at the same time. In fact, she can be characterized as attempting to avoid failure by succeeding. This student is highly anxious about her performance,

Motive to Avoid Failure		Low	High
	Low	Failure Acceptors	Success-Oriented Students
	High	Failure Avoiders	Overstrivers

FIGURE 2.1 Quadripolar Model for Need Achievement (Covington & Roberts, 1994)

often over-prepares for assignments and exams, and seeks extra credit whenever possible. Though in the short term, it may seem that she is successful as her grades are exemplary, in the long term, her excessive worry about failure and doubts about her adequacy may result in exhaustion and actual health problems.

• *Hopeless Henry/Failure Acceptor*: This student is low in both motives, reflecting an absence of both hope and fear. He is basically indifferent to achievement, believing that more effort and better learning strategies will make no difference in his history of academic failure. In addition to loss of hope, this indifference may also reflect hidden anger. He is not concerned about the implications of academic failure as at some point he has told himself that the lessons to be learned in school hold no relevance for his life.

Each of these students has a different set of beliefs and perceptions. Three of these students have motivational problems that limit their present and possibly future academic success. Defensive Dimitri is more concerned about failure than success and uses failure-avoiding strategies that often result in creating the very failure he fears. Hopeless Henry does not believe that anything he does will make a difference in succeeding in college. He has learned to be helpless. Anxious Anna wants to be successful but her constant worry causes considerable anxiety that interferes with her success and health.

Do any of these students resemble anyone you know? As you read this chapter, think about how the content can help you better understand each of these students. After studying this chapter, you will be able to:

• identify the factors that influence motivation;
• assess your beliefs and perceptions to account for your own motivation.

WHAT IS MOTIVATION AND WHAT FACTORS INFLUENCE IT?

Student motivation in the college classroom involves three interactive components as described in Figure 2.2 (adapted from Pintrich, 1994). The first component is sociocultural factors, made up of such influences as one's prior educational experiences, socioeconomic status, as well as peer,

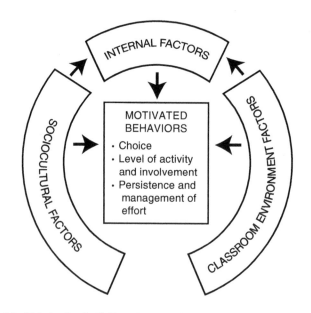

FIGURE 2.2   A Model of Motivation in College (adapted from Pintrich, 1994)

family, and cultural experiences. The second component, classroom environmental factors, includes the college and classroom environment, instructional methods and behavior, and type of assignments given to students. The third component in the model includes internal factors such as students' perceptions and beliefs.

Each of the three components has an effect on motivated behaviors, depicted in the middle of the model. You've heard the saying: "Actions speak louder than words." Based on this common wisdom, the best indicators of one's level of motivation are the actual behaviors, such as one's level of persistence when faced with obstacles. The internal factors, our perceptions and beliefs, naturally determine the degree to which we demonstrate motivated behaviors. For example, the more we value academic achievement (a belief), the more likely we are to choose (motivated behavior) academic tasks over attractive distractions, such as a last-minute invite to a party. Similarly, a classroom environmental factor, such as a well-designed academic task that is both interesting and challenging, is likely to bring about students' high levels of involvement. How do sociocultural factors, such as your prior educational experiences, influence your motivated behaviors?

As indicated by the arrows, the three components interact with each other in their effect on motivated behaviors. Clearly, a student's sociocultural background, such as one's family, leads to the development of the internal factors (i.e., one's perceptions, values, and beliefs). Similarly, classroom environmental factors, such as an enthusiastic professor, can lead to the development of certain perceptions and beliefs about the course topic.

We begin this section by discussing a definition of motivation (i.e., motivated behaviors). We will next discuss the sociocultural and classroom environmental factors, and finally, address the self-perceptions that influence motivated behaviors.

MOTIVATED BEHAVIORS

If you want to understand your own motivation, you might begin by evaluating your behavior in the following three areas:

- Choosing and starting an activity.
- Level of activity and involvement.
- Persistence and management of effort.

These behaviors are how you demonstrate your motivation. Students make choices every day about activities and tasks in which to engage. Many students choose to learn more about a subject or topic outside of class, whereas others limit their involvement to class assignments. The second author knew a student who could not say no when someone asked if he wanted to go to a movie or have pizza, even though he had to study for an exam or write a paper. The first author can also speak for herself and say that though she can plan to start revising a harshly criticized manuscript over a lunch hour, she can instead get distracted by the latest Netflix original. We do not have to be productive every moment. Having fun is part of life. However, the choices we make play important roles in determining the number of personal goals we will attain throughout life.

A second aspect of motivated behaviors is level of activity or involvement in a task. Some students are very involved in their courses. They ask questions during lectures, summarize their textbooks, spend considerable effort after class refining notes, outlining readings, and, in general, using different learning strategies to make sense of what they are learning. Other students are less engaged in their courses and do the minimal amount required to get by. They simply attend lectures and read their textbooks, expecting that these behaviors are sufficient to do well in a class. Of course, some students' level of activity involves not attending class regularly or skimming textbooks without trying to think critically about the content of what is read.

The third aspect of motivated behaviors is effort and persistence. The willingness of students to work hard and persist when tasks are difficult, boring, and unchallenging or when attractive distractions are available is an important factor in motivation and academic success. In many cases, students have to learn how to control their efforts and persistence in the variety of academic tasks they experience. Let's now examine the factors that influence motivated behaviors, in other words, what it is that gets us going, keeps us going, and ensures that we invest enough effort.

SOCIOCULTURAL FACTORS

The attitudes, beliefs, and experiences students bring to college based on their sociocultural experiences influence their motivation and behavior, and even their persistence or departure from college. Cultural groups may emphasize different norms, values, and expectations. For example, a minority group's perception of the college environment as accepting of their cultural values and norms is an important factor in determining whether they are likely to persist in college (Castillo et al., 2006). You also are influenced by your family experiences. Family characteristics such as socioeconomic levels, parental educational levels, and parental expectations can influence motivation and behavior.

The following is a description of the experiences of a middle-class student's preparation for college. Note how both her in-school and out-of-school activities influenced her, and how the student body composition, teachers' expectations, and parental and peer influence provided the motivation and knowledge to succeed once she arrived at college.

> Devon attended a high school where 85 percent of the students go to college. Her friends were very competitive and wanted to attend a prestigious college. As a result, they studied hard and challenged each other to do their best. Her teachers had high expectations for student success and demanded a great deal from her and her friends. Her teachers pushed them to take AP classes and get the most out of their high school experience. Since junior high school, Devon attended computer, soccer, and cheerleading camps, and took two different programs to improve her SAT scores. In her senior year, she met regularly with her counselor to discuss college options and receive information on opportunities for financial aid and on completing her college application.

She can't even remember when she decided to go to college because her parents expected her to do so as far back as she could remember. Both parents graduated from college and shared their experiences with her. In her junior year, her parents took her to visit different colleges.

Devon was accepted to the college of her choice, and by the time she walked on campus, she had a good understanding of what college would be like. For example, she was very familiar with how to register for classes, receive help from various academic support services, pledge a sorority, and schedule a meeting with professors to discuss exam results. In sum, she was prepared for college. She felt connected to the college and was very comfortable being a student.

It would be nice if all students had the same opportunities. Unfortunately, first-generation college students, that is, students who are the first in their immediate family to go to college, and students from low-income families tend to have different educational experiences than Devon. Data demonstrate that close to one-third of all students enrolled in post-secondary education are first generation (NCES, 2018) and are four times as likely to drop out of college after their first year, compared with their more advantaged peers (Engle & Tinto, 2008). What are the causes for these statistics? How does the experience of these students differ from the description of Devon and her peers?

While in the past, students from low-income backgrounds were usually labeled "at-risk," there is a growing emphasis on resilience and determining factors that enable these students to be "at-promise." We'll review the risk factors first and then discuss facilitative or protective factors. Morales (2010) explains these two different factors in the following manner: "Risk factors are existing constructs that have the potential to create roadblocks or impediments to academic success. Protective factors have the ability to offset or mitigate all the aspects of these risk factors" (pp. 3–4).

Risk Factors

The following are the major risk factors:

Lack of Access to Financial Resources   Research indicates that socioeconomic status (SES) plays a major role in determining achievement levels of different students. The schools in low-SES communities are historically poorer-performing and may not be able to provide students the extra educational experiences that benefit them. For example, low-SES students may not have regular access to computers and may not be able to attend SAT courses or obtain private tutors to help them best prepare for college-level study. In some low-SES schools, state and federal programs provide these opportunities for students. However, when they can't provide needed educational opportunities, parents often do not have the funds available to fill the gap (Morales, 2010).

Stereotype Threat   A distressing research finding is that African American and Latinx students from elementary school through college tend to have lower test scores and grades, and tend to drop out of school more often than White students (National Center for Education Statistics, 2018). In addition, regardless of income level, they score lower than White and Asian students on the SAT. For years, educators have been concerned with these statistics, especially when capable minority students fail to perform as well as their White counterparts.

Professor Claude Steele (1999) and his colleague (Aronson, 2002) believe they have identified one possible explanation for this dilemma. They coined the term stereotype threat to mean the fear of doing something that would inadvertently confirm a stereotype. The following is an explanation of this phenomenon.

> **Stereotype Threat:** The fear of doing something that would inadvertently confirm a stereotype. An example is an older person who takes an exam after being told that elderly individuals forget much of what they learn.

Stereotypes can influence an individual's motivation and achievement by suggesting to the target of the stereotype that a negative label could apply to one's self or group. For example, the commonly held stereotype that women are less capable in mathematics than men has been shown to affect the performance of women on standardized math tests. When female students were told beforehand of this negative stereotype, scores were significantly lower compared with a group of women who were led to believe the tests did not reflect these stereotypes (Spencer et al., 1999). In another investigation (Levy, 1996), half of a group of older adults were reminded of the stereotype regarding old age and memory loss, while the other half were reminded of the more positive stereotype that old people are wise. The older adults performed worse on a test of short-term memory when they were presented with the negative stereotype than when they were reminded of the more positive stereotype. Why do you think the women and older adults scored lower under the stereotype threat condition?

Now let's review the research as to how stereotype threat may help to explain the low achievement of certain minority group members. There exists a stereotype that many African American and Latinx students may not have the academic ability to succeed in college. As a result, many minority students may feel at risk of confirming this stereotype and wonder if they can compete successfully at the college level. Thus, just the awareness of the stereotype can affect a student's motivation and behavior. Steele and Aronson (1995) asked African American and White college students to take a difficult standardized test (verbal portion of the Graduate Record Examination). In one condition, the experimenters presented the test as a measure of intellectual ability. In the second condition, the experimenters reduced the stereotype threat by telling the students that they were not interested in measuring their ability with the test, but were interested in the students' verbal problem solving, a skill not related to intelligence. The only difference between the two conditions of the experiment was what the researchers told the students: the test was the same; the students were equally talented and were given the same amount of time to complete the exam.

The results of the experiment indicated a significant difference for African American students. When the test was presented in the non-evaluative way, they solved about twice as many problems on the test as when it was presented in the standard way. Moreover, there was no difference between the performance of African American and White test takers under the no-stereotype threat condition. For the White students, the way the test was presented had no effect on their performance. The researchers believed that by reducing the evaluative condition, they were able to reduce the African American students' anxiety, and, as a result, they performed better on the exam.

Aronson (2002) pointed out that in numerous investigations, researchers have found that the stereotype threat condition does not reduce effort, but in fact makes individuals try harder on tests because they want to invalidate the stereotype. As a result, students under the stereotype threat condition appear more anxious while taking a test. In addition, they also reread questions and recheck their answers more often than when they are not under stereotype threat. As a result of this test anxiety and unnecessary second-guessing, students placed in a stereotype threat condition become poor test takers!

Are you vulnerable to stereotype threat as a member of a minority group, a woman, or an older student who has come back to college a number of years after graduating from high school? Can student-athletes experience stereotype threat? Could the stereotype threat of an "absent-minded professor" influence your instructor's behavior? Has stereotype threat influenced your motivation or behavior in any way? Are you aware of such influence?

It is clear that stereotype threat has a detrimental effect on performance so what can you do about reducing the influence of stereotype threat? Aronson (2002) pointed out that stereotype threat appears to be especially disruptive to individuals who believe that intelligence is fixed rather than changeable. In Chapter 3, we will discuss this topic in more depth and provide you with ways to change your beliefs about intelligence. Additionally, Alter et al. (2010) established that when one is faced with stereotype threat, an effective way to erase the negative effect of it is to reframe the task as a challenge. For example, instead of looking at academic tasks as measuring intelligence (a potential threat), it is beneficial for students to frame them as helping them learn (challenge). There is also some evidence that stereotype threat may be reduced through cooperative learning and other forms of direct contact with other students.

In a successful program that improved the academic achievement of a group of African American freshmen at the University of Michigan (Steele et al., 1997), students lived in a racially integrated "living and learning" community in a part of a large dormitory. The students were recognized for their accomplishment of gaining admission to the university and participated in weekly group discussions to talk about the common problems they all faced. In addition, they participated in advanced workshops in one of their courses that went beyond the material in the course. All of these activities were useful; however, the weekly group discussions appeared to be the most critical part of the program. The researchers believed that when students of different racial groups hear the same concerns expressed, the concerns appear to be less racial. The students also may learn that racial and gender stereotypes play a smaller role in academic success than they may have originally expected.

It is important to realize that the researchers exploring the impact of stereotype threat are not saying that this phenomenon is the sole reason for underachievement by certain minority students. We have already discussed a number of other important factors that can make a difference between a successful and unsuccessful college experience. Nevertheless, stereotype threat must be considered an important factor in understanding underachievement of certain minority students.

Subpar Pre-College Preparation   As another risk factor faced by first-generation college students and students from low-income families, research indicates that teachers' lower expectations in low-socioeconomic schools compared with schools in more affluent neighborhoods may result in the students' lowered academic expectations of themselves. In addition, the students often take less rigorous courses and are not exposed to effective study skills. Recent data demonstrate that compared with students whose parents had a bachelor's degree, first-generation students were much less likely to have graduated from high school with an academically focused curriculum (16 percent vs. 37 percent) and had less Advanced Placement credits (18 percent vs. 44 percent) (NCES, 2018). One low-income, first-generation college student reflected back on her high school experience in the following manner.

> It seemed like we had gaps. It was like we were missing part of the picture … I kept thinking, "gosh, did I miss some lectures along the way?" But I didn't; they just weren't there.

(Richardson & Skinner, 1992, p. 32)

Lack of Family and Community Academic Role Models   Devon learned a great deal about college from her parents. Unfortunately, by definition, first-generation college students don't have this opportunity and must learn how to prepare for college and complete admission forms by themselves or with help from teachers and counselors. Transition to college can be difficult for any student, but when an individual has family members who have experienced this transition, he or she is less likely to feel lost in an unfamiliar environment.

Here is how one low-income, first-generation college student described his feelings about attending college:

> I remember being nervous as hell. … Most of my academic experience up to [this point] wasn't really good. So going to college was like, "What the hell am I doing here?" Parents didn't go to college. So I didn't have any background of what the hell college was. Really not understanding how academia works. And, you know, growing up and being in high school, I didn't have a great experience at all. I was really kind of made to feel like my ideas weren't good, and that was part of the reason for my nervousness.

(Jehangir, 2010, p. 19)

Attending college can be like traveling to a foreign country where you don't speak the language and don't understand the customs and culture of the country. Students who don't understand the college culture tend to feel isolated and even marginalized in the environment. These feelings can lead to anxiety and low motivation because some students may begin to feel that they will not be able to succeed.

Factors That Mitigate Risk and Facilitate Academic Performance

Despite the risk factors described in the previous section, many first-generation, low-income college students succeed in college. In fact, your authors have taught hundreds of such students who demonstrated high levels of motivation and academic competency. Though categorized as first generation and low income, these students achieved as well if not better than many students whose parents and/or siblings attended college. Morales (2010) identified some of the protective factors that lead to their academic resiliency and success.

Sense of Obligation to Family   For some students, a sense of obligation can act as a protective factor and have positive influences for them. The following comments are from an African American female student who shows how obligation to family can operate to support one's success.

> I have to be the first one in my family to graduate from college; I am seen as the golden child. My mother has high expectations of me, and I never want to let her down in any way. See, where I'm from, there are not many opportunities, so when I was given a scholarship to attend the university, I was given the opportunity of a lifetime. It is very important to me that I succeed at this college because I want to be able to get that good paying job, so that my mom won't have to struggle anymore. I want to be able

to set the bar and show people that it isn't impossible for an inner city kid who came from a low-class family to be able to graduate from a four-year college.

(Jehangir, 2010, p. 13)

Although some parents have not attended college, their high expectation for success and strong work ethic can be very inspirational for their children. You may be an adolescent who has experienced such support from your parents.

Caring High School and College Teachers and Counselors   These individuals act as mentors and help students deal with the uncertainty of school. They are likely to exist in all schools and play an important role in helping students succeed. Sometimes one person can make a difference and it is the responsibility of students to find this individual. Help seeking (discussed in Chapter 7) is what self-regulated students do.

Personal Attributes That Support Success   According to Morales' (2010) study of academically resilient (had completed at least 30 college credits with a minimum GPA of 3.0) low-socioeconomic students of color, some personal protective attributes were a strong obligation to their race and ethnicity and community of origin, and a strong future orientation, manifested by goal setting, self-motivation, and a high persistence at academic tasks. Morales found that academically resilient students of color were well informed about racism, discrimination, and bigotry, and were motivated to be in a position to benefit their racial-ethnic group, their families, and their communities. They saw their academic success as a form of political activism. Among the other personal attributes were high self-esteem and internal locus of control. We will discuss these under internal factors.

In summary, many students have certain advantages to help motivate and prepare them for the demands of college. If you are such a student, take advantage of these opportunities. Advantages, however, do not always lead to success. We have seen many students who experienced advantages but come to school undisciplined and perform poorly their first semester because they don't take personal responsibility for their behavior. Whether or not you entered college with the types of advantages discussed here, maintain your motivation and persistence, seek out help, and join college groups so that you feel connected to the college environment.

CLASSROOM ENVIRONMENTAL FACTORS

In an interesting book, *Making the Most of College*, Light (2001) interviewed hundreds of college seniors to identify contextual factors that make college an outstanding experience. One of the most important contextual factors in college is the nature of instruction. Here are some findings about college instruction that appeared to motivate students: First, the students reported that they learned significantly more when instructors structured their courses with many quizzes and short assignments. They liked immediate feedback and the opportunity to revise and make changes in their work. They did not like courses when the only feedback came late or at the end of the semester.

Second, the students reported that they liked classes where the instructors encouraged students to work together on homework assignments. They mentioned that some of their instructors created small study groups in their courses to encourage students to work together outside of class. This activity helped students become more engaged in their courses and helped them develop a sense of a learning community. Similarly, Zhao and Kuh (2004) found that participation in learning communities, focusing on cooperative learning, and greater student interaction, improved student motivation in the classroom.

Third, many students found that small-group tutorials, small seminars, and one-to-one supervision were the highlights of their college careers. They highly recommended that undergraduate students find internships and other experiences where they can be mentored by faculty members.

Fourth, students reported the beneficial impact of racial and ethnic diversity on their college experiences. They reported how much they learned from other students who came from different backgrounds—ethnic, political, religious, or economic.

Fifth, students who get the most out of college and who are happiest organize their time to include activities with faculty members or with other students (see Chapter 7 regarding seeking help and meeting with your professors). Below are comments of one student who sought help from a professor:

> First of all, organic chemistry is very difficult, it's too abstract, so you either know it or you don't know it, and so it was hard to begin it. He helped me out. And when I knock on his [the professor's] door, and he was always there, he always helped me. He tried to push to see who I was, where I was coming from, why I was there, and he's the only one who basically say [sic] "How are you doing? Are you doing all right? Okay, where are you going to be? What do you want?" He's the one who just sit [sic] in there and say, "Yes. You can do it but take little steps at a time, like little by little. Don't push too far, too hard." So that's why he stands out. … Not only me, he encouraged a lot of people. But he takes the time just to listen and he's always there. And he is always there, not only in the course but sometimes if you have a personal [concern] or a problem, he's at least [willing] to listen to you and [would] say, "Okay, this is what you can do, this is what you should do."

(Mullen, 2010, p. 145)

Most students need recommendations from faculty members for scholarships, jobs, or graduate study. Yet, they often fail to establish the kind of relationships with instructors that enable them to request a letter of recommendation. Light (2001) pointed out the advice he gives all his advisees: "Your job is to get to know one faculty member reasonably well this semester. And also to have that faculty member get to know you reasonably well" (p. 86). He reported that as his first-year advisees approach graduation, they tell him that this advice was the most helpful suggestion they received during their freshman year.

Professors differ as much as any other group of individuals; some are easy to approach, whereas others make it appear that they are trying to avoid students. In fact, in many large universities, a student has to work hard to make contact with some professors. Whether a professor is approachable or not makes a difference in student motivation. Mearns et al. (2007) found that if an instructor is approachable and sensitive to student needs, students are committed to working harder. Similarly, Bryson and Hand (2007) identified effective instructors as demanding high standards and challenging students but also making themselves available to students. Whether your professors appear approachable or not, think about the challenge of getting to know at least one instructor or professor well each semester. Not only will you find that the experience will motivate you to achieve in his or her class, but when the time comes for letters of recommendation, you will have a list of professors to ask. So, try not to be intimidated by your instructors: go to office hours, sign up for study sessions, and get a few students together and invite the instructor to lunch if you don't want to do it by yourself.

EXERCISE 2.1: SELF-OBSERVATION: ANALYZING MY PERSONAL AND SOCIOCULTURAL BACKGROUND

Directions: What attitudes and beliefs have you brought to college that could influence your motivation and academic behavior? Check either Yes or No for each of the questions listed and then write a summary statement about how your personal, social, and cultural experiences influence your present motivation. What do you see as your areas of greatest strengths in meeting your goals? What areas do you need to work on to ensure your success in college?

		Yes	No
1.	Did you like high school?		
2.	Were you active in social activities in high school?		
3.	Are you a member of a minority group with a small enrollment in your college?		
4.	Do you have parents and/or siblings who have attended college?		
5.	Do your parents want you to major in a specific area?		
6.	Are your aspirations the same as your parents' or other family members'?		
7.	Are you paying for your own education?		
8.	Do you have responsibility for caring for children while in college?		
9.	Are you older than most of the students in your classes?		
10.	Have you met students with common interests?		
11.	Have you been able to cope with the stressors of college life?		
12.	Have your expectations about college life been fulfilled to date?		

Summary Statement:

_____

_____

_____

_____ ■

EXERCISE 2.2: SELF-OBSERVATION: ANALYZING CLASSROOM EXPERIENCES

Directions: The following are some questions to consider about college courses. Select one of the courses you are taking this term and check either Yes or No for each of the questions listed. Think about how your responses could influence your academic motivation and behavior. Compare your responses with those of other students in your class who are taking the same or different courses. How can you be more active in making the most of your college experience?

		Yes	No
1.	Are you given freedom to select your own topics for papers and assignments?		
2.	Does the instructor offer an opportunity for discussion in class?		
3.	Is there an opportunity to work with other students?		
4.	Is the grading competitive (i.e., grading on a curve)?		
5.	Does your instructor or teaching assistant appear willing to meet with you?		
6.	Have you had a personal meeting with your instructor?		
7.	Does the instructor provide clear guidelines as to what is expected in the course?		
8.	Does this class have more than 50 students in it?		
9.	Does your instructor provide timely feedback on assignments?		
10.	Are you participating in group study sessions?		

Although it is important for students to understand that the classroom environment can influence their motivation, they need to take responsibility for their own behavior. The second author's daughter came home one day during her freshman year and told him that she received a low C on a midterm exam. In the same breath, she reported that she did not like the instructor, implying a relationship between the low grade and her dislike of the instructor. The second author responded that his expectations for her academic performance were not based on her like or dislike of courses or professors and told her she had to learn to do well in all types of situations.

In Chapter 1, you learned that self-regulated students learn how to overcome obstacles to increase the probability of their academic success. Think about some of the actions you can take to improve your academic learning when you don't like your instructor, find the course boring, or when the instructor spends all his or her time lecturing and doesn't encourage student interaction or small-group work.

INTERNAL FACTORS

Students' goals, beliefs, feelings, and perceptions determine their motivated behaviors and, in turn, academic performance. For example, if students value a task and believe they can master it, they are more likely to use different learning strategies, try hard, and persist until completion of the task. If students believe that intelligence changes over time, they are more likely to exhibit effort in difficult courses than students who believe intelligence is fixed. In this section of the chapter, we are going to explain why the answers to the following questions can provide insight to your own motivation:

- What is my value for the different academic courses and tasks?
- What are my hopes, expectations, and fears about the future?
- What are my goals?
- Why do I want to reach my goals? What is my goal orientation?
- Do I believe I can do well on different academic tasks?
- What do I believe to be the causes of my successes and failures?

Notice that all of the questions deal with beliefs and perceptions. You can learn a great deal about your motivation by examining your beliefs and perceptions. We will next explore the role of value orientation, possible selves, goals, goal orientation, efficacy, and attributions in understanding motivated behaviors: the degree to which we start tasks, persist at them, and invest the necessary effort to succeed (Figure 2.3).

FIGURE 2.3   Internal Factors Influencing Motivated Behaviors

What Is My Value for the Different Academic Courses and Tasks?

Values and interests play an important role in academic behavior. They affect students' choices of activities, as well as the level of effort and persistence they put forth on a task or assignment. Eccles (2007) and colleagues have found that the perceived value of learning tasks is determined by four factors: 1) the degree to which one expects to enjoy the task (intrinsic interest); 2) the degree to which the task is useful in the context of one's goals (extrinsic or utility value); 3) the extent to which engaging in the task is important for one's self-concept or identity (attainment value); and 4) the degree to which the benefits of engaging in the task outweigh the costs.

Let's consider three students in a chemistry course. The first student decides to take the course because it fulfils a general education requirement. She has very little interest in the subject. This is an example of a student having extrinsic or utility value for the task. The second student is enrolled in the course because she enjoys learning about science and would like to pursue a career in the health sciences. This student has both intrinsic and utility value for the task. The third student wants to learn chemistry because doing well can help her get on the dean's list and feeling competent is an important value in her life. The primary motivation for this student is attainment value. As you can see, you can have different value combinations for the same task.

Value Orientation: The different reasons for engaging in tasks such as enjoyment, usefulness, importance, and cost-benefit analysis.

All three of these students want to succeed but may behave differently during the term. At times, their different **value orientations** may influence them to make different decisions regarding their effort and persistence in the course. For example, during final exams, students often have to make decisions concerning where to place their greatest effort. Students who are taking a course just to complete an elective may decide to spend more time during finals on another course they enjoy and where higher achievement is more important.

Students who limit their involvement or effort in a particular class are not necessarily lazy or unmotivated. Sometimes, it is a matter of weighing the cost and benefits. If the cost of engaging in a specific class will require them to sacrifice time from other important classes or extracurricular activities such as athletics or social organizations, they may invest less effort. Sometimes, the cost can also be the anticipated anxiety of engaging in the task or loss of a positive self-image. College students do not develop a personal interest in or high value for all their courses. The task, however, is to manage motivation to successfully complete courses, even when there is little value or interest in them.

What Are My Hopes, Expectations, and Fears about the Future?

We have just discussed that students may have different values. Based on your values and your past and current success or failure in pursuing what you value, you are likely to have specific "possible selves" (Markus & Nurius, 1986; Oyserman, Destin & Novin, 2015). **Possible selves** are images of yourself in the future that you either dream about or expect to become, on the one hand, or hope to avoid becoming, on the other hand. When you view your hoped-for possible selves as attainable, they become expected selves. Your hoped-for or expected possible selves could include being a good student (e.g., "I will get through my freshman year with solid grades"), making the band, or obtaining a great job. Your fears could include failure in schoolwork (e.g., "I will flunk school"), not starting on an athletic team, loneliness, or poverty.

Possible Selves: Future-oriented images of self that individuals expect and hope to become as well as are afraid of becoming.

In addition to your values, your possible selves are influenced by many other factors already discussed in this chapter: your family's socioeconomic and educational level and expectations, your gender and ethnic background, and your relationship with your instructors in the academic setting. Think about how stereotype threat may influence your possible selves. When you examine your possible selves in Exercise 2.3, determine if any of your fears are dictated by a stereotype you are afraid of confirming.

Why is it important for you to become aware of your future-oriented hopes, expectations, and fears? Researchers (Markus & Nurius, 1986; Oyserman, Destin & Novin, 2017) have shown that possible selves play a role in directing your behavior, whether you are conscious of it or not. That is, if you have a hoped-for self of "me as a straight-A student," you are likely to only perform behaviors consistent with that possible self (e.g., using more meaningful strategies than simple memorization, and optimizing your physical and social environment for study purposes). Additionally, fears can be very motivating as well. For example, if you have a feared self of "being a drop-out," you may be more likely to work hard in college to avoid that possible self than students who have not seriously considered such an outcome. Interestingly, Oyserman and Markus (1990) found that hoped-for selves will be most effective as motivational resources when they are linked to feared possible selves, representing what could happen if the positive outcome is not realized (e.g., "I will finish college as a straight-A student because otherwise I will likely not get into the graduate school of my choice"). As a result, students are likely to select strategies that both increase the likelihood of hoped-for selves and decrease the likelihood of feared selves becoming a reality. On the other hand, if a student only has feared selves, a sense of hopelessness may prevail.

One of the problems some students face in college is that they either do not have academic hoped-for selves or only have feared selves as a student. Here is one student's statement: "I'm going to play professional football. Ever since I was a little kid my dream has been to be a great tailback. And that's what I think about all the time. Nothing else matters that much, especially school! Don't bother me about learning all this stuff. I just need to get by until I am ready for the NFL" (Hock et al., 2006, p. 205). This student is focused on his hoped-for self as an NFL player. It is possible that this student lacks academic possible selves because of a history of repeated failure and even ridicule in school, resulting in a complete loss of hope for himself as a student. Another possible explanation is that he is an outstanding football player and a good student, but he strongly believes that football is more relevant for his future than academics. Since he has no hoped-for selves as a student, academics is less important to him.

EXERCISE 2.3: POSSIBLE SELVES: MY HOPES, EXPECTATIONS, AND FEARS ABOUT THE FUTURE (ADAPTED FROM OYSERMAN & MARKUS, 1990)

Directions:

1. List below the things that you most *hope* you will become in the next year.
2. List below the things that you are most *likely* to become in the next year.
3. List below the things that you most *fear* you will become in the next year.

As you review your possible selves, answer the following questions: In what areas do I have hopes, expectations, and fears? In other words, what kinds of "roles" do I occupy (i.e., a student, a person, an athlete)? Do I have only fears or hopes in a certain area of my life or are they balanced? What is the source of my possible selves?

What Are My Goals?

Though possible selves are very important in determining our motivation, they do not always result in self-regulatory behavior as we may not be consciously aware of them or they may simply be too vague (e.g., "me as doing well in school next year"). Oyserman and her colleagues (2004, 2006) found that possible selves are only effective when associated with specific goals and self-regulatory strategies to achieve them.

Each year, we find many differences in the abilities of students to articulate their goals as we begin the "learning to learn" course. Some students have clear and well-defined goals. They know why they are in college and what they are attempting to attain. At the other end of the spectrum, some students lack academic possible selves, and have therefore not defined their personal goals and are not sure why they are in college. Some of our students who are raising families or who have returned to college after some absence appear to have more specific goals than some students who come directly from high school. How would you explain this difference?

Think about a musician, athlete, or businessperson who has hoped-for selves and wants to excel in his or her area of expertise but has no specific goals to direct his or her behavior. It is very difficult to be motivated without specific personal goals and therefore, it is important to set goals in different life areas because such goals serve to motivate behavior. Goals enhance performance in five major ways (Locke & Latham, 1990, 2013):

- *Effort:* The goals you set for yourself influence what you attend to and how hard you try to maximize your performance. The more difficult the goal, the harder you are likely to work to attain it.
- *Duration or persistence:* When you work on a task without a goal, you are likely to allow your attention to drift, become more easily interrupted, and even stop working without completing the task. When you have a goal in mind, you have a more clearly defined point in the performance that defines when it is time to quit or withdraw from the task (i.e., when the goal is attained).
- *Direction of attention*: Goals direct your performance toward the task at hand and away from unrelated or irrelevant tasks.
- *Strategic planning*: To accomplish a goal, you need to develop an action plan or strategy. Goal setting encourages strategic planning, because the presence of a goal encourages you to decide how to proceed.
- *Reference point*: When you identify where it is you are headed (i.e., have a goal) and receive feedback on where you are, you can evaluate your performance and determine what further actions need to be taken (if any). In fact, it is your satisfaction or dissatisfaction with this evaluation that may have the greatest impact on your motivation.

Have you identified some goals you would like to attain this term or year? If so, do you have goals in any of the following areas: academic, social, occupational, or personal? How has your success or failure in attaining previous goals influenced your motivation in different areas of your life?

Why Do I Want to Reach My Goals? What Is My Goal Orientation?

In addition to setting goals, it is important to be aware of the reasons or purposes for setting goals. Researchers (Ames & Archer, 1988; Berger & Archer, 2018) refer to this as goal orientation and have identified two types of achievement goals: mastery and performance. A **mastery goal** is oriented toward learning as much as possible for the purpose of self-improvement, irrespective of the performance of others. A **performance goal** focuses on social comparison and competition, with the main purpose of outperforming others on the task.

Mastery Goal: Learning as much as possible for the purpose of self-improvement, irrespective of the performance of others.

Performance Goal: An orientation toward learning in which outperforming others is a major concern.

Think about how you approach different classes. Are you interested in learning as much as you can in a class, or is your primary goal to simply do better than the majority of students so you can attain a satisfactory grade? It is not uncommon for students to have a mastery goal orientation in one class and a performance goal orientation in another. It is also possible to have a performance and mastery goal orientation in the same class.

An analysis of the distinction between mastery and performance goals in Table 2.1 shows how students define schooling and learning in different ways. The goal orientation that students adopt in a course influences the effort they exhibit in learning tasks and the type of learning strategies they use. Thus, when students adopt a mastery goal orientation, they are more likely to have a positive attitude toward the task (even outside the classroom), monitor their own comprehension, use more complex learning strategies, and relate newly learned material with previously learned material. In contrast, students who adopt a performance orientation tend to focus on memorization and other rote learning strategies and often do not engage in problem solving and critical thinking. In general, they do not think about what they learn, but rather look for shortcuts and quick payoffs. Students with performance goals want to look competent (e.g., Anxious Anna) or avoid looking incompetent (e.g., Defensive Dimitri).

In general, research suggests that adopting a mastery goal orientation has positive academic outcomes. However, it has been found that performance goals also can be related to positive academic performance in introductory college classes (Harackiewicz et al., 1997). To explain this finding, Elliot and Church (1997) found that performance goals can be differentiated into approach and avoid dimensions. Performance-approach oriented students are driven to experience success by demonstrating their superior ability while performance-avoid oriented students want to avoid the appearance of incompetence. For example, a student who wants to demonstrate to her instructor and other students that she is better at math than most of her peers is performance-approach oriented while a student who wants to avoid looking like he is poorer in math than most of his peers is performance-avoid oriented. Whereas a performance-approach orientation can have positive effects on achievement such as earning high grades, a performance-avoid orientation is always detrimental.

In addition to a student's individual goal orientation in a particular class, the learning environment also has an effect on whether one endorses mastery or performance goals. For example, large lecture classes where instructors grade on a curve and success is defined as outperforming others is very likely to instill a performance orientation in most students. Thus, the grading method and type of tests used may create a performance-oriented classroom environment. In the same investigation, the researchers found that mastery goals predicted interest in the introductory class, whereas performance goals did not. We have an interesting dilemma: each goal was related to one indicator of success (academic performance or interest) but not the other. In this situation, it appears that

TABLE 2.1
Two Definitions of Schooling

	Mastery	Performance
Success defined as …	improvement, progress, mastery, innovation, creativity	high grades, high performance compared with others, relative achievement on standardized measures
Value placed on …	effort, academic venturesomeness	demonstrating high performance relative to effort
Basis for satisfaction …	progress, challenge, mastery	doing better than others, success relative to effort
Error viewed as …	part of the learning process, informational	failure, evidence of lack of ability
Ability viewed as …	developing through effort	fixed

Adapted from Ames and Archer (1988).

students who endorsed both mastery and performance-approach goals were most likely to like the course and achieve well.

EXERCISE 2.4: IDENTIFYING MASTERY AND PERFORMANCE GOAL ORIENTATIONS

Directions: Based on the information in Table 2.1, classify the following statements as either mastery (M) or performance (P) goal oriented by writing an M or a P in the space provided:

1. "I enjoy finding extra material to read in this course."
2. "It is important to me to do better than my friends."
3. "If you don't have the ability to do well, more effort is a waste of time."
4. "I'm not doing as well as I can, but I will improve."
5. "My adviser thinks I should take another advanced math course, but I don't want to because it may lower my average."

Student Reflections

For years, my goal in all my classes has been to achieve a certain grade. The grade differed from class to class depending on my confidence for success in the course. This strategy has been my plan of attack since elementary school. Unfortunately, my goals have never changed, and I rarely participate in class just for the simple pleasure of learning. I enjoy a class once a discussion begins, but I usually prefer to be somewhere else. I am performance rather than mastery driven. I do not care to learn anything for the sake of learning. Schoolwork is just a means to an end: graduation and a degree.

Learning how to understand my own motivation has helped my self-regulation in school.

Every class is different, and I have learned to take its importance into consideration. Some classes are simply for utility purposes—a means to an end. In these classes, I set goals for myself based on performing at a level equal to or better than my peers. However, in my major courses, I am concerned with learning all that I possibly can. These classes are exciting, and I am strictly mastery oriented. By seeing my classes for what they are, I can set goals suitable for their purpose. Each one is different, and as I achieve in each class, my confidence is maintained because of the goals I set. Whenever I begin to feel discouraged with a low grade on an exam or paper in a class that I don't value, I remind myself of my goal for the course. In this way, I don't get down on myself.

In the Student Reflections section, two students present different views on goal orientation. The first student admits that his primary goal orientation is to meet requirements, not learn. The second student reports that his goal orientation is influenced by the value he placed on different courses. What factors influence your goal orientations?

Your goal orientation or orientations in a particular course can greatly impact your motivation, even before you ever open a textbook or take your first lecture notes. Analyze your goal orientation in each of the classes you are currently taking. Do you have the same goal orientation in all of your classes? Do you think you exhibit both orientations in some classes? Do you find that your learning behavior differs depending on your goal orientation? Also, think about a hobby or particular interest you have. How long can you persist on the task before getting tired or bored? How is your behavior related to your goal orientation?

Do I Believe I Can Do Well on Different Academic Tasks?

Values and goals determine students' reasons for engaging in different tasks. Another important belief is **self-efficacy**, which refers to the evaluation students have about their abilities or skills to successfully complete a specific task (Bandura, 1982, 2018). The key question that determines self-efficacy is: "Am I capable of succeeding at this task?"

Self-Efficacy: The belief that one can successfully complete a specific task.

Educational researchers have found that efficacy beliefs are among the most important predictors of student motivation and self-regulated behaviors (Hattie & Donoghue, 2015; Robbins, Lauver, Le, Davis, & Langley, 2004). Students with high efficacy are more likely than their low-efficacy counterparts to choose difficult tasks, expend greater effort, persist longer, use more complex learning strategies, and experience less fear and anxiety regarding academic tasks.

Self-efficacy is situation specific. You might have a different level of self-efficacy in a biology versus a political science course. Further, you are likely to have different levels of self-efficacy even in the same class. For example, you may have a high self-efficacy for completing a term paper in a psychology course but a low sense of efficacy regarding your performance on multiple-choice questions. Similarly, you may judge yourself to be very competent at basketball but not at tennis. We have efficacy beliefs about each task we undertake.

Bandura (2015) wrote that "one of the most powerful effects of self-efficacy beliefs is their influence on the choices people make" (p. 1036). He points out a decision about one's career as one of those choices. Therefore, while self-efficacy often predicts what goals we set and how well we perform in the moment, it also has long-reaching consequences for our personal identity and well-being.

We derive our self-efficacy beliefs primarily from four sources: our own previous performance on the task, observing similar others perform the same task, verbal and social messages we receive from others, and our physiological and emotions states (Bandura, 1977). The most influential source is our own previous performance on the task with success raising and failure lowering our self-efficacy. An effective way of raising self-efficacy is dividing the task at hand into small steps and setting short-term, reasonable goals that allow us to experience progress and success. In addition, as a student, it is important to surround yourself with successful similar others and people who believe in you.

We mentioned in Chapter 1 that our primary goal is to help you become a more successful learner. An important step is to help you feel more competent to excel in the different academic tasks you experience. Setting goals is one way to enhance your sense of efficacy. As you work on academic tasks, you should determine your progress by analyzing your performance according to your goals. Recognizing that you are making progress toward your goals can validate your initial sense of self-efficacy and maintain your behavior as you move toward goal attainment. Learning how to use different learning strategies is another way to enhance your sense of efficacy.

Monitoring your self-efficacy on tasks can focus attention on your beliefs about the effectiveness of your study methods. Zimmerman, Bonner, and Kovach (1996) suggested a procedure that can be used for quizzes or homework assignments (see Follow-Up Activity 3). Before taking your next quiz or exam, read all of the questions and estimate your ability to answer the questions on a ten-point scale. The lower the score, the less competent you feel; the higher the score, the more competent you feel. Compare your actual score on the quizzes or exams with your efficacy scores. Your self-efficacy ratings can operate like a thermostat, providing information you can use to modify or change your learning and study behavior. For example, how would you explain a situation in which your efficacy ratings are always higher than your actual test scores, or where your efficacy ratings are always lower than your actual test scores?

Self-efficacy monitoring helps you gain accuracy in predicting your learning. If quizzes or exams are more demanding than you expect, you may need to study harder to succeed. Rating your efficacy too low or being overly optimistic about your performance can be detrimental to your academic success. The more accurate your perceptions of competence or efficacy, the more likely you will be to use the information to make appropriate changes in your learning and study strategies.

WHAT DO I BELIEVE TO BE THE CAUSES OF MY SUCCESSES AND FAILURES?

When an event occurs, individuals can interpret it in different ways. Consider two college students of equal ability in the same class who just received a C on a term paper. The first student is very upset because he does not think the instructor's grading was fair, and further, that the instructor does not like him. He decides that there is not much he can do to obtain a high grade in the course. The second student determines that the grade reflected the amount of time he spent completing the task and decides that he needs to work harder in the future.

Attribution: An individual's perception of the causes of their own success or failure.

Why did the two students of equal ability interpret their experiences differently? One explanation is that the two students made different attributions about their performances on the term papers. An **attribution** is an individual's perception of the causes of his or her success or failure (Weiner, 1986, 2018). Attribution theory helps explain why individuals respond differently to the same outcomes.

The most common attributions for academic performance are ability ("I did well because I am smart" or "I did poorly because I am not capable") and effort ("I studied hard for the test" or "I did not study hard enough"). However, students often make other attributions, such as "I was lucky or unlucky," "The task was easy or hard," "I was tired," "I did not feel well," or "The instructor was unfair."

Weiner (1986, 2018), a leading motivational researcher, believes that how students perceive the causes of their prior successes and failures is the most important factor determining how they will approach a particular task in the future and how long they will persist at it. Causes can be categorized in broad terms as internal or external and controllable or uncontrollable. For example, students who believe their successes and failures are because of internal controllable causes such as their level of effort are likely to try harder in future situations and persist on difficult tasks. Morales (2010), in studying academically successful low-income students of color, identified their internal locus of control among the key protective factors. Students with an internal locus of control are more likely to seek assistance from their instructor if they do not understand the material and will attend extra-help sessions when necessary. Other examples of internal controllable causes are the quality of learning strategies used in test preparation and starting to study several weeks before the final exam rather than the night prior. In contrast, students who believe their successes and failures are external and uncontrollable (e.g., because of luck or the generosity of the teacher) are less likely to seek the help they need. One's ability is generally seen as due to heredity, and therefore, though internal, it is perceived to be uncontrollable. If a student believes that they simply do not have the ability to do well in a specific content area, they are not likely to seek help. After all, if they asked for help and still do not perform well, the embarrassment is worse.

Now that you know that attributions can have a powerful impact on your success and failure, we will discuss how you can use this information. One implication of this theory is to understand the role of attributions in your own learning. Remember that the fact that you attribute a cause to some factor does not mean that your attribution reflects reality. Think about a friend who has the tendency to attribute a low test grade to "tricky" questions or an unfair instructor when the grade was really because of poor preparation.

It is important to consider how you interpret your own behavior. Educational research indicates that self-regulated learners tend to attribute failure to corrective causes and attribute successes to their own personal abilities (Zimmerman, 2015). Ask yourself the following questions:

- "When I perform poorly, do I attribute my performance to uncontrollable factors such as low ability? Are there alternative explanations for the causes of my academic performances?"
- "What role do attributions play in my understanding of my achievement and motivation?"
- "Could I benefit from attributing a poor performance to lack of effort or failure to use appropriate learning strategies rather than to lack of ability?"

Many students have difficulty in courses because they lack prior knowledge, use inappropriate learning strategies, or fail to monitor their comprehension—all factors that are controllable. When students recognize that their behavior is modifiable, they will more likely feel motivated to achieve.

As the semester progresses, it is not uncommon for students to feel "up and down" at different times. Attribution theory can help students to better understand their own feelings. Attributions are related to different emotional responses. For example, whether individuals attribute failure to ability or effort influences how they will feel about themselves. Attributing failure to lack of ability elicits feelings of shame and humiliation; attributing failure to lack of effort leads to guilt and regret, which often leads to an increase in effort the next time. Emotions or feelings will change if attributions are changed. Therefore, individuals should carefully consider all the possible reasons for their performance before they draw any conclusions, especially when they do not perform as well as they expected. Most important, they should consider other causes besides lack of ability, especially effort.

COVINGTON'S SELF-WORTH THEORY

Self-worth is the need for students to maintain a positive image of themselves and their ability. It is similar to such terms as self-esteem or self-respect. According to self-worth theory (Covington, 1992; Covington, von Hoene & Voge, 2017), individuals learn that society values people because of their accomplishments. Success enhances the sense of worth. However, if a person fails at a task, the feedback evokes the possibility of a lack of ability and creates feelings of unworthiness and self-rejection. As a result, when individuals are faced with the possibility of failure, they will avoid the situation or develop strategies to prevent any inferences to a lack of their ability. It is this fear of failure and not lack of caring or interest in the subject matter that often leads to inappropriate academic behavior.

> **Self-Worth:** The need for students to maintain a positive image of themselves and their ability.

We use many different strategies to maintain our self-worth when low performance occurs. Covington (1992) identified a number of these strategies. Note how the following strategies function to change the attributional focus for failure to other explanations than lack of ability:

> *Procrastination*: If an individual studies at the last minute and does not have enough time to properly prepare for an exam, failure cannot be attributed to lack of ability.
> *Unattainable goals*: If an individual selects very difficult goals, failure is often assured. However, failure in such tasks reveals little about one's ability because most individuals would fail.
> *Underachievers*: If an individual avoids any test of his or her ability by just doing the minimum to get by, he or she can maintain an inflated opinion of ability: "I could do it if I really tried."
> *Anxiety*: If an individual argues that one's poor performance is the result of test-taking anxiety, then one can't blame the performance as the result of low ability. In other words, "It's better to appear anxious than stupid."

(Covington, 1992, p. 88)

Instructors like students who try. Do you feel worse about a grade on a test or paper when you have worked hard or when you exhibited little effort? Educational research indicates that students experienced greatest shame with a combination of high effort and failure and least shame with a combination of low effort and failure (Covington & Omelich, 1979). This research helps explain why failure-avoiding students often do not try. Expending effort and still failing poses a serious threat to one's self-worth. The student who does not try but fails can always rationalize that success could have been achieved through proper effort, thus maintaining a reasonable level of self-worth. Instructors, however, tend to reinforce students who demonstrate effort and are more critical of those who do not. Understanding the perspectives of both the instructor and the student helps reveal how effort can become a "double-edged sword" for many students. They must walk the tightrope between the threatening extremes of high effort and no effort at all. They must demonstrate some effort to avoid negative sanctions from their instructors, but not enough to risk shame should they try hard and fail. Some students use excuses to maintain a balance between these extremes. A popular tactic is to try hard but to use excuses to explain why trying did not help. Such behavior avoids any inference to low ability.

Hopeless Henry believes that his failures are because of a lack of ability. As a result, he does not believe that hard work will pay off. The problem with this belief is that he is likely to exert little effort even in situations in which effort would lead to success.

What is interesting about self-worth theory is that it offers a different explanation of failure. Many students are motivated, but for the wrong reasons—they are more motivated to avoid failure than motivated to succeed. They are driven by circumstances to protect their self-worth.

A college friend of the second author was a bright but anxious student. He always told everyone that he never had enough time to study before an exam. Everyone was impressed by the success he achieved with little apparent effort. However, in situations where his achievement was unsatisfactory, he would also remind us that he did not spend much time studying. It was not until years later that the second author learned he had always found time to study regularly during the term. His strategy was to protect his self-worth. The moral of this story is not to gauge the amount of time and effort you need to prepare by listening to the comments of others.

What strategies have you used to protect yourself from the possibilities of failure? Have you ever raised your hand early in a class period to answer a question, knowing that the instructor might not call on you later? Have you remained silent when asked a question by an instructor, hoping that if you paused long enough the instructor would rephrase the question once or twice until either the answer was given to you or someone else was called on?

We both can identify with the following situation, and it may be uncomfortably familiar to you, too. A common practice in language classes is to require students to take turns translating sentences into English. As the instructor moves down the row asking one student after another to translate, anxious students are not paying attention to each translation. Instead, they are counting down the row to locate the sentence they will have to translate and begin practicing the sentence. During this time, they have missed the translations of all the previous sentences. Learning the sentences is vital to the content of the particular lesson, but some students are more motivated to avoid failure than to master the content of the lesson.

Let's explore this notion of fear of failure in more depth. Cox (2009) also believes that students' past experiences with failure lead to fear. These experiences often are so influential that some students come to believe that they can't succeed and feel that at any moment their weaknesses will be exposed for all to see. For example, if students come to college with poor writing skills, they may constantly worry that eventually their instructors will learn about their deficiency. The student's beliefs, that is, the self-doubt and anxiety about succeeding in a course, result in disengagement strategies such as not asking for help when needed, avoiding interaction with instructors, or even setting lower academic goals for themselves.

Another major disengagement strategy used by students is not attending class regularly. After all, if you don't attend class, you will not be exposed to answering questions or participating in class discussions when you are not prepared or don't understand the material. Unfortunately, this strategy often backfires on students. A study (Crede et al., 2010) highlighted the importance of class attendance. The researchers found that class attendance was a better predictor of academic success than students' SAT scores, high school GPA, or study habits. Why does class attendance influence grades? The researchers believe that regular class attendance allows students to obtain information not found in textbooks or lecture materials presented online.

The fear of failure can also explain why many students refrain from asking questions in class. Many students tell us that they don't ask questions because they don't want to appear "dumb" or unintelligent and want to avoid embarrassment. One student explained his behavior by reporting that he likes to remain "hidden" or be just another face in the group. Another student reported that she felt pressure because when she asked a question everyone would turn around to look at her (Dieckmeyer & Dembo, 2007).

How did some of us come to be more motivated to avoid failure than motivated to succeed? Have we always been this way? Dweck made an interesting observation of infants:

> Infants stretch their skills daily. Not just ordinary skills, but the most difficult tasks of a lifetime, like learning to walk and talk. They never decide it's too hard or not worth the effort. Babies don't worry about making mistakes or humiliating themselves. They walk, they fall, they get up. They just barge forward.

(Dweck, 2006, p. 16)

Is it just a coincidence that infants learn so much during their first year of life; perhaps more so than any other time in their lives? Teachers observe a change in some students' behavior during early childhood. As students proceed in school, they are often more hesitant to respond in class, demonstrate anxiety, and are less likely to respond positively to challenging academic tasks. What do you think happens between infancy and early childhood, and even adolescence? What happens to students that cause changes in their motivation to learn? Is the difference related to how adults respond to infants' and adolescents' success and failure? What is your experience with ability and self-worth? Do you think society communicates to children early in their lives that unless they achieve, they are unworthy? Does self-worth theory help you understand the behavior of anyone you know? How do you deal with fear of failure in school, in sports, or any other endeavor in which you participate?

Eliminating Academic Fear of Failure

The following suggestions can help you reduce or eliminate your fear of failure (adapted from Martin, 2010). These suggestions emphasize the importance of thinking differently about your success and failure or low performance. It is faulty beliefs that cause you to spend considerable time and energy to protect your self-worth.

1 Focus on mastery and improvement to promote a success focus, which will help to minimize fear of failure and self-defeating behaviors.

Earlier in this chapter, we discussed different views of intelligence. If you hold a fixed view of your competencies, which means that you are unlikely to improve your knowledge or skills, you tend to be more focused on avoiding negative judgments about your behavior and use strategies to protect your self-worth. Students who view their competence as something that can be improved tend to see failure and poor performance as feedback they can use to improve future performance. We will discuss different views of intelligence or "mindsets" more in Chapter 3.

2 Expand your view of success to include improvement, personal bests, and new understanding in your academic work.

Students often focus entirely on the end product and not on how hard they worked or what they learned as they completed a task. It is important to expand your view of success to consider progress and improvement. This view provides encouragement and hope that you can improve your performance over time. Most important, this belief can reduce the use of failure-avoiding strategies and allow you to focus on how you can be a more successful learner.

> 3 Understand that your self-worth as a student is not dependent on your ability to perform, but more on your effort, learning strategies, and attitude.

Students who base their self-worth solely on how they perform are more likely to use strategies to avoid failure because they don't want to feel worthless. Instead, you should consider how hard you tried, and whether you have done your best in the given situation by using appropriate learning strategies and having a positive attitude.

> 4 Anticipate environments and situations that might trigger a fear of failure and attempt to focus more on what needs to be accomplished and mastery of the tasks—and less on how your work will be evaluated or compared with someone else's.

When you learn about a task or exam, begin planning what you need to do to succeed. Chapter 6 on time management will be a valuable resource for you. Determine areas that you need to spend more time on or with which you need assistance. Plan in advance and seek help from individuals who can help you. In sum, focus on what you need to do to succeed.

> 5 Minimize the extent to which your feelings about yourself are based on how other individuals respond to you or evaluate you.

When students overemphasize the importance of how others think of them, their self-worth is likely to increase and decrease on a regular basis. This fluctuation occurs because the opinions of others are likely to be inconsistent or not adequately informed. The point is that you can't allow the reactions of others to dictate your own self-judgments. In Chapter 1, you learned that one characteristic of a self-regulatory learner is to judge one's own performance. You can't always be successful or competent. Naturally, this does not mean that you are a failure! We are not saying that you should never listen to the criticism or negative feedback from instructors or peers. Instead, you should listen to feedback from others but also use your evaluation of your performance to determine your next steps. In this manner, you can learn to take charge of your own learning.

> 6 Attempt to obtain feedback on your academic work so you understand why you performed as you did. Link the feedback to your behavior (i.e., how hard you tried, the strategies you used to learn the material, and your attitude about the task). This information can be used to develop a plan to improve your performance or repeat your success on the next exam or task.

We often find that students do not take the opportunity to attend office hours to learn why they received the grade they were given on an exam or paper. Many students feel that once the exam is over there is nothing they can do to improve. What they fail to realize is how much information they can obtain that can help their study plans for the next exam or paper. You can't develop a plan to do better if you don't understand why you succeeded or failed to do well on the present exam or paper. We find that there are usually some identifiable reasons why students performed poorly that can be addressed the next time. Again, a poor performance should not reflect on one's worth as a person. Instead, it reflects some of the learning strategies students used, their preparation, and the nature of their effort. Chapter 7 provides some good suggestions for how to have effective meetings with your instructor when you seek help. This information is important in planning for the next academic task.

AM I MOTIVATED TO CHANGE MY ACADEMIC BEHAVIOR?

In the first chapters you learned what it takes to be a self-regulated learner. The major issue that you now face is whether you are actually motivated to change your academic behavior. No one, not your parents, friends, or college instructors, can make you change. You need to decide whether you want to learn and study differently in college than you did in high school. Of course, if you were an A student in high school, we would recommend that you not change many things. However, if you think there is some room for improvement, then you should consider what aspects of your academic behavior in college you want to change.

The next student reflection was written by a student in our learning strategies course about six weeks into the semester.

Wouldn't it be nice if all students were influenced in the same manner? Unfortunately, students react differently to change. Prochaska and Prochaska (1999) suggested four reasons why individuals have difficulty changing their behavior: they can't, they don't want to, they don't know what to change, or they do not know how to change. If you would like to change but have difficulties, think about how these reasons might apply to you. We'll discuss each of these reasons to help you analyze your own behavior by using the motivational topics we discussed in the chapter. You might want to review self-efficacy, attribution and self-worth theory, and goal orientation and value orientation before you read this final section.

Student Reflections

Last week I took my midterm of this semester.

Despite all the discussion in my learning and study strategies course, I basically studied the same way I have always been studying most of my life. I read over the material a few times, underlined some key points, and woke up early to review the material. It is not that I thought the new learning strategies would not be helpful, but it seemed to me that they took more time than it was worth. When I received a lower grade than I expected, I decided to try some of the new strategies. I now realize that I can cover the same amount of material in the same time or even shorter. Most important, instead of simply reading the material over and over again, I now understand the material much more because I am generating questions while I read and attempting to answer them. My mind does not wander as much as it did before because I have a purpose to my reading. I find that I can remember much more material after each study session.

I CAN'T CHANGE

A key factor to consider when you believe that you can't change is your level of self-efficacy regarding a specific task. Remember that researchers have found that your level of self-efficacy can predict behaviors such as choosing to engage in tasks and persisting at them in the face of difficulty. Therefore, if you hold a low sense of efficacy for a particular task, such as improving your note taking, you may avoid learning a new skill, give up easily when things get tough, and conclude that you cannot change that particular aspect of your academic behavior. However, if you put in the effort and experience success, your perception about your ability to master the skill will change.

Another factor that may contribute to a belief that you cannot change is that many of our behaviors become automated over time and we cannot change aspects of ourselves that we are not conscious of (Prochaska & Prochaska, 1999). Studies in psychology (e.g., Bargh, 2015; Bargh &

Chartrand, 1999) indicate that some behaviors become non-conscious and we have difficulty being aware when we engage in it and explaining how we do certain things. Try explaining how you bowl or how you hit a baseball or how you learn certain material for an exam. It is not as easy as you think. Without realizing it, you probably have automated your study habits through their repeated use during the 12 years of schooling prior to college. Changing such automated behaviors requires considerable commitment, effort, and time, leading some students to conclude that they lack the willpower and inner strength, and therefore cannot change. For example, when we teach a system of note taking in Chapter 9, some students report that they can't learn the new system because their old methods, though ineffective, are automated to the point where they function in a non-conscious way. What makes matters worse is that when students are under pressure, such as preparing for an important midterm exam, they often resort to their existing automated skills even when they know that these skills are not as useful or effective as the new skills they have learned or practiced. In summary, expect changing your academic behavior to not be an easy process, but know that you can change if you are willing to put in the effort and time to practice a new skill. Remember that you didn't become good at playing basketball, the piano, chess, or whatever interests you in just a few sessions of effortless practice.

I Don't Want to Change

We have found that most students identify this category for why they don't change their academic behavior. Let's look at some of the factors that contribute to this belief (Isaacson, 2002). First, students may have a high sense of self-efficacy in their abilities and the effectiveness of their existing study strategies. They tell themselves, "After all, I got through high school and was accepted into college!" This response is a reasonable approach to one's academic work and can lead to success for some students. There are, however, students who do not understand the difference in the required study skills between high school and college, and fail to realize what awaits them down the road. In fact, many of these students have such high self-efficacy that they are overconfident in their abilities. These students demonstrate displeasure when faced with a requirement to take a learning strategies course because it conflicts with their perception of the level of skills they possess for academic studies: Did you take this class as an elective or were you required to take it?

Students can demonstrate passive or active resistance in class. How would you analyze the behavior of the following student?

> I dislike this learning strategies class and I know that this is no reason for me to do poorly in the course. However, I still think my study strategies are as good as the ones that are discussed in class. Therefore, I do not see any reason for me to change.

Why does this student behave the way she does, considering the fact that she is not doing well in class? Why do some students persist in the same behavior in college even though they know their strategies don't work for them? Is this a way to protect their self-worth? Are they concerned that they may not be able to learn or apply the new study and learning strategies?

First-year students often fail to recognize that success in many college courses requires critical thinking skills: the ability to organize arguments and evidence from many sources that often disagree with one another. In his interview with college students, Light (2001) found that students who had academic difficulty pointed out that their high school courses did not demand much critical thinking, but in college courses, it is an important skill for success. When students have difficulty in courses that require critical thinking skills, they often blame or attribute their poor results to the instructor, as expressed in the following statement: "I always did well in high school. I can't believe these tests; they are so unfair." What often occur are explanations for failure that can be categorized as external attributions—usually the teacher or the test—not oneself. In high school, if failure occurred, it was the teacher who was asked to change. Common requests include: "Slow down," "Explain it again," "Be more concise," "Give me examples," and "Make the test easier." Isaacson (2002) stated that blaming others by attributing the responsibility for lower academic success or failure to others influences students not to take personal responsibility and take charge of their own learning. Thus, when an opportunity presents itself, like taking a learning strategies course in college, the students fail to recognize how it can help because they may not recognize that they are responsible for their own academic outcomes: What was your attitude when you registered for this course? Do you think you need to change any aspect of your learning and study behavior? Do any of the beliefs described in this section relate to your thinking? If not, explain why your attitudes or beliefs are different and what factors influenced your openness to the possibility of changing some of your own study behaviors.

In this chapter, we identified two major goal orientations—mastery and performance. In a mastery orientation, a person wants to learn as much as possible and improve one's academic performance. In a performance orientation, a person wants to perform better than others, or, as one student put it: "I simply want to get through this course." Adopting a performance orientation and simply wanting to "get through courses" may cause students to lower their value for a study skills course, resulting in a lack of interest and an unwillingness to acquire and practice self-directed learning skills. A person with a mastery orientation is more likely to use advanced rather than simple rehearsal strategies in their courses. Therefore, your goal orientation may be a factor in your perceptions regarding the desire or need to change academic behavior.

I Don't Know What to Change

Often, students come to class believing that they can and want to change their academic behavior but are not sure what they have to do to change. The purpose of the self-observation assessments at the beginning of each chapter is to provide information about your behavior.

Your instructor may ask you to take different study skill assessments to help you identify your strengths and areas of improvement. Knowing what to change requires an understanding of your learning and study strategies. The more you understand your strengths and weaknesses, the better you will be able to develop a plan for changing your behavior. One of the instruments we use is the Learning and Study Skills Inventory (LASSI; Weinstein et al., 1987). This instrument helps students compare their skills with other college students in such areas as attitude and interest, motivation, time management, anxiety, concentration, information processing, selecting main ideas, self-testing, and preparing for and taking tests. Which of these areas do you think are your strengths and weaknesses?

I Don't Know How to Change

Even though this course teaches learning strategies to bring about change in your academic behavior, you may not know how to change. There are many possible reasons for this problem. First, you may experience difficulty in transferring your newly learned strategies to other courses you are taking because you are not practicing these strategies in other courses. If you learn strategies but don't practice them in other courses, it is unlikely that you will become a more successful learner. Once you practice the learning strategies in different contexts, you can then make changes in how you apply the strategies in different courses and become a more successful learner.

Second, problems in knowing how to change can also stem from a lack of self-control. Examples of self-control in the academic context are self-instruction and attention focusing. Self-instruction or self-talk, an important aspect of self-control, is an important strategy that can help you guide your behavior. Research has shown that verbalizations, such as how to apply a mathematical formula, can improve students' learning (Schunk, 1982). We shall discuss the importance of self-instruction or self-talk in Chapter 5. Finally, in the discussion of self-worth in this chapter, we mentioned that some students are uncertain that they possess the adequate ability to succeed. As a result, they may actually handicap themselves by not studying and using other self-defeating strategies to have an excuse for failing that does not reflect poorly on their ability. Failing for a reason such as not adequately preparing for an exam is less likely to threaten self-worth than failing because of low perceived ability. Garcia (1995) found that college students who used self-handicapping strategies employed few practice and time-management strategies. Self-handicapping provides a significant obstacle to the intention of changing one's academic behavior. Even though a student may believe he or she can and wants to change, engaging in self-handicapping behavior instead of using effective learning strategies can lead to less successful academic outcomes. It is possible that, through self-handicapping, students who do not know how to change may actually start to believe that they cannot change. Here is a statement from a student who is afraid to change:

> The only reason that I think I have not changed is because I don't know how to change my ways. I feel that I have been studying and preparing for my tests and quizzes the same way for so long that I am afraid that it will be too hard to change, and if I try to change I might do worse with the new way rather than the old way.

There are many motivational factors that influence your beliefs about changing academic behavior. The more you understand the dynamics of change, the more you can learn to control your behavior and, ultimately, make the necessary changes to attain your personal and academic goals.

In summary, this chapter presented an overview of the various factors that influence your motivation, in other words, whether you choose to engage with tasks, persist at them, and invest the necessary mental effort to succeed. First, we discussed the external factors such as sociocultural and classroom environmental factors. Some of these factors are concrete and even visible, such as the presence or lack of resources or how a course is structured, while some are invisible, such as stereotypes that may exist about the group to which you belong. Second, we discussed internal factors, the beliefs and self-perceptions such as value orientation, self-efficacy, goal orientation, and attributions. While you cannot always control the external factors by being a self-regulated learner, you can become aware and manage the internal factors, and as a result, enhance your level of motivation.

Chapter Review

KEY POINTS

1 Researchers have identified four motivational profiles: success-oriented, overstriving, failure avoiding, and failure accepting students.
2 Motivated behaviors are determined by choice of behavior, level of activity and involvement, and persistence and management of effort.
3 Motivation is influenced by sociocultural factors, classroom contextual factors, and internal beliefs and perceptions.
4 Although first generation and low-income students face specific risk factors that have the potential to create roadblocks to their academic success, many of these students also possess certain factors that mitigate risk and facilitate academic performance.
5 Stereotype threat is the fear of doing something that would inadvertently confirm a stereotype. Stereotype threat can influence a student's motivation and achievement.
6 The college environment and instructors' teaching practices can influence students' motivation in the classroom.
7 The degree to which you value a task—or not—predicts your level of motivation. We can value tasks for different reasons: enjoyment, usefulness, importance, and cost-benefit analysis.
8 Hoped-for, expected, and feared possible selves play an important role in your motivation and behavior.
9 Goals enhance performance in five major ways: effort, duration or persistence, direction of attention, strategic planning, and as a reference point for evaluating performance.
10 It is difficult to be motivated to achieve in any area without goals.
11 A mastery goal orientation is more likely to lead to the use of more and more effective learning strategies than a performance goal orientation.
12 Performance goals can be divided into performance-approach and performance-avoid goals. There is evidence that a performance-approach goal orientation in introductory college classes leads to high achievement but low interest in course content.
13 Self-efficacy influences individuals' effort, persistence, and use of learning strategies.
14 Attributions to controllable causes such as level of effort are more effective than attributions to uncontrollable causes such as ability or luck.
15 Self-efficacy and attributions have an important influence on self-regulated behavior.
16 Many students are motivated for the wrong reason—to avoid failure rather than to attain success.
17 The fear of failure is a significant factor that explains why certain students behave in ways that are detrimental to their success in college.
18 There are four reasons why students have difficulty changing their academic behavior: they don't believe they can change; they don't want to change; they don't know what to change; or they don't know how to change.

FOLLOW-UP ACTIVITIES

1. Use the Self-regulation Process to Manage Your Motivation

The process for your self-study was identified in Chapter 1 and is explained in depth in Appendix B, with examples provided in Appendix C. This study focuses on motivation. Complete the following self-study during a period of two to three weeks. Your report should include each of the processes below and should be approximately five to eight typed pages in length.

Self-Observation and Evaluation. Am I satisfied with my academic motivation? Do I need to change my motivation? If yes, what problem(s) do I encounter? What are the symptoms of my problem (i.e., when, where, and how often does my problem occur)? How much of an impact does this problem have on my academic performance? What factors (e.g., beliefs, perceptions, feelings, physiological responses, or behaviors) contribute to this problem? What do I need to change to reduce or eliminate my problem?

Goal Setting and Strategic Planning. What are my goals? What strategies will I implement to improve my academic motivation? When will I use these strategies? How will I record my progress?

Strategy Implementation and Monitoring. What strategies did I use to improve my academic motivation? When did I use these strategies? What method(s) did I use to record my progress (e.g., documents, charts, logs, tally sheets, checklists, or recordings)? When did I use these methods? How and when did I monitor my progress to determine if my new strategies were working? What changes, if any, did I make along the way?

Strategic-Outcome Monitoring. Did I attain the goal(s) I set for myself? Have the modifications in my motivation improved my academic performance or personal life? What strategies were the most and least effective? What changes, if any, do I need to make in the future?

2. Identify Factors That Influence Motivation

Select two different courses you are currently taking—one that you perceive to be difficult and one less challenging, or one that you like and one that you don't like. Analyze your motivation in the two classes by discussing each of the following factors that determine students' motivated behaviors.

	Class 1	Class 2
Goals		
Value orientation		
Self-efficacy beliefs		
Mastery vs. performance goal orientation		
Attributions for academic performance		

3. Analyze Efficacy Scores

Students in a learning course are given ten-point quizzes each week before the class lecture. Before they begin writing their responses, they are asked to rate how well they think they will do on the quiz on a scale from one (low) to ten (high). The following scores represent the quiz scores and efficacy ratings for four different students for the first three quizzes of the term. Review these scores and describe each of the students' motivation and behavior as best you can. In what ways could these scores influence the students' motivation and study behaviors for future quizzes?

Student 1

Quiz Score	7	9	9
Efficacy Rating	4	7	6

Student 2

Quiz Score	2	5	4
Efficacy Rating	4	5	7

Student 3

Quiz Score	8	9	8
Efficacy Rating	9	9	8

Student 4

Quiz Score	3	5	4
Efficacy Rating	7	8	8

4. Discuss the Motivation Behavior of Different Students

At the beginning of the chapter, you were introduced to four types of students, three of whom had motivational problems. Suppose you were an adviser at the college or university they attend. Each student has made an appointment to see you. How would you explain their own motivation and behavior to them, using the internal beliefs and perceptions discussed in this chapter (value orientation, possible selves, self-efficacy, goals, goal orientation, attributions)?

Defensive Dimitri

_____
_____
_____
_____
_____
_____
_____

Anxious Anna

_____
_____
_____
_____
_____
_____
_____

Hopeless Henry

_____
_____
_____
_____
_____
_____
_____

5. Help Students Deal with Different Attributions for Their Behavior

Suppose you took a part-time job as a peer counselor and were asked to meet with students who had academic problems. How would you respond to students who attribute poor test performance to the statements in the left-hand column? In the right-hand column, write a response to each of the students.

Attribution	Suggested Responses
I lack ability.	
I didn't feel well.	
I wasn't in the mood.	
I'm not interested in the task.	
I don't do well on tests.	
The material was boring.	
The test was unfair.	
I didn't have enough time to study.	

6. Use Motivation Strategies

Here are some strategies that college students use to monitor and regulate their motivation (Wolters, 1998, pp. 228–229). The strategies are organized by category. Identify one of the strategies listed that you don't use but could incorporate in your repertoire of motivation strategies.

Performance Goals

"I would think about how I wanted a good grade."
"I would remind myself about how important it is to get good grades in college."

External Rewards

"Give myself rewards when I finish studying."
"Each time I successfully review a topic, I might give myself a break and do something relaxing like watch TV or nap."
"Tell myself that if I finish the next five pages of reading, I can go and talk to a friend."

Value Orientation

"I would find ways that it relates to my life."
"I would remind myself about why I am taking this class."
"I would try to relate it to my experiences or how I would feel in certain situations."
"Make studying into a game."
"Try to make it more interesting."

Help Seeking

"Ask to study with a friend."
"Talk to the (teaching assistant) or professor."

Environment Structuring

"Sit with the book in a quiet room with a soft drink."
"Take little breaks so I don't burn out."
"I'd take a break, completely forget the subject matter, and then return, hopefully refreshed."

Attention

"Study at a time when my mind is more focused."

7. Analyzing Your Educational Experiences

Write a short essay analyzing your educational experiences. Answer the following questions: In what ways has my family influenced my goals, motivation, and behavior? To what degree did my teachers and friends help me succeed? What was the school environment like? Was it supportive? Was preparation for college adequate? Why or why not? Which challenges am I facing in college? What am I doing to overcome these challenges?

Answers to Exercise 2.4

1. M   2. P   3. P   4. M   5. P

3 Understanding Learning and Memory

You are reading this book because you want to become a more successful learner and are attempting to acquire new learning strategies. Before we present research-based effective strategies, it is important to understand some basics about the human brain in terms of how we learn. Once you acquire important knowledge concerning the human brain in the context of memory and learning, you can better evaluate your own learning processes and may be even more motivated to replace or enhance your existing learning strategies with new skills presented in this chapter. This chapter describes the fundamentals of how the human brain functions; how information is received and processed in the mind; and how learning, remembering, and forgetting occur. After studying this chapter, you will be able to:

- understand and explain intelligence as a malleable trait;
- explain the benefits of a growth versus fixed mindset;
- identify how the information-processing system (IPS) operates;
- identify the flaws in human memory;
- explain why it is important to use a variety of learning strategies to learn different material;
- assess the effectiveness of your own learning and study strategies.

When it comes to learning and motivation, the organ that plays the most significant role by far is the human brain. Because research about the brain is still in its infancy, there are many questions and several myths about the brain and how it works. Here are a few of them:

"I inherited my intelligence from my parents. Am I stuck with what I have?"

"Isn't human intelligence fixed by the time a child starts kindergarten?"

"Are left-brain learners really better at math than right-brain learners?"

"My visual learning style is not suited to learn by listening to lectures. Will I not do well in college?"

In the last 20 years, research with animals, case studies of people with brain injuries, and advances in technology, such as using the electro-encephalograph (EEG) and magnetic resonance imaging (MRI), have given us the opportunity to explore and answer these questions. We know that all learning originates in and changes the brain. Indeed, education is practical neuroscience. That does not mean that every learner and teacher needs to memorize 100 neurotransmitters and 50 brain areas responsible for cognition, motivation, and emotion, but it does mean that as a learner, you can become more effective with some knowledge of how the brain senses, processes, stores, and retrieves information. The purpose of this chapter, therefore, is to serve merely as a primer to the brain. It is not our intent to overwhelm you with neurophysiological terminology but rather use it to frame our discussion about issues such as intelligence and learning.

WHERE DOES LEARNING TAKE PLACE IN THE BRAIN?

Looking at the brain in broad strokes, it has two hemispheres and four lobes: frontal, parietal, occipital, and temporal. Where does learning occur? The short answer is that learning takes place in several places. We know that the frontal lobes are largely responsible for conscious thinking, language, reasoning, planning, decision making, and self-monitoring. We know that the parietal lobes play a role in paying attention and processing word sounds, while the occipital lobes aid in interpreting and remembering visual information. The temporal lobes interpret and remember auditory information but also play a significant role when it comes to long-term memory (LTM) (Byrnes, 2001). As you see, there is no one area of your brain that is responsible for learning. We also know that the brain is not only a thinking brain but also the center of motivation and emotion. For example, a structure in the temporal lobe, the amygdala, figures prominently in negative emotions, such as stress, fear, and depression.

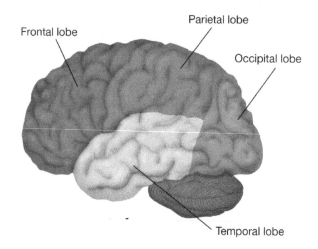

Our brain is also divided into the left and right hemispheres. To a certain extent, the two hemispheres have different specialties. The left side is largely responsible for controlling the right side of the body and vice versa. The left hemisphere is in charge of language, reading, and mathematical calculation, while the right side is more dominant in visual and spatial processing. In general, the left side is more apt to handle details, while the right side is better equipped for looking at and synthesizing concepts and ideas into an integrated whole. Based on these differences between the functions of the two hemispheres, it is no surprise that there is a popular myth about "left-brain" and "right-brain" learners, implying that people think predominantly in only one hemisphere of their brain. You have probably heard the statement that "right-brain" learners are more creative while "left-brain" learners are stronger at analytical thinking. Just do a search for "left-brained vs. right-brained" and see how many quizzes pop up to help you determine which side of your brain in supposedly dominant. In reality, the two hemispheres are joined together by a collection of neurons called the corpus callosum which enables the two sides to communicate and collaborate on a constant basis. For example, to find humor in a joke, you'll need the left hemisphere to handle the basics of syntax and specific word meanings and the right hemisphere to detect sarcasm and puns. In conclusion, we know from neuroscientific research that, first, no one is totally left-brained or totally right-brained, and, second, in order to be successful, you can and must develop both sides of your brain.

Related to the myth of left-brained and right-brained learners is the concept of learning styles. There are over 70 different models of learning styles that have been proposed over the last 30 years (Coffield et al., 2004). Chances are that you have been characterized as either a visual or a verbal learner at some point in your academic life. Indeed, some of us feel that we remember pictures better than conversations, indicating a potential differential strength in processing visual and verbal cues. But is it also true that as a visual learner, you are likely to learn better if written material is presented in a visual format, such as via images and graphs rather than simple text? Many researchers (Hussman & O'Laughlin, 2018; Kirschner & van Merriënboer, 2013; Pashler, McDaniel, Rohrer,

& Bjork, 2009; Willingham, Hughes, & Dobolyi, 2015) have concluded that, at this time, there is no evidence for the hypothesis that people learn and perform better when instruction is designed to match their learning style. Further, if you believe that you have a specific learning style, you may reject learning strategies that do not appear to match your style. For example, an auditory learner may avoid developing graphs or matrices as a means to support learning. This is problematic as the key to effective self-regulation is the ability to implement a wide variety of different strategies. Additionally, regardless of whether you have a learning style, chances are that this preference will not be matched by your instructor's teaching style! Therefore, in enhancing academic success, we recommend a focus on acquiring learning strategies that will enhance your performance regardless of your learning preferences.

IS INTELLIGENCE FIXED OR MALLEABLE?

What does it mean that someone has a high IQ? Some of you, no doubt, will immediately think that IQ—or intelligence—is highly heritable, not open to change, and pretty much fixed by the time a child starts kindergarten. Based on attribution theory discussed in Chapter 2, this is an internal but uncontrollable attribution. Recent research, however, has demonstrated that our brains are much more malleable than previously thought. Specifically, it was believed that all nerve cells or neurons a person would ever have are produced in the first few weeks of the prenatal period. We now know, however, that the formation of new neurons, as well as the development of new connections between the neural networks and the strengthening of existing ones, occurs throughout the life span. Modern brain imaging has demonstrated that when people acquire new skills the areas of the brain responsible for these skills become more dense with neural tissue. This process is known as **neuroplasticity**. The discovery of neuroplasticity disputed the claims that the brain does most of its maturation before kindergarten. We now know that the brain continues to develop throughout childhood and adolescence and even into adulthood.

> **Neuroplasticity:** The ability of the brain to grow and change as a result of input from the environment.

So which aspects of the brain continue to develop during your college years and beyond? We know that myelination, the coating of the long, slender nerve cell projections, continues into the twenties. The better the myelination, the faster your thinking. We also know that several parts of the brain, such as the frontal and temporal lobes, increase in size well into adulthood, enhancing your ability to pay attention, control impulses, and develop plans—all skills that are crucial to your academic and personal success. What is most important to know, though, is that neuroplasticity is dependent on environmental stimulation. In essence, our brains are malleable and experience-dependent, and intelligence is created when neural connections in the brain are changed because of challenge and learning. The good news is that this fact puts you in charge. By challenging your brain to think in new and deeper ways via the use of the effective learning strategies we are about to discuss, you can grow it!

WHY IS A GROWTH MINDSET MORE BENEFICIAL THAN A FIXED MINDSET?

Let's return to the belief that intelligence is fixed by the time you reach kindergarten—which, as you now know, is not the case. Recall our discussion about mastery and performance orientation in the previous chapter. We pointed out that students with a mastery orientation view ability as developing through effort, while performance-oriented students see it as fixed. The belief about the nature of your ability has profound implications for your learning and motivation—and indeed for the development of your brain. Professor Carol Dweck from Stanford University has conducted research for decades addressing beliefs related to the role of heredity in our intelligence. Dweck (2006) developed the idea of "mindsets" in reference to our beliefs about intelligence. Dweck found that

Fixed Mindset: An individual's belief that brain and intelligence cannot be developed and that success is dependent on the amount of intelligence one has to begin with.

Growth Mindset: An individual's belief that brain and intelligence can be developed and that success is dependent on the amount of effort applied.

we endorse either a **fixed mindset** or a **growth mindset** (sometimes called incremental). The individuals who possess a fixed mindset believe that the brain and intelligence cannot be developed and that success is dependent on the amount of intelligence one has to begin with. Based on attribution theory discussed in Chapter 2, this is an internal but uncontrollable attribution. People with a fixed mindset tend to worry about how smart they look, avoid challenges, become upset by mistakes, do not expand effort when needed, and ultimately achieve less in the long term. People with a growth mindset, on the other hand, believe that they can develop their brain and intelligence (an internal but controllable attribution), do not worry about how smart they look at any moment, welcome challenges, expect to expand effort, and have positive learning outcomes in the long term. The key difference between the two mindsets is their view of effort. People with a fixed mindset believe that you either have the ability or you don't, and there's little that can be done to improve in cases when you don't. Those with a growth mindset, on the other hand, see success as resulting from the expenditure of effort. It is important to point out that Dweck believes that one's mindset about intelligence itself is modifiable (Bandura, 2015).

Dweck found that the idea of mindsets applies not only to our intelligence, but to other qualities as well. In her book *Mindset: The New Psychology of Success* (2006), she looks at the application of the mindsets to the world of athletics and considers the differences between Michael Jordan and John McEnroe. The two elite athletes, though both clearly very successful, endorsed opposing mindsets about their ability and talent as an athlete. Can you guess who had the fixed and who the growth mindset? As Dweck points out, based on her analysis of McEnroe's autobiography *You Cannot Be Serious*, McEnroe saw talent as being something inherent that one either has or doesn't. Because he saw his talent as fixed, he looked to blame outside factors (ranging from eating too close to the match to it being too cold—or too hot) when things did not go well. McEnroe acknowledged, in retrospect, that he did not fulfill his potential. By contrast, Michael Jordan knew he had to work hard and develop his talent to succeed. He, in fact, embraced his failures and even stated in an ad for Nike, "I've missed more than nine thousand shots. I've almost lost three hundred games. Twenty-six times, I've been trusted to take the game-winning shot, and missed." For Michael Jordan, there was no one else to blame for his shortcomings and the only remedy was to practice more and expend more effort, key beliefs of someone with a growth mindset. As you see, the simple idea of mindsets makes all the difference. Complete Exercise 3.1, based on Dweck (2006, p. 12), to determine which mindset you endorse!

EXERCISE 3.1: SELF-OBSERVATION: ANALYZING MY MINDSET

Which mindset do you have? Answer the questions (Dweck, 2006, p. 12) about how you view intelligence.

Rate the statements below (1–5 disagree to agree scale):

1. Your intelligence is something very basic about you that you can't change much.
2. You can learn new things, but you can't really change how intelligent you are.
3. No matter how much intelligence you have, you can always change it quite a bit.
4. You can always substantially change how intelligent you are.

Statements 1 and 2 reflect a fixed mindset while statements 3 and 4 reflect a growth mindset. Which mindset did you agree with more? Next, ask yourself the following question: "When do you feel smart?" Write your responses in the lines below.

_____
_____
_____
_____
_____

Your answers could range from "It's when I don't make any mistakes" to "When I make a mistake and learn from it," and "When I finish something perfectly" to "When I work on something for a long time and start to figure it out" (Dweck, 2006, p. 24). Analyze which mindset you have based on the discussion about the differences between the two mindsets.

_____ ■

After completing Exercise 3.1, you now know what your mindset is. How can you change from a fixed mindset to a growth mindset? Dweck (http://mindsetonline.com) provides four steps for this process:

- Step 1: Learn to hear your fixed mindset "voice." What is the voice of your specific fixed mindset? Does it tell you that if you fail, you'll be a failure or that your peers will ridicule you for thinking you had the talent for a task at hand? Does it try to tell you that not getting an A in a class was not your fault? Get to know the internal monologue dictated by your mindset.
- Step 2: Recognize that you have a choice. It is up to you how you interpret setbacks and challenges. Do you conclude that you lack the intelligence to be successful, or do you tell yourself that with more effort you can perform better next time?
- Step 3: Respond to your fixed mindset with a growth mindset voice. For example, your fixed mindset may tell you that if you don't try you can protect yourself from failing. Challenge this with a growth mindset voice that says that if you don't try you will automatically fail.
- Step 4: Take the growth mindset action by learning from your setbacks and trying again, embracing challenges, and being receptive to constructive criticism.

Dweck, based on her years of conducting research about mindsets, suggests that the key to changing a fixed to a growth mindset lies in practicing hearing both voices and choosing to act on the growth mindset. Be sure to complete Follow-Up Activity 1 (p. 70), which gives you practice in responding to a fixed mindset voice with a growth mindset one.

Your mindset plays a critical role in how you will read the upcoming sections about learning strategies. It is likely that if you have a growth mindset, you will see how the strategies we discuss can be beneficial to your academic performance. If, however, you view intelligence as fixed, you may doubt that learning in new and more effective ways will make a difference for you. It is our hope and recommendation that you adopt a growth mindset voice as you continue to read the chapter.

HOW DOES THE INFORMATION-PROCESSING SYSTEM EXPLAIN LEARNING?

We now turn to how the human brain works in terms of learning and memory. Have you ever wondered why you remember certain information and why you cannot even remember the important ideas in a course you completed a few months or weeks ago? Many learning experts believe how individuals learn provides the answer to this question.

Information-Processing System: The cognitive structure through which information flows, is controlled, and is transformed during the process of learning.

Encoding: The process of transferring information from working memory to long-term memory.

Retrieval: The process of remembering or finding previously stored information in long-term memory.

Psychologists provide many different theories and explanations of human learning. One way to understand how information may be acquired or lost is to understand the **information-processing system** (see Figure 3.1). Needless to say, none of us has three boxes inside our heads. These boxes represent different functions of the human brain when it comes to information processing. It is also important to note that there is not one area of our brain that contains a specific memory store. For example, we know that the sensory register includes our auditory processing areas in the temporal lobe and the visual processing areas in the occipital lobe. We know that both the frontal and parietal lobes are involved with working memory and the temporal lobes play a significant role when it comes to LTM. The purpose of this model is to identify how our brain stores, encodes, and retrieves information. Storage is the process of placing information into memory. **Encoding** is the process used to change information in some way before it is stored, because information is not stored exactly as it is presented. For example, when an individual reads a textbook, he or she derives meaning from the words read and stores the meaning rather than the specific words on the page. Sometimes when a person reads, he or she remembers the information by changing the words to an image of the event. **Retrieval** refers to the process of remembering or finding previously stored information. Sometimes it is easy to recall information, whereas other times it takes considerable thought and effort to remember.

Three important points are emphasized in this chapter:

1. Learning involves getting information into LTM, a component of memory that holds knowledge and skills for long periods of time.
2. Much of what we think we have learned is soon forgotten or never really learned in the first place.
3. The specific strategies used to store information in LTM affect the likelihood that the information will be remembered. In other words, how we learn often determines what we remember.

SHORT-TERM SENSORY STORE

As shown in Figure 3.1, the flow of information begins with input from the environment, such as the visual perception of words in a text or the sound of your professor giving a lecture. Based

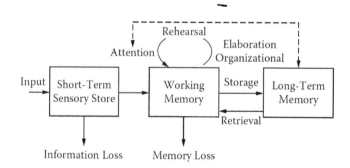

FIGURE 3.1   A Model of the Information-Processing System

on neuroimaging, we know that the occipital lobes play a key role in processing visual cues and the temporal lobes in processing auditory cues. Input from the environment enters the **short-term sensory store** (STSS). Information in the STSS is stored briefly until it can be attended to by the working memory (WM). Everything that can be seen, heard, or smelled is stored in the STSS, but it only lasts for a matter of seconds before it is forgotten.

> **Short-Term Sensory Store:** The part of the information-processing system that briefly stores information from the senses.

Many of the stimuli humans experience never get into our WM because we do not attend to them. We are constantly barraged with stimuli from our environment. For example, by the time an individual wakes up, gets dressed, and walks or drives to class, he or she observes hundreds, or perhaps thousands, of objects that cannot be recalled. If you drove to class today, do you remember the color or make of the car next to which you were parked? Do you remember the student who sat next to you in your first class? What did he or she wear? If you found the person attractive or interesting, you may be able to answer these questions, because you may have been attentive to such details. However, the fact is that we are not attentive to most of what we see or hear in our daily lives.

If you have not attended to information, there is little concern about retention or retrieval, because no information will have been acquired. When you attend a lecture and your attention fades in and out, you will fail to recall some of the important information presented by the professor. This is why it may be important for you to improve your attention.

Think about reading a textbook. As you read, you begin thinking about the party you are planning to attend next Saturday. When your mind goes back to the book, you realize that you covered two pages but don't remember a thing. You read but you do not remember anything, because you were not paying attention to the words in the textbook. When students say that they can attend to many things at one time, they really mean that they can switch their attention from one task to another. It is difficult to read a textbook and watch a TV show simultaneously. Information is missed from both sources.

In summary, unless special attempts are made to attend to and record information, much of the material in lectures and textbooks is never stored in memory. Therefore, the information is never learned. A similar situation occurs when you are introduced to someone and ten seconds later you cannot remember the person's name. The problem is not that you forgot the name but that you never learned it in the first place. When you mention to friends that you forgot important information during an exam, you need to consider whether the real problem was learning or forgetting.

WORKING MEMORY

Working memory is the active part of the memory system and has been described as the center of consciousness in the IPS. Whenever we are consciously thinking about something or actively trying to remember a forgotten fact, we are using our WM. Based on neuroimaging, we now know that the brain lobes that are directly involved with working memory are the frontal, temporal, and parietal lobes.

> **Working Memory:** The part of the information-processing system in which the active processing of information takes place.

Working memory screens and decides how to handle different stimuli. Three events can happen when material gets into the WM (Eggen & Kauchak, 1997):

- It can be quickly lost or forgotten.
- The content can be retained in WM for a short period of time by repeating it over and over (i.e., rehearsing).
- The content can be transferred into long-term memory by using specific learning strategies.

The WM is limited in two ways—capacity and duration. At any one time, the WM of an adult can hold only five to nine chunks of information. This limitation is referred to as the "7±2 Magic Number" (Miller, 1956). Through recent studies, some researchers (e.g., Cowan, 2005) have found that working memory capacity may be even lower, perhaps between three and five chunks. New information coming into WM will, if it catches the attention of the student, tend to crowd out old information already there. If information is believed to be important, it should not be left in WM, because it will be soon forgotten. It is the working memory capacity limitation that causes high levels of anxiety to be detrimental to the thinking process. Think about someone who has anxiety related to performance in mathematics. Perhaps this person is you. Based on research, we know that the anxiety reaction consists of intrusive thoughts (e.g., "I'm terrible at math") while attempting to solve mathematics tasks. The coupling of working memory being limited to begin with and the inability to ignore the anxiety-creating thoughts creates a situation where there is very little cognitive capacity available to actually process the mathematics task at hand, leading to lowered performance (Hopko et al., 1998).

Chunking: Grouping of data so that a greater amount of information may be retained in working memory.

A number of control processes operate at the WM level and provide it with some flexibility in dealing with information. **Chunking**, or grouping information, is one way of keeping more than nine pieces (7±2) of information in WM. For example, it is usually easier to remember a number such as 194781235 if the numbers are grouped in threes (194 781 235), because the original nine units are reduced to three chunks. When we read a word, we think of it as a single unit rather than as a collection of separate letters. For example, a sentence can be thought of as a single unit, or chunk, instead of a series of letters and words. By organizing information into larger chunks, the WM can handle more information, because the organization reduces memory load. Although our WM uses chunking strategies automatically and unconsciously, these strategies also can be learned.

EXERCISE 3.2: DEMONSTRATING THE CAPACITY OF WORKING MEMORY

Directions: Try this short memory experiment (Goetz et al., 1992, p. 323). Read the following list of letters once. Cover the page and attempt to recall them in order. Write your answers on a separate sheet of paper.

FB   IMT   VU   SAHB   OCIA

Check to see how many letters you recalled in the right order.

Now, let's look at another list. Again, read the list once, and then cover the page and write all the letters you can remember in order:

FBI   MTV   USA   HBO   CIA

How many letters did you get right this time? We bet you did much better the second time. Notice that the same letters are presented in the same order in both lists. The only difference is that the second list is arranged in familiar patterns. Because the letters are familiar and meaningful, each set can serve as a single unit, or chunk, in WM. Instead of trying to remember 15 separate letters, as in the first list, you only have to recall five familiar chunks in the second list. The first list exceeds the 7±2 guideline; the second list can be managed within your WM limits.

Because WM is characterized by a limited capacity, only a very small amount of information in the sensory store can ever be processed in WM. According to information-processing theory, information must be processed in WM before it can move on to LTM. This means the learner must do something active with the information to move it into LTM. However, because WM has a short duration (about 5–20 seconds), the processing must be completed fairly quickly, or at least rehearsed until it can be processed.

Another common control process is **maintenance rehearsal**. This strategy helps keep information activated for more than 20 seconds in WM by rehearsing the information mentally. For example, if an individual gets out of the car to obtain directions to a location, the information could easily be forgotten by the time he or she gets back into the car. Therefore, after receiving directions, individuals often rehearse or repeat, "Left–left–right–left" while driving away to prevent forgetting.

Maintenance Rehearsal: A strategy to keep information activated in the working memory by repeating the information mentally.

Sometimes during a lecture, we will point out some information about the upcoming exam or make changes in reading assignments. Some students fail to enter the information in their notes because they mistakenly believe they will remember the information. Unfortunately, they probably forget the information as soon as they leave the lecture. Days or weeks later, some students will ask, "When did you tell us that?"

Gagné (1985) estimated that individuals are likely to learn only about one to six new ideas from each minute of a lecture, a small number of the ideas that are typically presented during that time. Therefore, students must constantly make important decisions about what information to attend to and what information to neglect. It is difficult enough to obtain important information from a lecture while trying to be attentive. Imagine how much information is lost in lectures when students are not attentive.

One of the advantages of reading compared with note taking is that you do not have to make quick decisions about what is important, because you can read the material at your own pace and reread it as many times as necessary. Strategies to help you remember more information from lectures and textbooks are presented later.

Long-Term Memory

Long-Term Memory stores all the information we are not immediately using. The popular metaphor for long-term memory used to be that of a filing cabinet in which information is stored. It was once believed that unless information is carefully classified and placed in the correct file, it could be misfiled and not retrieved when needed.

Long-Term Memory: The part of the information-processing system that holds information for long periods.

Though aspects of this metaphor are still appropriate, modern neuroimaging has demonstrated that memory is far more complex than that. It appears that retrieving a memory involves activating brain-wide neural networks resembling a jigsaw puzzle more than pulling a file from one location in a file cabinet. Because of this, recalling a single memory may use many places in the brain at the same time. Is there a limit to how much we can learn and remember? While our working memory is limited by capacity and duration, it is generally believed that long-term memory can indefinitely store an unlimited amount of information and there is debate about whether we actually ever "forget" anything at all, or whether it's just that we are not always able to retrieve certain information and memories.

Information enters the LTM through the WM. While information must be repeated—or rehearsed—in order to stay in working memory, it must be elaborated upon and connected to information already in LTM in order to be effectively retrieved and used at a later time. It takes time and effort to build coherent, organized brain networks that allow us to access the necessary information and experiences to deal with both familiar and new situations. During the encoding process, several factors, such as storing facts in isolation and the presence of distractions, such as continuously texting while you are preparing for exams, can severely impair the retrieval process. On the other hand, the better the learning strategies you utilize, the better you are able to retrieve the necessary knowledge.

Another factor that affects effective storage in long-term memory is prior knowledge. In some courses, students bring a great deal of prior knowledge to class because they may have already taken a course in the subject or have done some reading in the area. In other courses, students may have little or no prior knowledge of the subject matter. As we stated previously, prior knowledge plays an important role in learning. For example, compare the ease or difficulty of taking lecture notes when you read prior to the lecture with another time when you did not read the material prior to the lecture. The more information you know before you attend a lecture, the easier it is to take notes and understand the material. This is why instructors ask you to complete reading assignments before lectures.

We can read textbooks in education and psychology with a great deal of understanding because of our good background in the content presented in these texts. Yet, junior high students can read an article in *Electronic Gaming Monthly* more rapidly and with greater understanding. We know the techniques and strategies for how to read, but do not have much knowledge about the topics discussed in *Electronic Gaming Monthly*.

You now have the basic understanding about how the human memory and learning work in terms of the information-processing system. Beginning with the environment, information flows to the short-term sensory store. The information that is attended to then proceeds to the working memory, from where it may be lost, modified, or stored permanently in the long-term memory. The process of retrieval effectively returns a long-term memory from storage to working memory, where it can govern thinking and behavior. Finally, the strengthened memory is then re-stored in long-term memory.

Before we move our attention away from the information-processing system, we should point out that like most models, this model has its share of criticism. The main criticism points out that the structure of working and long-term memory is not uniform but rather subdivided into several components. For example, there are differences in how different types of information such as knowledge of facts and knowledge of how to do things are stored as well as whether the storage of information necessarily occurs in only a linear fashion. However, for purposes of understanding how to best facilitate intentional and meaningful learning, the benefits of the model outweigh its criticism.

WHAT ARE THE FLAWS IN HUMAN MEMORY?

We mentioned above that currently, most psychologists believe that storing information in long-term memory is permanent. This, however, does not mean that memories are flawless. Unfortunately, no matter how young or old you are, there are certain memory flaws that can affect your behavior.

In his book *The Seven Sins of Memory*, Schacter (2001) explored the nature of memory's imperfections. We can all recall the problems we have in forgetting different types of information. For example, we often fail to recall information in a textbook, or forget our bank passwords or PIN identifications for the many websites we use on the internet. This type of forgetting, called *transience*, is only one of the seven flaws in our memory. Transience refers to the situation when individuals fail to remember a fact or idea. It is a weakening of memory over time. We will emphasize this type of memory problem in this chapter.

A second flaw in our memory is called *absent-mindedness*. It involves the breakdown between attention and memory. It often occurs when we are preoccupied with distracting concerns such as placing sunglasses down at a friend's home and forgetting to take them when we leave. Although this type of memory problem occurs more often in older adults, it is prevalent in individuals of all ages as well.

A third flaw is called *blocking*. It is the unsuccessful search for information that we may be desperately trying to retrieve, such as the name of an attractive woman or man we met at a party the previous night. Have you ever been in a situation where you are with a friend and see another person who knows you and you are embarrassed because you can't think of the person's name and thus can't introduce your friend to that individual? You start the conversation hoping that the individual will introduce himself or herself to your friend.

A fourth flaw is called *misattribution*. It involves assigning a memory to the wrong source, such as *incorrectly* remembering that someone told you something that you actually read about online. Or, you are sure that a friend told you something but find that he or she never mentioned a thing about the topic. We often see this flaw in cases of mistaken eyewitness identification.

A fifth flaw is called *suggestibility*. It refers to memories that are implanted because of leading questions, comments, or suggestions. Numerous examples of this flaw are special concerns in legal situations where suggestive questioning by law enforcement officials can lead to errors in eyewitness identification. This flaw also has been identified in cases of child abuse where psychotherapists have elicited memories of traumatic events that never occurred.

A sixth flaw is called *bias*. Schacter (2001) pointed out that we think of memories as snapshots that are retrieved in the exact way they were stored. Unfortunately, our memories do not work in the same manner as a photo, because we recreate or reconstruct our experiences rather than retrieve exact copies of them. Sometimes, in the process of reconstructing memories, we add or change feelings, beliefs, or even include new information. One of the ways in which bias works is that we change previous experiences based on what we now feel rather than what happened in the past. For example, if we are currently dissatisfied with a romantic relationship, we are very likely to recall previous negative experiences in that relationship.

The last flaw in our memory is *persistence*. It refers to remembering what we would prefer to omit from our memory. Have you ever had problems sleeping because you can't stop thinking about a poor grade on an examination or an unpleasant interaction with a professor? You can probably still remember a certain negative experience in your life and how you recalled the experience repeatedly in the days and weeks after it occurred, even though you would have liked to forget it. What causes us to remember negatively experienced and fear-producing events so well? The answer lies in our brains. When in a state of fear, our brain releases stress hormones, such as adrenaline. These chemicals activate the "fight or flight" response and stimulate the amygdala, the structure of the brain involved in processing negative emotions. When we experience a situation similar to the fear-producing one, our brain automatically responds by triggering the release of stress hormones.

Can you think of situations where you experienced one or more of these memory flaws? If so, share them with your classmates when you discuss this chapter in class or with your study group.

WHAT IS THE DIFFERENCE BETWEEN ROTE LEARNING AND MEANINGFUL LEARNING?

Learning, in many ways, is the process of acquiring knowledge. This process can be viewed on a continuum from basic to complex. Basic learning involves such things as recalling names and dates, associating a word in English to its equivalent in Spanish, and chronologically listing the events leading up to the Civil War. More complex learning involves understanding the main ideas in a story, solving verbal problems in algebra, or comparing and contrasting the poems of two different authors.

Many students do not realize that some of the strategies effective for learning basic knowledge may not be useful for learning more complex knowledge. Learning experts often make the distinction between rote and meaningful learning. In **rote learning**, the student learns through repetition without gaining a deep

Rote Learning: A process of learning whereby the student learns through repetition without gaining a deep understanding of material.

Meaningful Learning: A process of learning whereby the student attempts to make sense of the material so it will be stored in long-term memory and retrieved when needed.

understanding of material. An example of rote learning is memorization. In **meaningful learning, the student** attempts to make sense of the information so that it will be stored in LTM and retrieved when it is needed. One of the major problems in cramming for examinations is that students do not learn the material in a way that makes sense to them by relating the information to what they already know. The end result is that 24 hours after the exams, nothing, or very little information, is retained.

The other significant difference between rote and meaningful learning is that with rote learning, students tackle the same type of problem over and over again. An example of this would be repeatedly solving questions requiring the use of the same type of mathematical equation, one after another, while preparing for exams. It is no surprise that you may have adopted this strategy as most textbooks you have used to date rely primarily on blocked practice. Meaningful learning is studying mixed problem sets where the brain is essentially forced to figure out what is similar and different about the problems and, by doing that, creates a deeper understanding of the issue at hand. In this case, essentially, it is beneficial to mix and compare apples and oranges (Dunlosky, Rawson, Marsh, Nathan, & Willingham, 2013). Via several studies, this approach has been found to be effective in learning cognitive skills (e.g., Rohrer & Taylor, 2007). Researchers have demonstrated this approach to be true for motor skills as well. For example, Hall, Domingues, and Cavazos (1994) established that college baseball players had better hitting performance when they practiced different pitches than when they practiced the same pitch over and over before moving to the next pitch. It is important, therefore, to include the practice of rearranging and mixing your study problems in order to make your learning more meaningful.

WHICH LEARNING STRATEGIES PROMOTE LEARNING AND RETENTION?

Mnemonic: A memory technique that makes the task of remembering easier.

Before you begin reading this section, think about some content you remember from a course that you took some time ago. Why do you remember this information when so much other information in the same course was lost? If you learned the **mnemonic** "My very eager mother just served us nine pizzas" in elementary school, you have probably been waiting for years for someone to ask you to name the planets from the sun, in order: Mercury, Venus, Earth, Mars, Jupiter, Saturn, Uranus, Neptune, and Pluto. The beginning letter of each word corresponds to the first letter of each planet. We should mention that, today, Pluto is actually no longer considered a planet. It will be interesting to find out the new mnemonic for the order of planets. The second author also can identify the components and functions of the human digestive tract many years after taking biology. His instructor taught the class to first draw an outline of the human body and place the name of each component near its location. Finally, the students were told to write a short sentence describing the function of each organ below its name. The second author can still visualize each organ and function in the digestive tract. Think about some content that you learned in a course and still remember. What factors contributed to your retention of the content?

Earlier in the chapter, we discussed encoding—the process of putting new information into the IPS and preparing it for storage in LTM. The best way to prepare information for storage is to make it meaningful and to integrate it with known information already in your LTM. Some learning strategies are better than others for getting information into your LTM.

Table 3.1 identifies a number of important learning strategies to help you understand, learn, and remember course material. As you review the table, place a check next to the strategies you have used most often and circle the strategies you have used least often in school. If you are not familiar with one or more of the terms, complete this task after you read more of the chapter.

TABLE 3.1

Examples of Learning Strategies

Learning Strategies	Example	Learning Behaviors
Rehearsal	"I use note cards to learn definitions of terms."	Copying material Note taking Underlining text
Elaboration	"I try to relate new concepts to things I already know."	Summarizing Note making Answering questions
Organizational	"I try to separate main points from examples and explanations when I read a textbook."	Selecting main idea Outlining Representation (mapping)

REHEARSAL STRATEGIES

When we think of basic learning, we often imagine having information drilled into us through endless repetition. Whether memorizing a song or learning the capitals of each state in the United States, we have been told by our instructors that we must practice, practice, practice. But does it matter how we practice? Learning experts offer some advice as to how practice can be made more effective. A century of laboratory research has shown that **distributed practice** among frequent and short periods is more effective than a smaller number of sessions of **massed practice** (Carpenter, Cepeda, Rohrer, Kang, & Pashler, 2012; Kornell et al., 2010). If you want to remember the presidents of the United States without error, you should practice for many short sessions over an extended period of time, chunking the list and repeatedly saying the names. It is possible that in this process of revisiting the material over time, the brain has to relearn some of the content knowledge. In a sense, distributed practice demonstrates that "forgetting is a friend of learning" (Bjork, 2015). The classic all-nighter, of which we must admit we experienced a few during our own undergraduate days, is the best example of massed practice. Although this practice method may be effective in learning a large amount of basic information in a short time, it is a poor method of learning and remembering complex information and, really, gives you an illusion of learning. Massed practice is especially detrimental for learning in classes that are a part of your major. Have you experienced taking an advanced class and realizing that not only can you not remember the material from the prerequisite class, you feel as if you have never seen the material before? This is likely the result of massed practice.

> **Distributed Practice:** Learning is divided into short and frequent study sessions over a long period of time.

> **Massed Practice:** Learning is grouped into a few extended sessions over a short period of time.

Rehearsal strategies can be very effective in some types of learning. Copying material, taking verbatim notes, reciting words or definitions, and underlining material in handouts or textbooks are all examples of rehearsal strategies. However, the limitation in the use of rehearsal strategies is that they make few connections between the new information and the knowledge we already have in LTM. Therefore, if the information is not connected to anything when it is stored in LTM, it is difficult to retrieve. Your goal as a learner is to try to make the information meaningful if you want to increase the probability that you will remember it. Highlighting and underlining, some of the most popular learning strategies used by college students, are for the

> **Rehearsal Strategies:** The process of repeating information over and over in working memory to retain it.

most part rehearsal strategies. We'll address how to maximize the effectiveness of highlighting in Chapter 8. Let's now turn to the two major learning strategies that will help you learn more information—elaboration and organization.

ELABORATION STRATEGIES

Elaboration Strategies: Integration of meaningful knowledge into long-term memory through adding detail, summarizing, creating examples, and analogies.

Acronyms: Mnemonics that use the first letter in each word of a list to form a word (e.g., SMART goals).

Elaboration strategies help retention by linking new information to information already in your LTM. These strategies can be very useful for improving the recall of names, categories, sequences, or groups of items. One of the most popular elaboration strategies is the use of **acronyms**. Acronyms use the first letter in each word to form a mnemonic. Our earlier example about the order of the planets is an acronym. Here are some other popular acronyms:

HOMES

The five Great Lakes: Huron, Ontario, Michigan, Erie, Superior (geography)

ROY G. BIV

The colors of the spectrum: red, orange, yellow, green, blue, indigo, violet (physics)

King Phillip came over from Greece singing

The classification of organisms: kingdom, phylum, class, order, family, genus, species (biology)

Elaboration strategies for more complex learning from texts include paraphrasing, summarizing, creating analogies, writing notes in one's own words, and asking and answering questions. When someone asks us to elaborate on an idea we have expressed in discussion, he or she wants us to add more information to what we have said to provide detail, give examples, make connections to other issues, or draw inferences from the data. The additional information makes our point more meaningful to the listener and also is likely to make the point easier to remember.

Table 3.1 lists two terms—*note taking* and *note making* (i.e., developing questions from notes). Writing notes directly from a lecture is a rehearsal strategy, but asking questions and underlining the answers in the notes (note making) is an elaboration strategy. Chapter 9 discusses what is done with notes after a lecture is just as important as taking the notes in the first place. In that chapter, you will learn how to develop questions from your notes so you can check your understanding of lecture material.

We can elaborate when learning more complex information. As information enters WM, the successful learner thinks about the information: What does this new information mean? How does it relate to other ideas in the text and other information already learned? What type of analogies or examples can I generate?

A student learning that ancient Egyptian society depended on slavery may elaborate on this fact by adding details, making connections with other information, or drawing inferences. By way of providing detail, the student may notice that Egyptian slaves were largely prisoners of war.

The student may connect the concept of Egyptian slavery with what is known of antebellum US slavery, noting similarities and differences. The student may infer that life for an Egyptian slave was hard and held cheaply by Egyptian society at large. In this way, the learner integrates the new ideas into LTM by associating the new data with the old knowledge (Bransford, 1979). This procedure leads to improved understanding of the material and to an increased probability that the information will be remembered at a later time.

The following are other examples of analogies that promote connections between new ideas and existing student knowledge (cited in Ormrod, 1995).

- The growth of a glacier is like *pancake batter being poured into a frying pan*. As more and more substance is added to the middle, the edges spread farther and farther out (Ormrod, 1995, p. 298).
- The human circulatory system is similar to a *parcel delivery system*. "Red blood cells work like trucks, carrying needed materials from a central distribution point for delivery throughout the body. Arteries and veins are like roads, acting as access routes through which the various points of delivery are reached. The heart is like the warehouse or the central point in which vehicles are loaded and dispatched, and to which empty vehicles are returned to be reloaded" (Stepich & Newby, 1988, p. 136).
- A dual-store model of memory is like the *information selection and storage system you use at home*. Some things (e.g., junk mail) are discarded as soon as they arrive; others (e.g., bills) are only briefly dealt with; and still others (e.g., driver's license) are used regularly and saved for a long period of time (Ormrod, 1995, p. 298).

Have you ever used analogies in learning? If so, how did they help you recall information?

An important advantage of elaboration strategies is that they provide additional retrieval routes for remembering information. When you elaborate, you create additional ways of recalling the information. Therefore, if you cannot remember the original connection, you may be able to use other connections to retrieve the needed information.

Here is an example of elaboration in action (Gagné et al., 1993). A student reads in her political science textbook: "Political action committees (PACs) influence Congress with money." She already read that a PAC is a group whose purpose is to influence policy. Another student who came to the same section of the textbook about PACs goes one step further. She elaborates on the new information by thinking that the National Rifle Association has a PAC.

Suppose the following day the instructor asks the class what political action committees do. Both students may recall that they are groups whose goal is to influence policy. But suppose they cannot recall the purpose of a PAC. The student who thinks of the National Rifle Association may be able to infer what a PAC does from her elaboration that the National Rifle Association has a PAC. The organization tries to influence policy in Congress. This could lead her to conclude that PACs try to influence votes, thus answering the instructor's question correctly. This example illustrates the importance of providing additional retrieval routes for remembering information.

ORGANIZATIONAL STRATEGIES

Psychologists have found that it is difficult, and sometimes impossible, for humans to learn unorganized bits and pieces of information (e.g., definitions, dates, names, ideas) without imposing patterns of organization on the information (Gaskins & Elliot, 1991). By organizing information, connections and interrelationships are made within a body of new information. Learning is facilitated when a learner becomes aware of the inherent organizational structure of new material or imposes an organizational structure on material when no such structure initially exists. A body of new information to be learned is stored more effectively and remembered more completely when it is organized (Ormrod, 2011).

Internal organization of material helps learning and retention. An investigation by Bower, Clark, Lesgold, and Winzenz (1969) illustrated this finding in an investigation in which college students were given four study sessions to learn 112 words that were classified into four categories (e.g., minerals, plants). Some students had words arranged randomly, whereas others had words arranged in four different hierarchies (see Figure 3.2 for the minerals hierarchy). After one study session, students who had studied the organized words could remember more than three times as many words as those who had studied the randomized words. After four study trials, the students in the organized group remembered all 112, whereas the students in the random group remembered only 70.

EXERCISE 3.3: DEMONSTRATING THE IMPORTANCE OF CATEGORIZING KNOWLEDGE

Directions: Try the following experiment (Halpern, 1996, pp. 489–490). The following are two lists of words. Read the first list at a rate of approximately one word per second, cover the list, and write down as many of the words as you can remember, then repeat this process with the second list:

| Girl | Heart | Robin | Purple | Finger | Flute | Blue | Organ |
| Man | Hawk | Green | Lung | Eagle | Child | Piano | |

Now read the next list, cover it, and then write down as many of the words as you can remember from this list:

| Green | Blue | Purple | Man | Girl | Child | Piano | Flute | Organ |
| Heart | Lung | Finger | Eagle | Hawk | Robin | | | |

Stop now, cover the preceding list, and write down as many words from this list as you can remember.

Each semester, our students report that they remembered more from the second list. The two lists include the same words, but the second list is organized by category. Obviously, you did benefit from seeing the list a second time, but most of the improvement on the second list came from the organization provided by presenting the words in categories.

Categories can provide useful retrieval cues in many situations. For example, if you go to the supermarket with a shopping list, you can recall the items you need by checking different categories, such as dairy, meats, vegetables, drinks, and so forth. Think about courses such as biology, astronomy, or anthropology where learning classification lists are essential to success in the course. The research is clear: If you learn ways to organize material, you will be able to learn and retrieve the information more effectively.

Organizational Strategies:
Learning strategies that impose structure on material via hierarchical or other relationships among the material's parts.

Organizational strategies are as useful in remembering prose passages as they are in recalling lists. Outlines and representations (or maps) can be useful organizational strategies. These techniques enable a better understanding of text material by helping the learner analyze the text structure. Outlining is a strategy where major and minor ideas are written in abbreviated form using important

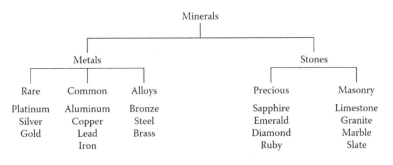

FIGURE 3.2   Example of a Hierarchy (Bower et al., 1969)

words and phrases. Representation is a process of drawing a diagram to picture how ideas are connected (see Figure 3.2).

EXERCISE 3.4: IDENTIFYING LEARNING STRATEGIES

Directions: The following behaviors represent different learning strategies used by students. Identify each type of strategy by placing the letter (R) for rehearsal, (E) for elaboration, and (O) for organizational in the space provided. Answers are on p. 72.

1 "In preparing for a chemistry test, I keep writing down major formulae until I remember them."
2 "I write a summary of each chapter in my political science book."
3 "I think of a computer when studying the information-processing system."
4 "I use a chart to compare different theories in my philosophy class."
5 "I ask myself questions after reading my history textbook."
6 "After taking notes in class, I write questions that the notes answer."
7 "I underline in my textbook while I read."
8 "I outline each chapter in my geology textbook."

One of the main points in this chapter is that there are different ways to learn and that some ways lead to greater information retention and retrieval. In Unit IV, you will learn how to use more elaboration and organization strategies in your learning and studying behavior. Our other goal in this chapter was to debunk the myth that your intelligence is fixed at some point in childhood. By adopting a growth mindset, we hope that you realize that you can cultivate your intelligence through effort. In many ways, your brain works like a muscle—it grows in strength and becomes, so to speak, "smarter." Acquiring and exercising effective learning strategies is one proven way to develop your brain.

Chapter Review

KEY POINTS

1 The brain continues to grow and change well into adulthood as a result of input from the environment. This process is called neuroplasticity.
2 Adopting a growth mindset about intelligence, as opposed to a fixed mindset, enables students to take on challenges, apply effort, learn from mistakes, and perform better in the long term.
3 The information-processing system is a model that is used to identify how individuals obtain, transform, store, and apply information. It comprises the short-term sensory store, working memory, and long-term memory.
4 Learning involves encoding information into long-term memory.
5 There can be no learning without attention.
6 There are seven flaws in human memory: transience, absent-mindedness, blocking, misattribution, suggestibility, bias, and persistence.
7 Memory is enhanced when the content is meaningful. When you learn something, try to relate it to something you already know.
8 Meaningful learning facilitates both organized storage and retrieval of information.
9 Many students use only rehearsal strategies in learning. As a result, they have difficulty understanding and recalling complex information.
10 Elaboration increases learning by linking new content to existing knowledge. It provides additional ways of remembering information.
11 Elaboration strategies include mnemonic devices, paraphrasing, summarizing, creating analogies and examples, writing notes in one's own words, explaining, and asking questions.
12 It is difficult to learn unorganized definitions, dates, names, and ideas without organizing the information.
13 Organizational learning strategies promote learning by imposing order on new content. Classifying, outlining, and creating representations or mapping are examples of such strategies.
14 How information is organized and elaborated influences one's ability to retrieve it when needed.

FOLLOW-UP ACTIVITIES

1. Challenge a Fixed Mindset

Provide a counterstatement to the fixed mindset voice. Possible challenges (based on mindsetonline. com) are included at the end of the chapter.

Fixed mindset	Growth mindset
"Are you sure you can do it? Maybe you don't have the talent."	
"What if you fail—you'll be a failure."	
"It's not my fault. It was someone else's fault."	

2. Identify the Memory Flaw

1. On your way back to the parking lot from class someone yells, "Hi!" and asks how you are doing. You know that you have met the person before, but don't know when or where.	
2. You tell your roommate that your mom always told you to refrigerate the ground coffee as it will taste fresher, but your mother insists she's never said that.	
3. While in the grocery store, you forget to give the cashier your coupons because you are busy texting a friend.	
4. Several weeks after the midterm, a friend asks about your essay answer. You begin to share your answer, only to find that there are several details you no longer remember.	
5. Everyone says that they wish they could go back to high school.	
6. You cannot study for an upcoming quiz because you keep remembering the game-winning home run you made yesterday.	
7. A friend is helping you prepare for an exam by quizzing you. She asks, "The answer to this question was discussed on the day we had the fire drill. Does that help you remember?"	

3. Analyze a Student's Behavior

Carla visited her biology professor to discuss her poor performance on the midterm exam. She was disappointed because she studied "very hard" for the exam. When the professor asked her to explain how she studied, she opened her book bag and produced more than 100 index cards with terms on one side and definitions on the other. She explained how she spent hours memorizing all the terms in the required textbook chapters. She did well on the multiple-choice questions, but poorly on the essay questions.

If you were the professor, what advice would you give her to prepare for the next examination?

4. Analyze a Student's Behavior

Read the following information concerning Ruben. Discuss the strengths and weaknesses of his motivation and learning strategies. What suggestions do you have for helping him become more successful?

Ruben is studying a chapter in his biology textbook for a quiz the next day. His experience taking biology in high school was mostly negative because his instructors focused on facts and definitions. As a result, he never developed much interest in the subject. He has been told that he will be asked to answer one essay question to test his knowledge of the material. He is not sure exactly what content will be tested but decides to develop a study plan to gain a general understanding of the main ideas and to recall the most important facts. He paraphrases each section of the chapter and underlines the important information. He realizes that he has difficulty comparing and contrasting some of the concepts discussed in class. Therefore, he decides to develop and write responses to short-answer essay questions he thinks may be on the test. He develops so many possible questions that he quickly becomes frustrated and only answers two essay questions. He then reads the chapter summary. Finally, he reviews the underlining in his textbook and decides it is time to move on to another subject.

5. Evaluate Your Learning Strategies

Think about the learning strategies you used in high school or in your last educational environment. How did you memorize basic material? How did you learn concepts in history, chemistry, and mathematics? If you had to do it over again, how would you improve your learning strategies in high school? Are you using the same strategies in college? What changes in your learning and study strategies do you think you have to make this year?

6. Prepare Study Materials

This chapter presented a number of strategies that promote learning. Identify a student in your class to review the content in this chapter with and together develop a plan for studying the material in the chapter. Identify each study strategy you will use and discuss how you will apply the strategy.

Answers to Follow-Up Activity 1

Fixed mindset	Growth mindset
"Are you sure you can do it? Maybe you don't have the talent."	"I'm not sure I can do it now, but I think I can learn to with time and effort."
"What if you fail—you'll be a failure."	"Most successful people had failures along the way."
"It's not my fault. It was someone else's fault."	"If I don't take responsibility, I can't fix it. Let me listen to what others have to say—however painful it is—and learn whatever I can."

Answers to Exercise 3.2

1. Blocking	2. Misattribution	3. Absent-mindedness
4. Transience	5. Bias	6. Persistence
7. Suggestibility		

Answers to Exercise 3.4

1. R   2. E   3. E   4. O   5. E   6. E   7. R   8. O

Part 2

Motivational Strategies

Chapter 4: Goal Setting
Chapter 5: Self-Regulation of Emotions

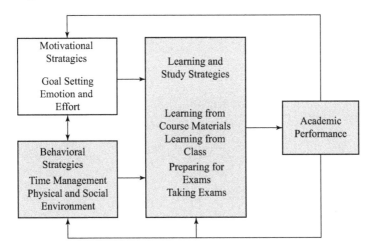

The purpose of this part is to present strategies that can be used to self-regulate motivation. Chapter 4 deals with goals and goal setting. The use of goal setting as a self-regulatory strategy is widespread in business, academic, and sports settings. Goals serve as the basis of motivation. Without goals, it is difficult to be motivated to achieve. More specifically, you learned in the chapter about motivation that goals influence whether we choose to engage with an activity as well as how much effort we invest and how long we persist at it.

Many individuals have experienced goal setting in areas that are challenging and interesting to them (e.g., a favorite subject, an athletic contest, or an artistic endeavor). However, goal setting can also be especially useful in uninteresting or unchallenging tasks. In these situations, goals can be used to counteract boredom and apathy by providing a sense of challenge and purpose (i.e., accomplishing the goal) that would otherwise be lacking. Hence, goal attainment can generate feelings of pride, satisfaction, or competence that may not be experienced by simply completing assignments or tasks (Reeve, 1996).

Chapter 5 covers additional motivational strategies that can be used to regulate your emotion and effort. Often high-pressure situations cause individuals to experience irrational and self-defeating beliefs, as well as anxiety (e.g., "I can't do it" or "I'm not good enough to compete with the students in my class"). These conditions interfere with the motivation to learn. Fortunately, these negative beliefs can be handled by changing the way individuals talk to themselves. The emotional dimension of anxiety can also be reduced using relaxation strategies.

4 Goal Setting

In this chapter, we will look at how to manage your motivation by setting effective goals. Before you actually set goals, there are other things to consider. For example, the importance of analyzing your identity before setting a goal cannot be overestimated. Similarly, understanding your governing values is an integral part of setting effective goals. This chapter will be organized as shown in Figure 4.1.

One of the major goals of the college experience is for students to develop a coherent sense of identity. According to Erikson (1968), developing identity involves the search for a consistent, self-constructed image of who one is and one's values and goals. All of us have various social identities, whether consciously or subconsciously. You might identify according to your gender, race, sexual orientation, socioeconomic status, religion, political affiliation, and body ableness or disability. Society privileges some identities but marginalizes others. Among the many dimensions, race and gender are the most prominent social categories. However, increasingly, both researchers (e.g., Pope & Reynolds, 2017; Shin et al., 2017) and practitioners are emphasizing the integration of our multiple identities and embracing our intersectional selves. Communities in higher education and elsewhere where the intersection of identity is recognized and celebrated, such as spaces for trans people of color or deaf women, have increased over time. These are important support structures as individuals with marginalized identities experience multiple oppressions.

Identity: A consistent, self-constructed image of who one is, what one values, and one's related goals.

Reflect on a personal experience where you encountered some type of active or passive oppression related to who you are. The oppression may have been personal or institutional. If you cannot identify a personal experience, then write about an experience of someone you know or something you have seen in the news. How did the experience impact you? How did it influence your values, principles, and beliefs?

A core feature of your identity is your values. Values are the fundamental beliefs that help us decide what is important to us; they guide our attitudes and actions. This chapter discusses the relationship between values and goals, and describes how to develop plans for attaining your goals. Figure 4.2 identifies the steps that lead from identifying values to engaging in daily actions. Everything starts with values. Have you thought about your own foundational values? What is

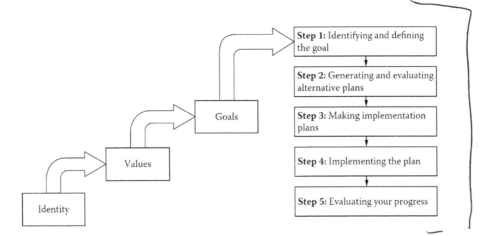

FIGURE 4.1 Outline of the Necessary Steps for Effective Goal Setting

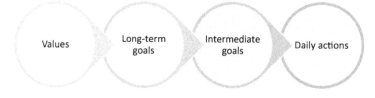

FIGURE 4.2   Translating Values into Daily Actions

important in your life? The following are some values that people have identified as of greatest importance in their lives:

- family
- wellness
- education
- non-discrimination
- respect for the environment
- work-life balance
- financial security
- religion
- integrity
- honesty
- service
- self-respect
- friendship
- courage

Our most important accomplishments are attained by translating our values into long-term goals. Long-term goals, in turn, are attained through a series of intermediate goals. Finally, the intermediate goals are attained through a series of specific, goal-oriented daily actions.

Suppose an individual values education and sets a goal to earn a college degree. To accomplish this long-term goal, the student needs to establish some intermediate goals. These intermediate goals often involve year-long goals (e.g., declaring a major and taking and passing a minimum number of classes), semester goals (e.g., exploring career possibilities and attending class regularly), monthly goals (e.g., meeting with an academic adviser and long-range planning for the completion of papers and other assignments), and weekly goals (e.g., short-term planning for the completion of papers, assignments, preparation for examinations, and using effective learning and study strategies).

WHY ARE VALUES AND INTERESTS AN IMPORTANT FOUNDATION TO GOAL SETTING?

Smith (1994) stated: "Values explain *why* you want to accomplish certain things in life. Long-range goals describe *what* you want to accomplish. Intermediate goals and daily tasks show *how* to do it" (p. 83). For example, a person may value health and fitness (the *why*). For this reason, he or she establishes a long-range goal of losing 20 pounds (the *what*), and an intermediate goal of losing five pounds by the end of the semester by developing a specific exercise program for one hour each day (the *how*). Each component—values, long-range goals, intermediate goals, and daily tasks—needs to be linked to the others.

If an individual's goals are not aligned with his or her values, the individual may never be satisfied with his or her accomplishments because he or she will be neglecting the things that matter most. Also, if the individual completes daily tasks that do not reflect long-range and intermediate goals, he or she will be busy doing things, but will not be productive.

The keys to goal setting and time management are governing values. Smith (1994) believes that one of the reasons many people are frustrated or stressed in their lives is because they ignore the first three levels of the pyramid. They complete many tasks, but do not base them on anything but urgency. As a result, they fail to get around to doing the things that are really important to them.

One of the ways in which your values manifest in college is by choice of major. For example, if respect for the environment is your core value, you might choose a major in the natural sciences. If non-discrimination is your core value, you might be interested in social sciences. Some students graduate with the major they first declared. However, if you are like about 80 percent of students, you will switch majors at least once while in college. The good news is that if you do change, you are in fact slightly more likely to graduate than students who never switched (EAB Student Success Collaborative, 2016)! This might be because your values and interests grow and change during college and your changed major is more closely aligned with your values and interests than your original one. As a result, you are more motivated and perform better than those who do not change their original major despite a change in their interests. Researchers (Allen & Robbins, 2010) call the alignment of interest with a major "interest-major congruence." Your college is likely to have a career center that has inventories designed to help you make a choice about a career and a major. It is also the case that choosing a major is not always the same as choosing a career. Though some majors, such as engineering and nursing, are career specific, many majors, such as biology and marketing, are career oriented and some, such as English and anthropology, are non-career specific. They do, though, build general skills such as verbal and written communication, critical thinking and problem solving, and organization which are required in many professional fields.

Reflect on the values that are most important to you and be prepared to discuss them with other students in your class. After studying this chapter, you will be able to:

- establish effective personal goals;
- develop and implement effective plans for attaining goals.

EXERCISE 4.1: SELF-OBSERVATION: IDENTIFYING YOUR VALUES

Directions: The purpose of this exercise is to help identify the activities you enjoy and determine whether you are finding time to participate in them. This exercise is based on Simon, Howe, and Kirschenbaum's (1995) *values clarification* program, based on the premise that many people do not know clearly what their values are:

- Make a list of seven to ten things that give you great pleasure or joy.
- After the name of each activity, write the date you last experienced it.
- Place a dollar sign after each activity that costs more than US$10.
- Now go through the list again and place a P after those activities that usually require considerable *planning*.
- Review your list and place an S after activities that you *share* with others.
- Finally, place an A after those activities that you do *alone*.

What does this exercise tell you about yourself? What are the activities valued by the students in your class? Why is it that some people find time to do the things they enjoy, whereas others do not? How do values influence goals?

My Activities List

_____

_____

_____

_____

_____ ■

WHY IS GOAL SETTING IMPORTANT?

In 2014, Serena Williams set herself a goal to break Chris Evert's and Martina Navratilova's respective 18 major tournament wins. After losing three Grand Slams, her coach encouraged her to change her mindset: "Why are you trying to get to 18 major wins? Your goal should be 30 or 40. 18 is such a low goal" (Bloomberg Radio, 2018). Williams reflected, "To me, it made so much sense. I set my goal for what was in sight. I think that subconsciously, a lot of people set their goal on what is already there. Why not reach for a higher goal? I really learned from that. Why would I reach for that when there's more." By 2018, with 23 Grand Slam wins, Williams beat Steffi Graf's record of 22 wins and has the distinction of being the greatest female tennis player of all time. The interview reveals the critical role of goal setting in Williams' success.

A goal is defined as "the behaviour or outcome that one is consciously attempting to perform or attain" (Zimmerman, Schunk, & DiBenedetto, 2015, p. 84). Goal setting, one of the key processes of self-regulation, refers to the process of establishing a standard for performance. Researchers (Locke & Latham, 2002, 2013) have demonstrated that people with goals outperform those without goals, and, generally speaking, when you have a goal, you are likely to perform better than when you do not have a goal. Think about something as simple as doing sit-ups. Would you really do 50 of them if you did not have such a goal? The same has been observed in activities as wide in range as learning text information, selling products, and losing weight.

What determines the level of goals we set for ourselves? A key determinant is our level of self-efficacy, discussed in Chapter 2 as an internal belief about task-specific self-confidence. As Bandura (2018) stated, "The higher their self-efficacy, the higher the goals people set for themselves" (p. 1026). Contrarily, if an individual doubts their ability, they tend to set low goals, give up quickly when faced with challenges and accept mediocre performance.

Most of us have goals in many domains: academic, social, occupational, and personal. Our goals have a time dimension: some goals are short term (e.g., earning an A on your sociology exam on Friday); others are long term (e.g., raising your grade-point average [GPA] to 3.0 this semester); and still others are very long term (e.g., becoming a human rights attorney or the No. 1 tennis player in the world). Long-term goals are very important, but from a self-regulatory perspective, short-term and intermediate goals are key to regulating motivation and behavior. Surely you have heard the saying "A goal without a plan is just a dream." A freshman journalism student might set his or her sights on becoming editor of the college newspaper during his or her senior year. The goal is four years away and represents a major achievement, so the student decides what needs to be done to work toward this long-range goal. An intermediate goal would be to become a section editor by his or her junior year. By setting intermediate goals that directly relate to the long-term goal, the student identifies a plan of action or path to follow to attain his or her ultimate goal. In addition to providing a path, intermediate goals play an important role in our motivation to pursue long-term goals. Long-term goals, such as becoming a college newspaper editor, may seem out of reach at times. Success at intermediate goals, however, gives you the self-efficacy to persist in giving the effort required to move closer to a long-range goal. This is further enhanced when others, such as your parents, peers, or coaches, give you positive reinforcement for meeting the intermediate milestones. The idea of goal setting and persistence despite obstacles is expressed in a reflection by a student with a learning disability:

> I just always knew that I was going to college and was going to graduate. I really never even thought of not doing it. Even with my problems with reading and writing, I think I've done a good job in school—all the way through. Part of my success in school, I think, is that I've always had a plan. I'm sure that some of this comes from my family. My brothers have both done really well in college. But, a lot of it is just me. I am determined. That really helps.

(Skinner, 2004, p. 100)

Goals can also be categorized into outcome versus process goals. Outcome goals refer to the result you'd like to achieve while process goals refer to processes you need to master to produce the result. One way to think about outcome goals is that they represent "what" and process goals represent "how." For example, in the context of dart throwing, a process goal involves using specific strategies to execute the throw while an outcome goal involves hitting the bull's eye (Zimmerman & Kitsantas, 1997). Experimental studies show that after setting an outcome goal (hitting the bull's eye), individuals who focused on process goals (specific strategy) first and then shifted to outcome goals produced the highest levels of performance (Zimmerman & Kitsantas, 1999). They did better than those who only focused on process goals (strategies), who in turn did better than those who only focused on outcome goals (hitting the bull's eye). There are several reasons for this, among them the fact that while the outcome is not always under your control, the process generally is. For example, it is not enough to set a goal such as "I want to lose ten pounds by the winter holidays" unless you also determine how you will accomplish this. Will you increase exercise? Decrease caloric intake? These actions are under your control while exactly how much weight you lose is not always under your control. For example, weight loss is impacted by the amount of sleep you get and stress in your life. While these factors are not always under your control, healthy habits such as increasing exercise and improving eating habits are—and in the long term, they will ensure success in losing weight. In the context of looking at goals in terms of outcome and process, the recommendation is clear: you need both.

Goal setting is a planning process and, as stated, an important aspect of self-regulation. This process puts meaning in people's lives, helps them achieve their dreams and ambitions, and sets up positive expectations for achievements. Students who set goals and develop plans to achieve them take responsibility for their own lives. Think about your own behavior. Are you in charge of your own behavior, or do you prefer that other individuals set goals and make important decisions for you? It is difficult to be a highly motivated individual without setting personal goals. Many athletes even mentioned that their coaches suggested they carry with them a list of their goals.

In team sports, coaches often meet with individuals to set both individual and team goals. In the business world, corporations set goals for sales and product development. In fact, the stock market is very sensitive to a company's performance goals. When a company announces its quarterly profits or losses, the investment world compares the performance with expected goals. The result often is immediate price fluctuation in the stock market.

Goals help us become aware of our values and help us determine what we are willing to do. As a result, they influence our attitudes, motivation, and learning. Think about your goals. Do your goals motivate you in a positive way to be a successful learner, or do your goals motivate you to get by doing as little work as possible? Are your experiences with goals similar or different from the student who reported the following?

Student Reflections

I never really gave much thought to developing personal goals. My dad always told me to set my standards high, and that if I put my mind to something, I could do anything. I never used to believe this statement, but I do now. Setting goals is something that I need to do so that I know where I want to go and develop a plan to get there. I have a friend who has a poster on his wall with five goals that he would like to accomplish this semester. I remember walking into his room and thinking to myself: "Wow, this guy has it together. He knows what he wants to accomplish." I know that I want to do well in college, but I do not have any specific goals. I want to set goals for the present and future so I have a way of showing myself that I have accomplished something. I feel better when I accomplish something that I set out to achieve.

WHAT PROPERTIES OF GOALS ENHANCE MOTIVATION?

Goal Properties: The more specific, proximal, and difficult goals are, the more effective they are likely to be.

Goal setting generally improves performance, but a key factor in this is the type of goals one sets. Schunk (1991) pointed out that the effects of goals on behavior depend on three **goal properties**: specificity, proximity, and difficulty. Goals that set specific performance standards, such as doing 50 sit-ups, are more likely to increase motivation than general goals such as "Do your best." Specific goals help the learner determine the amount of effort required for success and lead to feelings of satisfaction when the goal is attained. As a result, learners come to believe they have a greater ability to complete the task.

Goals also can be identified by the extent to which they extend into the future. Proximal goals are close at hand and result in greater motivation directed toward attainment than more distant goals. Sometimes, proximal goals are process-oriented while more distant goals are outcome-oriented. Pursuing proximal goals conveys reliable information about one's capabilities. When students perceive they are making progress toward a proximal goal, they are apt to feel more confident and maintain their motivation. Because it is harder to evaluate progress toward distant goals, learners have more difficulty judging their capabilities, even if they perform well.

Finally, a student's perception of difficulty influences the amount of effort they will invest in the task. Difficult goals energize behavior while easy goals stimulate little effort. Why set a goal of "staying in college" when you can "excel in college"? As students work and attain difficult goals, they develop beliefs in their competence. However, if they do not believe they have the ability to attain a goal, they are likely to have low expectations for success and not become involved in the task.

Think about how the specificity, proximity, and difficulty level in goal setting in each class might impact your motivation and perceptions of ability.

WHAT ARE THE STEPS IN THE GOAL-SETTING PROCESS?

The first learning strategy you will learn in this chapter is goal setting. Five important steps comprise this strategy (adapted in part from McCombs & Encinias, 1987). Begin this academic term by setting a few major goals in different areas of your life and developing an action plan to implement them.

STEP 1: IDENTIFY AND DEFINE THE GOAL

Think about all the things you would like to accomplish in the different aspects of your life (e.g., academic, personal, social, and career). Do you want to make the dean's list? Pass a difficult course? Become a leader in your community? Get a summer internship? Lose a few pounds? Ask yourself: "What areas of my life would I like to improve?" "What areas need to be worked on?"

Individuals set goals throughout their lives. As they attain one goal, they often identify another. In fact, one of the major ways individuals seek happiness is through goal attainment. When some students are asked what goal they would like to attain, they often mention being happy. Keep in mind that happiness is not a goal, it is a feeling or state of mind that occurs as the result of goal attainment.

Recently, the second author met a man in his fifties who always wanted to be a singer. He played some tapes of his songs at a party. His voice was outstanding! His problem was that he had a dream,

---

SMART Goals: An acronym identifying the criteria for setting goals—specific, measurable, action-oriented, realistic, and time-bound.

---

and indeed a long-term goal, but failed to set intermediate goals and daily tasks and develop any plans to attain them. As you set each of your goals, you want to make sure they are **SMART goals** (Smith, 1994): **S**pecific, **M**easurable, **A**ction-Oriented, **R**ealistic, and **T**ime-Bound.

A general goal would be, "Get in shape." But a specific goal would say, "Join a health club and work out three days a week."

- *Specific—describes what you want to accomplish with as much detail as possible.* If you establish vague goals, you lessen the possibility of attaining them. Describe the context (i.e., course, situation, or setting), as well as the specific outcome. Avoid general terms like "good," "well," "happy," "understand," and "know."

  Poor: "I want to *do well* in English."
  Better: "I want to *earn an A* on my next essay in English."

- *Measurable—describes your goal in terms that can be clearly evaluated.* If you fail to determine how a goal is measured, you will never know whether you attained it. Be sure to include a statement of the minimal level of performance that will be accepted as evidence that you have achieved the goal.

  Poor: "I want to *study* my biology textbook."
  Better: "I want to *read chapter 7* in my biology textbook and *answer all the discussion questions* by Tuesday of this week."

- *Action-oriented—identifies a goal that focuses on actions rather than personal qualities.* Be sure to identify your goal so that it includes an action to be completed; otherwise, you will not know how to accomplish it.

  Poor: "I want to *develop a better attitude* about studying."
  Better: "I want to *complete all my assignments* before class each day and *answer the chapter questions* for any readings."

- *Realistic—identifies a goal you know you are actually capable of attaining.* Goals can be challenging but unrealistic. Therefore, you must carefully analyze your goals to determine that you can reasonably expect to reach them. In thinking about general goal setting, there is some evidence that success-celebrating posts on social media such as images of a flawlessly fit body, perfect vacation, or a new car can pressure young people, particularly, to set unrealistic goals that can in fact bring about depression. Be sure to challenge yourself in goal setting but also be realistic. It is also important to be challenging but realistic in the academic context.

  Poor: "I want to *read five chapters* in my history textbook this evening and answer all the discussion questions."
  Better: "I want to *read two chapters* in my history textbook this evening and answer all the discussion questions."

- *Timely—identifies a goal that breaks a longer-term goal into a shorter-term goal(s) and clearly specifies a completion date.*

  Poor: "I want to *graduate* at the head of my class."
  Better: "I want to make the honor roll *this semester.*"

An important task in goal setting is to determine how much time each long-term goal will take and to establish some smaller steps, or intermediate goals, that will help you reach your final goal. One way to accomplish this step is to use a timeline. Write your final outcome goal on the right-hand side and identify the smaller, process-oriented goals that will help you reach this major goal. Estimate how long it will take to attain each intermediate goal.

Examples of SMART Goals

The following are examples of academic, social, occupational, and personal goals. Notice that each one of these goals is specific, measurable, action-oriented, realistic, and time-bound. Some of them also include both the outcome (what?) and process (how?) goal.

Academic
- "I want to complete an advanced mathematics course next semester, achieving a final grade of at least a B."
- "I want to earn a 3.0 GPA this semester by using effective exam preparation and exam-taking strategies."
- "I want to complete all my research papers this semester one week before handing them in so I have time to edit them."

Social
- "I want to meet new people this semester by attending a social event twice a month and introducing myself to at least two people at each event throughout this semester."
- "I want to volunteer at least five hours on Sundays by completing all my schoolwork between Monday and Saturday."
- "I want to spend at least one hour with my boyfriend/girlfriend each week this semester."

Occupational
- "I want to work at least ten hours per week this semester."
- "I want to obtain an internship in public relations by the end of May by applying for at least one internship every week."
- "I want to complete all my general education requirements by my sophomore year."

Personal
- "I want to work out four times a week for 40 minutes throughout the current semester."
- "I want to save US$500 this semester by cutting back on expensive coffee drinks and buying my lunch at the supermarket at least two times a week."
- "I want to meditate at least three days a week by getting up 15 minutes earlier than usual."

More about the value of meditation and how to do it in Chapter 5! Table 4.1 is a review of the procedures for writing SMART goals.

TABLE 4.1
Procedures for Writing SMART Goals

Procedures	Thought Process
Identify the area in which you wish to write a goal.	"I want to write a goal for my next composition paper."
Evaluate your past and present achievement, interest, or performance in the area to consider the extent to which your goal is action-oriented and realistic.	"I have been having some difficulty in the course and would like to demonstrate some improvement in the next paper."
State what you want to accomplish. Begin with the words "I want to" and include a specific outcome; describe the goal so that it can be measured and include a specific completion date (time-bound).	"I want to obtain a grade of A on the composition paper that is due on October 15."
State specific processes or strategies you will implement that will support you in reaching the outcome.	"I will earn a better grade by starting the composition paper early so I can create several drafts and turn in the final version. I will also seek help from the writing center to improve my sentence structure."
Evaluate your goal statement. Is it a SMART goal (i.e., specific, measurable, action-oriented, realistic, and time-bound)?	"Because my grades have been low on other composition papers, it may not be realistic for me to move to an A on the next paper. I will set my goal for a A– and then move to an A."
If necessary, make modifications in your goal statement.	"I want to obtain a grade of A– on the composition paper that is due on October 15 by writing multiple drafts and getting feedback from the writing center."

EXERCISE 4.2: WRITING PERSONAL GOALS

Think about the things you would like to achieve, obtain, or experience in life. Using the criteria and procedure for writing SMART goals, write at least four goals (include at least two major academic goals).

1.
2.
3.
4.

STEP 2: GENERATE AND EVALUATE ALTERNATIVE PLANS

You may have heard the saying "Good intentions have a bad reputation." Intending to do something does not necessarily translate into action. Just think of how many people actually accomplish their New Year's resolutions! Similarly, while it is important to create an effective goal statement, that in itself is not enough to bring about the desired results. Therefore, let's move on to the second step in the process—determining how you are going to attain your goal. The answers to the following questions can be very helpful:

- How would other people achieve this goal?
- Who can help me achieve this goal?
- How have I achieved similar goals in the past?

Let's consider a student whose goal is to attain a B on an English paper. Suppose the student has already written a few papers and is aware of his or her strengths and weaknesses. As part of developing an effective plan for the next paper, the student might ask him- or herself the following questions: Did I give myself enough time to complete the last paper? Do I understand the criteria for grading? Do I understand why my last paper was graded lower than expected? Do I understand my strengths and weaknesses? Would I benefit from having someone read the paper before I turn it in?

By asking these questions, the student begins to think about alternative ways to attain the goal and the advantages and disadvantages of each strategy. For example, the student might initially include in the plan time for two rewrites, but realizes he or she has an exam in another subject the same week. As a result, no matter how effective the plan might be for writing a better paper, the student probably will not do as well on the exam if he or she spends more time on the paper. Thus, the student needs to decide how best to spend his or her time. Our point is that one constantly has to weigh the advantages and disadvantages of one strategy over another.

STEP 3: MAKE IMPLEMENTATION PLANS

In Step 1, you learned why it is necessary to be specific in writing a goal. It also is important for your plan to be specific, so you know exactly what needs to be done to achieve your goal. This is the difference between an outcome and a process goal. It is not enough to have an outcome goal, you also need process goals. Sometimes, process goals include each of the necessary tasks that must be completed and the date by which the tasks will be accomplished. Setting deadlines for each task is helpful in ensuring that you continue to make progress toward your goal. Sometimes, a process goal might involve implementing a new strategy. For example, your goal may be to stop procrastinating and take advantage of your professor's offer to review research paper drafts. If you can predict that you will be faced with distractions, such as responding to text messages rather than staying on track with writing your paper draft, you may want to create an "if–then plan" (Gollwitzer, 1999). You could include "If I am writing my research paper draft, then I will ignore incoming text messages" (adapted from Wieber et al., 2011) as one of your tasks. Research in goal setting and implementation has demonstrated that the more attractive the distraction, the more necessary the "if–then plan" is for achieving your goal.

Table 4.2 presents an example of a checklist for identifying intermediate goals and tasks for writing a research paper. Research (Schunk, 1989) indicates that as you attain each of the intermediate goals, you will become more confident in your ability to complete the task. Thus, anytime you can break a major goal into several intermediate goals, you will be more motivated to move toward your major goal. Remember this finding whenever you get discouraged while thinking about completing a major task.

STEP 4: IMPLEMENT THE PLAN

The first three steps in the goal-setting process are planning steps. Step 4 requires you to put the plan into operation by completing each of the planned activities. Check your progress as you implement each task. Do not hesitate to make changes in your plan if you find that you miscalculated the time needed to complete a task. In some cases, you might find that you omitted an important task that needs to be added to your plan, such as researching a specific topic for a term paper. As you develop greater expertise in developing your plans, you will find they will require fewer modifications.

STEP 5: EVALUATE YOUR PROGRESS

In Step 5, you will evaluate your plans and progress. Ask yourself the following questions after you have attained your goal or when you begin to realize that your plan is not working effectively (McCombs & Encinias, 1987, p. 41):

- "How well did the plan work?"
- "How many tasks did I complete?"

TABLE 4.2
Making Implementation Plans: Intermediate Goals for a Research Paper

Intermediate Goal	Date Completed
Phase 1: Prewriting	
Identify topic	
Find sources for topic	
Use correct bibliographic notation for sources	
Phase 2: Drafting	
Organize paper around two subtopics	
Write draft of subtopic 1	
Write draft of subtopic 2	
Write introduction to paper	
Write conclusion	
Phase 3: Revising and Editing	
Review drafts for grammar and writing style	
Check transitions among subtopics	
Edit complete paper	
Prepare title page, bibliography, and table of contents	

- "With which task(s) did I have the most trouble? Why?"
- "What strategies worked well?"
- "What problems came up?"
- "What did I learn about myself?"
- "What didn't I plan for?"

If you do not attain your goal, you can evaluate what went wrong. Evaluation can help you rethink your strategy and determine another way to reach your goal.

Table 4.3 presents the five steps you should use when setting your goals. As you read this book, you will acquire more information about developing and implementing goals. As you practice the process, you will develop greater expertise and enhance the likelihood that you will attain your chosen goals.

TABLE 4.3
Procedures for Goal Setting

Procedures	Strategies
Identify and define the goal	Use SMART goals
Generate and evaluate alternatives	Answer the following questions:
	"How would other people achieve this goal?"
	"Who can help me achieve this goal?"
	"How have I achieved similar goals in the past?"
Make an implementation plan and related tasks	Use checklist to identify intermediate goals
Implement the plan	Use checklist to carry out the plan, and monitor progress, revising original plan as needed
Evaluate your progress	Answer the following questions:
	"How well did the plan work?"
	"How many tasks did I complete?"
	"With which task(s) did I have the most trouble? Why?"
	"What strategies worked well?"
	"What problems came up?"
	"What did I learn about myself?"
	"What didn't I plan for?"

Chapter Review

KEY POINTS

1 One's values, long-range and intermediate goals, and daily tasks should be aligned.
2 Goals influence motivation and learning.
3 Setting and attaining intermediate goals can motivate students to attain long-range goals.
4 In order to succeed, you need both outcome and process goals.
5 Three properties of goals influence motivation: specificity, proximity, and difficulty.
6 Each goal you set should be SMART: specific, measurable, action-oriented, realistic, and time-bound.
7 The following steps should be used each time you set a goal:
    a. Identify and define the goal.
    b. Generate and evaluate plans.
    c. Make implementation plans.
    d. Implement the plan.
    e. Evaluate your progress.

FOLLOW-UP ACTIVITIES

1. Establish a Goal and Implementation Plan

Identify a short-term goal you would like to attain in the next few weeks. Develop a plan for attaining it and write a brief two- to three-page report on the extent of your goal attainment. Use the five-step sequence identified in the chapter as headings in your paper. Be sure to focus on both the outcome and process-oriented aspects.

2. Analyze Student Behavior

Suppose you were working in your college counseling center as a peer counselor. Two students, Alan and Felicia, come to see you to discuss their problems. Read the brief description of each student and identify what you have learned to date that could be applied to each situation. Consider how you would start your discussion with Alan and Felicia? What issues would you raise? What advice would you give? Why?

Alan is a freshman music major who is an accomplished bass player. He has toured internationally with some of the best groups and is recognized as someone with a great deal of talent. His goal is to play professionally. He practices many hours a day and believes this activity is more worthwhile than taking general education courses. Alan believes he does not need a college education to attain his goal. Yet, his parents believe that the attainment of a college degree will benefit him throughout his life. He agrees to go to college to please his parents but is not very interested in some of his courses. As a result, his attendance is poor and his grades are low in freshman composition and psychology.

Felicia has always wanted to be a pediatrician. She is a freshman majoring in pre-medical studies and is having difficulty in her first chemistry course. Although she did well in her high school chemistry course, she finds her college course more difficult because it is taught differently. The exams require more problem solving and higher-level thinking than she experienced in high school. She begins to worry about her ability to excel in the sciences and to obtain admission to medical school.

Comments:

_____

_____

3. Translating Values into Daily Actions

Figure 4.2 illustrates the fact that one's values should serve as the foundation for determining personal goals and creating a daily task list that is related to the attainment of long-range and intermediate goals. Smith (1994) stated: "If your daily activities are guided in this manner by your fundamental values, you will feel the satisfaction that comes from succeeding at those things that mean the most to you" (p. 67). Identify one of your values and determine the degree to which your long-range and intermediate goals and daily tasks are aligned with this value. If your goals and daily tasks are not well aligned with what you value, develop a plan to better align them.

Comments:

_____

_____

5 Self-Regulation of Emotions

Academic emotions influence your learning and achievement. Positive emotions such as enjoyment of learning, hope, and pride predict high achievement, and negative emotions such as anxiety, boredom, anger, shame, and depression predict lower achievement (Pekrun, 2016). In the last decade, neuroscience has provided persuasive data that emotions are critical in the learning process. Indeed, neuroscientist Mary-Helen Immordino-Yang states that "emotions are, in essence, the rudder that steers thinking" (Woo, 2018, p. 6). In this chapter, the focus is on procedures to help you self-regulate your emotions. Regulation of emotions could mean curtailing and weakening negative emotions and intensifying positive emotions.

Researchers generally differentiate moods from emotions in terms of their intensity and duration. Moods are longer lasting, whereas emotions consist of short intense episodes (Pekrun et al., 2006). For example, if you are angry about a grade on a term paper, your anger usually disappears in a short period of time. When you are in a bad mood, this feeling may last for a whole day. In this chapter, however, we will not make a distinction between mood and emotion, and will instead use the term "emotion" to refer to both concepts.

After studying this chapter, you will be able to:

- understand the impact of academic emotions on performance;
- use self-regulatory strategies to address stress, anxiety, depression, and boredom.

EXERCISE 5.1: SELF-OBSERVATION: ASSESSING EMOTIONS

Directions: Assess your emotions by checking the appropriate response to each of the following questions. Write a summary statement in the space provided to describe the nature of your emotions.

	Always	Sometimes	Never
1. Do you get discouraged when you get a low grade on an exam or paper?			
2. Do you generally have a positive outlook on your ability to succeed in college?			
3. Do you find that panicky thoughts or worries frustrate your efforts to concentrate?			
4. Do you blame yourself when events do not go well for you?			
5. Do you easily get angry when people mess up?			
6. Do you have a high tolerance for frustrations?			
7. Do you get depressed?			
8. Do you feel pride regarding your accomplishments?			
9. How often do you feel bored?			

Summary Statement:

_____

_____

_____

_____

_____ ■

WHAT DO WE KNOW ABOUT COLLEGE STUDENTS' MENTAL HEALTH?

Each year, the American College Health Association surveys students to learn about factors influencing their academic performance. In the latest survey (ACHA, 2018), undergraduate students were asked to identify factors that caused them to receive an incomplete grade, drop a course, or receive a low grade in a class or on an exam. The ten top factors were as follows:

1 Stress.
2 Anxiety.
3 Sleep difficulties.
4 Depression.
5 Cold/flu/sore throat.
6 Work.
7 Concern for a troubled friend or family member.
8 Internet use/computer games.
9 Relationship difficulties.
10 Participation in extracurricular activities.

As you see, five of the top eight reasons are related, in some way, to emotions—stress, anxiety, sleep difficulties, depression, and concern for a troubled friend or family member. How does mental health impact achievement? In Chapter 3, we discussed the human brain as the center of learning and memory. However, our brain is not only involved with our thinking but also with our emotions.

Let's look at the link between mental health, the brain, and learning via one specific example, the top fifth factor, depression. Researchers have documented less activity in the areas of the brain that are responsible for the formation of new memories of individuals who are depressed versus those that are not. Based on this finding, students who are depressed "can be expected to learn less, not to learn as well, and to learn more slowly than their peers" (Douce & Keeling, 2014, p. 2). This chapter will discuss each of the most significant mental health problems, stress, anxiety, and depression, in dedicated sections.

Returning to the list of academic performance impediments, you'll note that internet use is among the top eight factors. Internet use refers to being on a laptop, tablet, smartphone, or other connected device. Internet use has many advantages, of course, such as the ability to quickly access knowledge, keep in touch with friends, and access different sources of entertainment. Unfortunately, researchers have begun to explore the problematic use of the internet, or internet addiction as it is sometimes called (Mihajlov & Vejmelka, 2017; Poli, 2017). Although these terms can be used to explain the loss of productive time, this overemphasis on screen time is also related to mental health issues. In one large study of over one million subjects, adolescents who spent considerable time on electronic communication and screens (e.g., social media, the internet, texting, gaming) and less time on non-screen activities (e.g., in-person social interaction, sports/exercise, homework, attending religious services) reported less happiness, lower self-esteem, and were less satisfied with their lives (Twenge, Martin, & Campbell, 2018). Further, Hunt, Marx, Lipson, and Young (2018) demonstrated that undergraduate students restricting Snapchat, Instagram, and Facebook to ten minutes a day produced significant drops in depression and loneliness. Do you have any ideas why excessive use of electronic communication and screen usage would have such an impact on mental health?

An important problem related to social networking was identified in a recent investigation by Tandoc, Ferrucci, and Duffy (2015), who found that constantly checking what your friends are up to and engaging in Facebook "surveillance" can lead to envy, which can ultimately lead to extreme sadness and depression. Some researchers have coined this the "Fomo Phenomenon"—the term "fomo" stands for "fear of missing out." Cheever, Rosen, Carrier, and Chavez (2014) also found heavy phone users feel very anxious if they can't use their smartphones. In addition, they feel anxious if they can't check their text messages or other mobile technology regularly. Table 5.1 presents strategies to minimize dependence on smartphones.

TABLE 5.1

Strategies to Minimize the Pitfalls of Smartphone Use

Make choices	Use your smartphone only for things you absolutely need it for (could you keep notes in a notebook or use a standalone alarm clock?).
Retrain yourself	Start seeing notifications as suggestions rather than demands. Avoid checking the phone first thing in the morning and during the day, gradually increase checking your phone from 15 minutes to 20 minutes, etc.
Set expectations	Break away from feeling that you need to be constantly connected. Be clear with family and friends about your response time.
Silence notifications	Turn off unnecessary notifications to reduce distractions and stress.
Protect sleep	Avoid using the phone late at night and turn off the phone when it is time for bed.
Be active	If you interact with social media sites, then contribute ideas, photos, and comments on other's posts. Being active is associated with higher well-being.
Don't text/email/call and drive	Place your phone out of reach. According to the National Highway Traffic Safety Administration, 3,450 people were killed by distracted driving in 2016.

Adapted from Weir (2017)

Here is another interesting finding: although a large number of students said it is better to resolve personal conflicts with a friend face-to-face, most of these students admit to using technology to avoid personal confrontations. This finding is supported by another study (Eagan et al., 2014) that found that students' time spent socializing with others has hit an all-time low, while time spent on interactions through online social networks has hit an all-time high.

The top third reason was sleep difficulties. Many college students underestimate the importance of sleep and how the lack of or disturbed sleep can impact their physical and psychological health and academic performance (Buboltz et al., 2006). One study that illustrates the impact of disturbed sleep was conducted by Hartmann and Prichard (2018), who investigated over 55,000 students. They found that students who experienced sleep problems raised the probability of dropping a course by 10 percent and lowered their cumulative GPA. The *National Sleep Foundation* recommends seven to nine hours of sleep for an adult between 18 and 25 years of age. If sleep is an issue you face, check out the Foundation's website and identify other resources on the internet or at your counseling center for suggestions in dealing with this problem.

Overwhelming stress is often the cause of sleep deprivation, as illustrated by another survey. In this study (Lund et al., 2010), about 68 percent of college students reported that their stress and anxiety concerning their academic and personal life kept them awake at night. Poor sleepers reported more problems with their health than good sleepers. One study found that 40 percent of students reported waking at night to answer phone calls, and 47 percent woke to answer text messages (Adams & Kisler, 2013).

WHAT TYPES OF SOLUTIONS ARE AVAILABLE FOR EMOTIONAL AND MENTAL HEALTH ISSUES?

Most colleges provide professional mental health services by licensed counselors, therapists, or psychologists. The services can be offered through counseling centers, student health centers, or both. If your college does not provide mental health services, contact your insurance company to determine your mental health care coverage. In more severe cases, professional mental health treatment is necessary and may involve counseling and psychotherapy, as well as medication. However, there are also ways in which you can help yourself regulate your emotions. We will provide specific strategies in this chapter to deal with the most common challenges faced by college students: stress and anxiety, as well as depression. Before we discuss college students' experience specifically and get to the solutions, let's discuss what causes our emotions.

What Causes Our Emotions?

There is an ongoing debate in science about whether emotions are primarily caused by biological or cognitive, thinking-related factors (Reeve, 2015). From the biological perspective, emotions are caused by biochemical and neurohormonal events in the brain. From the cognitive perspective, thinking is the prerequisite to emotion. Although both biology and cognition are important, this chapter will emphasize the cognitive explanation of emotions, especially as our thinking is something we can control and regulate. Specifically, we will discuss self-talk as the cause of some of our negative emotions.

How Does Self-Talk Affect My Emotions and Behavior?

Whether you realize it or not, you spend most of the day engaging in self-talk, your internal thought language. (Yes, you do talk to yourself!) These are the words you use to describe and interpret the events that happen to you and around you. In many ways, it is our interpretation of events and corresponding self-talk that determines our emotions, not the actual events that occur in our lives. Some of our self-talk serves as a productive motivator to try new tasks and persist in learning, whereas other forms of inner speech lead to unproductive behavior. For example, students interpret a poor grade on an exam in very different ways. Remember the discussion of attributions in Chapter 2? Upon receiving a poor grade, one student may tell himself, "I'll never pass this course and become an engineer," while another may tell herself, "If I study differently for the next time, I can do well on the exam."

A sports commentator once said that there was little difference in the ability (i.e., outer game) of the top 20 ranked tennis players in the world. What sets them apart is their mental approach to the game (i.e., their inner game). In sports, productive self-talk is related to improved learning, greater effort and persistence, and improved performance because it reduces anxiety (Oliver et al., 2009), especially in controlling pre-competition anxiety (Hardy et al., 2001). A good example of the impact of self-talk in sports is discussed by Gallwey (1974) in his book *The Inner Game of Tennis*. Gallwey said that tennis, like other sports, is composed of two parts, an outer game and an inner game. The outer game consists of mastering the techniques of how to play the game (e.g., how to serve and use one's backhand). The inner game takes place in the mind of the player and is basically the self-talk one uses while he or she is playing. Compare the dialogue of two different tennis players:

"I'm hitting my forehand rotten again today … Dammit, why do I keep missing those easy set ups … I'm not doing anything the coach told me to do in my last lesson."

"You were great rallying, now you're playing worse than your grandmother."

(Gallwey, 1974, p. 82)

"The last three of my backhands landed long, by about two feet. My racket seems to be hesitating, instead of following through all the way. Maybe I should observe the level of my backswing."
"Yes, I thought so, it's well above my waist … There, that shot got hit with more pace, yet it stayed in."

(Gallwey, 1974, p. 83)

How do you think such talk influenced each player's game?

Negative self-talk differs greatly from person to person but the following are eight irrational thinking patterns that influence individuals' emotions (McKay et al., 1997, based on Beck, 1976). As you read them, think of situations where you used any of the irrational thinking patterns.

1 *Filtering:* You focus on the negative details while ignoring all the positive aspects of a situation. Example: Your supervisor in a summer internship tells you that your work is good, but he thinks you socialize too much with the other personnel in the workplace. You go home thinking that your supervisor doesn't like you.

2 *Polarized thinking*: Things are black or white, good or bad. You have to be perfect or you're a failure. There's no middle ground, no room for mistakes. Example: You have an argument with one friend and explain the problem to the second friend. You tell the second friend: "Either you support me or you are not my friend."

3 *Overgeneralization*: You reach a general conclusion based on a single incident or piece of evidence. You exaggerate the frequency of problems and use negative global labels. Popular phrases for overgeneralization are all, every, none, never, always, everybody, and nobody. Example: You break up with your boyfriend or girlfriend and say: "No one will ever love me!"

4 *Mind reading*: Without their saying so, you know what people are feeling and why they act the way they do. In particular, you have a certain knowledge of how people think and feel about you. Example: "The professor thinks I am not very capable because he never looks at me."

5 *Catastrophizing*: You expect, even visualize, disaster. You notice or hear about a problem and start asking, "What if?" "What if tragedy strikes? What if it happens to me?" Example: While taking the SAT exam, you have trouble concentrating because you keep saying to yourself, "What if I don't get into college?"

6 *Magnifying*: You exaggerate the degree or intensity of a problem. You turn up the volume on anything bad, making it loud, large, and overwhelming. Example: "This term paper is ridiculous. I'll never finish it."

7 *Personalization*: You assume that everything people do or say is some kind of reaction to you. You also compare yourself to others, trying to determine who is smarter, more competent, better looking, and so on. Example: "Everyone in this class appears smarter than me."

8 *Shoulds*: You have a list of ironclad rules about how you and other people should act. People who break the rules anger you and you feel guilty when you violate the rules. Cue words used for this type of thinking are should, ought, or must. Example: "I never should appear hurt; I always need to appear happy and content."

EXERCISE 5.2: IDENTIFY IRRATIONAL THINKING PATTERNS

Directions: Write the letter of the thinking pattern identified in the second column by the statement in the first column. The correct answers are listed at the end of this chapter.

	Statement		Pattern
1.	I know that my friend is mad at me because I don't want to go to the concert with him.	a.	Filtering
2.	If my parents don't like my boyfriend, they don't care about me.	b.	Polarized Thinking
3.	My parents are spending a great deal of money to send me to this college. Therefore, I should only earn As.	c.	Overgeneralization
4.	I don't think I can do well in this class. Everyone seems so smart.	d.	Mind Reading
5.	I received an A on my term project, but I can't believe some of the negative comments my instructor gave me. I wonder if she really believes that I am an incapable writer.	e.	Catastrophizing
6.	I received a C on my first chemistry test. I will never become a doctor.	f.	Magnifying
7.	My parents were not pleased with my final grade in English. I can't do anything to satisfy them.	g.	Personalization
8.	My uncle has ulcers. It must run in my family, and I know that I am going to get ulcers.	h.	Shoulds

Student Reflections

When the notion of self-talk was first introduced in class, it sounded funny. After all, what normal person walks around talking to himself or herself? A week ago, I started to analyze my own self-talk. I never realized how much I talk to myself! I talk to myself about my weight, my appearance, my academic progress, and life goals. When I am studying, I wonder how I am doing in the subject or how well I will perform on the exam.

I find many examples of both positive and negative self-talk in my daily life. Recently, I was doing a scene in an acting class and I caught myself talking to myself, saying how bad I was doing. I was complaining to myself because I was not in the mood to do the scene. I stopped myself and just told myself to talk later and not now. My self-talk was not helping me get the job done.

Anxiety plays a different role in my life than I think it does for most other students. I do not experience much test anxiety, but I do experience task anxiety. When I am given an assignment for a class, I spend more time worrying about how and when I am going to get the assignment done than I do actually working on the task.

I understand that instructors expect more out of students when they are given take-home assignments. These assignments make me nervous, because I do not know whether I can live up to the instructor's expectations.

I am trying to deal with my anxiety by finding out the instructor's criteria for grading the assignment. In this way, I feel more in control of my destiny.

Having discussed our interpretations of events and self-talk as the primary cause of our emotions, let's now return to the main problems experienced by college students and suggest self-regulatory solutions.

WHAT DO WE KNOW ABOUT STRESS AND ANXIETY AMONG COLLEGE STUDENTS?

Everyone experiences stress and anxiety at one time or another. Is there a difference between the two? Although reported separately in the American College Health Association study (ACHA, 2018), stress and anxiety overlap considerably. Stress comes from specific events that make us feel worried, angry, or frustrated. Anxiety is a feeling of uneasiness or fear for which the source cannot always be identified. Extreme anxiety is a mental disorder; stress is not.

Based on the ACHA (2018) survey, 64 percent of students reported having felt overwhelming anxiety within 12 months before taking the survey and 22 percent reported being diagnosed or treated by a professional for anxiety in the last 12 months of taking the survey. In terms of stress, 44 percent of students reported experiencing more than average stress with 12 percent reporting tremendous stress. Data demonstrates that stress and anxiety levels among students have increased substantially since the 1990s. Among the most prevalent sources of stress and anxiety were academic demands, work, roommate issues, financial and career concerns, and family pressure to achieve. Though you may not have the stressors related to roommates, family, or work in your life, you have most likely experienced stress related to academic demands.

Worry: The cognitive aspect of anxiety, such as negative beliefs.

Emotionality: The physiological and psychosomatic aspects of anxiety, such as headaches and stomach distress.

Stress related to academic demands often manifests as test anxiety. Recent research has focused on the relative independence of two dimensions of test anxiety: **worry** versus **emotionality**. Worry is the major factor in the disruption of mental activity, whereas emotionality is more related to physiological distress. Worry reflects the cognitive aspects of anxiety—the negative beliefs, troubling thoughts, and poor decisions. Emotionality refers to the unpleasant affective reactions, such as tension and nervousness. Each of these dimensions can have differential effects on students. Although both dimensions can have a debilitating effect, the worry dimension has a stronger negative relation to academic performance than the emotional dimension. One reason for this finding is that emotionality tends to decrease once test taking begins, whereas worrisome thoughts often continue throughout the test and may be experienced for a period of time in advance of the examination. Also, achievement on the test suffers because attention is affected during test taking.

Anxiety can negatively impact academic performance in many ways. Ottens (1991) identified four interrelated characteristics of academically anxious students:

- **Disruption in mental activity**
  Remember the working memory capacity limitation? Recall also that the 7 ± 2 number may indeed really be 5 ± 2. Worry, as manifested in negative beliefs and troubling thoughts, takes up working memory capacity and begins to interfere with our ability to process the task at hand and recall what we have learned.

- **Physiological distress**
  Physiological distress is related to the emotionality aspect of anxiety referred to above. Common symptoms are a racing heart, sweaty palms, and an upset stomach. What are your physiological symptoms of anxiety?

- **Misdirected attention**
  Misdirected attention refers to problems with concentration or attention. No matter what the academic activity—taking notes, reading a textbook, studying, or taking an exam—anxious students easily lose their attention. This behavior handicaps students by not allowing them to complete their work efficiently. Defensive Dimitri's motivational problem is that he constantly encounters distractions when he begins studying for an exam. He constantly thinks about the possibility of failure, looking inadequate, and as a result forgets information. Anxious Anna, the overachiever, also has anxiety problems, but in her case, the anxiety leads to obsessive studying and preparation.

- **Inappropriate behaviors**
  The most common inappropriate behavior related to anxiety is procrastination. Other examples are quitting tasks before they are completed, conversing with a friend when time is running out to complete an assignment, or answering test questions in a rush to get out of the examination room as soon as possible. Defensive Dimitri, for example, deals with his anxiety by resorting to failure-avoiding strategies, such as procrastination.

Test anxiety is a specific form of anxiety related to the evaluation of academic ability. Educators are especially concerned about this type of anxiety, because it increases through the elementary grades to high school and becomes more strongly (i.e., negatively) related to indicators of intellectual and academic performance (Zeidner & Matthews, 2011). As students progress through college, the higher their anxiety, the more likely they will experience lower achievement.

WHAT ARE SOME SELF-REGULATORY SOLUTIONS FOR STRESS AND ANXIETY?

Though stress and anxiety are very common among college students, the good news is that they are the most well studied and understood academic emotions (Zeidner, 2007). We will now turn to how to regulate stress and anxiety.

A lot of stress and anxiety stems from negative self-talk, particularly from catastrophization and engaging in "shoulds." One way to deal with stress and anxiety is to dispute negative self-talk with positive, supportive statements. This requires writing down and actually rehearsing positive statements that directly refute your negative self-talk. There is evidence that engaging in talking aloud to yourself is even more effective than internal self-talk (Boroujeni & Shanbazi, 2011) because talking to yourself out loud can keep you better focused. The first author's husband always doublechecks himself by stating "keys, wallet, phone, laptop" whenever he heads out to work. If the first author did that as well, there'd be fewer detours back home to get the missing wallet! In addition, if you refer to yourself in the second ("You got this!") (or even third person), you may further decrease your stress and anxiety (Kross et al., 2014) because of "self-distancing." Can you think of a time when it was easy for you to give reassurance to an anxious friend and advise them on how to handle their challenge? Are you able to do that for yourself? By talking to yourself in second (or third person) may give you the distance you need to more clearly think through a problem you are facing.

Below are suggestions for how to deal with the tendencies to catastrophize and engage in "shoulds."

CATASTROPHIZING

Instead of expecting disaster ("I'll never get into graduate school with such scores") say, "So what, I can do better in these tests," and "I'll get better at this with practice." Or, even better, "You will get better with practice."

SHOULDS

Instead of demanding perfection ("I should always earn an A+") say, "It's okay to make mistakes. Setbacks are part of the process and an important learning experience."

Let's take a look at how recognizing and changing negative self-talk can alleviate stress and anxiety. One of the major sources of stress of college students is the new experience of living in residential halls and joining sororities or fraternities where you deal with all types of people, some of whom may be quite difficult. You may have an arrogant and inconsiderate roommate or annoying fraternity member. It is important to realize that it is not the unpleasant people who cause our distress, but the way we think about them and their behavior that is the root of our negative emotions. Instead of engaging in shoulds such as "My roommate should be just like me: always keep the kitchen clean and the dishes done," change the self-talk to "Overall, my roommate is nice. I am becoming frustrated over a small thing. I am not going to upset myself by demanding that she change her behavior and be just like me. This is not a perfect world."

While replacing negative self-talk with positive statements is a good strategy for dealing with worry (i.e., the cognitive component of anxiety), relaxation techniques are successful in dealing with the emotionality aspects of stress and anxiety (i.e., physiological symptoms and psychosomatic illnesses such as headaches and stomach distress). We'll describe some of them next but be sure to check out apps for them as well. Determine which technique might work best for you and you will surely find an app for that!

Relaxation techniques can be grouped into physical and mental techniques. For example, controlling one's breathing is an effective way to relax. When we are anxious, we tend to breathe in a shallow way by only drawing air into the upper chest area rather than throughout the lungs. Many experts in anxiety reduction teach individuals breathing exercises that involve long, slow exhalation. When we do that, the diaphragm expands and tenses when taking in air, and relaxes when the air is released. Thus, one physical way to relax is to increase the time you spend exhaling. This process is called **diaphragmatic breathing**. The following is a simple exercise to teach you to relax

Diaphragmatic Breathing: Deep breathing that is done either sitting or lying on one's back by contracting the diaphragm so that in breathing, the stomach moves but the chest remains as still as possible.

(Youngs, 1985). Experience the following technique by asking a friend to read each step so you can attempt it.

1 Get comfortable. Move your arms and legs around to make your muscles loose.
2 Close your eyes.
3 Take a deep breath in and count slowly: 1 … 2 … 3 … 4 … 5 … 6.
4 Let the air out very slowly, counting: 1 … 2 … 3 … 4 … 5 … 6.
5 Repeat Steps 3 and 4, but this time place your hands on your stomach and feel it filling up with air (pushing out) when you breathe.
6 Breathe in deeply while counting: 1 … 2 … 3 … 4.
7 Let the air out slowly while counting: 1 … 2 … 3 … 4 … 5 … 6 … (feel your stomach pull back in).
8 Repeat this a few more times.
9 Open your eyes.

Don't get too relaxed! You have more reading to do!

Another example of physical relaxation is **progressive muscle relaxation**. Jacobson (1938) wrote more than 70 years ago, "An anxious mind cannot exist within a relaxed body … a state of reciprocal influence exists between the brain and body" (Newman, 1996, p. 31). Jacobson developed a tensing and relaxing technique, progressive relaxation, to overcome many stress-related illnesses. His original program, involving each of the 16 muscle groups, took almost six months for an individual to complete. We will next describe a condensed, yet effective, version of Jacobson's technique (Newman, 1996):

> **Progressive Muscle Relaxation:** A systematic technique where muscles are tensed and relaxed in order to achieve a deep state of relaxation.

1 Take a deep breath and exhale. Inhale again and fill your lungs as full as you can.
2 Hold the breath and tighten all your muscles simultaneously. Feel the tension throughout your body. (Please note: Do not tighten any muscles to the point of pain.)
3 Maintain the tension for a count of 10, then relax everything quickly and completely. Release all muscle tightness, everywhere.
4 Breathe deeply and evenly. Notice how good it feels when you release the tension from every muscle, all at the same time.

Did you notice any muscles that remained tense despite your best efforts? Practicing progressive relaxation will help you become aware of the parts of your body where you hold your stress. With increased awareness, you can break the anxiety chain before it becomes overwhelming and out of control.

An example of mental relaxation is **meditation**, which includes a number of different methods. Basically, it involves assuming a comfortable position, closing your eyes, relaxing your muscles, concentrating on breathing, and focusing your attention on one thing at a time such as a candle, waterfall, or sound. This technique has been associated with reduced oxygen consumption, decreased respiration, slower heart rate, and lower blood pressure. Most importantly, research has indicated that meditation can alter one's mood and emotions (Travis et al., 2009).

> **Meditation:** A form of mental relaxation whereby individuals assume a comfortable position, close their eyes, focus on breathing, and attend to one sound or image at a time. There are many different forms of meditation.

Benson (1976), in his well-known book *The Relaxation Response*, developed his own version of meditation, which involved mentally repeating the word "one" with each exhalation of breath. The following is an adaptation of his procedure:

Pick a time and place where you will not be disturbed and lie or sit in a comfortable position.

Close your eyes and choose a center of focus. This is a word or phrase that helps shift your mind from a logical, externally oriented thought to an internal, passive center of focus and stops your mind from wandering. The most common focal point is a word such as "one", "calm", or "relax." However, a short phrase can also be used, such as "relax and be at peace."

Repeat your word or phrase each time you exhale. As you do this, adopt a passive attitude. This is the most important element of this method. Avoid concern about how well you are performing the technique and adopt a "let it happen" attitude. Your mind will occasionally slip away from its concentration on the word or phrase you have chosen. When this happens, don't panic or abandon your practice. Simply redirect your mind to your breathing and continue repeating your chosen word or phrase after each exhalation.

Practice for 10 to 20 minutes, then open your eyes and resume your normal activities.

(Peurifoy, 1995, p. 317)

Mindfulness: Awareness and acceptance of our thoughts, feelings, bodily sensations, and surrounding environment.

Recent evidence suggests that a specific type of relaxation, **mindfulness**, can not only reduce stress and anxiety but also improve memory and ability to focus. Mindfulness is defined as an awareness and acceptance of our thoughts, feelings, bodily sensations, and surrounding environment. In a study by Mrazek and colleagues (2013), undergraduate students were trained in mindfulness exercises and then required to integrate ten minutes of mindfulness exercises into their daily life for two weeks. One example of a mindfulness exercise consisted of sitting with legs crossed and counting up to 21 consecutive inhalations and exhalations. The goal of the different exercises was to allow the mind to rest naturally. The undergraduate students took the Graduate Record Examinations (GRE), the standardized tests considered for graduate school application, as well as tests of memory and distractibility, before and after the two-week mindfulness training. Data demonstrated that they significantly improved scores on all tests when compared with the control group of students who took a nutrition class instead of a mindfulness class.

In summary, in order to regulate the emotionality component of anxiety involving negative physiological reactions to stressful events, you will want to explore both physical and mental strategies. Be sure to check out apps such as Breathe2Relax, Headspace, Calm, and others. Your college counseling center or a reputable website is likely to have excellent recommendations. In addition to the strategies discussed, many students find engaging in mild to moderate exercise such as jogging or walking, or listening to music, helpful. Some other useful things to do to manage stress and anxiety are to eat a balanced diet, minimizing caffeine, and to confide in someone you trust. If you have a friend who suffers from anxiety, take the time to understand what your friend is going through and be tolerant, supportive, and non-judgmental, no matter how irrational the thinking may appear. As appropriate, encourage them to seek help and stay in treatment once it is begun.

WHAT DO WE KNOW ABOUT DEPRESSION AMONG COLLEGE STUDENTS?

Depression is a condition marked by sadness, commonly referred to as "feeling blue." Depressed students may lose interest in the activities they used to enjoy, have trouble concentrating and making decisions, and lose appetite or eat too much, and are likely to experience a loss of energy, among many other symptoms. Most college students experience mild depression where the feelings of sadness and anxiety dissipate within a couple of days. There are several reasons that may contribute to the feelings of sadness, such as a poor grade but also being away from home and missing your friends and family. Unless you deal with your homesickness or other reasons, your sadness may develop into depression over time.

What does data tell us about college students and depression? The American College Health Association (2018) survey found that 43 percent of students "felt so depressed it was difficult to function" at least once in the 12 months of taking the survey. Further, 18 percent reported being diagnosed or treated by a professional for depression within the last 12 months of taking the survey. In addition, 55 percent felt that "things were hopeless," 64 percent "felt very lonely," and 70 percent "felt very sad" within the 12 months of taking the survey. Clearly, depression and the related feelings of hopelessness and loneliness are significant issues for college students.

There are different levels of depression. In addition to mild depression that dissipates within a few days, minor depression lasts for about two weeks. Left untreated, however, it can develop into a major depressive disorder. This chapter offers self-regulatory strategies to deal with mild depression. If you experience depression symptoms that are disabling and interfere with everyday activities such as studying, eating, and sleeping for a few weeks or more, please contact your college counseling center or student health services—and let your family members know, as appropriate. These symptoms are important to be addressed.

WHAT ARE SOME SELF-REGULATORY STRATEGIES TO ADDRESS DEPRESSION?

There are some specific irrational thinking patterns that are likely to bring about or keep mild depression going. Magnifying and filtering, for example, is where individuals focus on the negative while ignoring the positive aspects of a situation. In fact, depressed individuals often see the world as if they were wearing negative glasses. For example, a student athlete may be reviewing a video of herself, notice some mistakes and fail to recognize any areas of success. Though it is important to locate areas of improvement, filtering out anything positive is distorted thinking.

Overgeneralization is another pattern that can promote feelings of hopelessness and sadness. For example, a college student may be rejected by someone he or she is attracted to and develop a belief that he or she is unattractive to all potential dates. This type of thinking is negative, unhealthy, and irrational, and can promote depressive feelings.

If you recognize your thinking as you review the irrational patterns, here are some questions to consider (Ellis, 1998):

- Where is holding this belief getting me? Is it helpful or self-defeating?
- Where is the evidence to support the existence of my irrational belief? Is it consistent with reality?
- What are the worst things that could actually happen to me?
- Is it really awful (as bad as it could be)?
- Can I really not stand it?

Let's take a look at some examples of negative self-talk and ways to dispute it. Remember that if you use the second (or third person) in your self-talk, it might be even more effective in helping you think clearly.

MAGNIFYING AND FILTERING

Instead of self-criticism such as "See, there was someone who did not see my effort as enough. There I go again, just can't get it right," say, "I am obsessing over one comment and ignoring all the great positive feedback I received. My report was overall very well received."

OVERGENERALIZATION

Instead of predicting a never-ending pattern of defeat as a result of one poor experience by statements such as "I'll never be able to do well in this," say, "I can continue to make progress one step at a time," "I acknowledge the progress I've made and will continue to improve."

In addition to using self-regulation to address the cognitive causes of mild depression by disputing negative self-talk and replacing the irrational thinking patterns you may engage in, it is important to engage in physical activity on a continuous basis, participate in your favorite activities, spend time with others, and confide in someone who knows you well and who you trust about your feelings. If you have a friend who you suspect is depressed, engage in active listening (addressed in Chapter 7), invite him or her out for walks and very importantly, ensure that your friend gets professional help if the depression lasts for more than a few weeks.

Now that we have discussed self-regulatory solutions to anxiety, stress, and depression, we wanted to point out again that the solutions in this chapter are intended for mild symptoms—if you have more severe symptoms such as insomnia or excessive sleeping, persistent thoughts of something bad happening, or thoughts of death or suicide, you need to see a professional health care provider.

WHAT IS THE IMPACT OF BOREDOM ON ACADEMIC PERFORMANCE?

We will close our discussion of emotions by focusing on boredom, a topic that is rarely discussed by instructors and students, but has an important impact on students' academic performance.

Many students complain that they are bored in school or in various courses they must take. Boredom is a problem because it can diminish attention and interfere with academic performance, motivation, and self-regulation (Pekrun, 2016). Boredom is caused by both dispositional factors (i.e., personality) and situational factors (e.g., classes and instructors). Some individuals are more prone to boredom than others. In fact, one study found that students who report a high frequency of boredom in school also experience high rates of boredom outside of school (Larson & Richard, 1991). Students report boredom for a number of reasons, including "the course has no meaning for me," "we do the same thing in each class," "the subject matter is too difficult or too easy," or "I don't like my instructor" (Daschmann et al., 2011). We find that students sometimes report to us that they find the material boring. When we try to discover what aspect of the material the students thought was boring, we often learn that the problem is not "boredom" but the lack of understanding of the material. Therefore, when students report that they are bored with the material, they often use this state of mind to escape from learning tasks that are perceived to be beyond their capabilities.

Boredom is often called the "silent emotion," as compared with other negative emotional states like anxiety and anger, which are more likely to be noticed by instructors, parents, or friends. Boredom is not only detrimental in school, but also has many non-academic consequences because it is related to alcohol consumption, drug use, stress and health problems, and dissatisfaction at work (Pekrun et al., 2010).

WHAT ARE SELF-REGULATORY STRATEGIES TO ADDRESS BOREDOM?

Can something be done about boredom? The answer to this question may depend on how students attribute the causes of their boredom. For example, if students believe boredom is caused by external and uncontrollable factors (e.g., an uninspiring instructor or course), they will be less likely to think they can do something about their feelings compared with students who attribute their boredom to internal and controllable factors (e.g., lack of understanding of the material or lack of effort). Successful students find ways to manage their boredom when they attribute it to controllable factors.

Your authors have a combined total of 50 years of teaching experience. We try hard to provide stimulating and interesting class lectures. Unfortunately, we realize that, at certain times, we may bore our students. You can't always depend on your instructors to provide interesting lessons, just like you can't depend on your job always to be stimulating and self-fulfilling. In general, you can't avoid facing some boring tasks in your daily life. Self-regulated learners attempt to take charge of their learning and do something about the onset of boredom so that it doesn't negatively impact their academic achievement.

Nett, Goetz, and Daniels (2010) completed an investigation where they studied students' strategies for coping with boredom. The following discussion is based on their research. Table 5.2 illustrates four categories of coping strategies, classified by two dimensions. The first dimension classifies the strategies as *approaching* or *avoiding*. This means that one can try to solve the problem or avoid it. The second classification is the type of coping—*cognitive* or *behavioral*. Cognitive strategies relate to changing one's perception of the situation, while behavioral strategies involve methods to change the situation or environment.

An example of a *cognitive-approach* strategy (i.e., changing perceptions) is when a chemistry student reminds herself that she needs to obtain a high grade in the course to be accepted into medical school. *Behavioral-approach* strategies are different in that they involve trying to change the boring situation. One such strategy occurs when a student asks her instructor to allow her to work on a paper more related to her area of interest than the paper topics provided by the instructor. It is an action strategy that attempts to deal directly with the problem.

Many students use *cognitive-avoidance* and *behavioral-avoidance* strategies. These strategies help students to forget or avoid the boring situation by thinking about other things (e.g., thinking about weekend activities with friends; a cognitive strategy) or doing something not associated with taking lecture notes (e.g., texting during class or talking with students seated near you in a lecture hall; a behavioral strategy). Thus, cognitive-avoidance strategies focus on thinking about things that are more interesting than the task or activity you find boring. Behavior-avoidance strategies, in contrast, occur when you *do* something unrelated to the task or activity that you find boring.

Now let's take some time for you to classify the coping strategies you use when you feel bored with an activity. It could be an academic or non-academic activity. Do these strategies fall into one classification, or do you use different classifications of coping strategies (Table 5.2)?

Do you want to make an educated guess as to which self-regulatory strategy proved to be most successful? The researchers assessed different boredom coping strategies before they conducted their investigation. From previous research, they knew that there is a strong negative relationship between the value of the subject or task and boredom. This means that if the task value is low, then it is likely that boredom will be high. Therefore, they predicted that strategies that encouraged valuing the situation might have the most impact on reducing boredom. So, which of the different strategies we discussed do you think is most likely to increase the value of a learning task? The answer: the cognitive-approach strategy (i.e., changing your thoughts or beliefs about the situation)! The researchers believed that this strategy worked best because it targeted the key aspect of boredom: perceived low task value. The cognitive approach strategies discussed in this chapter to deal with such emotions as anxiety and depression are based on changing individuals' perceptions or beliefs based on the underlying belief that our thinking is the primary cause of our emotions.

Behavioral approach strategies can also be useful: ask for help, locate reference books on topics that cause some difficulty in the course, talk to the instructor about the course, and study in a group. What other actions can you take to increase the value of the activities or tasks in a class?

In this chapter, we have identified a number of emotion-related challenges and provided solutions. As you become a more self-regulated learner and take charge of your learning, motivation, and emotions, you can become a more successful and happier student. Table 5.3 summarizes the chapter and provides procedures for the self-regulation of emotions.

TABLE 5.2

Classification System of Students' Strategies of Coping with Boredom

Type of Coping	Approach Coping	Avoidance Coping
Cognitive	Thinking differently to change the perception of the situation	Thinking of something else not associated with the situation
Behavioral	Taking actions to change the situation	Taking actions not associated with the situation

From Nett et al. (2010). Reprinted with permission from Elsevier Publishing

---

TABLE 5.3

Strategies for Self-Regulation of Emotions

Problem	Self-Regulatory Strategy	Example
Stress and anxiety	Replace negative self-talk and irrational thinking such as catastrophizing and shoulds with positive counterstatements.	Instead of demanding perfection ("I should always earn an A+") say, "It's okay to make mistakes. Setbacks are part of the process."
	Other general strategies:	Exercise, spend time with others.
	Relaxation techniques.	Engage in progressive muscle relaxation by tensing and relaxing muscles systematically.
		Engage in diaphragmatic breathing by breathing in deeply and letting air out very slowly so the stomach, not the chest, pushes out and pulls in.
		Engage in meditation and mindfulness by assuming a comfortable position, closing eyes, and focusing on breathing.
Depression	Replace negative self-talk and irrational thinking such as overgeneralization and filtering with positive counterstatements.	Instead of self-criticism such as "See, there was someone who did not see my effort as enough. There I go again, just can't get it right," say, "I am obsessing over one comment and ignoring all the great positive feedback I received."
	Other general strategies: Exercise, engage with favorite activities, spend time with others.	
Boredom	Change thinking to change perception of the situation.	Instead of telling yourself that chemistry is boring, remind yourself that you need to earn a high grade in order to become admitted to medical school.
	Take action to change the situation.	Instead of seeing the final assignment topic as not relevant for your goals, ask the instructor if you can write on a topic more related to your goals.

Chapter Review

KEY POINTS

1 Stress, anxiety, and depression are the most common mental health issues among college students.

2 Excessive use of electronic communication and screen usage can have a negative impact on mental health.

3 Lack of sleep can negatively impact physical and psychological health and academic performance.

4 There are eight patterns of negative self-talk, referred to as irrational thinking patterns, that influence our emotions.

5 Anxiety has two dimensions: worry and emotionality. Each dimension can have different effects on students. Worry has the strongest negative relation with achievement because it interferes with the storage and retrieval of information.

6 Anxiety can influence behavior by disrupting mental processes, producing physiological distress, misdirecting attention, and causing inappropriate behaviors such as procrastination.

7 Responding with positive counterstatements is an effective way to change negative self-talk. There is evidence that using the second (or third person) ("You can do this!") is more effective than using the first person ("I can do this.").

8 Physical and mental relaxation techniques can be used to regulate the emotionality aspect of anxiety.

9 Relaxation techniques such as diaphragmatic breathing, progressive muscle relaxation, mindfulness, and meditation can alter one's emotions.

10 Cognitive-approach strategies are most effective in dealing with boredom.

FOLLOW-UP ACTIVITIES

1. Change Irrational to Rational Thinking to Change Emotions

Select some event that disturbs you and demonstrate how you can change your irrational beliefs to more realistic beliefs, leading to a more positive outlook regarding the event. Like most of the learning and motivational strategies you are learning in this course, you need to practice this procedure many times before it becomes effective (adapted from Merrell, 2001).

Activating Event (the disturbing situation)

_____

_____

_____

Self-Talk (following the event)

_____

_____

_____

Consequence (how I felt)

_____

_____

_____

Replacing Negative Self-Talk with a Productive Statement (how I argue against the negative belief with a more realistic or rational belief)

_____

_____

_____

New Effect (the way I feel and will behave after I dispute the irrational beliefs)

_____

_____

_____

2. Identify Irrational Thinking

Individuals who experience negative emotions such as depression, anxiety, hopelessness, and shame tend to adopt irrational modes of thinking. Therefore, it is important to identify patterns of such irrational thinking. Review the examples of irrational thinking identified in this chapter and identify a situation where you used any of these thinking processes:

- filtering
- polarized thinking
- overgeneralization
- mind reading
- catastrophizing
- magnifying
- personalization
- shoulds

3. Use the Self-Regulatory Process to Reduce Anxiety

Complete the following self-study during a period of two to three weeks. Your report should include each of the following processes and should be approximately five to eight typed pages in length. See Appendix B for detailed information on how to conduct a self-regulation study.

Self-Observation and Evaluation. How does anxiety influence my academic and personal life? Do I need to change the way I deal with anxiety? If yes, what problem do I encounter? What are the symptoms of my problem (i.e., when, where, and how often does my problem occur)? What factors (e.g., beliefs, perceptions, feelings, physiological responses, or behaviors) contribute to this problem? What do I need to change to reduce or eliminate my problem?

Goal Setting and Strategic Planning. What are my goals? What strategies will I implement to reduce my anxiety? When will I use these strategies? How will I record my progress?

Strategy Implementation and Monitoring. What strategies did I use to reduce my anxiety? When did I use these strategies? What method(s) did I use to record my progress (e.g., documents, charts, logs, tally sheets, checklists, or recordings)? When did I use these methods? How and when did I monitor my progress to determine if my anxiety-reducing strategies were working? What changes, if any, did I make along the way?

Strategic-Outcome Monitoring. Did I attain the goal(s) I set for myself? Has the reduction in my anxiety improved my academic performance or personal life? What strategies were the most and least effective? What changes, if any, do I need to make in the future?

4. Assess Self-Talk

During the next week, monitor your self-talk and evaluate how it affects your motivation and self-confidence. Consider all the situations and tasks in which you engage—academic, athletic and recreational, social, occupational, and personal. Include in your report the following information: date, situation (e.g., academic), setting (describe where you were and what you were trying to accomplish), and report the self-talk as specifically as possible. Finally, discuss what strategies you used to deal with any negative self-talk.

Date: _____
Situation: _____
Setting: _____
Self-talk: _____
Strategy: _____

Date: _____
Situation: _____
Setting: _____
Self-talk: _____
Strategy: _____

Date: _____
Situation: _____
Setting: _____
Self-talk: _____
Strategy: _____

Date: _____
Situation: _____
Setting: _____
Self-talk: _____
Strategy: _____

Comments: _____
_____
_____
_____
_____

5. Explore Anxiety-Producing Situations in School

The following are common thoughts and worries expressed by individuals who have test anxiety (Smith, 1982, p. 179). Check those with which you can identify the most and then add additional thoughts in the empty spaces provided. Compare your thoughts and worries with those of other students in your class. Finally, discuss strategies you can use to deal with your negative thoughts.

a. Worry about performance
   I should have reviewed more. I'll never get through.
   My mind is blank, I'll never get the answer. I must really be stupid.
   I knew this stuff yesterday. What is wrong with me?
   I can't remember a thing. This always happens to me.

    b. Worry about bodily reactions
       I'm sick. I'll never get through.
       I'm sweating all over—it's really hot in here.
       My stomach is going crazy, churning and jumping all over.
       Here it comes—I'm getting really tense again. Normal people just don't get like this.

    c. Worry about how others are doing
       I know everyone's doing better than I am.
       I must be the dumbest one in the group.
       I am going to be the last one done again. I must really be stupid.
       No one else seems to be having trouble. Am I the only one?

    d. Worry about the possible negative consequences
       If I fail this test, I'll never get into the program.
       I'll never graduate.
       I'll think less of myself.
       I'll be embarrassed.

Effective Strategies

_____

_____

Answers to Exercise 5.2

    1. D   2. B   3. H   4. G   5. A   6. C or F   7. F   8. E

Part 3

Behavioral Strategies

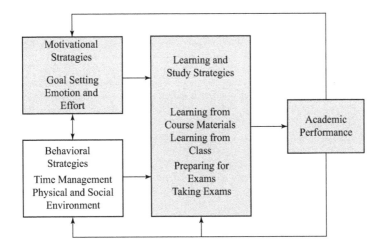

In this unit, we present strategies that will help you control your time and your physical and social environment. For the most part, these strategies involve behavioral changes that you can initiate to affect your learning. You cannot control your life without controlling your use of time. In Chapter 6, you will be asked to analyze your use of time and we will teach you a management system to use your time more effectively. In Chapter 7, we describe procedures to help you regulate or manage your environment. Many students have academic problems because they do not regulate their physical and social environments; instead, their environments manage, or better yet, control them. This is particularly the case in the context of the ever-present distractions such as texting and social media. We emphasize the cost of multitasking—or really, task switching—as an increase in time spent on a task and a decrease in the quality of engagement and the eventual product. The key aspect of regulation of the physical environment is one's study environment. Regulating one's social environment focuses on knowing when and how to seek and obtain help.

6 Time Management

In Chapter 1, we introduced time management as a category among the six aspects of self-regulation. The fact that time management claims its own category highlights its importance. In fact, recall that some research emphasizes that your time-management skills are better predictors of your GPA than your SAT scores (Britton & Tesser, 1991). Educational researchers (MacCann, Fogarty, & Roberts, 2012) have established that time-management skills are even more important for non-traditional students, such as part-time students who may be employed and have dependents. Time management is not only important at the undergraduate level—effective time-management skills that you develop now will help you in graduate school. In a study about medical school students (West & Sadoski, 2011), effective time-management skills such as avoiding procrastination, managing study periods, and prioritizing tasks emerged as more predictive of first semester academic performance than ability as measured by the Medical College Admission Test. In high school, time was structured for you because you were in school most of the day, spending about 30 hours per week in class and between 10 and 15 hours a week on homework. In college, you spend only about 12–16 hours in class per week, class times vary from day to day, and you may have several hours between classes. However, one of the things your college professor is likely to tell you when reviewing the class syllabus is to expect to spend between two and three hours studying for every hour spent in the classroom. This means that you have to manage more hours of study time and do not have your parents around to offer "suggestions" for how you should do it. You may also be taking an online class where you have no live sessions at all, and it is entirely up to you how you structure your time. You are also likely getting involved with college-related social opportunities (clubs, fraternities/sororities) and faced with the challenge of new responsibilities (chances are that you may be employed while in college). The problem for most students is not that they don't have enough time to accomplish what needs to be done, but that they do not know how to manage the amount of time available. The good news is that time-management skills can be taught. The purpose of this chapter, therefore, is to help you manage your time more effectively.

After studying this chapter, you will be able to:

- Analyze your use of time;
- identify your time wasters;
- develop a time-management system;
- use strategies to reduce procrastination.

WHAT IS TIME MANAGEMENT?

Smith (1994) defined *time* as "a continuum in which events succeed one another from past through present to future" (p. 20). The basic aspect of time is an event. Everything in our life is an event. Getting out of bed in the morning, driving or walking to class, and reading this book are all events. Time is the occurrence of all the events in our lives in sequence, one after the other. When we talk about time management, we are really talking about event or task management. After all, the purpose of time management is to ensure that we complete all of our important tasks each day. It is not simply to manage time. Smith (1994) stated: "Controlling your life means controlling your time, and controlling your time means controlling the events in your life" (p. 20).

HOW DO YOU USE YOUR TIME?

Time is a limited resource that some manage more effectively than others. As a first step in identifying how you use your time, we'll look at something we are all guilty of: wasting time. The purpose of the following exercise is to identify your major time wasters. Naturally, some of the potential time wasters identified in the exercise also have productive uses, such as relaxing after a long day of classes by playing your favorite video game. It is not difficult for them, though, to become time wasters and interfere with the attainment of your personal goals. For example, you may end up spending much more time playing the video game than initially planned because you are not always aware of the passage of time! Similarly, you may tell yourself, "I'll just reply to this one text!" Hanson et al. (2011) found that students in fact spent more time each week texting (14.35 hours per week on the average) than they spent on attending courses (12.35 hours), studying for courses (11.91 hours), or working (13.27 hours). Many students reported that they sent more than 200 texts a day!

Many of the potential time wasters are related to the use of the internet. Although internet facilitates life on one hand, it has brought new risks with it on the other. In fact, internet dependency has emerged as a concept of addiction. Wang (2001) developed a brief questionnaire to point out potential issues. Four of the ten items are presented below. Do you agree with any of the statements below about your use of the internet?

1 My grades have declined because I have been putting more time into net-related activities.
2 I have missed classes or work because of online activities.
3 I have tried to prevent others from knowing how much time I spend on the net.
4 Others, whom I trust, have told me I spend too much time on the net.

EXERCISE 6.1: SELF-OBSERVATION: ASSESSING TIME WASTERS

Directions: As you review the items, identify the time wasters that are most problematic for you. Rank them from 1 to 10, with number 1 as your greatest time waster.

Time Wasters	My Rank
1. Using social media (Instagram, Snapchat, Twitter)	
2. Watching television	
3. Surfing the web (e.g., YouTube)	
4. Visiting with friends/socializing (including the college party scene)	
5. Texting and/or talking on the phone	
6. Daydreaming	
7. Playing video games/online gaming	
8. Sleeping too much	
9. Waiting for others	
10. Procrastinating	

How you use your time can be classified into four quadrants based on whether the events in your life and the tasks you do are important or urgent, as shown in Figure 6.1. For example, completion of a research paper is an important task but may not be urgent at the beginning of the semester, while a next day quiz is both important and urgent. Changing the desktop design, in most cases, is neither important nor urgent, while many interruptions, such as scheduling conflicts in optional events, may seem urgent, but are not truly important.

As you see, time wasters, such as busywork, belong to Quadrant 4. Unfortunately, many people spend a significant amount of their time in this quadrant. Why do you think that is? The answer lies in the fact that tasks that are not important to us do not cause stress, while giving ourselves (and communicating to others) the illusion of being productive. In reality, of course, busywork only keeps us occupied.

Exercise 6.2: Self-Observation: Assessing Use of Time

Directions: Students who have difficulty with time management often lack awareness about how they spend their time. This exercise gives you an opportunity to evaluate your actual use of time. Fill in the following calendar with your activities last week.

My Use of Time

	Monday	Tuesday	Wednesday	Thursday	Friday	Saturday	Sunday
6–7 a.m.							
7–8							
8–9							
9–10							
10–11							
11–12							
12–1 p.m.							
1–2							
2–3							
3–4							
4–5							
5–6							

My Use of Time

	Monday	Tuesday	Wednesday	Thursday	Friday	Saturday	Sunday
6–7							
7–8							
8–9							
9–10							
10–11							
11–12							
12–1 a.m.							
1–2							
2–3							
3–4							
4–5							
5–6							

Time Analysis

Activities	Monday	Tuesday	Wednesday	Thursday	Friday	Saturday	Sunday	TOTAL
Eating								
Sleeping								
Class								
Studying								
Working								

Personal chores and responsibilities					
Social activities (face-to-face)					
Screen time (social networking, gaming, texting, TV)					
Physical activity (sports, working out, etc.)					
Miscellaneous					

Next, using the Time Activities Analysis table, determine how much time you spend in each activity listed for each day of the week, as well as the total for the entire week. When you total your time, round to the nearest half-hour (e.g., 9 hours and 20 minutes sleeping = 9.5 hours).

Let's pause here for a moment. We included sleep as a category as getting enough sleep has an important role not only in rejuvenating us physically but is critical to our ability to learn. Specifically, during sleep, the brain solidifies and enhances memories, including new learning from the day before. Sacrificing sleep in order to spend more time studying will therefore in fact backfire (Gillen-O'Neel, Hyunh, & Fuligni, 2013).

List the three activities on which you are spending the most time (other than sleeping):

1.
2.
3.

Summarize what you have learned about your personal time-use habits. Be specific (e.g., When do you study? Do you spend more than two hours a day on Facebook or talking on the phone? Do you tend to accomplish your goals?). Does your response differ from your original perception of time wasters reported in Exercise 6.1? What do you need to do to become more effective in achieving your goals?

QUADRANT 1: Important/Urgent	QUADRANT 2: Important/Not Urgent
Crisis Pressing Problems Projects Completed at the Last Minute	Planning Long-Term Projects
QUADRANT 3: Urgent/Not Important	QUADRANT 4: Not Urgent/Not Important
Interruptions Time-Specific but Non-Essential Events	Busywork Time Wasters (TV and Internet)

FIGURE 6.1   Urgent versus Important Tasks (adapted from Covey, 1990).

Many of you, no doubt, listed procrastination as your number one time waster in Exercise 6.1. Looking at Figure 6.1, in which quadrants do you think procrastinators spend a lot of time? Procrastinators distract themselves either by engaging in busywork or by responding to interruptions. Doing Quadrant 3 and 4 activities at the expense of Quadrant 1 and 2 activities is a clear sign of procrastination. We will talk more about procrastination later in this chapter and discuss why procrastinators avoid doing things that are important to them.

What, then, can you do to manage your time effectively? Clearly, we all have to handle things that are both important and urgent (Quadrant 1). The key to successful time management, however, is to set aside time every day to do some Quadrant 2 activities. For example, you may start a literature review for the semester research paper, start investigating graduate programs in your field long before you obtain your undergraduate degree, or simply take the first steps in gathering the documents necessary for your tax return. By accomplishing things that are important but not yet urgent, you avoid later crises, enhance the vision for your future, and have a sense of control over things that truly matter in the long term. In essence, by emphasizing Quadrant 2, you prevent fires, while living in Quadrant 1, you fight fires.

WHAT ARE SOME EFFECTIVE TIME-MANAGEMENT STRATEGIES?

SET REGULAR STUDY PERIODS

Setting a regular time to study each day helps "protect" you from constant conflicts with other tasks that you must complete. There always will be unexpected events that rob time from your studying. If circumstances arise that prohibit you from studying, adjust your schedule. If you do not establish a set time, the probability increases that you will become involved with other tasks. If it could be helpful, you can program your smartphone to prompt you that it is study time.

CREATE AN ENVIRONMENT THAT IS RELATIVELY FREE OF DISTRACTIONS AND INTERRUPTIONS

You live in a technologically rich world, using your smartphone to text and stream music, your tablet to read the required course material, and your laptop to stream video, often simultaneously. Although multitasking is typical and you may even perceive it to be a strength, problems occur when you believe that you can learn complex material effectively while engaging in other activities, such as texting. We will return to the problems associated with multitasking—or really, task switching—in Chapter 7. As you know, our attentional capacities are very limited. Remember the Magic Number? At any one time, the working memory of an adult can hold only a limited amount of information. Though you can learn new information while being distracted, the encoding process is much more superficial than when learning in a focused manner. This, of course, affects the quality of retrieval, such as when needing to access the learned knowledge for a quiz. In addition, dividing your attention among competing tasks ends up being costly in terms of the overall amount of time devoted to the target task. How costly is texting while reading academic material in terms of time spent on task? In an experimental study, Bowman, Levine, Waite, and Gendron (2010) found that those students who texted while reading spent 59 percent more time than students who did not text during reading. As a possible explanation, the researchers suggested that every time you distract yourself from reading a text, you have to reread portions of the text in order to get back on track.

In addition to turning off your phone while studying, analyze your present study environment and determine whether it is the best place for you. Most college students study in one of five locations: home, their residence hall, apartment, fraternity or sorority house, or library. Wherever you decide to study, consider the level of distractions present. If you find you are constantly distracted by discussions, telephone calls, music, or other factors, consider another location (see Exercise 7.1).

Schedule Tasks so They Can Be Accomplished in 30- to 60-Minute Blocks of Time

There are two major reasons for block planning. First, it is wise to develop intermediate goals and specific tasks for each major goal identified. Organizing time around intermediate goals and daily tasks helps lead to a greater sense of efficacy as each intermediate goal and task is completed. For example, in developing a plan for writing a paper, you may decide to spend 30 minutes outlining the paper and another 30 minutes to determine what topics will be covered. Second, many students miss great opportunities for studying by neglecting time between classes. A few short intervals quickly add up to an hour or more of study during the day. Consider short intervals of study as well as longer intervals when you plan your study schedule.

Take Short Breaks

How long you study is determined by your motivation and concentration. In general, most students need a short five- or ten-minute break each hour. However, you may be able to concentrate for longer periods of time. You need to adjust the study intervals according to your own personal needs. If you find you are easily distracted, you may need a two- or three-minute break after 30 minutes or so. You may have heard of the "Pomodoro" technique in which time-consuming tasks are broken down into smaller chunks of time with built-in breaks. Aside from a kitchen timer, there are several apps available based on this technique such as Be Focused. Taking breaks helps you maintain focus, decreases stress and frustration, and ultimately, increases productivity.

Be Specific in Identifying How You Plan to Use Your Time

It is not how long you study, but how you study that determines academic success. If you break your goal into tasks, as suggested earlier, you will find it easier to determine how you will spend your time. Do not just write the course name or study topic (e.g., psychology) in your schedule. Specify what you plan to do during the time. In other words, make sure your plan is SMART!

Alternate Subjects When You Have a Long Time Block Available for Study

Students generally believe that it is best to "park themselves" at a table and study one topic for as long as they can take it, the so-called "block study." In fact, there is evidence (Bjork, 2015) that most effective outcomes result from mixing topics. For example, you can focus on one topic such as philosophy for one hour and then shift to chemistry for the next hour instead of studying philosophy for two hours. Varying the type of material studied in a single sitting seems to leave a deeper impression on the brain than does concentrating on just one topic or skill at a time. Performers have used this approach for a long time. Musicians, for example, mix up scales, musical pieces, and rhythmic work in their practice sessions in order to perform at their best. Top athletes also work on different skills in combination with each other, and therefore their practice does not become repetitive and routine. We are now getting evidence that this strategy works in academics as well. You may find that you can better control your motivation and concentration by completing certain aspects of the assignment in one subject area and coming back to another part of the assignment at a later time.

Estimate the Time Needed for Each Assignment

Successfully estimating the amount of time needed for each subject comes with experience. The better you estimate time, the more realistic your study plan will become. However, no one can be on target every time. It often is not until you begin studying or writing that you find that you underestimated the time needed to complete the task. If this occurs, there is nothing wrong with adjusting your schedule the next day.

Prioritize Tasks

One of the most important factors in developing an effective time-management system is prioritizing tasks. Not everything you have to do is of equal importance. You need to decide what task should be completed first. As we discussed previously, it is important to distinguish between important and urgent tasks. An urgent task requires immediate attention. An example of an urgent task is a phone call. When a phone rings, you say to yourself: "I need to take this." Yet, how many calls do you receive each day that can be classified as important? And, if you do not recognize the number, chances are good that it is a "robocall." Don't let that distract your focus—if it is important, they'll leave a message. Similarly, most students leave on the texting capacities of their phone while studying and answer their texts immediately, interrupting their academic work in order to read and respond to texts that are purely social in content (Levine et al., 2007). While most texts may be important (if they are from good friends or family), they are likely not urgent—you can text back whenever you want! Can you distinguish between important and urgent tasks by providing some examples in your own life?

Do the Assignments for the Course You Dislike First

Do you have a tendency to put off difficult tasks? Do you recall stating the following: "I'll do it later in the day," or "I'll do it tomorrow"? If so, join the crowd! Individuals tend to do first what they like the most. Later in this chapter, we will talk about procrastination to help you deal with the problem of delaying tasks.

Consider studying for the course you dislike or have the most difficulty with first. There are many advantages in using this strategy: First, you become tired at the end of the day and should study difficult material when you are most alert. Second, one way to deal with the problem of procrastination is to deal with the disliked task immediately and get it out of the way instead of allowing it to "hang over your head." Finally, you often feel that you have something to look forward to when you leave the best for last. Just think of the analogy of eating dinner—it would not be a good idea to eat your dessert before you dig into those Brussels sprouts!

Work Ahead of Your Assignments When Possible

Before the week begins, assess the workload for the upcoming week or even month, especially major events that may require changes in your schedule. For example, suppose you know that you are going home for the weekend or have an important social event coming up. In addition, you see that you have a major midterm on Monday morning following the big weekend. You will need to consider changes in your study schedule to prepare for the exam. Also, some assignments, such as a major paper, may require more than one week of involvement. By knowing what future tasks are required, you can plan a strategy for completing them in a timely fashion and avoid the perfect storm!

TAKE DOWN ANY APPOINTMENTS AS SOON AS YOU MAKE THEM IN YOUR SMARTPHONE OR CALENDAR

Have any of the following events happened to you? You take an appointment card from your doctor or dentist for your next visit and place it safely in your wallet or purse. Unfortunately, you fail to look at it and miss your appointment. We remember the time when, if you did not have your bulky calendar handy, appointments were recorded on a piece of paper or in the palm of your hand, only to be discovered days later in the wash or, you guessed it, washed off. Those times are long gone with electronic time management being readily available. You just have to get into the habit of immediately recording any appointments you set! Most time-management systems will even send you reminders.

USE TECHNOLOGY TO MANAGE YOUR TIME

We have already referred to using your smartphone to help you manage time and suggested technology to help you implement the Pomodoro technique. Technology provides several different tools to help you become an efficient time manager. Some of the management tools include calendars where you can set up reminders as pop-up messages, pictorial mind maps where you can create lists and rearrange the list as necessary, and email management solutions where you can flag emails with priorities. New products and programs are continuously being created and existing ones updated for you to move forward with your time-management skills. But remember, while it is a valuable skill to use technology in managing your time, it is as important to manage your technology time!

HOW DO I DEVELOP A SYSTEM OF TIME PLANNING AND MANAGEMENT?

We now use the information presented in this chapter to develop a system for time planning and management. The following are three forms useful in planning your time: a semester calendar, weekly priority tasks list, and a weekly schedule.

Student Reflections

Things that worked for me in high school, I discovered, don't work for me in college. I really was unprepared for the amount of material that is presented here and the speed at which it is presented. It was a bit of a shock. Things I picked up quickly in high school I couldn't pick up as easily anymore.

Here at college I wasn't checked every day. I did not get off to a great start because I have never really learned to study this enormous amount of material in a systematic way. I tend to do one subject for a big time span and then neglect it for a week. Then I moved on to another subject and forgot about that for a week. So, there was no continuity within each course. That had a lot to do with it. Finally I figured it out. This year, I'm pushing myself to spend a little bit of time every day on each subject.

(from Light, 2001, p. 24)

Semester Calendar

The semester calendar should be used to identify due dates each month for assignments and papers, dates of tests, and important non-academic activities and events. This calendar should be on the wall in your room or on your desk. Semester calendars can be purchased in college bookstores and local stationery stores.

Weekly Priority Tasks List

This form allows you to make a "to do" list for all the tasks that could or should be done during the week, based on your goals. Each week you will decide on the priority of each task and determine its order of importance. The following is an example of one student's weekly priority tasks list, where A identifies the most important tasks to be completed, B identifies tasks needing to be completed only after the A tasks are completed, and C identifies tasks to be completed only after A and B tasks are completed. The number next to each letter further prioritizes the importance of each of the A, B, and C tasks. Your smartphone is likely to have a similar feature available.

Weekly Schedule

The final form is the weekly schedule, which identifies the time and order in which you will complete the tasks and activities for the week. This schedule is developed each week and reviewed each day to determine whether any changes are needed for the following day because of unforeseen circumstances (e.g., changes in appointments or the need for additional time to complete tasks). Naturally, a smartphone makes a similar feature available to you.

Semester Calendar						
Month						
Sunday	**Monday**	**Tuesday**	**Wednesday**	**Thursday**	**Friday**	**Saturday**
1	2	3	4	5	6	7
8	9	10	11	12	13	14
15	16	17	18	19	20	21
22	23	24	25	26	27	28
29	30	31				

Weekly Priority Tasks List

Week of _____ through _____

Tasks	Priority Rating	Day(s) Scheduled

Tasks	Priority Rating	Day(s) Scheduled
Upgrade my phone	C–4	Sat
Write poem for English	C–1	M–Th
Call cousin	C–2	F
Buy flowers for mother	C–3	Th
Composition paper—outline and write	A–3	W, Th
Calculus assignments		
Ch. 2—complete assigned problems	A–1	M
Ch. 3—complete assigned problems	A–2	W
Psychology research paper	B–3	Th, F
Read Ch. 2—outline main ideas	B–1	M
Answer end-of-chapter questions	B–2	T

NAME						WEEKLY SCHEDULE	
	Monday	**Tuesday**	**Wednesday**	**Thursday**	**Friday**	**Saturday**	**Sunday**
6–7 a.m.							
7–8							
8–9							
9–10							
10–11							
11–12							
12–1 p.m.							
1–2							
2–3							
3–4							
4–5							
5–6							
7–8							
8–9							
9–10							
10–11							
11–12							

Table 6.1 displays a summary of the procedures for developing and implementing a time-management plan.

TABLE 6.1
Procedures for Developing and Implementing a Time-Management Plan

Procedures	Examples
Establish a time for planning at the beginning of each week when you will not be interrupted. This time also should be used to review your prior week's use of time and performance.	Most students use Sunday night. Ask yourself the following questions: "Did I attain my goals last week?" "Did I plan for sufficient study time?" "Do I need to make changes in my goals or priorities?" "Do I need to make changes in my time management?" "What are my goals for this week?"
Enter all fixed activities in your weekly schedule.	Fixed activities are those activities over which you have little or no control (e.g., job, meals, classes, athletic practice, sleep, appointments).
Review your written goals to determine what tasks need to be started or completed to bring you closer to attaining your goals.	"I want to practice my guitar four times a week for 40 minutes." "I want to achieve an A in English this semester."
Check your semester calendar to determine whether there are any exams, papers, or other major assignments due in the next few weeks.	"I have a midterm in Spanish coming up in two weeks. I had better start developing a study plan to review all the material next week."
Identify all the personal and academic tasks you have to complete for the week on the weekly prioritized task list.	"I need to buy computer paper, complete my math problems, do my Spanish translation each day, write a short paper, and finish the assigned readings in sociology."
Prioritize the tasks list by giving a value ("A," "B," or "C") to each item on the list. Place an "A" next to items that must be done. Place a "B" next to any task that is important and should be done. That is, after all the "A" tasks are completed and you have time, you would work on the "B" items. Finally, write a "C" next to any task that is less important and could be done later. That is, after the "A" and "B" tasks have been completed, you'll do the "C" tasks.	"I am having some difficulty in Spanish so I can't afford to get behind (A). Therefore, I must spend extra time this week on my translations. My short English paper is due on Friday so I better write the first draft on Wednesday to give me time for a rewrite on Thursday (B)."
Give a numerical value to each item on the list. In other words, determine which "A" task is most important and label it "A–1." Then decide which "A" item is next most important and label it "A–2," and so on. Do the same for "B" and "C" tasks.	"I understood the sociology lecture, so I'll do the reading after I finish my math assignments (C–1) and the first draft on my English paper. I'll practice my guitar before dinner (C–2)."
Complete your weekly schedule by transferring the items on your priority tasks sheet to your weekly schedule forms. Put the "A" items first, followed by the "B" items, and finally as many of the "C" items you think you can accomplish.	
Check your weekly schedule each evening for the next day and make modifications as needed (e.g., changes in appointments, unexpected assignments, or unusual demands on time).	"I thought I could write the first draft of my English paper Wednesday but found I have to do more library research. I need to spend at least one hour in the library tomorrow."

WHAT IS PROCRASTINATION?

Although we've been putting it off, it is time to deal with the time waster identified earlier in the chapter—procrastination (pun intended!). Are there things you put off doing though you know you should not? Do you delay tasks beyond what is reasonable? Procrastination can be broadly defined as the voluntary delay of an intended course of action past the time most likely to produce the desired performance (Steel, 2007). In short, it is the postponement of tasks. Procrastination is universal and very common, with university students being perhaps the population most well known for engaging in this type of behavior. In fact, data shows that between 70 percent and 90 percent of college students engage in academically related procrastination, including delaying the start or finish of papers, studying for exams, registering for classes, making appointments with instructors, and turning in an assignment on time (Ferrari, 2001). As instructors, we often hear of last-minute "all-nighters" prior to our final exam. Though "cramming" for an exam may be seen as just a part of the college experience, it should be viewed as a detrimental behavior. Studies clearly demonstrate that procrastination can result in poor academic performance, negative emotions such as shame and guilt, stress, and depression (Steel, 2007; Steel & Ferrari, 2013).

Procrastination is particularly relevant from a self-regulatory perspective because it is sometimes referred to as the "quintessential self-regulatory failure" (Steel, 2007). Exploring the motivation of habitual procrastinators has revealed that they are more likely than non-procrastinators to make attributions with an external locus of control (Brownlow & Reasinger, 2000) and have lower self-efficacy to self-regulate (Klassen, Krawchuk, & Rajani, 2008). When it comes to brain function, procrastination is believed to be related to our executive functioning, the aspect of our brain that is integral to planning, organizing, strategizing, and managing time and space.

WHAT ARE THE CAUSES OF PROCRASTINATION?

As mentioned, procrastination on academic tasks can lead to low academic performance, including poor grades and course withdrawal. Although there are different reasons for procrastination, Ferrari, Johnson, and McCown (1995) identified two patterns that should be of concern to college students. The first pattern is classified as a lack of conscientiousness and is associated with such behaviors as poor time management, work discipline, self-control, and responsibility. The second pattern is classified as avoidance and is associated with fear of failure and anxiety.

Fear of failure was discussed in Chapter 2 under Covington's (1992) self-worth theory. He believes that academic procrastination serves the goal of preserving feelings of self-worth by avoiding situations in which students might fail. As our self-worth is invested in things that are important to us, procrastination mostly emerges in situations that are important to us. Recall the previous discussion where we stated that procrastinators spend time doing unimportant things in Quadrants 3 and 4 (Figure 6.1) at the expense of things that are important to them. Though unimportant things such as changing your desktop design at the expense of important tasks may make us feel better in the short term, they are eventually outweighed by the costs such as stress and lowered performance.

Closely related to fear of failure is perfectionism. Several authors have suggested that procrastination and perfectionism are related (e.g., Burka & Yuen, 1983). This relation is explained as follows: An individual procrastinates to gain additional time to produce the best product. Unfortunately, if the procrastinator has unrealistic or too high standards, he or she is rarely satisfied with the product and fails to turn it in on time. Psychologists have traced perfectionism back to experiences growing up in families where parents tend to be very demanding and critical of their children's behavior (Flett et al., 1995). Another characteristic in the second pattern of procrastination is anxiety. If students are anxious, procrastination is seen as a way of avoiding the anxiety associated with studying or completing the assigned task.

It is beyond the scope of this book to determine specific diagnoses of procrastination problems. If you believe procrastination is a serious problem affecting your behavior and none of the following strategies identified in this chapter help you deal with your particular problem, you may want to consider discussing it with a counselor at your counseling center.

PROCRASTINATION AND TECHNOLOGY

As mentioned previously, though technology is an important tool, it can also generate negative "side effects." How often do you tell yourself, "I'll just do a quick search for another reference" and find yourself spending an hour in fascinating but irrelevant diversions? If so, you may have become one of the millions of "mouse potatoes" and "cyber-slackers" (Lavoie & Pychyl, 2001, p. 439). Procrastinating in the manner pointed out previously is especially insidious because you may deceive yourself into believing that by following the diversions you are actually productive. In addition, you may rationalize "just one more website" as justified because engaging in a quick detour does not appear to be harmful for the completion of a pressing task. On some occasions, you might not even pretend to look for references and instead become one of the folks who get caught up in watching cats online. Did you know that in 2014, the more than 2 million youtube.com cat videos had nearly 26 billion total views (Marshall, 2014)? We wonder how many of those views were manifestations of procrastination.

Using social media has emerged as one of the main ways to procrastinate. This is not a surprise as social media satisfies one of our basic needs: to connect with each other. But, when that connection is readily available and indeed, sometimes intrusive such as via instant messages and push notifications, it is an attractive way to procrastinate.

Procrastination using technology presents a high cost not only in terms of individuals' performance, such as a student's grades, but also in terms of business performance. Similar to your time in college being largely unstructured, jobs are becoming more and more self-structured and productivity is increasingly dependent on the employees' level of self-regulation. In addition, the internet is the common mediator between the employee and employer. Why sit under the watchful eye of your supervisor when you can telecommute from a satellite office that is more convenient? Though the computer in both academic and professional settings is intended for higher productivity, it also contains an enormous amount of temptations (YouTube and online gaming, anyone?). Avoiding procrastination when it comes to using the internet is a true self-regulatory challenge, for all the reasons pointed out previously.

WHAT CAN I DO ABOUT MY TENDENCY TO PROCRASTINATE?

To begin, developing an effective time-management plan is a good first step. Second, the self-talk strategy discussed in Chapter 5 can also be effective in dealing with procrastination. In Chapter 7, we also identify attention and concentration strategies that can be helpful in dealing with procrastination.

In this chapter, we discuss two additional strategies that you will find helpful. The first category of strategies involves taking some action to reduce or eliminate the tendency to procrastinate. The second strategy is an extension of self-talk procedures whereby you attempt to challenge and change some of the misperceptions that lead to procrastination.

PROCRASTINATION ELIMINATION STRATEGIES

The following are some procrastination elimination strategies to help you keep on task (Ellis & Knaus, 1977; Ferrari, 2001; Lewis, Jr. & Oyserman, 2015):

- *Time-Telling*: Procrastinators have difficulty estimating the time needed to complete tasks. For the most part, they underestimate the time necessary to perform a task. Practice estimating time needed to complete tasks and compare the accuracy of your estimation over a series of tasks. You can also get an on-screen timer for time-telling.

- *Reframe Deadlines into Smaller Units of Time*: If something is due in three days, think of it as being due in 72 hours. If something is due in one month, think of it as being due in 30 days. When we think of time in smaller units, it makes the future feel closer and we are much more likely to take action.
- *Prompts/Reminder Notes*: Use physical reminder notes (e.g., Post-it® notes) placed in specific locations to remind you to finish a particular task. For example, place a note on a bathroom mirror, in your appointment book, or smartphone.
- *Reinforcement*: Make an agreement with yourself that after a period of working on a task, you will reinforce yourself. For example: "If I study for 50 minutes, I'll get myself an ice cream." Similarly, rather than viewing the YouTube video of the day before starting your assignment, use the internet as a reward for your most challenging academic tasks.
- *The Bits-and-Pieces Approach*: Divide the task into component parts such as reviewing the assignment guidelines, conducting research, writing an introduction and a conclusion. You can also simply divide the task into pages written per day. Then, rather than ignoring the assignment, commit to completing one or two pages per day.
- *The Five-Minute Plan*: Agree to work on a task for five minutes. At the end of five minutes, decide whether you will work on it for another five minutes. Often momentum builds as you near the end of the first five minutes, so you want to maintain your focus on the task.
- *The 80 Percent Success Rule*: Don't expect to go from "total non-completion" to "total completion" of all tasks. Instead, take a realistic approach by setting a goal to complete at least 80 percent of the task. Give yourself some reinforcement when you reach this goal and plan the completion of the final 20 percent of the task.
- *Social Support for Task Completion*: Work with students who tend to complete tasks. These individuals can serve as positive models instead of fellow procrastinators who help maintain procrastination.
- *Establish a Set Time for a Routine*: Setting a precise time during the day for completing a task can help you get it done. For example, deciding to exercise soon after you wake up can help you establish regular exercise behavior.
- *Modify the Environment*: Your working environment can directly influence procrastination. For example, if you need to complete some reading or write a short paper, a room with a TV or a coffeehouse with free Wi-Fi may not be the best place to begin and sustain motivation to complete the task. Changing the setting by going to another room in your home or going to the library, where you may find fewer distractions, can help you focus on the task.

Challenging and Changing Beliefs and Misperceptions

Another way of dealing with procrastination involves challenging and changing beliefs and misperceptions. The following misperceptions are frequent among most procrastinators (Ferrari et al., 1995):

- Overestimation of the time left to perform a task.
- Underestimation of time necessary to complete a task.
- Overestimation of future motivational states. This is typified by statements such as "I'll feel more like doing it later."
- Mistakenly relying on the necessity of emotional congruence to succeed in a task. Typical is a statement such as "People should only study when they feel good about it."
- Belief that working when not in the mood is unproductive or suboptimal. Such beliefs are typically expressed by phrases such as "It doesn't do any good to work when you are not motivated."

Some misperceptions increase anxiety about a task, leading to a feeling of futility or hopelessness regarding the ability to complete it (e.g., "It's too late to complete this task"). Other misperceptions are characteristic of individuals who are not very conscientious about completing tasks (e.g., "I do my best work when I do it at the last minute").

EXERCISE 6.3: CHALLENGE IRRATIONAL BELIEFS

The following is a list of rationalizations and corresponding suggestions for challenging the first three misperceptions (adapted from Ferrari et al., 1995, p. 198). Provide your own challenges for the remainder of the beliefs. As you attempt to deal with reasons for procrastination, ask yourself the following: Is my belief or explanation reasonable? Is my belief accurate? Am I being objective? What argument or statement can I use to discredit my irrational belief?

Irrational Beliefs	Self-Talk Challenges
It's too late to complete this task.	"It's never too late! If I get started now, I can make good progress and get the task done."
I'm very good at getting things done at the last minute, so I don't have to worry.	"I fool myself in thinking that I do a good job when I wait until the last minute. The truth is I rush to find all the material I need; I don't have time to review a draft of the assignment and make necessary changes. My main concern is finishing the task rather than determining how I can do the best job."
I won't get this task done unless I relax first or get in the right mood.	"I need to stop kidding myself. I may never be in the mood to complete the assignment or get in the mood after the assignment is due. If I get started on the assignment, I may get in a better mood to do it."
I'm too nervous or stressed to get this task done.	
I've missed so many opportunities so far, so why should I bother?	
I'm not smart enough to do this task.	
If I don't think about doing this task, I won't have to worry as much.	
I'm too tired to do this task well, so why bother?	
I can't work without (a specific person, study room, etc.) being available.	

■

Chapter Review

KEY POINTS

1 Individuals control their lives by controlling, whenever possible, the timing of events in their lives.
2 Students with better time-management skills tend to have higher grade-point averages.
3 The problem for most individuals is not lack of time but poor time management.
4 Assessing present use and waste of time is essential before changing or modifying a daily or weekly schedule.
5 How you use your time can be classified based on whether the events in your life and the tasks you do are important or urgent.
6 Individuals must always consider personal goals before scheduling tasks in a time-management plan.
7 Three forms are needed for time planning and management: a semester calendar, a weekly priority tasks list, and a weekly schedule.
8 One of the major problems in time management is failure to prioritize tasks.
9 Two major patterns of procrastination are lack of conscientiousness and avoidance associated with anxiety and fear of failure.
10 Strategies for dealing with procrastination include improving time management, maintaining attention and concentration, using specific behavioral changes such as the five-minute plan, reducing anxiety, and challenging irrational beliefs.

FOLLOW-UP ACTIVITIES

1. Use the Self-Management Process to Improve Your Time Management

Complete the following self-study during a period of two to three weeks. Your report should include each of the following processes and should be approximately five to eight typed pages in length. See Appendix B for detailed information on how to conduct a self-management study.

Self-Observation and Evaluation.   How do I manage my time? Do I need to change the way I plan and manage my study schedule? If yes, what problem(s) do I encounter? What are the symptoms of my problem (i.e., when, where, and how often does my problem occur)? How much of an impact does this problem have on my academic performance? What factors (e.g., beliefs, perceptions, feelings, physiological responses, or behaviors) contribute to this problem? What do I need to change to reduce or eliminate my problem(s)?

Goal Setting and Strategic Planning.   What are my goals? What strategies will I implement to improve my time management? When will I use these strategies? How will I record my progress?

Strategy Implementation and Monitoring.   What strategies did I use to improve my time management? When did I use these strategies? What method(s) did I use to record my progress (e.g., documents, charts, logs, tally sheets, checklists, or recordings)? When did I use these methods? How and when did I monitor my progress to determine if my new time-management plan was working? What changes, if any, did I make along the way?

Strategic-Outcome Monitoring.   Did I attain the goal(s) I set for myself? Have the modifications in my time management improved my academic performance or personal life? What strategies were the most and least effective? What changes, if any, do I need to make in the future?

2. Identify Your Escapist Techniques

On a separate sheet of paper, create a chart using the following headings and jot down all of the methods you use in a one-week period to avoid doing your work. What can you do to keep from repeating these avoidance patterns (taken from Van Blerkom, 1994, p. 52)?

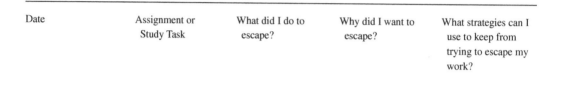

Date	Assignment or Study Task	What did I do to escape?	Why did I want to escape?	What strategies can I use to keep from trying to escape my work?

3. Identify How You Spend Your Time

Based on Exercise 6.2, where you assessed your use of time, categorize the events in your calendar from the previous week according to the quadrants below. Categorize attending classes as belonging to Quadrant 1. Determine the quadrant in which you spend most of your time. Is spending time in that quadrant leading to the attainment of your long-term goals? Next, look at how much time you dedicate to planning (Quadrant 2) and how much time you waste (Quadrant 4). Lastly, assess whether there are any changes you want to make about how you spend your time.

Quadrant 1: Important/Urgent   **Quadrant 2:** Important/Not Urgent
Quadrant 3: Urgent/Not Important   **Quadrant 4:** Not Urgent/Not Important

4. Identify Your Favorite Procrastination Beliefs

The following is a list of common beliefs and misperceptions of procrastinators (Bliss, 1983). Identify your top *five* cop-outs and write a challenge for each of them.

1. It's unpleasant.
2. It's not due yet.
3. I work better under pressure.
4. Maybe it will take care of itself if I just don't do anything.
5. It's too early in the day.
6. It's too late in the day.
7. I don't have any papers with me.

8. It's difficult.
9. I don't feel like doing it now.
10. I have a headache.
11. Delay won't make much difference.
12. It may be important, but it isn't urgent.
13. It might hurt.
14. I really mean to do it, but I keep forgetting.
15. Somebody else may do it if I wait.
16. It might be embarrassing.
17. I don't know where to begin.
18. I'm too tired.
19. I'm too busy right now.
20. It's a boring job.
21. It might not work.
22. I've got to tidy up first.
23. I need to sleep on it.
24. We can get by a little longer as is.
25. I don't really know how to do it.
26. There's a good TV program on.
27. As soon as I start, somebody will probably interrupt.
28. It needs further study.
29. My horoscope indicates this is the wrong time.
30. Nobody is nagging me about it yet.
31. If I do it now, they'll just give me something else to do.
32. The weather's lousy.
33. It's too nice of a day to spend doing that.
34. Before I start, I think I'll take a break.
35. I'll do it as soon as I finish some preliminary tasks.
36. My biorhythms are out of sync.
37. The sooner I fall behind, the more time I'll have to get caught up.
38. I'll wait until the first of the year and make a New Year's resolution.
39. It's too late now, anyway.

Cop-out #1: _____
Challenge Statement: _____

Cop-out #2: _____
Challenge Statement: _____

Cop-out #3: _____
Challenge Statement: _____

Cop-out #4: _____
Challenge Statement: _____

Cop-out #5: _____
Challenge Statement: _____

7 Self-Regulation of the Ph and Social Environment

As a college student, you participate in many different learning environments. You may attend classes on the physical campus space and spend countless hours studying at the library or in a study hall. You may also connect to a virtual environment for a fully or partially online course—or your professor's office hours. In addition, you may participate in student-generated social learning spaces via blogs, wikis, and social networking. Whatever the learning environment, the skills we discuss in this chapter related to improving attention and concentration, seeking academic help, making study groups more productive, and improving communication skills are critical for optimal academic performance.

Whatever the learning environment, you can take actions to adapt to your environment, as well as change your environment to fit your needs. For example, although you cannot control the room assignment for a course, you often can determine where you sit, as well as your level of concentration during the period. If you sit near students who are carrying on a conversation during a lecture, you can move your seat. If you are in a discussion and there is considerable noise outside, you can ask to shut the window or close the door. In other words, even when you cannot select the optimal learning environment, you can take steps to adapt or modify the physical environment.

Some of the students in our classes are athletes and fraternity or sorority members who are required to attend a "study table" for a number of hours per week to study under supervision in a specific location. Because of their many time pressures, the requirement of a specific place for study is not a bad one. However, many students report that their mandated study environment is often not conducive for effective study. Some complaints include too many individuals in the room, high noise levels, and friends more interested in talking or listening to music than studying. This is a situation where management over one's physical environment is not an easy task but can be achieved with some ingenuity. The following strategies have been used by students in this environment: setting specific study goals for each evening, selecting a location in the room that is most conducive for study, reducing visual contact with certain individuals, limiting socializing to breaks outside the room, and noise-canceling headphones.

While we are on the topic of where you study, there is a longstanding debate in memory research about whether it is better to vary your study context (e.g., by studying in different places) or whether it is better to keep the environmental context as similar as possible (i.e., always study in the same location). A classic set of experiments (Smith et al., 1978) found that college students who studied a list of 40 vocabulary words in two different rooms (one windowless, the other with a nice view) performed better on a memory test than students who studied the words twice in the same room. As an explanation for this difference in memory performance, the authors hypothesized that when the learning environment is varied, the brain is forced to make multiple different associations with the same material. This process may enrich the information learned, enhance learning, and diminish forgetting. There are other studies (e.g., Xue et al., 2010), however, that challenge the benefit of creating diverse contexts in which study takes place. So, the jury is still out on this issue. What should you use as a guideline of where to study? Should you mix up where you study or choose the same location every time you study? Our recommendation, as already alluded to in the discussion above, is, first and foremost, choose a physically and socially distraction-free environment that allows you to fully concentrate on the topic at hand.

Self-regulation of the social environment also relates to the ability to determine when you need to work alone or with others, or when it is time to seek help from instructors, tutors, ers, and non-social sources such as a reference book, additional textbooks, or the internet (Zimmerman, 2015).

A recent experience, mentioned earlier in the text, provides a good example of the need for self-regulation in this area. A student mentioned in class that she did not do well on her biology exam, because she did not prepare for the type of questions it contained. The second author suggested she meet with her instructor to discuss her present performance and learn more about future exams. She agreed. When she returned to class the following week, he asked her about the meeting. She stated that she went to the instructor's office, but because other students were waiting to see him, she left and did not return. In Chapter 1, we mentioned that when self-regulated learners confront obstacles, they find ways to succeed! If a meeting with an instructor can lead to higher academic performance, you must develop strategies to obtain the information. This may mean making an appointment in person, by phone or online, waiting outside the office, finding out when the instructor arrives in the morning, or walking with the instructor to his or her next class. In other words, your job is to obtain the information. It is easy to convince yourself that you tried sufficiently to complete a task or that the task was too difficult. Unfortunately, these attributions do not help you obtain the information you need.

Motivational beliefs and perceptions often play an important role in explaining individual differences in the willingness and ability to manage physical and social environments. For example, as reported in Chapter 2, students who perceive themselves as academically competent feel in control of their academic success and have a mastery orientation view to help-seeking as an effective learning strategy and are more likely to seek help (Karabenick & Newman, 2011). In a study of the characteristics of students who attend voluntary review sessions, Ames and Lau (1982) found that students' participation was related to their attributional patterns and past performances. Students who did poorly on earlier exams, but attributed their poor performance to low effort and a lack of knowledge rather than to low ability or intelligence, were much more likely to seek help than students who attributed their poor performance to lack of ability, the difficulty of the exam, or the instructor. After studying this chapter, you will be able to:

- improve your attention and concentration;
- select or modify study environments;
- work more effectively in groups;
- prepare for and benefit from meetings with tutors and instructors.

WHAT ARE THE COSTS OF TASK SWITCHING?

Multitasking: Performing two tasks that require conscious processing simultaneously, switching from one task to another, or performing the tasks in rapid succession.

Task Switching: The brain switching back and forth while performing two or more complex tasks.

Have you kept up with social media while sitting in a lecture, sent several texts while doing homework, or played a game while listening to your instructor's taped lecture? If so, you have engaged in mental juggling known as **multitasking**, or really **task switching**, and often noted as the number one killer of productivity. Though it is possible to juggle several tasks at once if they are simple and do not require the same mental resources, such as walking and listening to music, switching between more complex tasks that require conscious processing is simply not possible. Try this experiment. Start writing, on a computer or paper, about your day. As you get into the groove, start reciting the alphabet backward. Can you do both tasks at the same time? Instead of multitasking, what in fact happens is quick switching between tasks that may seem like you are performing them simultaneously—but you are really not (Kirschner & De Bruyckere, 2017). In essence, if you believe you are "good at multitasking," you have developed an ability to quickly switch between multiple tasks—but that comes with a price of lowered productivity and performance. In fact, even walking and talking on the cell phone depletes our attentional resources. Researchers (Hyman et al., 2009) found that cell phone users walked slower, changed directions more frequently, and were less likely to notice a unicycling clown than individuals who walked while listening to music, without electronics, or talking to each other. Seventy-five percent of folks on their cells were blind to the fact that there was a unicycling clown complete with a vivid purple and yellow outfit, large shoes, and a bright red nose! Remember our discussion of the Information Processing System and the limitation of our working memory? Recall that current estimates place the capacity limit of working memory at 4±1 units of information. No wonder, therefore, that we are only able to pay adequate attention to one task at a time. Whether you are a "digital native" who grew up task switching or not, we all have "information-processing bottlenecks" in the brain (Kirschner & van Merriënboer, 2013). Recent research (as cited by Kirschner & De Bruyckere, 2017) demonstrates that in addition to reducing performance, continuously switching between tasks may result in long-term loss of ability to focus on a single task, loss of ability to ignore distractions, and even affect brain development.

So what are the costs of task switching? First, although it may take only a few seconds or even milliseconds per task switch, these small increments of time add up quickly. There are estimates that shifting between tasks can cost up to 40 percent of productive time (Rubinstein, Meyer, & Evans, 2001). Second, when you switch between tasks, you make more mistakes than if you engage in one task at a time.

The prevalence of technology in our daily lives has brought about the new phenomenon of media multitasking. We know that distractions are readily available and our recommendation is clear: when it comes to academic work, focus on monotasking, not multitasking!

IS THERE A DIFFERENCE BETWEEN ATTENTION AND CONCENTRATION?

Related to the topic of multitasking is the discussion of the differences between attention and concentration. Although these terms are often used interchangeably, there is a slight difference in meaning. **Attention** is a selective process that controls awareness of events in the environment. During the discussion of the information-processing system (Chapter 3), we pointed out that the nature of attention determines the stimuli that are processed or neglected. Because of our limitations in attention span and ability to focus on a stimulus, it is necessary to constantly refocus on the stimulus or message.

Attention: A selective process that controls awareness of events in the environment.

Concentration is the term used to identify the continual refocusing on a perceived stimulus or message. Note that *focus* is the key word identifying attention and *refocus* is the key word identifying concentration (Wolff & Marsnik, 1992). Multitasking and task switching, in essence, is the antithesis of concentration.

Concentration: The process of continual refocusing on a perceived stimulus or message.

Chapter 3 discussed the key to learning as attention. Information cannot be acquired unless one is attentive. Unfortunately, many students are not aware when they are not paying attention. Aside from switching between different tasks, have you ever caught yourself daydreaming as you turned pages in a textbook and realized that you did not recall anything you read? Have you tried to study but had so many things on your mind that it was impossible to accomplish anything? If you answered yes to any of these questions, you will benefit from the information in this chapter.

EXERCISE 7.1: SELF-OBSERVATION: EVALUATING STUDY ENVIRONMENTS

Directions: The purpose of this exercise is to help you identify your best study environment. You may study in many different locations: your residence hall room, apartment, home, fraternity, sorority, athletic study hall, or library. Identify two or three different study locations that you have used to study this term and rate your behavior in each location on a five-point scale. Identify the location by writing it next to the letters A, B, or C. Complete your ratings by writing in the number 1, 2, 3, 4, or 5 for each location.

A:

B:

C:

1	2	3	4	5
Very descriptive of my behavior		Moderately descriptive of my behavior		Not at all descriptive of my behavior

Behavior	Locations		
	A	B	C
1. I begin studying immediately.			
2. I study with little interruption from others.			
3. I avoid spending time on my phone (talking, texting).			
4. I avoid spending time daydreaming or sleeping.			
5. I find the temperature conditions satisfactory.			
6. I find the chair, table, and lighting satisfactory.			
7. I concentrate on what needs to be accomplished.			
8. I take the appropriate number and length of breaks to maintain concentration.			
9. I return to studying immediately after my breaks.			
10. I attain my study goals.			
Average Rating			

Average your ratings for each of the locations you rated. The lower the score, the better you rated the location. Which location did you rate the best? Is the information consistent with your perceptions? How can you make use of the information in this exercise? Do you need to alter or change your study environment? If so, what changes might you make?

_____

_____

_____

_____

WHAT FACTORS INFLUENCE ATTENTION AND CONCENTRATION?

Students have difficulty concentrating on tasks because of both external and internal distracters. External distracters are environmental sources of interference (e.g., noise, such as the TV), interruptions (e.g., phone calls and texts), uncomfortable study areas (e.g., clothes and books piled all over the room), and disruptive roommates. Internal distracters refer to sources of interference from within, such as irrelevant thoughts (e.g., "I forgot to return my library books today"), worry (e.g., "I don't know if I can learn this material"), physiological and emotional distress (e.g., headache), and daydreaming (e.g., thinking about next weekend's party).

EXERCISE 7.2: SELF-OBSERVATION: BECOMING AWARE OF MISDIRECTED ATTENTION

It is important to identify the types of distracters that tend to interfere with attention (Ottens, 1991). Think about academic situations in the present or past where your attention was misdirected. In the following table, identify the situation and type of distraction. Consider the following questions: Do your distractions tend to be more internal or external? Do your distractions tend to occur in certain situations (e.g., tests or lectures) or locations (e.g., studying at home or school or in the library)?

Where Attention Got Misdirected	Type of Distraction (Internal or External)

■

EXERCISE 7.3: SELF-OBSERVATION: BECOMING AWARE OF YOUR LISTENING HABITS

Directions: Assess your current listening habits by checking the appropriate response to each of the following statements. Write a summary statement about how often you find yourself engaging in these ten bad listening habits (adapted from Robertson, 1994).

	Always	Sometimes	Never
Calling the subject matter uninteresting and not paying attention			
Criticizing the speaker's delivery (e.g., accent) or mannerisms and not listening to the message			
Getting over-stimulated by something the speaker says (e.g., disagreeing with something the speaker says and no longer listening to the speaker)			
Listening primarily for discrete facts and missing the overall take-home message of the speaker's presentation			
Trying to outline everything that is being said rather than listening to the main points			

Faking attention to the speaker

Creating or allowing interfering distractions

Ignoring difficult material and only listening to points that
are easy to comprehend ("the principle of least effort")

Daydreaming

Comments:

HOW CAN I IMPROVE MY ATTENTION AND CONCENTRATION?

You will be better able to enhance your concentration if you deal with known distracters before you begin studying, reading, or listening to a lecture; adopt strategies that encourage concentration; monitor your concentration as you study; and deal with distractions when they occur. Aside from improving concentration, removing distractions is also important for reducing the tendency to procrastinate. When distractions abound, it is easy to replace your intention to begin the task you have been putting off with an attractive distraction, such as checking out a funny video your friend sent you instead of starting the draft for your final paper. Table 7.1 contains a list of suggestions to help you manage both external and internal distractions. In addition, you can use technology and apps to improve concentration and boost productivity. Remember the discussion about the Pomodoro technique where work is broken into focused blocks of time, separated by a short, usually five-minute break? This strategy allows your mind to stay fresh, complete tasks quicker—and be more productive.

TABLE 7.1

Improving Attention and Concentration

Carefully determine when you will study in your time-management plan.	If you get tired late in the evening, don't schedule study times when you are likely to be tired or don't attempt to study during your dinner hour.
Monitor daydreaming.	Make a checkmark on a notepad whenever you catch yourself daydreaming. Monitoring concentration can help keep you on task.
Deal with boredom.	Alternate different subjects when you study. Take study breaks at least every 50 minutes or so.
Instead of worrying, take action.	Talk to the instructor or teaching assistant about course issues or problems, find a tutor, call your girlfriend or boyfriend to resolve a recent disagreement before you begin studying.
Monitor concentration.	Constantly ask yourself questions like: "Did I understand what I just read?" "Am I beginning to daydream?" "Am I trying to understand the lecture?"
Use self-reminders or self-directives.	"You're starting to worry again about your test performance, just relax and get back to the question" or "I better start asking myself questions because I didn't understand what I just read."
Set goals.	"I want to complete chapter 4 this evening and answer all questions in the study manual."
Have a set start and end time.	Instead of setting aside an entire night to study, set time limits. You will be more productive as you have a deadline.
Manage your time.	"I need to find three hours in my study plan this week to research library material for my paper."
Take breaks.	Take a ten-minute break at least for every 50 minutes of study or work longer if you can maintain your concentration.
Use active learning strategies.	Write and answer questions, outline, or summarize material. When listening in class, determine the main points and distinguish them from supporting details. Remain active by taking effective notes. Make mental summaries as you listen.

EXERCISE 7.4: DEALING WITH DISTRACTERS

For each of the following situations, identify the type of distracter by placing an I (for internal) or an E (for external) in the space provided. Next, refer to the suggestions in the previous section on ways to improve concentration and recommend how each student could improve his or her concentration.

1. Alicia is about to study for her history exam when her roommate comes rushing in to tell her about her date for Saturday night.
   Recommendation:

   _____

2. While Tony is working on his calculus assignment, he remembers that he forgot to deposit money in his checking account and his tuition check will bounce.
   Recommendation:

   _____

3. While Ralph is taking notes in his biology class, workers start drilling outside the window of the lecture hall.
   Recommendation:

   _____

4. Each time Carole starts studying for her French exam, she is reminded of her low quiz scores and wonders if she is going to pass the course.
   Recommendation:

   _____

5. As Mary is reading her economics text, she realizes that she turned five pages and does not remember one thing she read.
   Recommendation:

   _____

6. Alex has trouble concentrating when his professor starts talking too fast. He gets frustrated with the professor and stops taking notes.
   Recommendation:

   _____

7. Felicia starts studying at about 10 p.m. and soon finds she is too tired to complete her history assignment for the next day.
   Recommendation:

   _____
   _____
   _____

Student Reflections

I was never one to receive help in high school. If I could not understand subject matter, I just told myself that it was too complex for me. I thought that students who sought extra help in subjects they did not understand were people who were "teachers' pets." I often believed them—that they were too concerned with their academic learning. I reasoned that these types of students developed into nerds, because they did nothing but study. My fear was that if I gained extra help I would become one of them too.

Table 7.2 summarizes the procedures for monitoring and dealing with attention and concentration problems.

HOW DO I SEEK ACADEMIC HELP?

Help-seeking is unique among learning strategies because students may feel that it implies that they are incapable of completing an academic task without assistance, which can be threatening to self-worth. As a result, many college students fail to seek needed help, considering it embarrassing, an admission of defeat, and something to be avoided whenever possible (Karabenick & Dembo, 2011).

There is substantial evidence, however, that more resourceful and proactive learners are more, rather than less, likely to seek help when needed (Karabenick, 1998; Karabenick & Knapp, 1991; Karabenick & Newman, 2011; Zimmerman & Martinez-Pons, 1990). For those students, seeking help is considered preferable to stoically maintaining their independence.

Almost 30 years ago, in an interesting investigation, Karabenick and Knapp (1991) illustrated the concern that students have about having to ask for help. Many colleges offer courses that are taken online without direct interaction with an instructor. This type of learning can have a direct influence in reducing the concern of appearing less competent when seeking help. The learner can have anonymity. As a result, he or she can receive help without the instructor or classmates knowing

TABLE 7.2
Procedures for Monitoring and Dealing with Attention and Concentration Problems

Procedures	Examples
Review your time-management plan and determine which tasks you will attend to during each study session.	"I need to read and study two chapters in my psychology textbook today."
Before you begin studying, determine whether there are any distracters that may influence your concentration.	"I have one internal and one external distracter that will interfere with my reading. My two roommates are playing videogames and I must call my mother and wish her a happy birthday."
If a distracter is present, determine whether it is internal or external and refer to the list of strategies to deal with it. If no distracter is present, begin using strategies that encourage concentration.	"I'll go to the library tonight to study and call my mother before I leave."
Monitor concentration as you study.	"I have turned two pages but don't remember what I read."
If attention gets misdirected, refer to the list of strategies to maintain concentration. If concentration is broken, maintain your use of learning strategies and take short breaks during the study session.	"I better start asking myself questions so I can maintain my focus on the material."
At the end of the study session, make a check next to each task that you completed in your time-management plan.	"OK, I'm finished with my math problems and research for my anthropology paper. What's next on my list?"

who is asking for and receiving help. In this research study, one group of learners received help from a computer program and another group from an assistant. More than twice as many students requested help from the computer (86 percent) than from the assistant (36 percent). The knowledge that another person (even though the learners never met the person) was providing the help was apparently sufficient to reduce help-seeking.

Earlier in the chapter, we presented research to indicate that students who perceive themselves as academically competent and who feel in control of their academic success are more likely to seek help. The paradox is that students who need the most help are often the least likely to obtain it. Students who are comfortable with and capable of eliciting help from others are often able to solve their problems and, in addition, acquire greater knowledge of how to obtain help in the future.

Newman (1991) provides some good advice about seeking help. He identified a sequence of decisions and actions that play an important role in both help-seeking and the self-regulation of learning:

- *Awareness of a Need for Help.* The student is aware that knowledge is lacking or comprehension is incomplete. Awareness is a key factor in both seeking and benefiting from help. Individuals are not likely to seek help if they do not know what they do not understand. You should not wait to be jolted by a low exam score or poor grade on a paper to decide that you need help. Instead, you should evaluate your understanding of the content in each of your courses on a regular basis throughout the semester.
- *Decision to Seek Help Rather Than Taking Alternative Actions.* When some students realize they are in trouble, they head for the registrar's office to drop a course rather than consider alternative strategies such as obtaining a tutor, joining a study group, or meeting with the instructor or teaching assistant. At times, many self-regulated learners have academic difficulties. However, they learn how to use the services and resources available to them. Are you aware of the services provided by your college or university? Do you have a learning center for academic assistance? Are tutoring services available?
- *Decision Regarding the Type of Help to Seek.* Some problems can be solved by seeking non-social assistance. For example, students in math or science courses can benefit from purchasing review books that provide numerous opportunities to solve different types of problems or locating reputable online sources. They can also borrow other textbooks from the library that explain information in different ways.
- *Decision Regarding the Target Person from Whom to Seek Help.* The target person could be a friend, study group, professor, or tutor. Keep in mind that you're not limited to one source of help. Ask yourself: How soon do I need the help? Who is most likely to provide help in the shortest time frame? Who is most competent in providing the help?
- *Employment of a Help-Seeking Strategy.* Prepare before you meet with the person who can help you. First, determine what it is that you do not understand about the material. Second, make an appointment (if possible) with your tutor, teaching assistant, or instructor. Third, carefully review the content and make a list of the specific questions you want answered at the meeting. Categorize the different problems you have trouble solving (e.g., underline foreign language passages that you have trouble translating or list terms that you don't understand). You will benefit more from these sessions if you are prepared for the meeting. It is not acceptable to walk into a session and say something like: "I don't get it" or "I don't know what is going on in this course." Many times, you will spend more time *preparing* for a productive session than you spend with the person in the session.
- *Processing of the Help.* Good notes should be taken concerning the advice obtained so they can be referred to after the session. You may wish to record the session using your smartphone if the instructor is open to it so you can listen and think during the session instead of writing. Consider the advice you received when you sought help in terms of how it could change your learning and study behavior for the remainder of the course. What did

you learn that could be applied to new chapters or units in the course? What are some immediate changes you should make to improve your performance in the course? How can you best keep pace with the new material in the course?

Newman's suggestions help you deal with any fear or anxiety caused by seeking help. The key is to develop a plan of action. By the way, when contacting your professor, err on the side of being formal. In her first years of teaching, the first author would periodically get emails that started with "Hey, Helena." You can guess that these relationships did not get off on the right foot. It is always safest to call your professor "Professor" until they tell you otherwise, start your emails with "Dear Professor" and write using full words and sentences rather than act as if you were texting.

WHAT MOTIVES DO STUDENTS HAVE FOR COMMUNICATING WITH THEIR INSTRUCTORS?

Martin, Myers, and Mottet (1999) have identified five motives students have for communicating with their instructors: relational, functional, excuse-making, participation, and sycophancy. They explain the motives behind each of the communication purposes as follows:

> When students communicate in order to *relate*, they are trying to develop personal relationships with their instructors. Communicating for *functional* reasons includes learning more about the material and the assignments in the course. Students also communicate to offer *excuses*, attempting to explain why work is late or missing or to challenge grading criteria. A fourth reason students have for communicating is for *participation*. Students want to demonstrate to their instructors that they are interested in the class and that they understand the material. A fifth reason is *sycophancy*, which involves getting on the instructor's good side. Students may communicate in order to make a favorable impression or to get the instructor's approval.
>
> **(Martin et al., 1999, p. 159)**

What are the different motives that influence you to interact with your instructors? Review the description of the five motives and provide examples for how you communicated with a high school or college instructor. Your second author used the participation motive when he took classes where the instructor included student participation as part of the grading in the course. Your first author can remember focusing on the relational motive when she wanted to obtain recommendations from his instructors. There is no one best way to communicate. Instead, there are different reasons or motives to interact with instructors, and in any given academic year, you might be influenced by all or most of the motives.

HOW CAN I ESTABLISH EFFECTIVE RELATIONSHIPS WITH INSTRUCTORS?

It is important to have good relationships with your professors, especially those that teach in your major. Before you know it, you will be needing recommendation letters for employment or graduate school. Though you clearly need professors as discussed previously, it is helpful to understand what they need from you. Anderson and Carta-Falsa (2002) found that both students and instructors desire an "open, supportive, comfortable, respectful, safe or non-threatening, and enjoyable interpersonal climate" (p. 136). What can you do to go about establishing such a relationship? First, you might want to get to know your professor by searching the school's faculty directory. Being a professor is usually more than a job; it's who they are in the professional sense. Your professor likely dedicated somewhere between seven and ten years to become an expert in their field. Show an interest in their work! Some professors also discuss their hobbies in the bio—you might even find that you have similar interests and experiences! Second, use the syllabus to determine if the professor has regular office hours or only schedules meetings by appointment. The meetings can take place in person or online. Third, make an appointment. Approaching a professor before or after class without an appointment may not be effective as you do not know their schedule. Fourth, show up on time to your appointment or if you have to cancel, give adequate notice if possible. You can start the appointment by telling the professor your "agenda": the items you'd like to discuss such as clarifying a specific aspect of a theory (i.e., functional motive), getting to know them better (i.e., relational motive), or other reasons. It helps to look organized and to the point. By the way, if your goal is to discuss a grade (i.e., functional motive), it goes without saying that you want to leave your attitude at the door. Trust us on that one. Generally, the best approach is to ask the professor for guidance on how to do better on the next test. If you have a constructive attitude and are not perceived to be "grade lawyering," they might even give you an opportunity to earn more points on the test you came to discuss! In summary, aim to create a respectful and enjoyable relationship with as many professors as you can.

HOW CAN I WORK MORE EFFECTIVELY IN GROUPS?

Each semester, when we introduce a group project, one or two students will ask to work individually because of negative experiences with group projects. Many students do not realize that it is difficult to escape from team involvement in the workplace. That is to say, it is unlikely that one would approach his or her supervisor and ask: "Can I work on a project by myself?"

Recently, the second author had an opportunity to teach an educational psychology course to training specialists working for some of the most successful computer companies in the country. During a discussion in class, the students mentioned that their companies had no difficulty hiring bright mathematicians, scientists, or computer specialists. Their problem was that while there was a heavy reliance on team-based projects, some of their personnel did not function well in group settings. As a result of problems in interpersonal relations, there are often delays in completing projects.

One of the most productive sources of social support is working in learning or study groups. Reports from studies indicate that cooperative learning can promote higher academic achievement, higher level thinking skills, and greater ability to transfer learning from one situation to another (Johnson, Johnson, & Smith, 2013). Group learning, though, should not replace studying and reflecting on your own. An effective way to use group work is to first study on your own and then use group work to test each other's knowledge and work through challenging material together. Listening, speaking, teaching, and testing each other are effective ways to determine what you understand and if you have any gaps in understanding. Groups can meet in person or online, making getting together in a group very convenient. Table 7.3 presents some recommended procedures for forming and studying in groups (Frender, 1990). The following are examples of how one student found different ways to use cooperative learning in different classes.

Student Reflections

During the course of the semester, I have found group studying to be an essential part of my success in my different classes. The following are examples of how I have used group study this semester:

- Before a test in biology, I met with two friends to review the material for the exam. We heard that the professor's exams came straight from his lectures. Therefore, we basically went straight through the notes and discussed what was presented each day. As we proceeded, we learned some information from each other that we did not have in our notes. Also, discussing the material helped us learn it more thoroughly.
- There are practicals in my biology laboratory in which students are required to identify different things seen in the lab and perform different tasks learned in lab throughout

the semester. I studied in a group for my practical so we could quiz each other. We used pictures and drew diagrams and asked each other to label them. We wrote down different procedures learned in lab as we discussed how we did them. Most important, we discussed the reasons behind each activity that occurred during the lab.

- In chemistry, there are many problems that must be done after reading a chapter to prepare for a test. My friends and I usually read the chapter by ourselves, then get together to do the problems. This way, if we don't understand something, we can ask each other and get help solving the problems. This procedure speeds up the learning process because we don't need to go back and refer to the chapter as much.

- In math, I meet with my friends to discuss problems that we couldn't solve individually. The individual who solved a problem correctly explains to the rest of the group how he or she did it.

- In my English course, I get together with one of my friends to read each other's papers. Usually after I write a paper, it is hard for me to identify my own errors. When someone else reads it, he can tell me what parts he doesn't understand and what needs improvement so I can make the necessary adjustments.

TABLE 7.3

Procedures for Forming and Studying in Groups

Notice who is in your class. Identify two, three, or four interested students. Contact the students to arrange a meeting time and place.

At the first session:

- Exchange names and phone numbers.
- Conduct an overview of the subject matter.
- Discuss each member's particular interest in a topic.
- Assign each member an equal number of text pages or notes to lead the discussion of each topic in the course.
- Discuss possible test questions.

Before you end the first meeting:

- Make sure every member has a clear set of goals for the next session.
- Be certain that each member understands his or her particular assignment.
- Discuss any problems that occurred during the first session.

At the second meeting, discuss the content and begin testing each other. (Smaller groups may begin testing each other during the first meeting if they complete their planning over the phone or in person before the meeting.) Identify topics or sections of the content that the group had difficulty understanding. Decide how the group members can obtain additional help, if needed (e.g., one group member may contact the instructor or teaching assistant to answer questions, another member may decide to research a question or topic in greater depth).

HOW CAN I HELP MAKE MY STUDY GROUP MORE PRODUCTIVE?

Social Loafing: The tendency of individual group members to reduce their work effort as groups increase in size.

Not all group experiences are as positive as the examples identified in the student reflection section. Although common wisdom would state that many hands make light work, research has demonstrated that quite the contrary can occur. One of the problems that emerges in group work is social loafing. **Social loafing** refers to the finding that individuals exert less effort when their efforts are combined than when they are considered individually (Latané et al., 1979). Why does that occur? Classic research by Latané et al. (1979) demonstrates that when individuals pool their efforts, their individual contributions are less noticeable and thus they, unlike individuals that perform solo, are able to "hide in the crowd." Being less noticeable, these individuals experience less pressure to work hard. Latané conducted interesting experiments that illustrated the phenomenon of social loafing. In one experiment, he compared two variations of the cheering task. In one setting, people sat in a circle around a single microphone. When groups cheered, only an overall sound level could be measured and each person's contribution was non-identifiable. Latané observed that the more people were in the group, the less effort each participant invested in cheering. However, when each person had an individualized microphone on a headset and a sound level reading could be taken for each person, there was no social loafing effect.

You have probably experienced working in group settings where a few students do most of the work while everyone gets the credit. It can be infuriating and discourage you from ever wanting to work at a task as a group again. However, as mentioned previously, not working as a group may not be an option. So what can you do to avoid social loafing as you are engaged in group work? The following are specific conditions that can be set in place to ensure that everyone contributes.

Ensure Group Size Stays within Four to Six Students

The bigger the group, the more likely social loafing.

Make Each Group Participant Identifiable

As stated in Table 7.3, it is important to conduct introductions at the very first meeting so that people are less likely to feel that they can hide in the crowd. In a bigger group (over six people), it may also be wise to have everyone wear nametags for the first few meetings to further reduce the potential for social loafing.

Make Each Group Participant Accountable

It is important that each group member leaves each meeting with a specific, individual set of goals. Ideally, each group member should have an assigned role with corresponding responsibilities. When a group member feels that his or her individual contribution is indispensable, social loafing will diminish.

Offer Incentives for Good Individual Performance

Offering formal acknowledgment where appropriate can inspire a group member to work hard and keep from loafing. Even offering informal, simple social rewards such as expressing liking and approval for individual performance can result in the greater expenditure of effort.

HOW CAN I IMPROVE MY COMMUNICATION SKILLS?

Sending Messages Effectively

One of the most important functioning skills in group dynamics is learning how to send messages effectively. Johnson (2003) identified some key skills for this purpose:

Clearly "own" your message by (a) using personal pronouns such as I, me, and my, and (b) letting others know what your thoughts and feelings are. You "disown" your messages when you use expressions such as: "most people," "some people," and "our group," making it difficult to tell whether you really think and feel what you are saying or are simply repeating the thoughts and feelings of others.

Describe the other person's behavior without including any judgment, evaluation, or inferences about the person's motives, personality, or attitudes. When reacting to the behavior of other people, be sure to describe their behavior ("You keep interrupting me") rather than evaluating it and communicating character flaws ("You're a rotten, self-centered egotist who won't listen to anyone else's ideas").

Describe the ways the relationship can be changed to improve the quality and quantity of interaction among the individuals involved. To maintain and improve a relationship, the quality of the relationship needs to be discussed and reflected on periodically.

Make the message appropriate to the receiver's frame of reference. This same information will be explained differently to an expert in the field than to a novice, to a child than to an adult, or to your boss than to a coworker.

Ask for feedback concerning the ways your messages are being received. To communicate effectively, you must be aware of how the receiver is interpreting and processing your messages. The only way to be sure is to seek feedback continually as to what meanings the receiver is attaching to your messages.

Describe your feelings by name, action, or figure of speech. When communicating your feelings, it is especially important to be descriptive. You may describe your feelings by name ("I feel sad"), by actions ("I feel like crying"), or by figures of speech ("I feel down in the dumps").

Use nonverbal messages to communicate your feelings. Nonverbal messages are very powerful but inherently ambiguous. When people cry, for example, it may be because they are sad, happy, angry, or even afraid. When utilized with verbal messages, however, nonverbal messages clarify, strengthen, enrich, emphasize, and frame the message.

Make your verbal and nonverbal messages congruent with each other. Every face-to-face communication involves both verbal and nonverbal messages. Usually these messages are congruent, so by smiling and expressing warmth nonverbally, a person can be saying that she has appreciated your help. Communication problems arise when a person's verbal and nonverbal messages are contradictory; if a person says, "Here is some information that may be of help to you," with a sneer and in a mocking tone of voice, the meaning you receive is confused by the two different messages being sent simultaneously.

Be redundant. Repeating your message more than once and using more than one channel of communication (such as pictures and written messages, as well as verbal and non-verbal cues) will help the receiver understand your messages.

(Johnson, 2003, pp. 132–133)

I-Messages: Assertive statement that focuses on the sender's needs and feelings, rather than the traits and behaviors of the receiver, in order to raise the odds another person can hear you clearly.

One very effective way of clarifying for yourself and the other person just what you are feeling when you have difficult negative feelings is to do it through **I-messages** (Gordon, 2001). This type of communication is called an I-message because the focus is on you and the message is about yourself. This is in contrast to a You-message, which focuses on and gives a message about the other person. Compare the two statements below and determine which one you think will be received more effectively by the other person:

- One roommate to another: "You need to put your books and papers away from the table after you finish doing your homework!"
- One roommate to another: "When you leave your books and papers on the table after you finish your homework, I feel very frustrated because I cannot find enough room to do my homework."

We think you agree that the first, You-message, lays blame, conveys criticism, and is in essence a verbal attack that is likely to put the other person immediately on the defensive. The second, I-message, on the other hand, focuses on the sender, not the other person, does not assign blame but simply expresses how the sender feels. The essence of the You-message is "You have a problem" while the essence of an I-message is "I have a problem."

There are three parts to an I-message:

- Part 1: State the feelings that the behavior produces for you "I feel very frustrated ..."
- Part 2: Describe the behavior which is interfering with you "when you leave your books and papers on the table after you finish your homework ..."
- Part 3: State the consequence "because I cannot find enough room to do my homework."

You may conclude the I-message by telling the other person what you want and what you prefer they do. For example, in the instance addressed here you may simply wish to say something like "Please clean up after yourself!" Very often, though, the receiving individual is likely to figure out what you want to see happen and you do not need to state it.

There are some common mistakes that undercut the effectiveness of an I-message. For example, you may be sending a disguised You-message ("I feel that you are a jerk!") and therefore communicating a judgment instead of a feeling. Also, when your non-verbal body language contradicts your words (for example, smiling when you are irritated), the I-message will likely not be effective.

RECEIVING MESSAGES EFFECTIVELY

One of the most important skills in receiving messages involves giving feedback about the message in ways that clarify and encourage the continuation of discussion. Gordon (2001) provided some helpful information when he encouraged listeners to become **active listeners**. This means letting others know that we recognize the feelings behind what they are saying. Read the following possible dialogue between you and a friend. Which comment do you think will gain the most response from your friend? Why?

> **Active Listeners:** A type of communication in which the listener summarizes and paraphrases what he or she has heard from another individual so the individual feels that he or she has been understood.

Friend: "That was the worst test I ever took."
You: "Don't worry about it. Let's get a pizza!"
Friend: "That was the worst test I ever took."
You: "You are really upset about the test."

Gordon believes that the second dialogue would most likely encourage greater dialogue, because you attempt to communicate that you understand your friend's feelings. Active listening involves recognizing the feelings and meaning of others, and then restating this meaning so others feel understood and accepted. This type of listening provides a sort of mirror for the person to see himself or herself more clearly.

Many individuals do not use active listening. Instead, they want to give advice as to what others should do about their situation without recognizing feelings. In fact, in some families, students grow up without being able to openly express their feelings. Here's an example:

Student: "I can't complete all the work demanded in my courses."
Parent: "I have many pressures in my job, too. I wish I was in college and all I had to think about was my courses!"

Is this the type of response that will encourage you to discuss your feelings, or is it more likely to encourage you to walk away or change the topic? Think about your closest friends. Are they more likely to recognize your feelings than other individuals in your life? If you were the student's parent, what type of active listening response would you give? Remember, don't start by trying to give advice.

The following are other examples of active listening:

Message: "I can't complete all the work demanded in my courses."
Response: "You seem upset about your course work."
Message: "I can't believe it that my boyfriend [or girlfriend] said that I was an inconsiderate person!"
Response: "Sounds like your boyfriend [or girlfriend] really hurt you."
Message: "I finally made the dean's list."
Response: "You seem proud of yourself. Way to go!"

As you can see from these examples, the responses reflect back the meaning of the message in a clear manner. The listener focuses on the feeling expressed and avoids trying to solve problems for others. This strategy helps to confirm and validate an individual's feelings, as well as to set the stage for any necessary problem solving by getting individuals to discuss the reasons behind their feelings. Try using active listening with a member of your class, close friend, or parent, and evaluate the nature of your communication with this individual.

Chapter Review

KEY POINTS

1 Self-regulated learners restructure their physical and social environments to improve their learning.
2 Multitasking by switching between many tasks that require cognitive resources is not possible due to working memory limitations. Task switching causes us to make errors and take longer to complete tasks.
3 Self-regulation of one's social environment relates to the ability to determine when one needs to work alone or with others; to seek help when needed from instructors, tutors, or peers; or to seek help from non-social sources (e.g., textbooks and reference materials).
4 Students may lack the self-regulation to overcome environmental distractions, anxiety, or competing emotional or physical needs.
5 Motivational beliefs and perceptions account for individual differences in the willingness and ability to control one's physical and social environment.
6 Students have difficulty concentrating on tasks because of external and internal distracters.
7 Social loafing is a significant problem that emerges in group work settings. There are specific procedures for forming groups and reducing the potential of social loafing that make group work an effective process.
8 Students have different motives for communicating with their instructors. These motives include relational, functional, participation, excuse-making, and sycophancy.
9 Students can improve their communication skills by learning how to send and receive messages more effectively.
10 Learning how to send I-messages and become an active listener can improve communication with others.

FOLLOW-UP ACTIVITIES

1. Use the Self-Regulation Process to Improve Attention and Concentration

Complete the following self-study during a period of two to three weeks. Your report should include each of the following processes and should be approximately five to eight typed pages in length. See Appendix B for detailed information on how to conduct a self-regulation study.

Self-Observation and Evaluation. What problem(s) do I have regarding attention and concentration? What are the symptoms of my problem (i.e., when, where, and how often does my problem occur)? Do I multitask and task switch? If so, how often? How much of an impact does this problem have on my academic performance? What factors (e.g., beliefs, perceptions, feelings, physiological responses, or behaviors) contribute to this problem? What do I need to change to reduce or eliminate my problem(s)?

Goal Setting and Strategic Planning. What are my goals? What strategies can I use to reduce distracters and maintain concentration? When will I use these strategies? How will I record my progress?

Strategy Implementation and Monitoring. What strategies did I use to improve my attention and concentration? When did I use these strategies? What method(s) did I use to record my progress (e.g., documents, charts, logs, tally sheets, checklists, or recordings)? When did I use these methods? How and when did I monitor my progress to determine if my new plan was working? What changes, if any, did I make along the way?

Strategic-Outcome Monitoring.   Did I attain the goal I set for myself? Have the modifications in my attention and concentration improved my academic performance or personal life? What strategies were the most and least effective? What changes, if any, do I need to make in the future?

2. Assess Group Dynamics

Use the procedures for forming and studying in groups discussed in this chapter and evaluate the effectiveness of one of your study groups. Make recommendations on how your group could function more effectively.

3. Visit with an Instructor

Newman (1991) identified a sequence of decisions and actions that play an important role in both help-seeking and self-regulation of learning. Use Newman's suggestions discussed in this chapter to meet with one of your instructors. Write a summary of how you used his or her recommendations and evaluate the effectiveness of the meeting.

4. Create an I-Message

Instead of attacking the other person as described in the You-message below, create an I-message with its three parts.

You-message:

When you did not show up last night, you ruined our plans for studying! This is such an important exam, how could you?

I-message:

5. Practice Active Listening

The following is a series of statements made by our college students. Provide responses to each statement that demonstrate active listening responses:

1 This course sucks!
     Response:
2 I don't know how I will ever finish this term paper.
     Response:
3 I can't believe my girlfriend left me!
     Response:
4 I'm so tired, I can't study any longer.
     Response:
5 My instructor must think I am an idiot by asking me such an easy question.
     Response:
6 It doesn't matter how much I try, I can't get higher than a C in my writing course.
     Response:

Answers to Exercise 7.4

1. E   2. I   3. E   4. I   5. I   6. E   7. I

Part 4

Learning and Study Strategies

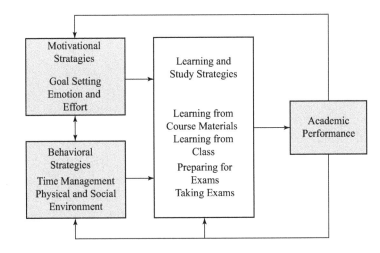

This unit includes four chapters focusing on important study strategies used to learn, remember, prepare, and take exams. One of the important ideas presented in this unit is that preparation for exams begins when students first take notes or read the first chapter on a topic. Exam preparation should not begin when an instructor announces an exam! The manner in which one takes notes and reads textbooks determines how much information is learned and remembered. Therefore, the more content one understands and remembers while moving from one topic to another in a course, the easier it is to prepare and perform successfully in an exam.

It is often difficult to make up for ineffective learning by studying. Reviewing incomplete information, confusing theories, or improper procedures for solving problems generally leads to less than satisfactory results on examinations. At times, intensive studying or cramming can help students get through certain exams that simply require regurgitation of basic material. However, as questions become more complex and require a greater understanding of the material, it is more difficult to succeed without using effective learning and study strategies.

An important issue to consider is motivation. What is the goal in taking a course and learning its content? Is it simply to get through the material or learn it? If the goal is to master the material, cramming is not an efficient study strategy. Ask yourself: "How much of the material do I understand? Could I adequately explain the content to others and answer questions about it?"

Another important idea emphasized in this unit is that reading or taking notes and remembering are two separate activities. Just because one reads a textbook or takes notes does not mean that he or she will remember what was read or written down. Additional steps are needed to ensure the material learned is remembered. These steps involve the use of elaboration and organization strategies to move information into long-term memory (Cortina et al., 1992).

A final point before beginning the unit. There are common learning strategies used in both learning from class and textbooks that should be undertaken before, during, and after each learning session. These strategies make the difference in how information is learned and remembered, whether you are learning from traditional or e-textbooks, live lectures or pre-recorded ones. The strategies involve preparing for learning, paying attention to specific signals provided by a lecturer and author to identify main ideas, keeping track of main ideas, and identifying organizational patterns within the material (Pauk, 1993). Many of the same learning strategies used to learn and remember material in textbooks apply to learning by lectures and vice versa. Remember that individuals learn best when they recognize or impose patterns of organization on content rather than studying isolated bits and pieces of information.

8 Learning from Course Materials

Your courses are likely to include different materials: traditional textbooks, e-textbooks, PowerPoints, articles, and videos. We will dedicate the majority of this chapter to processing information from the most traditional source, textbooks. Textbooks can be either traditional printed ones or e-textbooks. At the end of the chapter, we discuss effective ways of learning from video captured lectures and PowerPoint slides as well. The majority of strategies for effective learning from textbooks work well for learning from other sources as well. The key, as we will discuss, is to become actively involved with the material before, during, and after.

Individuals spend a good deal of time reading throughout their lives. They read for enjoyment, relaxation, or knowledge. As a result, they often read differently depending on the purpose for reading. For example, students do not read a college textbook the same way they read popular websites, magazines, or best-sellers. Have you ever watched people read a magazine or review their favorite news outlet on their smartphone? How often do you see them taking notes on what they read? For the most part, these individuals do not care about how much they remember, because they do not expect to be tested on the material. Yet, because of their interest in the material, they often remember a great deal of what they read. College students are expected to read and remember material in courses whether or not they are interested in the content or believe it has any relevance to their future occupational goals. Success in different courses depends on learning to use effective reading strategies for a variety of college textbooks.

For example, let's assume you were expected to read a chapter on social psychology for a quiz in class. Please read the passage below, using any helpful strategies you currently know:

> Three different accounts have been proposed to explain why stereotypes develop. The first, the shared distinctiveness account, is a purely cognitive account; it proposes that the tendency to form stereotypes of people is a natural consequence of the way we process information. In particular, David Hamilton has proposed that a phenomenon well-known in general psychology, the illusory correlation, can explain the development and maintenance of stereotypes without needing to posit that we have any motivational biases at all with regard to our thinking about groups of people. The second account also sees stereotypes as a consequence of the way we think about people, but it suggests that stereotyping depends on our having categorized people into ingroups and outgroups. The essence of this account, the outgroup homogeneity account, is that once we divide people into ingroups and outgroups, we are likely to form stereotypes of the outgroups. The third account, the cultural account, argues that we cannot understand the stereotypes we have of various groups in cognitive terms alone; it suggests that the stereotypes we have are a consequence of the specific way our culture has structured interactions between ingroups and outgroups. According to this view, the history of a culture determines the particular content that various stereotypes have. Let us consider these explanations one at a time.
>
> **(Sabini, 1995, p. 125)**

PROBLEMS IN USING COMMON READING STRATEGIES

How successful would you be in answering a quiz question that asks you to point out the main difference between the three accounts for the development of stereotypes? As you are reading this paragraph, you may not recall much of the information you read less than a minute ago. In fact, you may have forgotten much of what you read by the time you finished reading the passage. The reason for this outcome is that, often, college students view reading a textbook as a passive task, "something akin to hearing (as distinguished from listening), as though the text author is tell-ing and they, as readers, are supposed to sit back and just receive the information" (Armstrong & Newman, 2011, p. 17). Which strategies did you use to make your learning effective when reading the passage above? Did you read every word aloud? Did you reread the passage a few times? If so, you were indeed behaviorally active (i.e., talking) but were not necessarily cognitively active (i.e., you were not necessarily making sense of the material) (Mayer, 2008). Less skilled readers might view the passage above as a list of facts and use behavioral strategies (e.g., only reading the passage out loud or rereading it a few times) to carefully study every word. A more skilled reader will view the same passage as an organized body of knowledge and use learning strategies to make sense of it. In addition to reading aloud, she may relate the material to her prior knowledge about the topic, summarize the author's main points in her own words, create a representation to organize the material, or self-test herself by asking and answering questions about what she just read. The learning strategies we share in this chapter are designed to assist you in becoming a cognitively active reader.

One of the strategies you may have used to read the passage above is underlining or highlight-ing. For the rest of the chapter, we'll use the two terms interchangeably. Over half of our students underline/highlight passages in their textbooks as they read. Some students even use complex, multicolor highlighting systems where one color is for key words, another for examples, and a third for supporting details. Unfortunately, no matter how complex your highlighting or under-lining approach, both of them are rehearsal strategies that do not require much thinking about the content and, as a result, do not help move material into long-term memory. Another problem is that irrelevant information is often highlighted/underlined along with relevant information. When it comes time to review the understanding of the text, the highlighting or underlining may be confusing. Thus, it is possible to spend considerable time underlining or highlighting a textbook and still not remember most of the important ideas in a chapter. Finally, there is some evidence that highlighting can actually hurt performance on some high-level tasks. It may be that highlighting focuses the learner's attention on individual concepts at the expense of reflecting on connections between the different concepts. For the reasons listed, underlining/highlighting, along with rereading, emerged as the least effective strategy from among ten most commonly used strategies (Dunlosky, Rawson, Marsh, Nathan, & Willingham, 2013) and must be used in concert with other reading strategies.

In this chapter, we ask you to assess your present reading strategies and determine how success-ful they are in helping you achieve your academic objectives. After studying this chapter, you will be able to use effective learning strategies to improve your reading comprehension and retention.

WHAT DOES RESEARCH TELL US ABOUT SKILLFUL READERS?

Skillful readers attempt to comprehend and remember what they read by using specific learning strategies to manage their understanding. The following is a summary of these strategies (Dole et al., 1991):

- Determining importance. Skillful readers identify main ideas and separate them from examples and supporting details. Less skilled readers often underline or highlight text as they read and do not differentiate between important and less important ideas.
- Summarizing information. Skillful readers summarize information by reviewing all the ideas in a passage or chapter, differentiate important from unimportant ideas, and then synthesize the ideas to create a statement that represents the meaning of the passage or chapter. Less skilled readers do not stop to summarize what they have read.
- Drawing inferences. Skilled readers use inferencing extensively to fill in details omitted in a text and to elaborate on what they read. In other words, they ask questions like: What is the author implying? What is the implication of the actions suggested in the passage?

How do these ideas relate to other points of view on the issue? Less skilled readers rarely go beyond the written words in the text.

- Generating questions. Skilled readers maintain active involvement by generating questions and attempting to answer them while they read. Less skilled readers tend to be more passive and fail to generate such questions.

- Monitoring comprehension. Skilled readers are not only aware of the quality and degree of their understanding but know what to do and how to do it when they fail to comprehend material. Less skilled readers fail to monitor their understanding. As a result, they frequently rely on others to determine their degree of understanding.

The five reading activities just described have an important element in common. Reading for understanding and remembering requires an active involvement on the part of the reader. Exercise 8.1 provides an opportunity to evaluate your own reading strategies.

EXERCISE 8.1: SELF-OBSERVATION: ASSESSING READING STRATEGIES

Directions: For each question, place a check in the corresponding box that best describes the strategies you presently use to complete your reading assignments. When you have responded to all of the items, write a brief summary statement describing what this brief assessment tells you.

	Always	Sometimes	Never
1. I preview all my textbooks to review the learning aids provided by the authors.			
2. I preview each chapter before I read.			
3. I think of questions as I read.			
4. I underline or highlight my textbook as I read.			
5. I look for main ideas as I read.			
6. I use maps or charts to organize the content I read.			
7. I complete exercises or answer questions at the end of each chapter when I am finished reading.			
8. I make notes to identify material I don't understand.			
9. I constantly monitor my understanding as I read.			
10. I read my assignments before attending lectures.			

Summary Statement:

_____

_____

_____ ∎

Compare your reading strategies with the student responses on the following page. How are your strategies similar or different from the behavior reported?

WHAT LEARNING STRATEGIES CAN I USE TO IMPROVE MY READING COMPREHENSION AND RETENTION FROM TEXTBOOKS?

Now that you know what it takes to become a skillful reader and have evaluated your own reading behavior, let's discuss reading strategies for textbooks. The strategies discussed in this section are separated into activities to be completed during three stages of reading: before, during, and after (adapted from McWhorter, 2010).

1. Preview the Book for Learning Aids

If you were to review each of your textbooks, you would find that they differ greatly in design and readability. Think about two different textbooks you are currently reading. What makes one appear more "reader friendly" and another less "reader friendly"? Are you influenced by color, large type, headings, pictures, summaries, or wide columns?

Student Reflections

When I started college, I mostly underlined and highlighted everything I thought was important (which unfortunately happened to be just about every other sentence). This strategy proved to be detrimental in studying for exams. I even thought that highlighting phrases in different colors would make a difference; instead, this strategy was worse. I ended up with endless pages that looked like rainbows of pink, blue, yellow, and green marks. I could never decipher the information any better than I could before I highlighted it.

* * *

High school textbook reading was certainly an easier task than it is in college. College-level reading requires more time and energy in absorbing ideas and information. In high school, I always read assigned reading once and highlighted and memorized vocabulary words and facts. Now that I am in college, I allocate more time to study and read all the necessary information. I begin looking over all the headings throughout the chapter, both headings and subheadings. I then review vocabulary and boldface terms in each chapter. Following readings, I review the key points at the end of the chapter. I answer questions given at the end of the chapter, as well as the questions I developed from the reading.

* * *

A majority of high school reading is related to worksheets and other assignments where you are required to find specific details to finish an assignment. This demand got me into the habit of reading just for the specific facts, which didn't focus on the big picture. In college, you are often asked higher level questions on exams that require much more thought about the topic. It is helpful to own your own textbooks, because you can mark in them.

Have you considered the learning aids included by the author to help you comprehend the material? The following are some of the most common learning aids provided in textbooks:

- Chapter objectives or questions
- Glossaries
- Boldface or italics
- Answers to problems or exercises
- Summary or review sections
- Tables and figures
- Research or application boxes

Think about how each of these learning aids helps you learn. Objectives and questions help you determine what you learned in each chapter. When you are finished reading, you need to determine whether you attained the objectives of the chapter. If questions are presented at the beginning or end of the chapter, you can check to determine whether you can answer the questions. If you cannot answer the questions, you did not learn the material. A glossary defines the key terms in a textbook and often is listed in the back of the book. Some books have what is called a running glossary, where key terms are defined on the page where they first appear. Some authors boldface all words in the glossary and use italics or bullets to identify an important term or phrase. These elements are used to signal important information. Answers to problems and exercises are very useful in mathematics, business, and science courses, where solving problems is an important objective of the course. Most authors only provide answers to the even or odd problems in the textbook. Summary and review sections help identify the main points in the chapter and serve as a useful reminder of what should have been learned. Tables and figures can be useful in summarizing a large amount of information on a topic. Finally, research or application boxes either describe specific investigations that have been conducted by researchers or provide special insights regarding the relevancy of the information to daily life.

In summary, authors include various learning aids in textbooks to help you comprehend and retain information. Recognizing and using these aids can help you check your understanding and encourage you to become more actively involved in your reading assignments. Can you identify the learning aids provided in this textbook?

2. Survey the Assigned Material before Each Reading Session

Before you begin reading a chapter, survey the table of contents and read the major headings. Then read the chapter summary and any questions posed by the author. This surveying will help you identify some of the main ideas, topics, or issues of the chapter before you begin reading.

When you first preview a textbook, look for learning aids. When you survey a chapter before reading, you are preparing to make some decisions. Surveying is analogous to viewing the coming attractions for a film. The film preview gives the viewer an idea of the type of movie he or she will view in terms of the plot and characters. It prepares an individual for the viewing of the movie. Surveying a reading assignment not only provides insights for what you will learn, but it also helps you evaluate the difficulty of the material. This evaluation helps you determine whether you should read the entire chapter at one time or divide the reading into several sessions.

A very important aspect of surveying the assignment before reading is relating the reading assignment to your prior knowledge about the topic. Exercise 8.2 is designed to have you experience the importance of prior knowledge.

EXERCISE 8.2: UNDERSTANDING THE IMPORTANCE OF PRIOR KNOWLEDGE

Directions: Two learning experts (Bransford & Johnson, 1972) presented college students with the following passage to read. Read it for yourself and then see how much you can remember.

> The procedure is actually quite simple. First you arrange things into different groups depending on their makeup. Of course, one pile may be sufficient, depending on how much there is to do. If you have to go somewhere else due to lack of facilities that is the next step, otherwise you are pretty well set. It is important not to overdo any particular endeavor. That is, it is better to do too few things at once than too many. In the short run this may not seem important, but complications from doing too many can easily arise. A mistake can be expensive as well. The manipulation of the appropriate mechanisms should be self-explanatory, and we need not dwell on it here. At first the whole procedure will seem complicated. Soon, however, it will become just another facet of life. It is difficult to foresee any end to the necessity for this task in the immediate future, but then one never can tell.

(Bransford & Johnson, 1972, p. 722)

Surely you recognized all the words in the paragraph. Yet, you probably still had difficulty under-standing what you were reading. Don't be disappointed if you did not understand the passage or remember much of the content. Most people don't remember one thing after the first time of reading it.

Now, read the passage again, but this time keep the title "Washing Clothes" in mind. You should be able to make more sense of the passage because the title provides a meaningful context or frame-work for understanding the text.

■

What does this simple experiment reveal? Any time readers gain information about a reading pas-sage or section in a textbook and relate the information to something they already know, they are better able to understand the incoming information. This is why certain authors provide outlines or questions before chapters or questions imbedded in the text. These components help readers think about the topics in the chapter they are about to read. When readers read outlines or think about the questions before they begin reading, they take advantage of important aids to facilitate comprehen-sion and memory (Halpern, 1996). The effect is the same when students read assigned material before taking lecture notes. Note taking is easier when students know something about the material being presented.

But are you ready for something quite radical? Richland, Kornell, and Kao (2009) found that pre-testing, essentially trying to answer questions about material you have not even seen yet is effective in improving learning. The findings suggest that the process, even if often unsuccessful in produc-ing correct answers, enables "productive failure" (Kapur, 2012) and creates a "fertile ground" for processing the material when it is available.

3. Read Questions That Are Provided at the Beginning or End of Each Chapter in Accompanying Study Guides or Provided by Your Instructors

These questions provide important guidelines for what you are expected to learn in the chapter. By reading questions before you begin reading the chapter, you have a better idea of what to focus on.

DURING READING

1. As You Begin Reading, Think of the Text as a Conversation Between the Author and Yourself

Ask the following questions: What is the author trying to tell me? For example, in the passage about the development of stereotypes on pages 195 to 196, the author was providing three different accounts for the phenomenon. Which sentences state the main ideas? How do these ideas relate to other points of view on the issue?

2. Turn the Headings in Your Textbook into Questions and Answer Them

Write questions in the margin of a textbook if there are no headings, or between the headings if there are long sections of text. Although during reading it may seem like extra work, creating ques-tions and answering them pays off when it comes to preparing for exams. We'll address this in Chapter 10.

There are two broad levels of questions: lower level and higher level. Lower level questions tend to focus on factual information and ask you to retrieve information that was previously presented. They require you to remember and understand facts, dates, terms, or lists. The following are exam-ples of lower level questions:

- What are the three explanations for why stereotypes develop? (Remember)
- What is the definition of a molecule? (Remember)

- What are the three major categories of marine life? (Remember)
- Why do experimental psychologists formulate hypotheses before beginning research investigations? (Understand)
- How does the human ear function? (Understand)

Higher level questions require you to apply the information that you learned in a new situation, analyze information, evaluate the value of the information, and create a novel plan or solution. The following are examples of higher level questions:

- What is the density of iron if 156g of iron occupies a volume of 20 cm^3? (Apply)
- Why does the temperature of the water influence the velocity of sound? (Analyze)
- What are the differences between the cognitive and cultural explanation for why stereotypes develop? (Analyze)
- How effective was the president's State of the Union address in urging Congress to increase the defense budget? (Evaluate)
- How would the map of the world look after World War II if the Ribbentrop–Molotov treaty was never signed? (Create)

As you attempt to determine the main ideas presented by the author, think about the level of questions that might be asked on exams. In this way, you will move beyond factual or low level questions. Students who spend considerable time studying for an exam and still do not do well often find that they failed to ask appropriate higher level questions in their exam preparation. Underline the answers to your questions.

The headings in a textbook often indicate the subject matter of a series of paragraphs. Therefore, if you can answer the questions generated from the headings, you will focus on the main ideas and supporting details in the specific passage in the textbook. For example, if you are reading a book and come to the heading "Physical Properties of Matter" you should ask yourself: What are the different physical properties of matter? As you read the passage, you will learn that they are solid, liquid, and gas. If your question is on target, you can write it as part of the heading and underline or highlight the answer in the textbook. If you develop a question and find that the passage focuses on something else, you can change your question and underline the answer to the alternative question. For example, you read the heading "Taxation" in an economics textbook but have no specific idea as to what about taxation the author will discuss. You read on and learn how the federal government uses tax policy to allocate different resources. You then go back to the heading and write: "How does the government affect the allocation of resources through tax policy?" You then go back to the text and underline the answer to the question. Sometimes you can ask more than one question. For example, if you find the heading "Gun Control" in a political science book, you might want to know: What are the different views on gun control? What organizations support and oppose gun control? What legislation currently exists regarding gun control?

The following are examples of headings in textbooks turned into questions:

Headings	Questions
Improving Listening Skills	What methods can students use to improve their listening skills?
Interest Groups	How do interest groups influence political elections?
Gender Identification	What is gender identity? What are the different theories of gender identification?

The following are two excerpts from textbooks where a student has turned the heading into a question and underlined relevant phrases in the passage to answer the question. Notice the selective use of underlining. After reviewing these examples, you can return to the passage about stereotypes on pages 193 to 194, determine a good question, and underline or highlight the phrases that answer the question.

How Did the Postwar Reconstruction Impact Southern Cities and Southerners?

Even as the rural Sound stagnated economically, southern cities experienced remarkable growth after the Civil War. As railroads penetrated the interior, they enabled merchants in market centers like Atlanta to trade directly with the North, bypassing coastal cities that had traditionally monopolized southern commerce. A new urban middle class of merchants, railroad promoters, and bankers reaped the benefits of the spread of cotton production in postwar South.

Thus, Reconstruction brought about profound changes in the lives of southerners, black and white, rich and poor. In place of the prewar world of master, slave and self-sufficient yeoman, the postwar South was peopled by <u>new social classes – landowning employers, black and white sharecroppers, cotton producing white farmers, wage-earning black laborers, and urban entrepreneurs</u>. Each of these groups turned to Reconstruction politics in an attempt to shape to its own advantage the aftermath of emancipation.

(Foner, 2017, pp. 574–575)

---

3. Underline/Highlight and Annotate Textbooks

In the introduction to this unit, we mentioned that underlining and highlighting were ineffective learning strategies. The purpose of underlining/ highlighting is to identify main ideas and supporting details (e.g., examples, facts, and illustrations). When underlining/highlighting is done without determining the main points, or if too much material is underlined or highlighted, both relevant and irrelevant information is emphasized. Therefore, it is often difficult to make sense of the underlining/highlighting, because everything appears to be important. It is not necessary to underline or highlight each word in a sentence to capture the idea in a passage. One way to test for successful underlining/highlighting is to read through highlighted passages to determine whether the main ideas have been identified. You accomplish this task by determining whether you have answered the questions asked in the textbook or answered the questions generated from the headings in the text. Sometimes you find that it is necessary to underline or highlight more information.

Underlining/highlighting must be a selective process. The most important advice we can give about underlining/highlighting is to underline or highlight after reading a paragraph or passage, not during the reading. The main idea in any paragraph can be in the first sentence or the middle or end of the paragraph. If underlining/highlighting is begun as the reading is started, the critical phrases in the passage may be missed. The basic rules of underlining/highlighting are to read first and then underline/highlight and select only the main ideas and supporting details.

Underlining or highlighting, though generally ineffective, can be the first step in effective learning. For example, you can combine highlighting with a meaningful learning strategy such as creating self-tests for the highlighted information (Dunlosky, Rawson, Marsh, Nathan, & Willingham, 2013).

In some situations, it may be important to do more than generate questions and underline the main ideas. Another strategy to improve comprehension is to annotate or mark textbooks. Annotations are words or symbols usually written in the margin of the textbook that help one to organize and remember important information. There are many different ways to mark or annotate a textbook. Consider the following guidelines:

- Mark selectively. Do not highlight complete sentences.
- Mark pages only after they have been read.
- Develop symbols that make sense.

Symbol	Explanation
?	Use a question mark to show material you don't understand.
*	Use a star to identify important ideas.
def	Use an abbreviation to identify definitions.
|	Use a vertical line to identify important ideas that are several lines in length.
O	Use a circle to identify unknown words.

FIGURE 8.1   Types of Annotations

Figure 8.1 identifies various types of symbols for annotations in textbooks. Other types of annotations include summary words or phrases in the margin that identify key ideas in the text, such as "causes of the illness" or "three characteristics of ...." Finally, you can write critical comments in the margin to help prepare for discussion of essays, short stories, or poems. Do not annotate a book that you do not own, especially library books.

4. Monitor Comprehension

Many beginning college students "tend to read on 'automatic pilot', and do not realize when they have trouble comprehending or truly digesting text" (El-Hindi, 2003, p. 360). The following is a question you should ask yourself each time you read: "How well am I understanding what I am reading?" If you are not understanding what you are reading, stop. Ask yourself why. The following are some common reading problems and possible strategies to solve them (adapted from Cortina et al., 1992, p. 34).

Problem	Strategy
There are words that I don't know.	• Try to use the rest of the sentence or paragraph to figure out the meaning of those words. • Check a glossary or a dictionary. • Ask someone.
I am having difficulty concentrating.	• Identify what is bothering you and take some action (read Chapter 7).
The topic is difficult because I know nothing about it.	• Reread the passage. • Read ahead to see if it becomes clearer. • Read supplemental material or simpler material on the same topic (perhaps an encyclopedia, another textbook, a book from the library, or a reputable website). • Ask someone to explain the material.

AFTER READING

Many students make the mistake of assuming that they are done once they read the last paragraph in their assignment. This is the critical time to take the necessary steps to ensure that you remember what you have just read. Because forgetting occurs very rapidly, it is important to get the information you read into long-term memory immediately. Here is what you can do.

1. Answer out Loud the Questions You Generated from the Headings Printed in Your Textbook, or Given to You by Your Instructor

If you cannot answer a question, you do not understand part of the content. Go back and reread the section of the textbook where the answer should be found. Once you find the answer, check your underlining/highlighting or annotations to ensure that the answer is identified.

2. Consider Summarizing the Material

A summary is a brief statement that identifies the major ideas in a section of a textbook, play, newspaper article, or story. For example, writing a summary of the plot in a novel incorporating information describing who did what, when, and where can be useful in determining that you understood the reading. Summarizing as a learning strategy is particularly useful in preparing for essay exams as opposed to multiple-choice and other objective tests that depend on recognition (Dunlosky, Rawson, Marsh, Nathan, & Willingham, 2013). The key to summarizing being an effective strategy, though, is that it indeed summarizes all the main points and excludes unimportant material.

The following are some suggestions for writing summaries (McWhorter, 2010, p. 344):

- Start by identifying the author's main point; write a statement that expresses it.
- Next, identify the key information the writer includes to support or explain his or her main point. Include these main supporting ideas in your summary.
- Include any definitions of key terms or important new principles, theories, or procedures that are introduced.
- Try to keep your summary objective and factual. Think of it as a brief report that should reflect the writer's ideas, not your evaluation of them.

3. Consider Outlining the Material

At times, answering questions is sufficient to confirm that you remember what you read. However, sometimes, because of the complexity of the material, you may decide to outline or graphically represent (i.e., map) the information. Both strategies organize the material by identifying the relation between main ideas and supporting details.

The easiest way to show the relationship between ideas and details in an outline is to use the following format:

I. Major Topic

A.   First main idea
    1   First important detail
    2   Second important detail
    3   Third important detail
B.   Second main idea
    1   First important detail
       • Minor point or example
    2   Second important detail

II. Second Major Topic

A.   First main idea

◼

Notice that the most important ideas are closer to the margins, with less important ideas or examples indented toward the middle of the page. The purpose of this format is to be able to look at the outline and quickly determine what is most important.

McWhorter (2010, p. 338) made the following suggestions for developing an effective outline:

- Don't get caught up in the numbering and lettering system. Instead, concentrate on show-ing the relative importance of ideas. How you number or letter an idea is not as important as showing what other ideas it supports or explains. Don't be concerned if some items do not fit exactly into outline format.
- Be brief; use words and phrases, never complete sentences. Abbreviate words and phrases where possible.
- Use your own words rather than lifting most of the material from the text. You can use the author's key words and specialized terminology.
- Be sure that all information underneath a heading supports or explains it.
- All headings that are aligned vertically should be of equal importance.

Here is a brief outline of the passage presented at the beginning of the chapter about the develop-ment of stereotypes.

1. *Three Accounts for the Development of Stereotypes*

A. Shared distinctiveness—Cognitive account
   1 Caused by nature of information processing
   2 No motivation to develop stereotypes
   3 Illusory correlation
B. Categorization into ingroups and outgroups
   1 Caused by outgroup homogeneity
C. Structured interactions between ingroups and outgroups—Cultural account
   1 Caused by history of culture

■

Here's a brief outline of the information-processing system discussed in Chapter 3.

I. *Information-Processing System*

A. STSS
   1 Memory lasts few seconds
   2 Capacity is large
B. WM
   1 Memory limited in capacity and duration
      a. 7 ± 2 (or even 4 ± 1)
      b. Memory lasts 5 to 20 seconds
C. LTM
   1 Storage of info is permanent
   2 Organization is like a jigsaw puzzle
   3 Flow of info in two directions

■

4. Consider Representing or Mapping the Material

Surely you have heard the expression "a picture is worth a thousand words." In learning, students often find it helpful to represent knowledge in terms of maps or diagrams to show how a topic and its corresponding information are related. Sometimes academic content is more easily learned by using a visual display of its organization rather than reviewing an entire chapter or section of a textbook. Consider, for example, how much discussion it would take to describe the functioning of a human heart. A good graphic representation in the form of a diagram can quickly illustrate the key components of a heart and the flow of blood through it.

Information in texts and lectures is often presented linearly, one idea at a time. Many students view academic subjects in terms of a large number of isolated facts. No wonder little information is remembered. Learning involves constructing meaning by combining ideas so that relations and patterns are apparent. When students view information solely in a linear format, they miss important relations among ideas.

One of the advantages of recognizing different organizational patterns used by authors and lecturers is that it allows the reader or listener to anticipate the type of information likely to be presented. A second advantage is that understanding how ideas and information are organized makes it easier to remember the information. If the author's or lecturer's organization patterns are understood, more of the material will be understood and remembered (Cortina et al., 1992).

Hierarchies: Organization of ideas into levels and groups.

Sequences: An organization that shows the order of steps, events, stages, or phases.

Matrices: An organization that displays the comparative relations existing within topics and across topics.

Diagrams: A visual description of the parts of something.

The discussion in this section is based on the work of Kiewra and DuBois (1998), who have developed a useful approach to the representation of knowledge. They identified four different representations—**hierarchies, sequences, matrices,** and **diagrams**—and provided suggestions for constructing them. This information is appropriate both for learning from reading and lectures. Kiewra and DuBois favor representations over outlines. They believe that representations provide better comparison of content and a more precise overview of the structure of the content than outlines. Each of the four representations is reviewed here.

Hierarchies   Hierarchies organize ideas into levels and groups. Higher levels are more general than lower levels. Hierarchies are organized around class-inclusion rules. These rules are based on the notion that something is a part of or a type of something else. Examples of class-inclusion rules are the classification of reptiles as part of animals and neutrons as part of atoms.

Take another look at the hierarchy of minerals that was first introduced in Chapter 3 (Figure 3.2). Level 1 represents the class (minerals), Level 2 includes two types of minerals (metals and stones), Level 3 includes three types of metals and two types of stones, and Level 4 includes specific examples of each of the types of metals and stones. The number of levels in a hierarchy can vary from one to more. It is important to reflect all the important levels and groups in any hierarchy that is developed.

The following is an excerpt from a child psychology textbook that will be used later in the chapter to illustrate how sequences and matrices can be used to organize information. Read the excerpt before moving to the next section of this chapter.

Stages of Development. Piaget was a stage theorist. In his view, all children move through the same stages of cognitive development in the same order. Each stage is a qualitatively distinct form of functioning, and the structures that characterize each stage determine the child's performance in a wide range of situations. There are four such general stages, or periods, in Piaget's theory.

The sensorimotor period represents the first two years of life. The infant's initial schemes are simple reflexes. Gradually, these reflexes are combined into larger, more flexible units of action. Knowledge of the world is limited to physical interactions with people and objects. Most of the examples of schemes given earlier—grasping, sucking, and so on—occur during infancy.

During the preoperational period, from roughly two to six years, the child begins to use symbols to represent the world cognitively. Words and numbers can take the place of objects and events, and actions that formerly had to be carried out overtly can now be performed mentally through the use of internal symbols. The preoperational child is not yet skilled at symbolic problem solving, however, and various gaps and confusions are evident in the child's attempts to understand the world.

Many of these limitations are overcome when the child reaches the period of concrete operations, which lasts approximately from ages six to 11. Concrete operational children are able to perform mental operations on the bits of knowledge that they possess. They can add them, subtract them, put them in order, reverse them, and so on. These mental operations permit a kind of logical problem solving that was not possible during the pre-operational period.

The final stage is the period of formal operations, which extends from about age 11 through adulthood. This period includes all of the higher-level abstract operations that do not require concrete objects or materials. The clearest example of such operations is the ability to deal with events or relationships that are only possible, as opposed to those that actually exist. Mentally considering all of the ways certain objects could be combined, or attempting to solve a problem by cognitively examining all of the ways it could be approached, are two operations that typically cannot be performed until this final stage.

(Vasts et al., 1992, p. 31)

Sequences   Sequences order ideas chronologically by illustrating the ordering of steps, events, stages, or phases. Sequences usually appear in a left-to-right pattern, with arrows between steps. Figure 8.5 provides an example of the stages of cognitive development described in the preceding excerpt. Timelines in history can also be used to visualize the sequence of events by drawing a horizontal line and marking it off in intervals. The times when different events in history occurred can be illustrated by adjusting the intervals at which the dates are placed on the line.

Matrices   Matrices display comparative relations and can be used successfully in very different content areas as shown in Figures 8.2 and 8.3. They are developed from a hierarchy or sequence and have three parts: topics, repeatable categories, and details located inside the matrix cells. These parts are shown in Figures 8.2 and 8.3. The topics appear across the matrix (e.g., amphetamines, depressants, and hallucinogenics; the functions of sine, cosine, and tangent of θ). The repeatable categories appear down the left margin. They are the characteristics by which the topics are compared (e.g., function, street terms, and example; unit circle, circle, and right triangle definitions). They are called repeatable categories, because each category is repeated for each topic. The author often identifies repeatable categories. However, sometimes categories will have to be identified from the information provided by the author. The details are the facts that pertain to the intersection of topics and repeatable categories. They appear inside the matrix in the cells at the intersection of topics and repeatable categories.

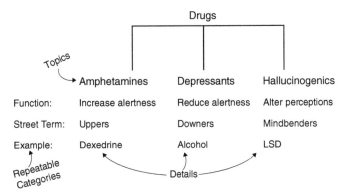

FIGURE 8.2   Components of a Matrix

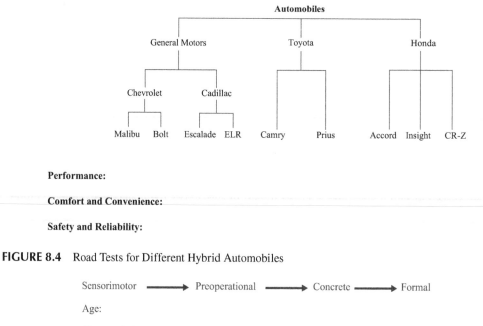

Functions	sine of θ	cosine of θ	tangent of θ
Abbreviation	sin θ	cos θ	tan θ
Unit Circle Definition	y	x	$\dfrac{y}{x}$
Circle (with radius r) Definition	$\dfrac{y}{r}$	$\dfrac{x}{r}$	$\dfrac{y}{x}$
Right Triangle Definition	$\dfrac{opposite}{hypotenuse}$	$\dfrac{adjacent}{hypotenuse}$	$\dfrac{opposite}{adjacent}$

FIGURE 8.3   Definitions of Trigonometric Functions

Automobiles

General Motors   Toyota   Honda

Chevrolet   Cadillac

Malibu   Bolt   Escalade   ELR   Camry   Prius   Accord   Insight   CR-Z

Performance:

Comfort and Convenience:

Safety and Reliability:

FIGURE 8.4   Road Tests for Different Hybrid Automobiles

Sensorimotor ⟶ Preoperational ⟶ Concrete ⟶ Formal

Age:

Characteristics:

FIGURE 8.5   Stages of Cognitive Development

Any hierarchy or sequence can be extended downward to form a matrix. Figures 8.3 and 8.4 illustrate a hierarchy extended into a matrix framework, and Figure 8.5 illustrates a sequence extended into a matrix framework from the reading on cognitive development. In Figure 8.5, the repeatable categories (i.e., age and characteristics) are provided for you. Fill in the details for each of the four stages of cognitive development and compare your representation with a classmate.

Diagrams   Diagrams display or illustrate the parts or components of different objects and are useful in almost every subject area. Diagrams can be drawn in biology to recall the location of different organs in the body or to identify different parts of organs such as the brain. In geography, a map of the European countries can be sketched to help assist recall of the location and approximate size of each country. In mathematics, diagrams of different geometric shapes are useful in solving problems when measurements are placed in the proper locations.

HOW CAN I CONSTRUCT REPRESENTATIONS?

IDENTIFY AND USE SIGNAL WORDS

Signal words provide clues as to how content is related and what representation (hierarchy, sequence, matrix, or diagram) to construct. A representation should not be selected solely on a signal word without the entire passage being read to confirm the representation. Table 8.1 includes examples of different signal words. Signal words for diagrams include parts, appearance, position, and movement.

EXERCISE 8.3: REPRESENTATIONS IN ACADEMIC CONTENT

Directions: The following are brief statements that introduce discussion of various topics. For each of the statements, identify which representation would most likely depict the information to follow by writing H for hierarchy, S for sequence, M for matrix, and D for diagram in the space provided. The answers are provided on p. 169.

1 Three different accounts have been proposed to explain why stereotypes develop.
2 There are a number of similarities and differences between mitosis and meiosis.
3 After food has been chewed, it is swallowed and passed down the esophagus to the stomach. Next, food enters the intestinal system.
4 There are several issues that students may face in college, some of them classified as eating disorders (comprising obesity, bulimia, and anorexia nervosa) and emotional problems (comprising depression and anxiety).
5 There are several perspectives on gender identification. They can be compared and contrasted based on how these perspectives interpret the influences of nature versus nurture.
6 The development before birth, called gestation, takes place in three stages: germinal, embryonic, and fetal.
7 The cerebellum is the coordinating center of voluntary movements and is located behind the cerebrum.
8 The framers of the Constitution devised alternative methods of selection and terms of service for national officials.

TABLE 8.1
Examples of Signal Words

Hierarchy	Sequence	Matrix
kinds of	first	like
types of	before	similarly, equally
classified as	in the center	in contrast
composed of	lower	on the other hand
parts of	outside	alternatively
groups of	after	similar
properties of	next	in comparison
characteristics of	last	
perspectives	steps, stages, phases, cycle as a result, consequently, therefore	

Adapted from Kiewra and DuBois (1998)

Identify and Develop Repeatable Categories

Signal words are useful in determining what representation will be used (i.e., a hierarchy, sequence, matrix, or diagram). However, because all hierarchical and sequential representations can be extended to form matrix representations, it is important to learn how to identify the matrix's repeatable categories.

It is important to be aware of the structure of different academic disciplines. For example, history courses tend to focus on who, what, why, and when questions that can be developed into repeatable categories such as causes, major battles, resolution, and so forth. In literature, short stories have a plot, a setting, and characters that can be used as common characteristics for comparing stories. In psychology, learning theories are used to explain how students learn. Therefore, repeatable categories to consider might be the definition of learning, role of the teacher, role of the student, and factors that influence motivation.

Often authors and lecturers identify the repeatable categories. Suppose you read about gender identity and the author points out that he will discuss four different theories of gender identification and the key processes and basic beliefs of each theory. Once you have completed the opening paragraph of the section in your textbook, you have already identified the repeatable categories: key processes and basic beliefs.

In some cases, you will read considerable material and have to identify the repeatable categories on your own. Suppose you read in a history book about different Asian cities. The author provides information about living conditions in the cities but does not specifically categorize the differences. For example, you may find reference to the congestion in one city, the slow pace of the inhabitants in another location, and so forth. If you were to develop a matrix of the information, you might consider lifestyle as a repeatable category to compare the cities you studied.

Like any other skill you develop, learning to construct representations takes practice. Some applications might come handy such as Lucidchart and Creately, though new ones will likely emerge by the time this textbook is published. As you read textbooks this week and take notes, think about how the information you are learning can be organized more effectively. As you begin constructing representations, you will find it easier to understand important relationships in the content of your courses.

EXERCISE 8.4: SELF-OBSERVATION: CONSTRUCTING DIFFERENT REPRESENTATIONS FOR THE MATERIAL

Directions: Read the following passages from different academic textbooks and, in the space provided, construct a complete representation for the material.

> Cells are composed of molecules. Some of the chemicals of life (bio-chemicals) are so large that they are called macromolecules.
>
> The major that make up and fuel cells include carbohydrates (sugars and starches), lipids (fats and oils), proteins, and nucleic acids. Cells require vitamins and minerals in much smaller amounts.
>
> Carbohydrates provide energy and contribute to cell structure. Lipids form the basis of several types of hormones, provide insulation, and store energy. Proteins have many diverse functions in the human body. They participate in blood clotting, nerve transmission, and muscle contraction and form the bulk of the body's connective tissue. Enzymes are especially important proteins, because they facilitate, or catalyze, bio-chemical reactions so that they occur swiftly enough to sustain life. Most important to the study of genetics are the nucleic acids DNA and RNA, which translate information from past generations into specific collections of proteins that give a cell its individual characteristics.

(Lewis, 2007, p. 22)

Representation:

Stocks and Bonds

Our discussion of the earnings of an investor in corporate securities introduces a subject of interest to millions of Americans—*stocks* and *bonds*, the financial instruments that provide funds to the corporate sector of the economy.

> **Common stock** represents ownership of part of a corporation. For example, if a company issues 100,000 shares, then a person who owns 1,000 shares actually owns 1 percent of the company and is entitled to one percent of the company's dividends, the corporation's annual payments to stockholders. The shareholder's vote counts for one percent of the total votes in an election of corporate officers or in a referendum on corporate policy.
>
> **Bonds** differ from stocks in several ways. First, the purchaser of a corporation's stock buys a share of its ownership and some control over its affairs, whereas the purchaser of a bond simply lends money to the firm and obtains no part of its ownership. Second, whereas stockholders have no idea how much they will receive for their stocks when they sell them, or how much they will receive in dividends each year, bondholders know with a high degree of certainty how much money they will be paid if they hold their bonds to maturity (the date the firm has promised to repay the loan). For instance, a bond with a face value of $1,000, with an $80 coupon that matures in 2010, will provide to its owner $80 per year every year until 2010 and the firm will repay the bondholder's $1,000 in 2010. Unless the company goes bankrupt, this repayment schedule is guaranteed. Third, bondholders legally have a *prior claim* on company earnings, which means stockholders receive no money until the firm has paid its bondholders. For all these reasons, bonds are considered less risky investments than stocks.

(Baumol & Blinder, 2012, p. 180)

Representation:

■

Table 8.2 contains a review of the different reading procedures discussed in this chapter.

TABLE 8.2
Procedures for Learning from Textbooks

Before Reading

1. Preview the book for learning aids.
2. Survey the assignment before each reading session.
3. Read questions at the beginning or end of each chapter or study guide that may accompany your textbook, or that are provided by your instructors.

During the Reading of Each Passage or Section

1. As you begin reading, think of the text as a conversation between the author and yourself. Ask the following questions: "What is the author trying to tell me?" "Which sentences state the main idea?"
2. Turn the headings in a textbook into questions and answer them. If there are no headings, write questions in the margin of the textbook.
3. Underline the answers to your questions and annotate the textbook.

After Reading Each Passage or Section

1. Answer out loud the questions that you generated from the headings printed in your textbook and given by your instructor.
2. After you have underlined the material, reread the questions to check whether underlining provides sufficient clues to answer the questions. If necessary, make modifications in underlining.
3. Consider summarizing, outlining, or representing the material.

WHAT LEARNING STRATEGIES CAN I USE TO BEST LEARN FROM E-SOURCES?

Your instructor is likely to give you an option of whether to purchase a traditional, printed textbook, or an e-textbook. The advantages of an e-textbook are its lower cost than a printed textbook, rich features, and ease of availability. But are there drawbacks to learning from a traditional versus e-textbook? One study (Daniel & Woody, 2013) found that although students who read a traditional versus an e-textbook scored similarly on reading-based tests, reading time was significantly higher with e-textbooks. This could be because students reading e-textbooks multitasked significantly more by engaging in other computer-based activities such as using social media. A recent study (Kong, Seo & Zhai, 2018) concluded that though there appear to be no differences in reading speed, reading on paper is better than reading on screen in terms of comprehension. So, the verdict seems to be out, but it looks like you cannot go wrong with a traditional textbook—you might read faster and comprehend more!

If you do decide to purchase an e-textbook, many, if not all, the strategies of learning from textbooks work for learning from e-books as well. For example, you want to use highlighting very purposefully and sparingly for the reasons previously discussed in this chapter. Similarly, you want to engage in determining importance, summarizing information, drawing inferences, generating questions, and monitoring comprehension. Also, consider factors that impact reading quality such as whether the screen image is of high quality, whether there is glare, and whether the color and font size are optimal. Reading from a screen may also place more strain on the eyes. To avoid that, position your screen in book-like positioning.

WHAT LEARNING STRATEGIES CAN I USE TO BEST LEARN FROM POWERPOINT SLIDES?

The vast majority of college instructors use PowerPoint to deliver lectures and some of them share their slides before the lecture. Below, see suggestions of how to adapt the strategies we discussed for learning from textbooks to learning from PowerPoint slides. In most cases, you will also have read a textbook chapter or articles on the same topic as the PowerPoint slides, so build on the knowledge from these other sources as you work with the PowerPoint slides.

Before Lecture:

- If the professor shares the PowerPoint slides ahead of lecture, preview them, just like you would a textbook chapter. This will activate any prior knowledge you have about the subject and improve your learning during the lecture.
- If you feel you understand the content well, perhaps based on the other sources regarding the subject, consider turning the slide headings into questions. This will prepare you to listen for the answers and enhance your learning during lecture.
- If you like to take notes by hand, be sure to print out the slides and ensure you leave enough space to take notes. It might be best to print out one slide per sheet of paper and use both the front and back to take notes.

WHAT LEARNING STRATEGIES CAN I USE TO BEST LEARN FROM VIDEO CAPTURED LECTURES?

More and more US colleges and universities use video lecture capture software such as Articulate Storyline or Adobe Captivate to "flip" instruction (Campus Computing Project, 2018). In flipped instruction, you watch lectures recorded by your professor or other experts before class and then apply the knowledge during class. The main goal in flipping a class is to move activities traditionally considered homework into the classroom and through that, create the space for deeper, richer learning experiences for students when the professor is present to guide the learning. In "flipped instruction," you are looking at a lot of video. Simply watching a video is a passive activity and as we have discussed, meaningful learning does not result from passive involvement. To combat that, become actively involved by applying the learning strategies presented in this chapter: determining importance, summarizing information, drawing inferences, generating questions, and monitoring comprehension. Below, see suggestions of how to adapt the strategies before, during, and after viewing a video captured lecture.

BEFORE VIEWING

- If the video is accompanied by a PowerPoint presentation, download and review it ahead of time to determine how the lecture is organized.
- Prepare for a way to take notes, whether in the notes section of PowerPoint slides or in printed out format.

DURING VIEWING

- Think of the lecture as a conversation between you and the presenter.
- Turn the slide headings into questions and answer them.
- Pause the video every time you identify a main idea and take notes about it. Include elaborative material such as examples and illustrations.

AFTER VIEWING

- Summarize and synthesize the key points.
- Consider representing the material via a diagram, sequence, hierarchy, or matrix.
- Test yourself by answering the questions you generated.
- Work with peers to clarify any misunderstanding and test each other as you likely generated different questions. However, note that any knowledge checks such as quizzes to be completed before class are usually designed to be taken individually!

In this chapter, we discussed learning from different course materials: traditional and e-textbooks, PowerPoints available before class, and videos such as in flipped instruction. Although the media of delivery will keep changing with the advances of technology, remember that the key to learning is not the media in which material is delivered but the degree to which you actively and meaningfully engage with the content before, during, and after.

Chapter Review

KEY POINTS

1 Skillful readers use specific learning strategies to manage their understanding.
2 Simply highlighting or underlining textbooks as one reads is not an effective learning strategy unless it is used with the generation and answering of questions.
3 Reading or taking notes and remembering are two separate activities. Just because you read or take notes does not mean you will remember what you read or write down.
4 Learning from course materials involves activities undertaken before, during, and after each activity.
5 Skillful readers monitor their understanding as they read.
6 Summarizing, outlining, and representing course content are useful strategies for learning and remembering material.
7 Information in textbooks and lectures is often presented in a linear fashion, one idea at a time. This form of presentation obscures the relation among ideas.
8 To construct meaning, it is especially necessary to organize information.
9 The four types of representations that can help learners understand relationships include hierarchies, sequences, matrices, and diagrams.
10 The active learning strategies of determining importance, summarizing information, drawing inferences, generating questions, and monitoring comprehension apply in different media such as traditional and e-textbooks, video captured lectures, and PowerPoint slides.

FOLLOW-UP ACTIVITIES

1. Use the Self-Regulation Process to Become a More Successful Reader

Complete the following self-study during a period of two to three weeks. Your report should include each of the following processes and should be approximately five to eight typed pages in length. See Appendix B for detailed information on how to conduct a self-regulation study.

Self-Observation and Evaluation.   What are the different media through which I learn course material? How effective are my reading and learning strategies? Are they more effective in some media (such as traditional textbooks) than others (such as video captured lectures)? Do I need to change the way I read and study? If yes, what problem(s) do I encounter? What are the symptoms of my problem (i.e., when, where, and how often does my problem occur)? How much of an impact does this problem have on my academic performance? What factors (e.g., beliefs, perceptions, feelings, physiological responses, or behaviors) contribute to this problem? What do I need to change to reduce or eliminate my problem(s)?

Goal Setting and Strategic Planning.   What are my goals? What strategies will I implement to improve my comprehension while learning? When will I use these strategies? How will I record my progress?

Strategy Implementation and Monitoring.   What strategies did I use to improve my comprehension? When did I use these strategies? What method(s) did I use to record my progress (e.g., documents, charts, logs, tally sheets, checklists, or recordings)? When did I use these methods? How and when did I monitor my progress to determine if my plan was working? What changes, if any, did I make along the way?

Strategic-Outcome Monitoring. Did I attain the goal(s) I set for myself? Have the modifications in my comprehension strategies improved my academic performance? What strategies were the most and least effective? What changes, if any, do I need to make in the future?

2. Assess Reading Behavior

The self-regulation model at the beginning of the textbook (p. 23) indicates that the use of motivational strategies (i.e., goal setting and mood and effort) and behavioral strategies (i.e., time management and physical and social environmental control) influence learning and study strategies. Explain how motivation and behavioral strategies impact your reading behavior. In addition, explain what steps you could take to deal with your reading concerns.

3. Analyze Use of Reading Strategies

At the beginning of this chapter, you learned about the strategies that skillful readers use: determining importance, summarizing information, drawing inferences, generating questions, and monitoring comprehension. Select a chapter in a textbook in another course and explain how you used these strategies in comprehending the material. If you did not use one or more of the strategies, explain the reason for your decision.

4. Improve Reading Comprehension and Retention

Directions: The following passage is taken from a college textbook. Read the passage and (a) generate a question; (b) underline relevant parts of the passage that answer the question; (c) identify the type of representation you could use to comprehend the material, including the topics and repeatable categories; and (d) circle the signal words in the passage. You will not be able to complete the representation, because the paragraphs do not include all the details you would need.

Types of Organisms

Although there is a great diversity of marine life, it is commonly separated into only three major categories: plankton, nekton, and benthos. These subdivisions are based solely on the general habit of the organisms and have nothing to do with their scientific classification, their size or complexity, or whether they are plant or animal.

The plankton are organisms that live within the pelagic zone and float, drift, or swim feebly; that is, they cannot control their position against currents. The plankton include plants, which are called phytoplankton, and animals, which are called zooplankton. Nekton are those organisms that swim. Only animals are included in this group. The benthos are those organisms that live on or within the bottom, the benthic environment.

The plankton are the most diverse and numerous, with the benthos not too far behind. Many groups of organisms spend a portion of their life cycle in more than one of these modes of life. It is common for a particular group to be planktonic in the larval or juvenile stage and then nektonic or benthonic as adults.

(Davis, 1986, p. 129)

5. Construct a Representation

Construct a representation for a textbook you are currently reading. Copy the pages in the textbook where the information came from. Identify the type of representation you used and include the repeatable categories and details.

Answers to Exercise 8.3

1. M   2. M   3. S   4. H   5. M   6. S   7. D   8. M

9 Learning from Class

Institutions of higher education have started to move from a reliance on only the instructor-led lecture to an inclusion of student-centered activities such as discussion sessions and student presentations. In other words, your professor may aim to be less of a "sage on the stage" and more of a "guide on the side." We will discuss strategies to approach planning and delivering individual and group presentations in Appendix A.

As we discussed in the previous chapter, some professors "flip" the course by taping their lecture material ahead of time to be viewed on a learning management system such as Blackboard. This enables them to spend class time on discussing the content with the students as well as engaging in activities that used to be homework, such as the application of content to problem solving and collaborative projects. Whether your course is instructor or student-centered, effective note taking is critical to learning. The note taking, really note making, strategies we discuss in this chapter can be adapted to the different ways in which information is presented in class.

Before we discuss effective strategies for learning in class, we'd like to say a few words about classroom etiquette or really, netiquette. If you are like the vast majority of students, you own a cell phone and bring it to every class period. Chances are that you own a laptop or tablet as well. Professors have different expectations about using electronic devices during class. Some professors completely ban the devices, some even offer extra credit if you agree to give up your cell phone for the entire lecture while others integrate devices into instruction. Be sure to determine where your professors stand. Either way, when in class, make it standard practice to turn off your ringer, remove your ear buds, and don't text or engage in social media. As much as you think you can hide it, staring at your lap generally gives you away.

No matter what the form of delivery and interaction in class, effective note taking is key to your success in college. Why? Remember the discussion of the information-processing system in Chapter 3? Because human memory fades quickly (do you remember which memory flaw this is?), it is important that you learn how to record major ideas and supporting details. In fact, the famous psychological concept of the "forgetting curve," established by Ebbinghaus in 1885, tells us that the human ability to recall new information drops to below 50 percent in an hour and to about 25 percent in 48 hours. Have you found yourself being in class but not paying attention to what was being talked about? Taking class notes ensures that you do not only "hear" the instructor but also "listen" to the information presented. That is, not only is your short-term sensory store passively registering the sound of the instructor's voice, but your working memory is actively and intentionally processing the information. Taking notes engages not only your sense of sound but also your sense of sight and touch. The more senses you engage in the process, the more enhanced the learning. In short, taking class notes is not only beneficial, but vital for your success in college.

One of the major differences between learning from texts and any course-related video versus learning in class is that in reading and reviewing video, you can control the flow of information. If you do not understand something, you can reread, put down the text or pause the video and return to it at another time. However, in class, the pace is controlled by the instructor. As a result, you need to use strategies to capture the main ideas more rapidly.

How do you take notes in college? Do you go traditional by using pen and lined paper, or do you use the modern alternative of digital note taking such as your laptop or tablet? There are several benefits to digital note taking. You may be like the authors in that you can type much faster than you can write. In addition, your handwriting may have "atrophied" from lack of use and is by now virtually illegible even to yourself. Typing is certainly a viable solution in this case. Additional important benefits of digital note taking are that your notes become indexable and searchable, you can organize the notes as you take them, and you can more easily integrate notes about the same major topic from different classes. And you guessed it, there's an app for that: check out Notability, Evernote, or Microsoft OneNote as examples of apps that enable you to take and organize your notes.

If you want to combine the traditional pen and paper writing with the digital benefits, you may want to look into digital pens. A digital pen saves your hand-written text in electronic form. Some digital pens synchronize your writing with digital recordings of what is going on around you while you are writing. After taking notes, you can store them on your computer without actually having to take your computer to class. Before you record the class, though, you must seek permission to do so from your instructor.

Despite all the excellent alternatives, we find that many students we teach still prefer taking notes longhand on lined paper. Why, with all the seemingly excellent gadgets out there? Some of our students state that they know that if they brought a laptop to class, they would be "cyberslacking" and multitasking in no time. They report that taking notes longhand keeps them from daydreaming, getting bored, or engaging in multitasking by checking social media, YouTube, or other distractions. Research findings demonstrate that students who multitasked on a laptop during lectures performed significantly worse on a comprehension test than those who did not multitask (Sana, Weston, & Cepeda, 2013). Worse, multitasking also proved detrimental for nearby peers who sat in the direct view of a multitasker! They too scored significantly lower than those peers who were not in direct view of peers engaged in multitasking. In fact, in a nationwide survey (Dahlstrom & Bichsel, 2014), almost half (47 percent) of undergraduate students and 67 percent of faculty report that in class use of mobile devices is distracting. It is not surprising, then, that 55 percent of faculty nationwide ban or discourage mobile device use.

Whether banned from using their laptops or not, many of our students prefer pen and paper. Research gives credibility to taking notes longhand. Researchers from Princeton and UCLA (Mueller & Oppenheimer, 2016) found through an experimental study that even if laptop use is limited to taking notes, it may in fact be detrimental to academic performance. When tested about the lecture content in terms of the complex ideas rather than the straightforward facts, pen-and-paper students always performed better. It appears that typing leads to taking verbatim notes, shallow processing, and lower quality of learning while longhand writing promotes listening, selecting the main ideas, processing information at a deeper level, and ultimately, a higher quality of learning. Although note taking via a laptop may be easier, it can actually cause lower performance outcomes. And, of course, there is the temptation to multitask. In fact, Mueller and Oppenheimer note that students may spend as little as one-third of classroom time taking notes, while the other two-thirds are spent on social media and other non-class distractions.

Considering research, our recommendation is to take notes via pen and paper or a digital pen rather than a laptop. Whether you choose to take notes longhand or digitally, the strategies presented in this chapter are highly applicable to both.

In this chapter, you will learn that what you do with your notes is just as important as how you record them. Educational research indicates that students who take notes and review them shortly after class learn more than students who take notes but do not review them (Kiewra, 2004). Part of the benefit of reviewing notes is that it allows further elaboration and integration of the material. Therefore, you should not simply skim your notes, but think actively about the ideas in the notes and relate them to other information you already know.

We notice that the number of notes students take in class is related to our instructional methods. When we deliver our lectures standing in front of the podium presenting information, students take many notes. However, if we move away from the podium and lead a discussion, note taking is reduced. What many students fail to realize is that a great deal of information is presented during discussions. It is the students' responsibility to capture the main ideas presented or discussed in all classes.

After studying this chapter, you will be able to:

• Evaluate your present note-taking practices;
• Use an effective method for taking and reviewing notes, also referred to as note making.

EXERCISE 9.1: SELF-OBSERVATION: ANALYZING NOTE-TAKING STRATEGIES

Directions: Assess your current note-taking strategies by checking the appropriate responses to each of the following questions. Be prepared to discuss in class your perception of the effectiveness of your current strategy. Think about why each of the questions in the table is relevant to taking effective notes.

		Always	Sometimes	Never
1.	Do you complete the assigned readings and other materials such as any video to be viewed before each class?			
2.	Do you try to sit as close as possible to the lecturer?			
3.	Do you take effective notes from PowerPoint-based lectures?			
4.	Do you doodle during a class?			
5.	Do you avoid listening when difficult information is presented?			
6.	Do you condense the main ideas rather than write complete sentences?			
7.	Do you use abbreviations?			
8.	Do you daydream in class?			
9.	Do you separate main ideas from examples and other secondary information?			
10.	Do you make a notation in your notes for information you don't understand?			
11.	Do you attempt to control distractions around you?			
12.	Do you try to determine the organization of the class?			
13.	Do you review your notes each day after class?			
14.	Do you understand your notes when you begin preparing for an exam?			

Comments:

_____

_____

_____

_____

_____ ■

Read the following student reactions to their experience with note-taking strategies. Are your experiences different or similar to the following comments?

Student Reflections

Note taking is far more difficult in college than in high school. The note-taking strategy that I learned in high school would be inappropriate and ineffective if I used it in a college course. High school teachers often spoon-fed the notes and emphasized what was important for you in the lecture. You were guided very thoroughly on what the specific main points and supporting details were. Key points were often written on the board, were illustrated in worksheets, and repeated many times. In addition, teachers would interact regularly with students while lecturing, allowing them to ask questions freely while emphasizing important information.

* * *

In college, taking notes requires more critical thinking and concentration. Good listening skills are essential for effective note taking because you have to determine the main points for yourself. Professors often move through a lecture with lightning speed, forcing you to determine key points quickly.

My note-taking strategies were very poor in high school. I would write down everything the teacher said and what was on the board. I thought that if I got everything written down on my paper, it would be easier for me to study, even if I did not know what the notes were about. At least I wrote all the information down! My notes were very disorganized, and I had no idea of the main purpose or ideas of my notes. Everything appeared to be thrown together, and it was very difficult to return to my notes, because I didn't know where to find certain things, and sometimes I really don't know the meaning of the information I wrote.

In high school, my notes were very confusing to me. I would just write down whatever I felt like at the time. My notes had very little structure to them. They would consist of very fragmented thoughts. When trying to review them for tests, I had a very hard time trying to figure out what went on in that particular lecture. I wouldn't even date my notes to know when a particular topic was discussed in class. At the time when I was in high school, I thought that my notes were just fine. I now look back on them, and they don't do the job.

HOW CAN I TAKE BETTER CLASS NOTES?

Note Making: The active and meaningful engagement with class notes by elaborative strategies such as creating mirror and summary questions.

There is more to taking class notes than recording ideas in a notebook or on your laptop. Similar to reading textbooks and learning from other course content, effective note taking and remembering what was written also involves activities in three important stages: before, during, and after the lecture. In fact, in Chapter 3, we introduced the concept of **note making**. As you may recall, taking notes in class by itself (note taking) is a rehearsal strategy, but the active engagement with the notes after they have been taken by creating questions and underlining the answers (note making) is an elaboration strategy. Therefore, taking notes is only the first stage in the process. We will next discuss the three important stages that transform note taking into note making in depth.

BEFORE CLASS

1. Complete Assigned Readings before Class

If you read textbook assignments related to the specific week or unit before class, you will learn more from the class for the following reasons (Ormrod, 2015). First, you will be able to direct your attention appropriately. One of the most important tasks in a class is to determine the main ideas. If you have already read the textbook, you will have a better idea of what is important than will another student who knows nothing or very little about the topic. Second, you are more likely to engage in meaningful rather than rote learning. That is to say, you will be better able to make sense of information delivered in class. Third, you will be able to organize the information because you will have a framework for understanding the material. Fourth, you will be able to use information from the textbook to elaborate on the information by filling in missing details or clarifying ambiguities.

2. Review Notes from the Previous Class

This activity should not take more than five or ten minutes, but the time is very worthwhile. Understanding previous material often provides a foundation for learning new material. The more information you do not understand, the more difficult it is to make sense of new material. Look up definitions of terms you do not understand and review computations in math and science courses after each class.

3. Bring All Necessary Materials (e.g., Notebook and Pen, Laptop, Handouts, Syllabus, and Textbook) to Class

Prepare at least 20 sheets of notepaper in the following format: draw a line down a sheet of paper, allowing for a three-inch margin on the left-hand side of the page. Write notes in the wide right-hand column and reserve the three-inch margin for questions derived from the notes. Many college bookstores sell notebooks with three-inch margins.

Keep your course syllabus in your binder or notebook, because instructors sometimes change assignments or dates of examinations. Placing changes directly in your syllabus will ensure that you do not miss some important information.

Instructors often mention material in the textbook, use the text for class discussions, or follow the text closely in class. Therefore, if you bring your textbook, you can mark the text or identify specific pages in your notes.

Here, it is important to also note what you may consider not bringing to the classroom or at least not having readily available during class. We already discussed the direct impact of multitasking on academic performance. One study (Tindell & Bohlander, 2012) reported that while in class, 91 percent of students had their phone on vibrate and only 9 percent had it turned off, 92 percent of students admitted to sending or receiving at least one or two messages during class, and 10 percent even admitted to sending or receiving a text during an exam! In deciding which items to bring to class, be aware of the "productive" and "distractive" contributions of all your devices!

4. Sit toward the Front of the Room If You Have Difficulty Concentrating

The closer you sit to the instructor, the better able you are to see and hear him or her and to maintain eye contact. The further you sit from the instructor, the easier it is to be distracted by other students talking or multitasking on their phones and laptops.

5. Date and Number Each Day's Notes

There are two major reasons for dating and numbering notes. The first is to be able to check the notes with the assigned textbook reading. The second is to obtain notes for days when you are absent. It is difficult to identify information in your notes when you do not know the exact day of class. If you have a friend in class, it is easier to discuss your notes when you can easily locate any given specific class session.

DURING CLASS

If you have completed all the steps outlined previously, you are now ready to fully benefit from the class, right? Unfortunately, Hanson et al. (2011) found that instead of taking notes, many students used class time to text and keep in touch with friends, study for other classes, or even catch up on sleep. In fact, several studies (e.g., Titsworth & Kiewra, 2004) demonstrate that students record fewer than 40 percent of the important lecture notes. Since taking complete lecture notes is positively correlated with achievement, taking incomplete lecture notes due to multitasking (or sleeping) naturally results in lower achievement. We'll next point out how to ensure you are taking complete notes.

1. Listen Carefully to the Instructor and Take Notes That Focus on Main Ideas and Supporting Details

Be alert for signals that indicate the importance of information and suggest possible representations you can construct after class.

Different instructors have different ways they communicate the importance of class material. The following are signals that indicate you should copy information in your notes:

- If the instructor *repeats* or *emphasizes a point*, you can usually assume it is important. You might write "R" (repeat) or place an asterisk (*) in the margin to mark the importance of the information.
- Copy whatever the instructor writes on the board or emphasizes via a PowerPoint.
- Always write definitions and listings, such as: "The three steps in this process are ..." "The two effects were ..." "Five characteristics are ...."
- Listen for *important comments*, such as: "This is an important reason ..." "Don't forget that ..." "Pay special attention to ...."

In the previous chapter, we discussed four different representations—hierarchies, sequences, matrices, and diagrams. Listen for the signal words listed in Table 8.1. The same words used by authors to signal organizational patterns are also used by instructors. When you hear a signal word in class, make a notation in your notes to review the information for a possible representation after class. Leave room in your notes for the construction of the representation.

We mentioned at the beginning of the chapter that it is as important to take notes in discussion-based sessions and other student-centered instructional activities as in typical lectures. In a student-led presentation, for example, look at your peers as the instructors and implement the same effective strategies of identifying main ideas and supporting details. Additionally, be sure to take notes on anything your professor adds or corrects during the student presentation.

While during lectures, an instructor typically makes main points and then supplies supporting details with examples, whereas discussion sections tend to be structured around questions posed by either the instructor or students. Van Blerkom (2012, p. 142) offers some helpful tips. Instead of writing down the main points, record the question asked. Then, write down the different points made during the discussion. You may also want to note who made which point. For example, you can simply write "P" in front of any question or statement made by the professor and "S" in front of any questions or points contributed by students. In essence, your notes from lecture versus discussion sessions could look like this:

In lecture:
   Main points made by instructor at the margin
       Supporting Ideas
           Examples

In the discussion section:
   Question posed by professor (P) or student (S)
       Points made during the discussion with supporting ideas
           Examples

2. Condense the Main Ideas and Supporting Details into Short Phrases or Sentences, Using Abbreviations Whenever Possible

As a side note, we don't think you will struggle with abbreviations as chances are your preferred way to connect with friends is texting, a channel of communication largely based on shorthand.

Instructor "There are three parts to the information processing system: the short-term sensory store, working memory, and long-term memory."
Condensation Three parts to IPS—STSS, WM, LTM

Words	Abbreviations
Pound	Lb
And	&
Positive	+
Negative	–
Without	w/out
Compare	Comp
Example	e.g.
Feminine	Fem
Masculine	Masc
Point	pt.
Introduction	intro.
that is	i.e.
Versus	vs.
equal to	=
Number	#
Achievement	Ach
Continued	cont'd

3. Use an Indenting Form for Writing Notes

Start main points at the margin and indent secondary ideas and supporting details. Further indent material that is subordinate to secondary points. The outline format helps you see how class was organized and helps identify the relative importance of the content when studying for an examination (see Figures 9.1 and 9.2). If the instructor's presentation is not well organized, do not spend too much time during class trying to figure out the outline. Get the main ideas down in your notes and reorganize them after class.

When the Instructor Moves to Another Idea or Topic, Show This Shift by Skipping Two Lines

One of the most confusing aspects of analyzing notes after class is following the instructor's main ideas. By skipping lines in your notes, you are alerted to the fact that the instructor moved on to another idea or topic. This procedure helps make sense of your notes.

AFTER CLASS

The most important part of note taking is the activities that are completed after you take notes. This is the stage that transforms note taking into note making. The activities presented here were developed by Heiman and Slomianko (1993). They involve generating and answering two types of questions from notes. The first is called a **mirror question**, because it directly reflects the information in your notes (see Figures 9.1 and 9.2). The second is called a **summary question**, because it reflects the major theme or main idea of the total class. If you know the answers to these questions, you understand your notes.

Mirror Question: A question that reflects the information in notes.

Summary Question: A question that reflects the major theme or main ideas of the total class.

What are the different chambers of the heart? What are the functions of the different chambers?	**Biology–Heart–9/17**
	
	Heart–muscular pump that provides pressure to pump blood throughout body
	
	Four chambers
	
	   rt. & left atria–<u>collect blood from major veins and empty it into ventricles</u>
	
	   <u>right & left ventricles–muscles whose contract forces blood to flow through arteries to all parts of body</u>
	
	Atrioventricular valves–between atria and ventricles that allow blood to flow from the atria to the ventricles, prevent flow in opposite direction.
	
	   Semiliunar valves–valves in aorta and pulmonary artery
	
	   aorta–carries blood from the left ventricle to body
	
	   pulmonary artery–carries blood from the right ventricle to the lungs

What happens if the valves in a heart are damaged?	*<u>If valves are damaged, the efficiency of the heart as a pump is diminished.</u>* *person may develop sympt. such as enlarged heart. Diagnosed by abnormal sounds as blood passes through them–heart murmurs.*
What happens if the ventricles in a heart are damaged?	*<u>If vent. are weakened by infection, lack of exercise, etc. the pumping efficiency of the heart is reduced.</u>* *Symptoms–chest pain, shortness of breath* *pain caused by heart not getting suff. blood.* *Portion of heart muscle not receiving blood will die in time*

Summary question (for complete lecture):

How does the heart function?

FIGURE 9.1   An Example of the Note-Taking Method in Biology

You need to set aside about five to ten minutes shortly after class to review your notes and complete the following activities:

1 Add any important information you remember the instructor saying but you did not write down.
2 Locate information you did not understand in class from the instructor, another student, or the textbook.
3 Play a form of academic Jeopardy and think about notes as answers to questions.

What are the different budget strategies that a president can use?	**Presidential Budget Strategies–9/15** *Veto strategy–often used as a defensive weapon that prevents Congress from funding at a higher level than the president wants* *president lack line item veto would allow them to veto particular items rather than whole measure* *Impoundment strategy–have the Congress and the OMB withhold funds from agencies* *president Nixon made most use of this strategy* *Reconciliation strategy–a method of changing budget politics*
What strategies did Reagan use?	*Types of* *fast track–budget committee compiles a single, omnibus reconciliation bill allowing proposed budget shifts all at one time* *national agenda–use public opinion to develop support for policy*
Why did early reconciliation work for Reagan?	*Outcome* *Reagan was able to dominate budget politics by compressing process.* *A single package made budget cuts highly visible– susceptible to national agenda made it difficult for party members to go against him.*
Summary question (for complete lecture): How do budgetary strategies allow presidents to implement their political agendas?	

FIGURE 9.2   An Example of Note-Taking Strategy in Political Science

After class, carefully read over the notes. Write mirror questions (in complete sentences) that the notes answer in the left-hand column of your notepaper (see Figures 9.1, 9.2, and 9.3).

Ask yourself: "If the information I wrote in my notes was an answer to a test question, what would the questions be?" In general, you should have three to four questions for each page of notes. If you cannot think of questions for certain parts of your notes, you probably do not understand the content or did not write enough information to make sense of the specific section of the notes. Write a question mark in the margin and ask a friend or the instructor about the information.

In science and math classes, it is important to identify the type of problem in the left-hand margin and the solution of the problem in the right-hand column. For example, if your math instructor is demonstrating the procedure to find the reciprocal of different numbers, the right-hand side of your notes identifies the procedure and the left-hand side lists the question: How do you find the reciprocal of different numbers?

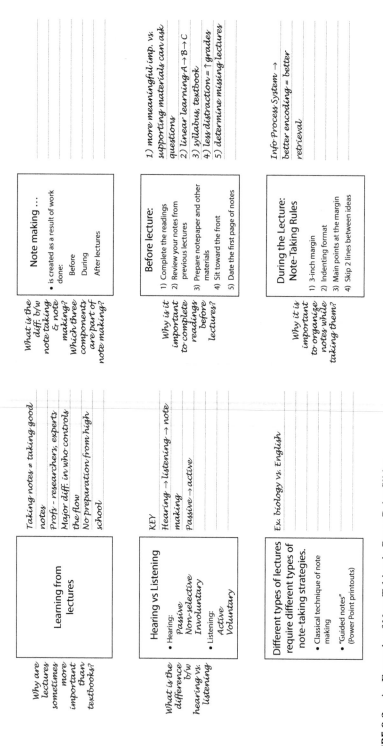

FIGURE 9.3   An Example of Note Taking in PowerPoint Slides

4 Once a question has been identified, return to the class notes and underline a key term or phrase that triggers an answer to the question.

When given the same notes, different students may underline different words or phrases, because the information that triggers an answer for one person may do nothing for another. As in reading textbooks, do not underline too much. Focus on only enough information to help answer the mirror question you wrote. The following are additional procedures to help you learn the content in your notes:

5 Read the key terms or phrases to verify that they help you recall the information in the notes. If the key terms or phrases trigger only partial answers to the questions, underline more information.
6 Cover the notes with a blank sheet of paper and attempt to answer the questions.
7 If appropriate, construct representations to depict the organization of class material.
8 Write a summary question for the total class at the end of your notes for the day.

Place a circle or box around this question so it will be easily recognized when you review your notes. Here you want to ask: "What is the one major question that reflects the purpose of today's class?" or "What is the relationship between my mirror questions?" If you can answer both of these questions, you will understand the theme or main idea of the total class. Think about the usefulness of summary questions in studying for essay examinations. In some classes, you may be able to predict 75 percent or more of the essay questions on your examinations.

EXERCISE 9.2: PRACTICING THE NOTE-TAKING STRATEGY

Directions: The following is a lecture excerpt on the psychology of learning. Take notes on this passage in the space provided. Be sure to use the indenting format. After taking notes, write one or more mirror questions in the left-hand margin and, finally, underline parts of your lecture notes that answer your mirror question(s). If possible, have a friend play the role of the instructor and read the lecture to you as you take notes.

I would like to begin my presentation this morning by comparing three major perspectives on human learning. Each of these perspectives has generated a great deal of research on human learning. Contemporary behaviorists view environmental factors in terms of stimuli and resultant behavior in terms of responses. They attempt to demonstrate that behavior is controlled by environmental contingencies of external reward or reinforcement, which are links between behavioral responses and their effects (or stimuli). Teachers who accept the behavioral perspective assume that the behavior of students is a response to their past and present environment and that all behavior is learned. For example, classroom troublemakers "learn" to be disruptive because of the attention (reinforcement) they get from peers; withdrawn students "learn" that their environment does not reinforce gregariousness, and they become reserved and silent. As a result, any behavior can be analyzed in terms of its reinforcement history. The logical extension of the behavioral principle of learning is a method to change or modify behavior. The teacher's responsibility, therefore, is to construct an environment in which the probability of reinforcing students for correct or proper behavior is maximized. This goal is best attained by carefully organizing and presenting information in a designed sequence. In contrast to the behavioral perspective, cognitive psychologists focus more on the learner as an active participant in the teaching–learning process. Those who adhere to this perspective believe that teachers can be more effective if they know what knowledge the learner already has acquired and what the learner is thinking about during instruction. More specifically, the cognitive approach tries to understand how information is processed and structured in an individual's memory. Many cognitive psychologists believe that teachers should instruct students in ways to use techniques or strategies to learn more effectively. Weinstein and Mayer (1986) state that effective instruction "includes teaching students how to learn, how to remember, how to think, and how to motivate themselves" (p. 315). Humanistic psychologists believe that how a person feels is as important as how the person behaves or thinks. They describe behavior from the standpoint of the believer rather than of the observer, and they are especially concerned with "self-actualization"—the growth of persons in whatever area they choose. The humanistic teacher is interested in creating an educational environment that fosters self-development, cooperation, and positive communication because of the belief that these conditions will foster greater learning.

(adapted from Dembo, 1994)

Psychology 101–Learning–Sept. 25

HOW CAN I ASK GOOD MIRROR QUESTIONS?

When students first begin writing mirror questions, most of the questions tend to be factual. As you write and answer mirror questions, it is important that the level of your questions reflects the same level of the instructor's focus. For example, if the main purpose of a class is to compare and contrast differences in major wars during the last century, the instructor is likely to focus on content that will be answered by such questions as: "What is the difference between …?" "What were the causes of …" "What might have happened if …?" However, if most of your questions focus on factual information like "What is …?" or "Who are …?" you are going to miss the major focus of the class and may not be properly prepared for the examination.

As discussed in Chapter 8, there are two broad levels of questions: lower level and higher level. Lower level questions tend to focus on remembering and understanding factual information, and involve responses regarding facts, dates, terms, or lists. Higher level questions require you to apply the information (e.g., by solving problems), analyze information, evaluate the information, or create a novel plan or solution. Be sure to generate both lower and higher level questions.

EXERCISE 9.3: IDENTIFYING THE DIFFERENT LEVELS OF QUESTIONS IN CLASS

Directions: For each of the questions identified below, write an L for lower level question or an H for higher level question in the space provided.

Indicate also which cognitive process (remember, understand, apply, analyze, evaluate, create) is being targeted in the question.

1 How many individuals died in the 9/11 attacks?
2 Should Khalid Sheikh Mohammed have been waterboarded in the interrogation process for his role in the 9/11 attacks?

3 What arguments would you use if you had to defend Khalid Sheikh Mohammed in court?
4 How many commercial passenger jet airliners were hijacked for the 9/11 attacks?
5 Why were the Twin Towers of the World Trade Center chosen as one target of the 9/11 attacks?

■

HOW DO I DEAL WITH PARTICULAR NOTE-TAKING PROBLEMS OR ISSUES?

The following questions and responses were adapted, in part, from Heiman and Slomianko (1993) and McWhorter (2010):

Should I copy over my notes?	No. Recopying notes is primarily a rehearsal strategy that requires little thinking. Your time is better spent writing and answering questions about the notes using the system described in this chapter.
Should I take notes in my textbook?	Generally, no. Most classes do not follow information directly from textbooks. Therefore, you will miss information by trying to locate the material in the textbook.
	One exception to this advice is books in literature classes. If the instructor refers to specific lines or pages while discussing a play, poem, or novel, notations in the margin may be helpful.
Should I record the class, especially if it is a lecture?	Generally, no. Listening to the lecture again takes up considerable time from other more useful study methods such as organizing the information. However, if English is not your primary language and you have serious difficulty following lectures, you might consider taping lectures for a short time until you improve your language skills. Be sure to ask your instructor's permission to tape!
Should I try to listen and not write when I don't understand something?	No. Keep taking notes; use blanks to indicate that you missed some material and question marks to indicate that you didn't understand something. Ask another student or your instructor to explain material you didn't understand.
I can't write as fast as my professors talk. What should I do?	Do not try to take verbatim notes. Paraphrase and use abbreviations. Insert blank lines and ask a student in your class for the notes you missed.
How can I better concentrate in class?	Sit in the front of the room. Be certain to preview assignments. Think about questions you may be expected to answer on exams.
How do I deal with an instructor who constantly wanders from one topic to another?	Be sure to read the textbook to discover organizing principles and attempt to organize notes after class. Compare your notes with those of other students.
What can I do about all the technical terms used in class that I can't spell?	Write them phonetically, the way they sound; fill in correct spellings during editing.

Table 9.1 presents a summary of the note-making procedures discussed in this chapter.

TABLE 9.1
Procedures for Note Making

Before Class

1. Complete assigned readings before class.
2. Review notes from the previous class.
3. Bring all necessary materials (notebook and pen, laptop or tablet, handouts). Prepare at least 20 sheets of notepaper in the following format: Draw a line down a sheet of paper allowing for a three-inch margin on the left-hand side of the page. Write notes in the wide right-hand column and reserve the three-inch margin for questions derived from class notes.

During Class

1. Listen carefully to the instructor and take notes that focus on main ideas and supporting details. Be alert for signals that indicate the importance of information.
2. Condense the main ideas and supporting details into short phrases or sentences using abbreviations whenever possible.
3. Use an indenting form for writing notes. Start main points at the margin and indent secondary ideas and supporting details. Further indent material that is subordinate to secondary points.
4. When the instructor moves to another idea or topic, show this shift by skipping two lines.

After Class

1. Add any important information you remember the instructor saying but you didn't write down.
2. Locate information you didn't understand in class from the instructor, another student, or the textbook.
3. Play a form of academic Jeopardy and think about notes as answers to questions. Shortly after class, read the notes over carefully. Write the questions that the notes answer in the left-hand column of your notepaper.
4. Once a question has been identified, return to the notes and underline a key term or phrase that triggers an answer to the question.
5. Read the key terms or phrases to verify that they help you recall the information in the notes. If the key terms or phrases trigger only partial answers to the questions, underline more information.
6. Cover the notes with a blank sheet of paper and attempt to answer questions.
7. If appropriate, construct representations to depict the organization of class material.
8. Write a summary question for the total class at the end of your notes for the day.

Chapter Review

KEY POINTS

1 Taking good notes and remembering what was written involves activities in three important stages—before, during, and after class. Engaging in all stages turns note taking into note making, a meaningful learning strategy.
2 Note making is important in both typical instructor-led lectures and during student-centered activities such as discussion sessions and student-led presentations.
3 Use an indenting form for writing notes. Start main points at the margin and indent secondary ideas and supporting details.
4 Be alert for signals that indicate the importance of information.
5 Think about notes as answers to questions.
6 Write mirror questions (in complete sentences) that the notes answer in the left-hand column of notepaper.
7 Create both lower and higher level questions.
8 Once a question has been identified, return to the notes and underline a key term or phrase that triggers an answer to the question.
9 Write a summary question(s) that reflects the theme or main ideas of the total class.
10 Use mirror and summary questions to prepare for exams.

FOLLOW-UP ACTIVITIES

1. Use the Self-Regulation Process to Become a Better Note Taker and a Note Maker

Complete the following self-study during a period of two to three weeks. Your report should include each of the following processes and should be approximately five to eight typed pages in length. See Appendix B for detailed information on how to conduct a self-regulation study.

Self-Observation and Evaluation. How effective is my note-taking strategy? Do I need to change the way I take notes? If yes, what problem(s) do I encounter? What are the symptoms of my problem (i.e., when, where, and how often does my problem occur)? How much of an impact does this problem have on my academic performance? What factors (e.g., beliefs, perceptions, feelings, physiological responses, or behaviors) contribute to this problem(s)? What do I need to change to reduce or eliminate my problem(s)?

Goal Setting and Strategic Planning. What are my goals? What strategies will I implement to improve my note taking during class? What strategies will I use to turn my note taking into note making? When will I use these strategies? How will I record my progress?

Strategy-Implementation and Monitoring. What strategies did I use to improve my note taking? When did I use these strategies? What method(s) did I use to record my progress (e.g., documents, charts, logs, tally sheets, checklists, or recordings)? When did I use these methods? How and when did I monitor my progress to determine if my new note-taking strategy was working? What changes, if any, did I make along the way?

Strategic-Outcome Monitoring. Did I attain the goal(s) I set for myself? Have the modifications in my note taking improved my academic performance? What strategies were the most and least effective? What changes, if any, do I need to make in the future?

2. Analyze Note-Taking Experiences

Identify your easiest and most difficult class in which you take notes. Why did you select these classes? Do the classes mostly include an instructor-focused lecture or other instructional activities such as discussion and student-led presentations as well? Explain what steps you have taken (or will take) to deal with the problems in the "most difficult" class.

Comments:

_____

_____

_____

_____

3. Edit and Review Your Notes

Select notes from a recent class. Instead of choosing a class with only an instructor-led lecture, consider choosing one that includes other ways of delivering information such as a discussion-based class or one that includes student-led presentations. Assess the completeness of your notes. You might want to compare your notes with a peer who you know takes effective and complete notes. Rewrite your notes to be complete and fit the format discussed in this chapter. Submit both sets of notes and write an analysis of the difference in the two sets of notes.

4. Analyze Your Instructors' Clues for Signaling Important Information

Instructors differ in the way they signal important information. Identify each of your instructors and list the verbal or non-verbal clues that he or she uses to signal main ideas or other important information presented in class.

Instructor Clues:

_____

_____

_____

_____

5. Compare Notes with Another Student

Select a specific class session at which another student was in attendance and took notes. Compare the number of main ideas identified by each of you and the mirror questions written after class. Discuss how the two sets of notes differ.

Model Answer to Exercise 9.2

	Psychology 101–Learning–Sept. 25
What are the differences between the beh., cog., and humanistic theories of learning?	Behaviorist
	S and R
	beh. controlled by environ.
	all. beh. is learned reinforcement
	Cognitive
	learner as active partic.
	information processing
	teach sts. how to learn
	Humanistic
	self-actualization
	develop educ. environ.
	feeling is important

Answers to Exercise 9.3

1 Lower level (Remember)
2 Higher level (Evaluate)
3 Higher level (Analyze or Create)
4 Lower level (Remember)
5 Lower level (Understand)

10 Preparing for Exams

Although the goal of this chapter is to discuss specific steps that are critical for a successful study plan, exam preparation really needs to begin on the very first day of the class. In fact, it's good practice to predict potential exam questions every time you study. While there are effective strategies to review the material, there simply is no substitute for ongoing learning.

We titled this chapter "Preparing for Exams" but an alternative title could be "Studying." All of the self-regulation processes discussed thus far are factors that can be used to plan and implement more effective study sessions (Zimmerman, 1998a). For example, to self-regulate academic studying, students must determine whether they will study and deal with the potential distractions and anxiety interfering with studying (motivation), plan how much time to spend studying (time management), determine how to study (methods of learning), select or create effective environments for study (physical environment), and ask instructors and other students to assist in learning (social environment).

Early in a term, most instructors remind students of a scheduled exam. It is not uncommon for many students to think: "Already … the class just started!" If you were to listen in on a conversation about exam preparation, you might hear the following: One student mentions she will set aside next Sunday to study, the day before the exam; a second student mentions that he began studying last week; a third student asks about organizing a study group. When the students begin talking about what material to study, one student remarks that he only plans to study his notes because he heard that the instructor stresses class notes over textbook readings; a second student states that she hopes much of the test comes from the textbook because she did not take many notes and has difficulty understanding the notes she took; a third student mentions that she plans to review the summary section of each chapter of the book and read through her notes a few times.

Students use a variety of study strategies for exam preparation. These strategies lead to different levels of success. In general, it is difficult to become a successful student by selectively studying course material. Yes, at times, some students will correctly predict the questions on an exam, but at other times, they will have wished they took a different approach. Our advice is to approach exam preparation with the notion that all relevant content will be reviewed. In this way, you will be prepared no matter what the instructor asks on an exam.

Sometimes a student can acquire some valuable tips from friends about exam preparation. However, students' comments also can negatively impact self-confidence if a student assumes that other students better understand the content or know more about exam preparation. Although it is helpful to discuss the content or even study with classmates, be sure to develop your own plan for success on an exam.

Each year we hear the following comment (although in different forms): "I can't believe this grade. I studied so hard!" or "I thought I really knew this stuff. I can't believe I didn't do well on the exam!" Baker (1989) called this "the illusion of knowing." The term describes the fact that some students think they know something when they really do not. Such an illusion occurs when students do not accurately test their knowledge to determine whether or not they understand and can recall the necessary content. Unfortunately, they wait for feedback from the instructor, who grades the exam, to find out whether or not they learned the material. An important aspect of exam preparation is to learn how to self-assess one's understanding of the course content. The primary method of self-assessment is predicting and answering questions. Simply stated: If a student does not generate and answer questions during study sessions, he or she is not adequately preparing for an exam!

Remember the discussion of the information-processing system in Chapter 3? The goal of learning is to move material into long-term memory, where it can be stored for retrieval. This goal can best be reached by using elaboration and organizational strategies rather than rehearsal strategies. Therefore, students who only use reciting, recopying, or rereading (i.e., rehearsal strategies) are likely to have difficulty recalling information or answering higher level questions during an exam. An important goal of this chapter is to encourage you to use a variety of study strategies appropriate for the different types of questions asked on exams.

Finally, the material in Chapter 10 and Chapter 11 is interrelated. You will learn that after you take an exam you should evaluate the effectiveness of your preparation. As you learn more about taking exams, you should apply this knowledge to improving your preparation.

After studying this chapter, you will be able to develop and implement effective study plans for examinations.

EXERCISE 10.1: SELF-OBSERVATION: ASSESSING EXAM PREPARATION

Directions: Assess your current exam preparation strategies by checking the appropriate responses to each of the following questions. Think about why each of the questions is relevant to effective preparation and summarize your exam preparation strategies in the following space.

		Always	Sometimes	Never
1.	Do you determine what content material is to be covered before you begin studying?			
2.	Do you set goals for what you hope to accomplish each time you study?			
3.	Do you set aside sufficient time to prepare for exams?			
4.	Do you develop a plan to study over a number of days?			
5.	Do you identify the specific study strategies you will use in each of your study sessions?			
6.	Do you select a quiet environment in which to study?			
7.	Do you study in groups?			
8.	Do you use study strategies other than rehearsal (e.g., reading over notes and textbooks, underlining content in textbooks, reciting definitions)?			
9.	Do you review your mistakes on past exams or quizzes?			
10.	Do you write questions to answer while studying?			
11.	Do you combine information from your class notes and texts together according to themes or topics when you study?			

Summary Statement:

_____

_____

_____

_____ ∎

HOW DO I DEVELOP A STUDY PLAN?

Successful athletes, musicians, artists, and writers often develop plans for how they will practice, prepare for performances, or make progress toward attaining their goals. For example, novelists often write many outlines and develop scenes and characters before they begin writing. Musicians set daily practice session goals and work carefully on separate passages of a composition. Students also plan for their performances, which are judged by examinations of the knowledge acquired in their courses. Therefore, sufficient time must be given to developing a "game plan" to prepare for each examination.

An effective study plan includes what, how, and when content will be reviewed. It organizes and separates material into small sections for study over a period of days. In addition, it includes a variety of learning and study strategies that will help the student respond correctly to both lower and higher level questions. As you might expect, time management plays an important role in the development of a study plan.

We'll now review a six-step procedure for how you can develop a study plan for each of your scheduled exams. In each step of the process, be sure to eliminate or at least minimize distractions such as texting and reviewing electronic notifications as they will impact the quality of both planning and executing your plan. Switching between different tasks, as we have discussed, is costly!

STEP 1: DETERMINE THE CONTENT COVERAGE AND QUESTION FORMAT OF THE EXAM

Exam questions come from many different sources. Omitting any of the following sources can result in incomplete information for exam preparation.

Course Syllabus. The course syllabus is a good place to start to determine the specific course content covered during the term. It is normally distributed at the first or second class session and includes all (or most of) the assignments (e.g., textbook chapters, exercises, and papers), as well as exam dates. Some instructors provide more information than others in a syllabus. This is why syllabi can range from about two pages to ten or even more pages. A review of the course syllabus will help you determine the exact content covered on the exam. If there are questions about the information in the syllabus, they can be raised in class. This review will prevent you from realizing midway through an exam that you failed to study some of the content covered on the exam.

Textbook Chapters. Many instructors use textbook chapters to organize the course units. The textbook chapters may be accompanied by other course materials such as journal articles and videos. After checking the topics covered in an exam, make sure the instructor did not announce any changes during the term. If the instructor failed to emphasize certain chapters or other sources such as articles and videos, do not assume they will not be covered on the exam. If you have questions, ask the instructor whether he or she will emphasize certain material in the course. Finally, assess how well you understand the material in each chapter and determine which chapters need more extensive study.

Class Notes. Whether the course you are studying for has lectures or discussions, review your class notes to determine if you have all of them and if they are complete. When notes are dated, it is easy to determine whether any notes are missing. If notes are missing or incomplete, borrow them from another student. Finally, ask your instructor or classmates questions about confusing aspects of your notes.

Previous Exams and Quizzes. Some instructors hand out copies of past exams, place them on reserve in the library, or allow students to review them in their office. If no mention is made of such exams, ask your instructor if it is possible to review an exam. The purpose of reviewing past exams is to identify possible topics or issues that are likely to appear on future exams. Although reviewing past exams can be helpful, do not assume that the exam coverage will be the same. Instructors often change textbooks or course content, and their exams reflect these changes.

The following are some questions you might want to consider when reviewing past exams: Does the instructor tend to ask questions from all the major areas in the course, or does he or she tend to focus on specific areas? Do the questions reflect both the textbook and other course materials such as lectures and articles, or is one source of information favored over the other? What types of questions are asked? Do they tend to be factual, or do they ask you to engage in higher level thinking such as solving problems, giving opinions, or analyzing information?

Instructor's Handouts. Do not limit your review to class notes, textbooks, and other course materials. Many instructors pass out or post summaries, outlines, lists of terms, sample problems, maps, or charts that provide information for exams. Any information that your instructor gives you is likely to be important. Date and label handouts as you receive them. The labeling should identify the class topic to which the material corresponds. It is important to save these handouts so you do not lose them.

Information from Other Students. Did you miss any classes during the term? Is there information you do not understand? Do not hesitate to ask students in your class questions about the course content. In addition, consider whether you could benefit from participating in group study sessions.

Information from the Last Class before the Exam. Review the content covered for the exam before class so you will be better prepared to ask questions in class and understand the instructor's reply to other students' questions. Although students can learn important information about a course from each class, the last class before an examination is especially important for several reasons. First, instructors may give a brief overview of the exam by discussing both content and format (i.e., number of essay and objective test questions). Second, instructors may provide last minute suggestions, such as "Pay particular attention to ..." or "Be sure to look over ...." Third, instructors may provide important information by the manner in which they reply to students' questions.

Information about the format of the exam can be helpful in determining the study strategies selected. Is the exam a combination of essay and objective questions (e.g., multiple-choice or true–false), or will the exam include only one type of question? The instructor can cover a broad field of knowledge by using objective questions, because they can be answered quickly. However, essay questions usually cover a limited field of knowledge, because they take longer to answer. The selection of study strategies for an exam depends on both the format and nature of the course content. For example, focusing on the summary questions after each class may be more important in preparing for an essay exam, whereas focusing on factual information may be more important when studying for certain objective exams.

STEP 2: ORGANIZE AND SEPARATE THE CONTENT INTO PARTS

Many students open their textbooks and notes and proceed sequentially through the content. They focus on dates, facts, formulae, or definitions found in textbooks or class notes. Often, studying textbooks and studying class notes are viewed as separate activities. The problem in this approach is that it is easy to lose sight of the important ideas and issues in the course. An alternative approach is to use *thematic study*, which involves organizing all relevant content, no matter where it is found, around specific topics or themes. For example, a unit covering different wars in history might be organized as follows: causes, major battles, military leaders, and political and economic consequences (repeatable categories in a matrix). All the factual information could be studied within each of the repeatable categories.

The advantage of thematic study is that it forces students to determine which topics are most important and to integrate the information from class, chapters in the textbook, and other course materials. Here are some suggestions for using this approach. First, review the course syllabus, introductory chapter, and class notes to determine whether the instructor or textbook author identified themes or topics for the course. A review of the table of contents in a textbook can be helpful in identifying themes. Second, identify how the class notes relate to the material in the textbook and other sources. Finally, integrate related material into themes. Identify the fundamental ideas that have been emphasized throughout the course and organize your materials around these ideas. In a US history exam, for example, fundamental ideas might be about national identity, migration and settlement, politics and power, the relationship of the United States with the world, and other core ideas.

As illustrated in the earlier example of the study of wars in history, one useful way to determine major topics and themes is to use representations for as much of the material as possible.

Such representations can be helpful in organizing the material and provide help in generating possible exam questions.

STEP 3: IDENTIFY SPECIFIC STUDY STRATEGIES

Remember from the previous chapters that many students use rote learning strategies such as rereading and highlighting that have limited effectiveness on long-term learning and retention. It is possible that these strategies are hugely popular because they are relatively easy for students to do. However, studies clearly point out that their effects of learning are not long-lasting (Dunlosky, Rawson, Marsh, Nathan, & Willingham, 2013). Let's take a look at a few meaningful learning strategies that have been demonstrated to be effective:

Self-Questioning and Self-Explanation. An example of elaboration, a meaningful learning strategy, is asking and answering "why" questions and generating explanations of what you have learned. Make a specific effort to relate new knowledge to your prior knowledge by asking questions such as "How does this information relate what I already know?" and "What new information does what I just learned add to my existing understanding?" Researchers rate these strategies as effective because they encourage you to become actively involved in exam preparation and, as a result, improve comprehension and retention (Dunlosky et al., 2013).

Self-Testing. While we are sure you prefer to take as few tests as possible, research findings clearly demonstrate that self-testing enhances learning and retention. **Testing effect** is the well-established research finding that retrieving information from memory such as in self-testing

> **Testing Effect:** The phenomenon that when information is retrieved from memory such as via self-testing and quizzes, one's memory of the retrieved information is strengthened.

strengthens our memory and consequent learning of that information (Roediger & Bulter, 2011; Rowland, 2014). In fact, after reviewing 700 scientific articles about the most common learning strategies, self-testing emerged as one of the most effective study strategies (Dunlosky et al., 2013). Why does self-testing work? It helps you identify gaps in your knowledge and understanding (remember from Chapter 8 that failure can be productive), produces better organization of knowledge, and facilitates retrieval of information for when you are actually taking an exam (Roediger & Pyc, 2012). Self-testing could involve strategies such as predicting and answering exam questions, answering questions at the end of a textbook chapter, and testing recall using note cards. If you follow the procedures for reading texts and taking notes in class described in Chapter 8 and Chapter 9, respectively, you already have been generating and answering questions related to the content in your courses. Therefore, you do not have to start from scratch. Your mirror and summary questions for each class will be useful for study. The questions in your textbook or the self-generated questions from the headings are another useful source. As you are answering the questions, use your own words as much as possible and think about personal examples that relate to the content. If you are working with someone else, consider explaining your answers to them and have them ask clarifying questions. This strategy will reveal any knowledge gaps you have and direct further study. Finally, the representations developed after reading or note taking can help you generate questions. If you have not developed such representations, you should consider doing so during your final preparation for an exam.

In addition to the general approaches just discussed, Table 10.1 identifies a list of effective preparation and review strategies that can be used in a study plan. You may use one or more of these strategies in the preparation for exams depending on the difficulty of the material and your own experience as to which strategies work best for you.

In earlier chapters, you were taught to write questions from your notes and turn headings in textbooks into questions. The purpose of this elaboration strategy was to help you become actively involved in the content so you would focus on the most relevant material when preparing for exams. The extra work that you did to complete these tasks will now pay off as you use these questions for self-testing.

TABLE 10.1
Study Strategies for Use in a Study Plan

Preparation Strategies	Review Strategies
Create representations and identify possible exam questions	Replicate representations or answer self-generated questions
Outline	Recite main points from outline
Summarize	Recite out loud
Predict essay questions	Answer essay questions
List steps in a process	Recite steps from memory
Read textbook questions	Answer textbook questions
Identify self-generated questions from textbooks	Answer self-generated questions
Prepare material for study group	Explain material to group members
Make question cards	Recite answers
Make formula cards	Practice writing formulae
Make problem cards	Complete work problems
Identify mirror and summary questions from notes	Answer mirror and summary questions from notes
Make self-tests	Take self-tests

Adapted from Van Blerkom (2012)

Naturally, in order for self-testing to be optimal, the questions you formulated from your class notes and textbook material need to accurately cover the possible questions that could be asked on an exam. Additionally, your self-testing questions should reflect the types of questions that will be on the exam. For example, if the exam requires an essay response targeting higher level thinking, then creating only lower level self-test questions may leave you unprepared for the exam. Remember from Chapter 8 that lower level questions involve responses regarding *facts*, *dates*, *terms*, or *lists*. Questions beginning with Who …? What …? When …? and Where …? are appropriate for lower level questions.

Higher level questions require you to *apply* the information that you learned to a new situation (such as solving problems), *analyze* information (such as comparing and contrasting information), *evaluate* the value of the information, or *create* a novel plan or solution. The following examples are stems for higher level questions: Why …? How …? What if …? How does A affect B? What are the advantages or disadvantages of …? What are the strengths or weaknesses of …? What are the differences between …? What is your opinion of …? Make a list of other higher level questions that could be asked on exams in the different courses you are taking.

Figure 10.1 presents different types of study cards students can develop for different courses. Note that the study cards can include both lower and higher level questions. A study card can focus on one major point or can combine a great deal of information about a topic. In this way, you can reduce the number of cards you need to produce.

When you approach the last evening before an exam, you should not be rereading the textbook or class notes, but instead use the representations you developed, along with questions, note cards, and summaries, as your primary review material.

Step 4: Identify the Amount of Time Needed for Each Strategy

Different study strategies involve different amounts of time. For example, making study cards to review definitions of terms often requires less time than developing a representation of content in a chapter or summarizing a short story. Therefore, after you determine how you will study for an exam, it is important to estimate the amount of time needed. No one can accurately predict the exact time needed for projected study sessions. Base your projections on previous experience and modify them as you acquire greater skill in using a strategy.

Front of Card	Back of Card
What were the causes of {...}	The causes were 1. 2. 3.
What are the differences between ——— and ————?	The differences are 1. 2. 3.
Convert .742 kg to grams	.742 kg × 1000g/1kg = 742g
Learning strategies	Techniques or methods students use to acquire information. Rehearsal (e.g. underlining) Elaboration (e.g., analogy) Organizational (e.g., outline and map) Certain learning strategies are more effective in moving information to LTM.

FIGURE 10.1   Examples of Different Types of Study Cards

STEP 5: ALLOCATE TIME FOR EACH STUDY STRATEGY IN A MONTHLY OR WEEKLY SCHEDULE

In the chapter about learning and memory, we pointed out that cramming or massed practice does not work because of the limitations of human working memory. Cramming may enable you to "regurgitate" the knowledge for an exam on the next day but does not produce long-term learning. Additionally, sacrificing sleep to cram is counterproductive and costly as the less you sleep, the poorer your performance on tests (Gillen-O'Neel, Fuligni, & Huynh, 2013). So what is a better approach? Experimental research has established beyond a shadow of a doubt that distributed practice promotes meaningful, long-term learning (Dunlosky et al., 2013; Kornell et al., 2010). Therefore, it is important to consider how much time each of the study strategies you plan to use will take and then identify time in your monthly or weekly schedule for each of the strategies. For example, in some cases you may need one or two days to prepare for short quizzes or exams, whereas for more comprehensive exams you may need a week or more to prepare.

Van Blerkom (2012) makes another important point about distributed practice. Many students believe that simply distributing the chapters or themes to be studied over several days constitutes distributed practice. However, distributed practice in fact means studying the same material over a period of days. For example, on the first day of your study plan for a course based on this textbook, you may spend one hour preparing the material for the information-processing system (IPS) and the related learning strategies. On the next day, you may spend one hour preparing the material for the time-management and procrastination chapter as well as spend ten minutes reviewing the IPS-related material. This could involve reviewing the key terms at the end of Chapter 3. On the third day, you will tackle a new theme but also take five minutes to review IPS and ten minutes to review time management and procrastination. Distributing the material in this manner gives you opportunities to rehearse, elaborate, and organize the material, which supports long-term memory encoding and, ultimately, learning.

STEP 6: MODIFY THE PLAN AS NECESSARY

The key to success with distributed practice is to follow your study schedule. The first author considered her study schedule in undergraduate and graduate school as her full-time work schedule, as something she had no choice but to follow. Do your absolute best to not let disruptions get you off track. However, the fact that you developed a study plan does not mean you always will follow it as planned. Many different factors influence the need for change, such as the unavailability of certain study material or the realization that you need to review certain material that you do not understand or cannot recall. Additionally, students make changes in their initial plans because of an underestimation or overestimation of time needed to study different content. The following student reflection discusses the benefits of distributed practice but also emphasizes the need to be flexible.

Student Reflections

I took the course based on this book several months ago and it has changed the way I prepare for exams. Going into the course, I wasn't too optimistic. I considered myself to have strong study skills already and I didn't think making adjustments was necessary. However, the strategies taught in the course and book about how to create successful study plans in preparing for exams were extremely helpful. In all honesty, my exam preparation was decent and perhaps slightly above average, but the book's strategies really gave me the extra boost necessary for college. I learned to set up a study plan with at minimum an entire week and a half before the exam.

For my Calculus 2 final, I laid out a two-week schedule and assigned a particular number of sections to be covered each day. What made this more effective was that each day built on the other, ensuring that rote learning was not taking place due to all the connections I would make between the concepts. Of course, it is tough to be perfect, so there were days where maybe I wouldn't get done what was scheduled. As the book suggests, when this happens, you just re-adjust your plan according to the time you have left until the exam. And finally, as the book suggests, I set the last three days aside for self-testing. Trying to emulate the testing environment as much as possible benefited me a great deal. I took at least five or six practice exams over the last three days.

After not giving the book much credit at the beginning, I now look back and I am extremely grateful for it as my study skills improved significantly right at the needed time. The key to making a change to your study skills is to stick with your plan as much as possible. Yes, sometimes certain tasks will not get done, but you must keep at it. It may be a trite statement, but practice makes perfect, and the more you practice, the more likely these practices will become habits.

The following student reaction illustrates that learning any new strategy takes time. How would you respond to the question asked in the last sentence?

Student Reflections

I have read the chapter on test preparation and I am trying to implement the strategy of generating and answering questions for my next exam in anthropology. I am outlining the required chapters, studying the vocabulary words, and generating some questions that I think will be on the exam. I think I am doing everything possible to prepare for the exam. Why don't I feel confident? There are so many possible questions that could be on the exam. I don't know if I am generating enough questions. My instructor makes it sound like test preparation is easy when it is not. I am never sure what an instructor will ask on an exam. Everything seems important to me! How do I deal with this situation?

AN EXAMPLE OF A STUDY PLAN

Figure 10.2 presents a study plan developed by a student in a child development course. As you review the procedures, think about how you could develop your own plans for exams in different courses.

CONTENT COVERAGE AND QUESTION FORMAT

Janis prepared for an examination in Human Development, which included 30 multiple-choice and four short-essay questions. Her instructor announced that the exam would include two chapters on adolescent development and related class notes. Janis read one of the chapters thoroughly and

Day	Study Strategy	Time	Completed
Monday	Reread Chapter 10 and generate questions from headings (A)	2 hrs	X
	Develop study cards for key terms (B)		X
	Make a list of major research findings (C)		X
Tuesday	Answer questions generated from Chs. 10 and 11 and related lecture notes (D)	2 hrs	X
	Review study cards (E)		X
Wednesday	Develop three representations from content and generate and answer possible exam questions (F)	1½ hrs	X
	Review lecture material not emphasized in textbook (G)		X
Thursday	Review summary section at the end of each chapter (H)	3 hrs	X
	Make a short list of possible essay questions from summary questions, lectures, representations, and textbook (focus on theories and developmental characteristics) (I)		X
	Outline or develop representations to assist in responding to the questions (J)		X
	Review study cards (K)		X
	Review list of major research findings (L)		X
Friday	Take exam		

FIGURE 10.2 Janis' Study Plan

skimmed the second chapter. She realized from her dated notes that she needed to obtain a copy of one day's notes from her friend.

ORGANIZE THE CONTENT FOR STUDY

The two chapters and class notes were on physical, intellectual, personality, and social development in adolescence. Janis reviewed the textbook and class notes and decided that the best organizing topics or themes for her review should be based on the four topics. The textbook was already organized around these topics, and the class notes needed to be reorganized to fit this organization. Because she used a three-ring binder for all her class notes, it was easy for her to place the notes in a different order from that in which they were originally presented.

Based on meeting with her instructor and her review of the course syllabus, Janis decided that she needed to learn (a) the key terms found in the readings and class notes, (b) important research findings, (c) theories of development, and (d) typical behavior of adolescents in each of the four areas.

IDENTIFY SPECIFIC STUDY STRATEGIES

Janis decided to make study cards for all the major terms in the two chapters, as well as the terms introduced by her instructor. The definitions were written in her own words rather than verbatim from the text, so she was sure that she understood each term. She also added examples, when appropriate, to enhance her recall of specific course content. For example, one key term was *personal fable*, which is defined as a belief in adolescence that one is special, unique, and not subject to the rules that govern the rest of the world. Janis wrote on the back of the study card: belief that one is special such that bad things affect others, not oneself (e.g., other people have sex and get pregnant, but not you).

One of the topics discussed in the readings and class notes was eating disorders. She decides it would be important to compare the three types of eating disorders—obesity, anorexia, and bulimia—in a matrix form. Figure 10.3 includes the matrix she developed.

From the matrix, she identified both multiple-choice and essay questions that could be asked about the material. Figure 10.3 lists examples of some of the questions she generated and answered in her study notes from the representation.

Eating Disorders

	Obesity	Anorexia	Bulimia
Description:	Overweight	Self-starvation	Eating binges/self-induced vomiting
Cause:	Overeating	Possibly related to societal pressure/psych. disorder	Possibly related to brain chem./psych. disorder
Health Risk:	Early death/chronic health problems	Death/depression	Depression/gastric irritation/skin prob./loss of hair
Treatment:	Diet/exercise	Therapy/hospitalization	Therapy

FIGURE 10.3   A Matrix Depicting Different Eating Disorders

MULTIPLE-CHOICE

Which one of the following eating disorders is difficult to treat without hospitalization?

a. Obesity
b. Anorexia
c. Bulimia
d. All of the above

Self-starvation is a major problem in adolescents with

a. Gonorrhea
b. Anorexia
c. Bulimia
d. Herpes

If you are studying in a group and your assignment is to write a few multiple-choice questions, you would want to include the incorrect responses. However, if you are attempting to generate many multiple-choice questions on your own, you may not want to spend the time writing the incorrect responses.

ESSAY

1 Compare and contrast the three different types of eating disorders experienced by adolescents.
2 Discuss the causes for different eating disorders identified in adolescents.

She developed a second matrix comparing physical development in males and females and a third on common sexually transmitted diseases. Finally, she constructed a sequence representation on different stages of moral development. She found the sequence helpful in understanding and recalling this important theory of development. In each case, she attempted to predict test questions that might appear on the exam.

Because she carefully read, generated questions from headings, and underlined the answers for the first chapter, she only had to review the answers to the questions. However, for the second chapter, she needed to reread the material, generate questions, and underline the answers in her textbook.

Finally, she reviewed the questions generated from her notes and attempted to identify material that was not covered in her questions from her textbook. Because her instructor was interested in cultural differences in adolescent development, there was considerable material in the class notes that was not included in the textbook.

IDENTIFY THE AMOUNT OF TIME NEEDED FOR EACH STRATEGY

In determining the amount of time needed for each strategy, Janis considered (a) her experience and knowledge using a strategy and (b) the time she thought she needed to spend on each strategy. For example, she believed that writing definitions for the key terms on study cards could be done in 30 minutes but developing three representations could take one and a half hours. Because she turned headings into questions for one chapter, she believed that the chapter could be reviewed in 20 minutes. However, she did not generate questions when she read the second chapter. She needed to reread the chapter and write questions, which she estimated would take at least an hour.

ALLOCATE TIME FOR EACH STUDY STRATEGY IN A WEEKLY SCHEDULE

Janis was taking four other courses and could not stop reading and studying in her other courses to prepare for her child development course. For example, she also had a math quiz and had to write a short essay for English. Her task, therefore, was to integrate her exam preparation with her other learning and study activities.

Janis labeled all the activities in her study plan from A to L. This labeling allowed her to identify each activity in her weekly schedule by a letter. Using this procedure, she did not have to recopy the description of the study activity in her weekly schedule. She simply referred to her study plan when it was time for the activity. Notice in Figure 10.2 that she prioritized her study sessions by starting with the chapter she did not carefully read. Janis also included time during the day to study for her child development exam so that she would have some time each evening for her other courses.

Janis' study plan was presented to provide a concrete example for how to develop such a plan. Such plans can greatly differ from course to course and student to student, depending on the nature of the content and ability of the student. For example, a study plan for a math course would involve the identification of the different types of problems studied in the unit, with problem solving as the major study activity. In a science course, the study strategies would focus both on learning the content knowledge and on solving problems.

Janis did not choose to study in a group for this exam but has formed study groups for other exams in the same and other courses she is taking. In general, she has found group study very helpful in reviewing answers to questions and reviewing solutions to problems.

Finally, once you start developing your own plans, modify the format to fit your own needs. The most important factor is not the format of the plan, but the selection and use of learning and study strategies to improve your retention and retrieval of information on the exam. Table 10.2 provides a summary of the procedures for developing a study plan.

TABLE 10.2

Procedures for Developing a Study Plan

Procedures	Examples
1. Determine the content coverage	"I never miss the class before an exam because the instructor usually reviews the content coverage. I also take the time to check that I have all the needed resources (i.e., books, notes, and handouts) before I begin studying."
2. Organize and separate the content into parts	"I have identified six different types of problems I need to learn how to solve in chemistry. I'll work on the problems in three different study sessions."
3. Identify specific study strategies	"I decide which study strategy is most helpful for the different content I must learn. For example, I prefer to use representations for more complex material and note cards for factual content."
4. Estimate the amount of time needed for each strategy	"During my first term in college I underestimated how much time I needed to review course content. I now begin to study for exams much earlier because I can't review a large amount of content in a day or two."
5. Allocate time for each study strategy in a weekly schedule	"When I have an exam, I try to schedule study time during the day and evening so I have time to complete my other assignments."
6. Modify the plan as needed	"I never realized how many unexpected events occur that interfere with my study time. I review my study plan each night and make needed changes."

Chapter Review

KEY POINTS

1   The primary activity during study is to test yourself by predicting and answering potential exam questions, answering questions in the textbook, and testing recall using note cards.
2   Self-explanation and self-questioning are effective study and exam preparation strategies.
3   A student needs to prepare for different levels of questions on an exam.
4   A study plan should be developed for each exam.
5   Different types of study strategies should be included in a study plan, especially elaboration and organizational strategies.
6   Representations can be a useful method for generating test questions.
7   Time management is an important factor in implementing the activities in a study plan.
8   Distributed practice is an effective study strategy where the student distributes the material over many study sessions in a monthly or weekly plan. This is in contrast to massed practice, where the student conducts study immediately prior to the exam in long sessions.
9   A student should focus on review material (i.e., note cards, representations, questions, and answers) during the last day(s) before an exam, rather than rereading books and notes.

FOLLOW-UP ACTIVITIES

1. Use the Self-Regulation Process to Improve Exam Preparation

Complete the following self-study during a period of two to three weeks. Your report should include each of the following processes and should be approximately five to eight typed pages in length. See Appendix B for detailed information on how to conduct a self-regulation study.

Self-Evaluation and Monitoring.   How effective are my current exam preparation (i.e., study) strategies? Do I need to change the way I plan and study for exams? If yes, what problem(s) do I encounter? What are the symptoms of my problem (i.e., when, where, and how often does my problem occur)? How much of an impact does this have on my academic performance? What factors (e.g., beliefs, perceptions, feelings, physiological responses, or behaviors) contribute to this problem? What do I need to change to reduce or eliminate my problem(s)?

Goal Setting and Strategic Planning.   What are my goals? What strategies will I implement to improve my exam preparation? When will I use these strategies? How will I record my progress?

Strategy Implementation and Monitoring.   What strategies did I use to improve my exam preparation? When did I use these strategies? What method(s) did I use to record my progress (e.g., documents, charts, logs, tally sheets, checklists, or recordings)? When did I use these methods? How and when did I monitor my progress to determine if my new exam preparation plan was working? What changes, if any, did I make along the way?

Strategic-Outcome Monitoring.   Did I attain the goal(s) I set for myself? Have the modifications in my exam preparation improved my academic performance? What strategies were the most and least effective? What changes, if any, do I need to make in the future?

2. Develop a Study Plan

Select a study partner and develop a study plan for an examination on one chapter in this book. Identify the different strategies you used in your plan and compare it with the plan of another pair of students.

3. Develop Questions from a Representation

A student developed the following representation in a physics course. Generate two multiple-choice and two essay questions that an instructor could ask from this representation (Figure 10.4).

4. Compare Study Plans

Develop a study plan for a science or math course and compare it with a study plan for a course in the humanities or the social sciences. Discuss how the study plans differ.

STATES OF MATTER

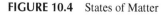

	Solid	*Liquid*	*Gas*
Shape	Its Own	Of Container	Of Container
Flow	No	Yes	Yes
Volume of substance	Smallest	In-between	Largest
Speed of sound in substance	Fastest	In-between	Slowest

FIGURE 10.4   States of Matter

11 Taking Exams

Effective test-taking strategies do not only involve what you do during the actual exam. Importantly, make sure you get enough sleep throughout the semester but also on the night before the exam. In Chapter 6, we discussed that during sleep, the brain solidifies and enhances learning, and therefore, sacrificing sleep will backfire (Gillen-O'Neal, Hyunh, & Fuligni, 2013). In addition, sleep deprivation decreases your ability to concentrate (Brown, 2017).

Although in this chapter, you will learn a number of strategies to help you succeed in exams, it is important to remember that these strategies are most effective when you prepare properly for an exam. Simply stated: test-taking strategies cannot make up for ineffective exam preparation. In discussing effective test-taking strategies, we will focus on two different types of tests: objective and essay. Objective tests include true–false, completion, matching, and multiple-choice questions. They are referred to as "objective" because they have right or wrong answers, and therefore, can be graded objectively. On the other hand, essay exams require students to construct their own, subjective responses to writing prompts. Most instructors use combinations of these two major categories of questions.

How many times have you heard the following statements: "The test was tricky," "I really knew that question, but I misread it," or "I knew the answer, but I did not organize my response adequately." Although many instructors will often empathize with your predicaments about taking tests, they grade exams on what was checked, circled, underlined, or written. It is your performance that is evaluated, not your intentions, beliefs, or test-taking strategies.

Test anxiety plays a role in exam performance as well. Some nervousness before and during a test is normal and may even increase your concentration and ultimate ability to do well. However, when it begins to negatively impact your performance, it can be defined as test anxiety—and you will want to address it. In order to determine if you have test anxiety, answer the following questions:

- Have I prepared adequately to perform well on this test?
- During the test, do I have trouble remembering material I studied and know?
- Do I have trouble concentrating during the test due to anxiety?
- Do my grades often not reflect how well I really know the material?

If your answer to the first question was "no," you have rational, justified test anxiety and will benefit from the strategic exam preparation approach presented in Chapter 10. It is, however, the case that some students, despite having effectively prepared for the test, have test anxiety and habitually "choke under pressure." This is irrational test anxiety. In Chapter 5, we discussed irrational thinking patterns such as filtering, catastrophizing, overgeneralization, and others. These can lead to negative self-talk such as "What if I don't earn a passing grade on this exam and have to drop the course?" or "I'm going to fail for sure." These irrational thoughts and the corresponding anxiety during taking the exam compete for the available working memory resources which, as you recall, are very limited to begin with. If you are one of the students who experience irrational test-taking anxiety in the sense that you are well prepared but still highly anxious, be sure to review and implement the anxiety-reducing strategies we discussed in Chapter 5: relaxation strategies such as diaphragmatic breathing and progressive muscle relaxation, and cognitive strategies such as replacing negative, irrational self-talk with positive counterstatements. For example, instead of "what if," try "I can handle this" and "I can be anxious and still do this." In addition, researchers recommend this seemingly counterintuitive idea: take ten minutes to write down your thoughts and feelings regarding the content of the exam immediately before the test.

Sounds surprising? Wouldn't you want to "turn off" your anxiety-related thoughts and feelings instead? Turns out that "writing alleviates the impact of worries on performance" (Ramirez & Beilock, 2011, p. 213), particularly for students who are habitually anxious in test-taking situations. Writing down thoughts and feelings about the exam may avail working memory resources to be focused on the exam, rather than the anxiety-related rumination. This allows for better performance.

The information in this chapter concerning taking exams is also helpful when writing and answering test questions in preparing for examinations. For example, the more you practice writing good essay responses before an exam, the more likely you will be able to demonstrate the same good responses on actual exams.

After studying this chapter, you will be able to use test-taking strategies to improve performance on objective and essay questions.

EXERCISE 11.1: SELF-OBSERVATION: ASSESSING TEST-TAKING STRATEGIES

Directions: Assess your current test-taking strategies by checking the appropriate responses to each of the following questions. Think about why each of the questions is relevant to successful performance on exams and write a summary statement about your test-taking strategies in the space provided.

	Always	Sometimes	Never
1. Do you preview your entire exams before beginning?			
2. Do you allocate time for each section of your exams before beginning?			
3. Do you carefully read the directions before beginning?			
4. Do you carefully read all of the response options in multiple-choice questions before selecting the best response?			
5. Do you outline or represent content for essay questions before you begin writing?			
6. Does test anxiety influence your performance on exams?			
7. Do you change a large number of correct answers to incorrect responses?			
8. Do you proofread your responses to essay questions?			
9. Do you review your responses to the exam before turning it in?			

Summary Statement:

_____

_____

_____

_____ ∎

WHAT STRATEGIES CAN I USE TO ANSWER OBJECTIVE TEST QUESTIONS?

Before we review specific test-taking strategies for different types of objective questions, it is important to review some general strategies to use for all objective questions.

How Should You Manage Your Time?

To properly manage your time, adhere to the following guidelines:

- Always know how much time you have for the test.
- During the test, check the exam location clock once in a while so that you will know how much time is left. Many exam locations, though, do not have a wall clock and chances are that you do not even own a watch. The only way most students we teach tell time is by using their cell phone. This could be problematic as most instructors do not allow any access to cell phones during the exam to avoid potential cheating. Our recommendation is to have an alternative way to tell time by investing in a watch for your college career. With fewer and fewer customers actually purchasing watches, you are sure to find some great bargains!
- When you begin the test:
  - Answer questions you know first.
  - Do not spend too much time on hard questions. Try not to get anxious when you cannot answer a hard question.
- Skip hard questions and go back to them at the end of the test.
- When you have answered all the questions, go back and check your work.

How Should You Approach Each Question?

Use the following guidelines to approach each question:

- If you do not know the answer to a question, read the question again.
- Read each of the answers.
- Mark the best answer only after you have read all of the answers.
- If you cannot figure out the answer to a question, guess.
- Be sure you mark one answer for each question. Do not leave a question blank.

When Should You Change an Answer?

You should change an answer:

- When you know you made a mistake.
- When you think another answer is better. A few minutes after you start taking a test, you sometimes get into the swing of the test, start retrieving the content from your long-term memory more effectively, and see things in the questions that you did not notice at first. After you finish the test and start going back over the questions, if a different answer seems better, you should change your answer.

Let's now review specific strategies for improving performance on true–false, matching, completion, and multiple-choice questions.

Strategies for True–False Questions

True–false questions are statements that you must decide are correct (true) or incorrect (false). Answer the following true–false question by writing True or False in the space provided:

Efficacy beliefs refer to a student's attitudes about an academic subject.

The answer to this question is "False," because efficacy beliefs refer to the perceptions students have about their ability to master a specific task.

The following are strategies for answering true–false questions:

- Carefully read key words such as all, most, some, always, little, none, completely, better, and more. A key word is a single word that can determine the overall meaning of the statement.
- Do not read too much into the statement. Base your response on the information provided in the statement, not additional knowledge you may know about the topic.
- Carefully read questions that have two-part statements. Remember that both parts of a statement must be true for you to correctly mark it "True."
- Look at the following statement:

Working memory is part of the information-processing system and can hold from seven to ten units of information at one time.

The first part of the statement is correct, because the working memory is part of the information-processing system. However, the second part of the statement is incorrect, because the capacity is from five to nine units of information—if not even lower. Thus, the response to the statement must be "False."

- Assume a statement is true unless you determine it to be false.
- Do not make decisions regarding a question based on the pattern or number of true and false statements. Incorrect responses to previous questions make such assessments inaccurate.
- If you do not know the answer, guess. You have a 50:50 chance of being correct!

EXERCISE 11.2: IDENTIFYING KEY WORDS

Directions: The following is a list of true–false questions that you might encounter in an introductory psychology course. The list is designed to point to commonly held misconceptions. The answer to each of these true–false questions is "False." Here's a clue: Each statement includes an "absolute" term that makes the statement false. An absolute term implies that there are no exceptions. What you need to do is to pick out the key words that make them false. When you are finished, check your selections with the answer key on page 282 (adapted from Deese & Deese, 1994, p. 62).

Key Words

1. Geniuses are always neurotic.
2. You can accurately tell what someone is thinking from facial expression.
3. Cats can see in total darkness.
4. There is a clear distinction between normal people and emotionally disturbed people.
5. Your IQ is completely determined by heredity.
6. It has been proven that animals can sense a coming earthquake.
7. Slow learners remember better what they learn than fast learners.
8. Darwin was the first person to advocate a theory of evolution.
9. It is possible to classify everyone as either extroverted or introverted.
10. Studying mathematics will necessarily make you a better thinker.

■

STRATEGIES FOR MATCHING QUESTIONS

Matching questions require you to associate or match one term or idea with another. A series of items appears in one column and the responses in another. You must select the option that is correctly associated with the item. The following is an example of such a question from a psychology course.

In the left-hand column are brief definitions associated with Chapter 3 about memory and learning. For each definition, choose a term from the right-hand column and place the letter identifying it on the line preceding the number of the term. Each letter is used only once.

1.	A selective process that controls awareness	a.	Encoding
2.	Grouping of data in working memory	b.	Rote learning
3.	Transferring information into long-term memory	c.	Working memory
4.	Learning through repetition	d.	Meaningful learning
5.	Learning through making sense	e.	Chunking
		f.	Attention

The following are strategies for answering matching questions:

- Make sure you understand the directions for matching the items on the two lists. For example, determine whether you can use an answer more than once.
- First match the items you know and cross them off the list before considering other terms on the list.
- Work from one side only. Crossing off items in both columns can be confusing.
- Eliminate any items on the answer list that clearly are not related to any of the definitions.
- Draw a line through all items that you have matched so you do not use any item more than once.

STRATEGIES FOR FILL-IN-THE-BLANK QUESTIONS

A completion, or fill-in-the-blank, item confronts students with a statement for which they must supply the missing word or phrase. This type of item emphasizes recall of previously learned material rather than recognition. An example of this type of item follows:

The Civil War began in _____.

The following are strategies for responding to fill-in-the-blank test items:

- Read the questions carefully and look for clue words (e.g., as, an, the, and, these), especially just before the blanks. Make your response grammatically correct.
- Do not leave any blanks. If you cannot think of the exact word, write a synonym for the word or phrase. You might receive partial credit for your response.

STRATEGIES FOR MULTIPLE-CHOICE QUESTIONS

The multiple-choice item contains a stem, which identifies a problem situation, and several alternatives, or options, which provide possible solutions to the problem. The alternatives include a correct answer and several plausible wrong answers, or distracters. The stem may be stated as a direct question or as an incomplete statement. An example of the two different types of multiple-choice questions follows. Circle the correct answer as you read each question.

Stem	1.	*Research has indicated that the students who are most successful in school tend to be*
Alternatives	a.	careful learners
	b.	sincere learners
	c.	passive learners
	d.	active learners
Stem	2.	*Which of the following behaviors is not a rehearsal strategy?*
Alternatives	a.	underlining
	b.	copying
	c.	representing
	d.	repeating

The answers to Questions 1 and 2 are d and c, respectively.

The following are strategies for answering multiple-choice test questions:

- Follow the directions to determine if there is any special information for answering the questions, such as a choice in the number of questions to be answered.
- Determine how much time you will allot for answering the questions. Use the rule: percentage of total points = percentage of total time. This means that a question worth 20 percent of the exam would be allotted 20 percent of your test time.
- Read the stem and all of the choices before determining the best answer. Many students quickly select an answer without reading all the alternatives. In most multiple-choice tests, you are often asked to select the best answer. Therefore, you may conclude that there is more than one correct answer, but that one choice is the best answer.
- Skip difficult questions at the beginning of the exam.
- Review choices that are very similar. Many students complain that multiple-choice questions are "tricky," because two items appear to be similar. Try the following strategy: Translate the similar choices into your own words and then analyze how the choices differ.
- Use caution when "all of the above" and "none of the above" are included as choices. Look carefully at each choice. If you can eliminate one choice, you can eliminate "all of the above" as a response. Likewise, if you are certain that one choice is correct, you can eliminate "none of the above" as a response.
- Review difficult questions before you hand in the exam.
- When in doubt, guess. If there is a penalty for guessing, still guess if you can omit at least two of the alternatives.
- Whenever possible, review exam results.

EXERCISE 11.3: TAKING A MULTIPLE-CHOICE EXAM

Directions: Use the strategies for taking multiple-choice exams by answering the following questions. Circle the letter representing the best response for each question.

1. The five-minute plan is useful in dealing with
   a. test preparation
   b. reading comprehension
   c. note taking
   d. procrastination

2. The best study method involves
   a. reading over the assigned material many times
   b. creating and answering questions about the material
   c. spending at least three hours preparing for each exam
   d. outlining as much of the material as possible

3. One of the most important methods in time management is to
   a. wait to study when you feel motivated
   b. listen carefully in class
   c. spend an equal amount of time on all courses
   d. prioritize tasks

4. Improving your reading and note taking involves certain activities that must be completed
   a. before, during, and after reading and note taking
   b. after learning
   c. before exams
   d. before quizzes and exams

5. To improve your concentration, you need to analyze distractions in terms of
   a. school and home
   b. internal and external
   c. independent and dependent
   d. simple and complex

6. One of the major mistakes students make while reading is that they
   a. think of questions to answer as they read
   b. underline as they read
   c. try to determine what is important
   d. constantly check on their understanding

7. All of the following are related to good test preparation except
   a. identifying what must be learned
   b. deciding how to study
   c. rewriting notes so they are better understood
   d. planning and organizing study time

8. Effective note taking involves
   a. writing down everything the instructor says
   b. separating main ideas from supporting details
   c. writing down only what the instructor says is important
   d. recording only information that interests you

9. One of the most important factors in becoming a more successful student is
   a. being liked by your teachers
   b. having good roommates
   c. taking charge of your own learning and motivation
   d. having educated parents

10. Highly motivated people usually
    a. don't need to think much about their own behavior
    b. set personal goals
    c. spend a lot of time with personal trainers or other motivators
    d. achieve their goals easily without too much effort

WHAT STRATEGIES CAN I USE FOR ANSWERING ESSAY WRITING PROMPTS?

Let's now shift to the second type of exams—essay exams. Essay writing prompts are statements or questions that are designed to test your analytical and writing skills. For example, you might find these essay exam prompts in a US history course: Assess the strengths and weaknesses of the Union and Confederacy, and compare and contrast the Populist Movement and the Progressive Movement. Some essay prompts may be worded as questions: Should reason alone be used to categorize actions as either morally right or morally wrong?

The following strategies are helpful in responding to essay prompts.

READ THE DIRECTIONS CAREFULLY AND DO EXACTLY WHAT IS ASKED

Often, students are given a choice of writing prompts to answer, such as three out of four. If a student answers all the prompts, only the first three would count. The following is an example of a writing prompt that needs to be carefully read:

Explain one effect of the Industrial Revolution on each of three of the following:

Transportation
Capitalism
Socialism
Population growth
Scientific research

READ EACH PROMPT CAREFULLY TO DETERMINE WHAT IS EXPECTED IN THE RESPONSE

Circle key words (i.e., list, describe, compare) in each prompt and take notes as you read. Many prompts require more than one type of response, and to receive full credit, the complete question must be answered. Observe the multiple responses required in each of the following prompts:

List several categories of speeches and describe their primary functions and uses.
For the US invasion of Panama, discuss the (a) causes, (b) immediate effects, and (c) long-term political implications.
Discuss how the Equal Rights Amendment was developed and explain why its passage has aroused controversy.
List the six components of self-regulation and discuss three of them in depth, explaining your own degree of self-regulation in these areas.

Reflecting on our experience with the last prompt, it is unfortunately not rare that students do an A+ job with the first two key words (list, discuss) but fail to explain their own degree of self-regulation, losing valuable points. Another difficulty is that some students do not understand key terms in essay prompts, and as a result, fail to do what is asked for in the prompt. The list of key words and their meaning given in Table 11.1 will be helpful in responding to essay prompts (adapted from Jefferson County Schools, 1982). Also, when you predict essay prompts before exams, use the list to write different types of prompts.

Let's take a key word from the table and work through how you could structure your essay to address it. If you were answering a US history essay prompt, Evaluate the impacts of legislative and judicial decisions in the 1850s, you would need to identify and discuss the specific decisions. You would next need to weigh the pros and cons of their eventual impact. Finally, you would need to render a well justified, evidence-based judgment as to whether, overall, the decisions promoted or hindered US unity.

TABLE 11.1
List of Key Words and Their Meanings for Essay Exams

If you are asked to …	You should do the following
Analyze	Break down or separate a problem or situation into separate factors or relationships.
Categorize	Place items under headings.
Classify	Place items in related groups, then name or title each group.
Compare	Tell how things are alike; use concrete examples.
Contrast	Tell how things are different; use supporting concrete examples.
Criticize	Make a judgment of the reading, work of art, or literature, and support your opinion.
Define	Give the meaning.
Describe	State the particulars in detail.
Diagram	Use pictures, graphs, or charts to show relationships of details to main ideas.
Discuss	Consider the various points of view by presenting all sides of the issue.
Distinguish	Tell how something is different from others similar to it.
Enumerate	List all possible items.
Evaluate	Make a judgment based on the evidence and support it; give the good and bad points.
Explain	Make clear and plain; give the reason or cause.
Illustrate	Give examples, pictures, charts, diagrams, or concrete examples to clarify your answer.
Interpret	Express your thinking by giving the meaning as you see it.
Justify	Give some evidence by supporting your statement with facts.
List	Present information in a numbered fashion.
Outline	Use a specific and shortened form to organize main ideas, supporting details, and examples.
Paraphrase	Put ideas in your own words.
Predict	Present solutions that could happen if certain variables were present.
Prove	Provide factual evidence to back up the truth of the statement.
Relate	Show the relationship among concepts.
State	Establish by specifying. Write what you believe and back it with evidence.
Summarize	Condense the main points in the fewest words possible.
Support	Back up a statement with facts and proof.
Trace	Describe in steps the progression of something.
Verify	Confirm or establish the truth or accuracy of a point of view with supporting examples, evidence, and facts.

Let's take a look at another example. The prompt, Summarize and criticize Maslow's hierarchy of needs, requires that you first summarize the different levels of needs from the most fundamental ones up and then, point out what Maslow may have missed in attempting to understand what motivates people.

DETERMINE HOW YOU WILL USE YOUR TIME

Read all the essay prompts on the exam before responding to a single prompt. If all the prompts are of equal difficulty and value (in terms of the number of points), you should divide your time equally for all the prompts. For example, you should allot 30 minutes for three prompts each worth ten points on a 90-minute exam.

Budgeting time does not necessarily mean giving an equal amount of time to each prompt. You need to consider both the difficulty level and value of the prompt in terms of the number of points. Determine how much time you need to spend and actually write down the time you began writing your response. If you finish a question early, you can use the extra time with another prompt.

Determine the Order in Which You Will Respond to the Prompts

Individuals differ on the strategy they use to respond to prompts. Some individuals like to begin with the easiest prompt first to build their confidence and reduce test anxiety. Other individuals prefer to begin with a more difficult prompt to get the worst part of the exam over. Still other individuals start with the prompt worth the most points to ensure they spend sufficient time on a prompt with the greatest payoff.

Organize Your Response by Making an Outline or Representation (Map)

Identify main ideas and supporting details or examples. When you begin writing, you can organize your essay by paragraphs, each with one main idea and several details or examples. This format makes it easy for the grader to follow your response.

Write Your Answer Following Specific Procedures

- Begin with an introductory paragraph that defines terms or describes how you will respond to the prompt.
- After the introductory paragraph, state your first main idea and back it up with supporting details (i.e., facts, dates, and examples). Go to the next main idea and do the same. Use the ideas, facts, and theories discussed in the course in your response to the prompt and be sure to support your arguments or point of view with factual information.
- Add transitional words such as first, second, third, moreover, in addition, similarly, also, however, therefore, on the other hand, nevertheless, finally, in short, to conclude.
- Add a summary.
- Proofread and revise your answer.

If Given an Opportunity, Review Your Exam Results

It is important that you analyze test errors, often called an error analysis, to improve future test performance. The answer to the following questions will help in your analysis: Why were points deducted from my answer? Did I answer all parts of the essay prompt? Can I easily identify my main ideas? Did I omit examples or supporting details? How well did I answer lower and higher level questions? What were the sources of my errors (e.g., class notes, textbooks, or handouts)? How will I adjust my study plan for the next exam? What study strategies were the most and least effective?

The student reporting the following experience indicates that analyzing test results can be beneficial.

Evaluating the Two Essay Responses

Read this section only after you have evaluated the two essay responses. The response to the essay on the proposed flat tax requires the student to discuss and describe. If you refer to the list of key terms presented earlier, you will see that discuss requires the student to consider the various points of view by presenting all sides of the issue, whereas describe requires the students to state the particulars in detail.

Student Reflections

A couple of weeks ago I took a history exam. I used a number of new study strategies and went into the exam with the confidence that I was going to do well. I had studied hard and thought I knew all the important information to be covered. In fact, I came out of the exam with a smile on my face, thinking that I had done a good job.

When I got the test back, I scored much lower than I had expected and was very upset and disappointed. I went back to my dorm and complained to my roommate. He suggested that I speak to the instructor. After some resistance, I agreed to make an appointment with him to talk about my exam.

We went through each question on the exam. I received a very high score on the multiple-choice section, but missed points on the short essay questions. The answers I gave were correct, but they did not answer the specific questions. My instructor came to the conclusion that it wasn't that I didn't know the material, but that I didn't understand the depth that he expected in the responses to the questions. He gave me some hints for studying for my next exam. I left the meeting feeling much better about myself and the effort I put in studying for the exam.

EXERCISE 11.4: EVALUATING RESPONSES TO AN ESSAY PROMPT

Directions: Review the strategies for writing a response to an essay prompt and then read the responses to the following essay prompt. Take notes as you read and determine the strengths and weaknesses of each response.

Discuss the proposed flat tax and describe what effects it might have on the US economy.

RESPONSE 1

In light of the public's dissatisfaction with the size and scope of the tax code and the government's reach into the purses of individuals, families, and businesses, a growing number of economists and politicians are calling for the elimination of the present tax system and the institution of a flat tax. Such a tax would apply a single rate (15%, for example) to all tax-payers and would eliminate most or all deductions, exemptions, and the like. A state sales tax would be an example.

Proponents believed that most people would save money, because the effective tax rate would be lower than what it presently is, citizens would appreciate the ease of the new system (the tax form would be not larger than a postcard), and it would be fairer, as everyone would pay the same rate and the rich would be prevented from circumventing their responsibility of paying their fair share by taking advantage of loopholes in the present tax code.

Opponents claim that a single rate would be an undue burden on lower income citizens as they are ill prepared to pay a percentage of their income that could go to food or rent. In addition, they argue that if allowances are made for poverty status, medical and home mortgage interest deductions, and other kinds of exceptions, it will not take very long for the new system to resemble the old one.

The proposed flat tax would immediately change the nature and operation of tax accounting in this country. With deductions and exemptions eliminated, there would be no need for tax specialists looking for ways to save people and business money. On a larger scale, people may or may not become more honest in reporting their income. If they stand to pay less in taxes with a flat tax than they had in years past, then citizens probably will report their income. If, however, they stand to lose money because of the elimination of loopholes, then much of the nation's business transactions and economy may go underground.

In conclusion, the flat tax, although clearly simpler, is not considered by all to be fairer or an improvement on the present system. Although it may solve some problems (greatly simplifying the code, for example), other problems may arise and might even make things worse (loss of needed deductions, regressive effect on the poor). Ultimately, a flat tax will only succeed if people believe that they are keeping more of their income, that governmental services are not being curtailed, and that everyone is paying their fair share. Defining fair share is at the heart of the issue.

Response 2

The flat tax means that people will no longer have to spend long hours and lots of money trying to figure out how much they owe (or how much they should get back from) the government each year. Instead of some people paying nothing, others paying 28%, and still others paying 39% of their income, the flat tax would have everyone pay the same rate. Many people feel this is the best way of dealing with the problem of paying for the government. Because all citizens, rich and poor, receives the benefit of paved streets, the protection of armed forces, and public schooling. It seems logical that everyone should have to pay, no matter how little they might be able to afford. Perhaps, for some people, any amount of taxation would prove to be a severe burden; in these rare instances, it would be wise to exempt such individuals from paying taxes until such times as they are financially better off. Still what drives this whole issue is the population's perception that things are not fair as they are. People feel that they are paying too much money and are receiving too little in return. The rich seem to have ways to hide or shelter their income, and the poor see what little they earn shrink under an ever increasing tax burden. The flat tax will not solve the whole tax problem in one step, but will help to create more fairness for everyone who has to pay taxes. An example of a flat tax is state sales taxes; rich and poor pay the same percentage, but not the same amount. The rich pay more in total dollars because the items they buy cost more.

The following guidelines were presented for writing an essay. Begin with an introductory paragraph to define terms or describe your approach to answering the prompt; state each main idea and back it up with supporting details or examples; add transitional words such as first, second, third, moreover, in addition, in conclusion, and therefore; add a summary or conclusion; and proofread and revise your answer.

In Response 1, the student's introduction describes why some individuals are interested in the flat tax and defines what it would accomplish. In the next two paragraphs, the student presents the pros and cons of the flat tax (i.e., satisfying the "discuss" aspect of the question). In the fourth paragraph, the student describes the effects it may have on the US economy, the second part of the question. In the fifth paragraph, the student uses the information presented in the earlier paragraphs to reach some important conclusions regarding the flat tax. The response is well organized, with each paragraph serving an important function in answering all parts of the question. The essay is well written and does not include any serious grammatical or spelling errors.

In Response 2, the student fails to organize his or her response to the essay prompt. The response is essentially one paragraph without attention to the two parts of the prompt. The single paragraph includes many ideas that could have been subdivided. The discussion aspect only includes the writer's point of view, omitting any reference to the oppositional arguments. The example of the flat tax is placed at the end of the first paragraph instead of the beginning. In addition, the preachy or narrow point of view does little to support a balanced response to the question. This point is clearly seen in the conclusion in the final paragraph. Finally, the student should have changed *receives* to *receive* in the sixth line of the essay.

Did you have any other comments regarding the two essays? If the essay was worth ten points, how would you score each essay? Table 11.2 reviews the procedures for answering multiple-choice questions, the most common objective question format, followed by procedures for answering essay prompts.

TABLE 11.2

Procedures for Answering Multiple-Choice Questions and Essay Exams

Procedures for Answering Multiple-Choice Questions	Examples
1. Carefully read the directions to determine if there is any special information for answering the questions.	Directions: Answer all questions. There is no partial reduction for incorrect answers.
2. Determine how much time you will allot for answering the questions by following the rule: Percentage of total points = Percentage of total time.	"Let's see, I have 50 multiple-choice and two essays to answer in 120 minutes. The multiple-choice questions are worth one point each and the essays are each worth ten points—that's 70 points. The multiple-choice questions are worth 50/70 or 0.71 of the exam. I better allot about (120 × 0.71) 85 minutes for the multiple-choice and about 17 minutes each for the two short essays."
3. Read the stem and all the choices first before determining the best answer.	"I was about to choose 'careful learners' until I read the better choice 'active learners.'"
4. Skip difficult questions.	
5. Review choices that are very similar.	"I'm going to read the stem and each alternative before I make a choice. I will cross out each alternative that I know is incorrect and focus only on the alternatives that are left. If necessary, I will redefine terms in my own words to help me make my final choice."
6. Go back over difficult questions.	
7. When in doubt, guess. If there is a penalty for guessing, still guess if you can omit at least two of the alternatives.	"I know the meaning of decoding and encoding, but I am not sure of the other two terms. What is my best choice of the remaining terms?"
8. If given an opportunity, review your exam results (error analysis).	"Most of the questions I missed were higher level questions and came from class notes."

Procedures for Answering Essay Exams	Examples
1. Read the directions carefully and do exactly what is asked. If given a choice, determine which prompts you will answer.	Directions: Answer prompts 1 and 2 and either 3 or 4.
2. Read each prompt carefully to determine what is expected in the response. • Circle key words in each prompt. • Make notes as you read.	Describe the functions of the Speaker of the House of Representatives and evaluate his or her performance. Be sure to provide support for your evaluative comments.
3. Determine how you will use your time.	"I have 90 minutes to answer three essays each worth ten points. This means that I should spend about 30 minutes per essay. If I finished a question in less time, I will have more time for the other two essays. I will also leave some time for outlining and editing each question."
4. Determine the order you will respond to the prompts.	"I like to begin with the easiest prompt. It builds my confidence."
5. Organize your response by making an outline or representation (map).	"I want to present three main ideas."
6. Write your answer in the following manner: • Begin with an introductory paragraph. • State your first main idea and back it up with supporting details or examples. Go to the next main idea and do the same. • Add transitional words. • Add a summary. • Proofread and revise your answer.	
7. If given an opportunity, review your exam results.	"My major problem was that I failed to provide supporting evidence for the ideas I discussed."

Chapter Review

KEY POINTS

1 Test-taking strategies cannot make up for poor exam preparation.
2 There are two types of test anxiety: rational and irrational. Rational anxiety can be addressed by effective exam preparation. Managing irrational anxiety involves both relaxation and cognitive strategies.
3 Carefully read the directions before beginning an exam.
4 Plan how you will use your time before beginning an exam. Many professors do not allow telling time using cell phones during exams so be sure to have an alternative way to tell time.
5 Look for key terms to determine how you will answer the question.
6 Be aware that some essay prompts may include more than one aspect that needs a response.
7 Carefully organize responses to essay exam prompts.
8 Conduct an error analysis after each exam to determine how you can improve your performance on future exams.

FOLLOW-UP ACTIVITIES

1. Use the Self-Regulation Process to Improve Test-Taking Strategies

Complete the following self-study during a period of two to three weeks. Your report should include each of the following processes and should be approximately five to eight typed pages in length. See Appendix B for detailed information on how to conduct a self-regulation study.

Self-Evaluation and Monitoring. How effective are my current test-taking strategies? Do I need to change the way I take tests? If yes, what problem do I encounter? What are the symptoms of my problem (i.e., when, where, and how often does my problem occur)? How much of an impact does this problem have on my academic performance? What factors (e.g., beliefs, perceptions, feelings, physiological responses, or behaviors) contribute to this problem? What do I need to change to reduce or eliminate my problem(s)?

Goal Setting and Strategic Planning. What are my goals? What strategies will I implement to improve my test-taking strategies? When will I use these strategies? How will I record my progress?

Strategy Implementation and Monitoring. What strategies did I use to improve my test taking? When did I use these strategies? What method(s) did I use to record my progress (e.g., documents, charts, logs, tally sheets, checklists, or recordings)? When did I use these methods? How and when did I monitor my progress to determine if my new test-taking strategies were working? What changes, if any, did I make along the way?

Strategic-Outcome Monitoring. Did I attain the goal(s) I set for myself? Have the modifications in my test-taking strategies improved my academic performance? What strategies were the most and least effective? What changes, if any, do I need to make in the future?

2. Analyze a Response to an Essay Prompt

Directions: Using the criteria for writing an essay exam, review the following prompt and evaluate the quality of the student's response.

Question: Identify and explain the factors that distinguish successful from less successful learners.

Successful learners can be distinguished from unsuccessful learners in three ways. The first difference is goal setting. The second difference is how they plan and organize their studying. The third difference is how they prepare for and take exams.

Successful learners establish long-term and short-term goals that direct their behavior. This helps them maintain their motivation as they attempt to reach their goals.

Successful learners realize that learning is best accomplished by planning and using different study skills. Rather than leaving things to the last minute, successful learners allocate sufficient time each day to read chapters, answer questions, and work on large projects. For example, if the assignment is to write a history term paper, successful learners dedicate time to obtaining the materials, allowing enough time to read and understand them, and writing the report early enough to allow enough time to edit the report.

Successful learners also plan for and take tests in a systematic manner. They allocate time for study. They realize that tests that are very important or difficult require more time and effort than easier exams. Therefore, they use different study methods to learn the material. Also, before they begin answering exam questions, they carefully determine what specific information is asked for in each question.

In summary, successful learners take charge of their own learning. They set goals, plan and organize their daily tasks, and prepare for and take exams in an orderly manner. Successful learners are not born, they learn to be successful.

Evaluation:

_____

_____

_____

_____

3. Conduct an Error Analysis on an Exam

Select an exam you recently took and use the criteria presented in the chapter for conducting an error analysis for objective and essay questions. Use the format in the following chart to categorize your errors, write a brief analysis of the data you collected, explain what you learned from the analysis, and describe what steps you can take to improve your exam performance. The actual number of rows in your chart will depend on the number of questions missed on your exam.

Question Missed	Type of Item (Higher or Lower Level)	Topic or Chapter	Error Source (Textbook or Class)

4. Practice Writing Responses to Essay Prompts

Use the information presented in this chapter to generate and answer essay prompts in this course. Select a partner and together write an essay prompt that could be asked on an exam. Next, write your response to the prompt independently using the following criteria. Begin with an introductory paragraph, state your first main idea and back it up with supporting details or examples, go to the next main idea and do the same, add transitional words, add a summary, and proofread and revise your answer. Finally, read each other's response and provide feedback. Discuss how each essay could be improved.

Answers to Exercise 11.2

The key words for each question are as follows: (1) always; (2) accurately; (3) total; (4) clear; (5) completely; (6) proven; (7) better; (8) first; (9) everyone; and (10) necessarily.

Answers to Exercise 11.3

1. D   2. B   3. D   4. A   5. B   6. B   7. C   8. B   9. C   10. B

Afterword

We are about to complete our journey toward helping you become a more successful learner. In Chapter 1, we began by introducing the concept of self-regulation, which would be used as the framework for determining the factors that influence academic success. The components of self-regulation include the following variables: motivation, methods of learning, use of time, control of one's physical and social environment, and the ability to monitor one's performance. The book was then organized around these components. The self-observation, exercises, and follow-up activities provided an opportunity for you to better understand and apply the information you learned. We now would like to complete the book by helping you integrate some of the most important ideas we introduced so you can better apply them in your learning.

Table 1 identifies the self-regulation components, academic challenges, and the chapters where each academic challenge is discussed. Our purpose is to briefly review some of the major research findings and concepts that were discussed in the book. This chapter is *not* meant to be a summary or review of the total book. Reviewing the key points at the end of each chapter can assist you in your review of all the major concepts in the book.

Self-regulation is the ability to control or manage the factors influencing learning. Self-regulatory learners establish optimum conditions for learning and remove obstacles that interfere with their learning. No matter how difficult the material or how clear the textbook, or the quality of instruction, the self-regulatory learner finds a way to excel. The research is clear in that students' inability to self-regulate learning behaviors is a major reason for their lack of learning. The fact that you know the components of self-regulation allows you to develop the specific skills to overcome obstacles or challenges in your academic learning. In fact, these same skills are relevant to challenges on the job or other life-skills necessary to help you succeed in any endeavors you may face outside of the college classroom.

You were fortunate that in elementary and secondary education you were guided by teachers, parents, and other caregivers in your learning. In college, you are expected to manage your own learning in such areas as motivation, what to learn, how to learn, when to learn, and where to learn. If you don't develop the self-regulatory skills needed for the demands of college learning, you will be at a serious disadvantage in college. Now that you are toward the end of your quarter or semester in college, you have already applied some of the self-regulatory skills introduced in the book. We hope that you have found the skills helpful and are on your way to becoming a more successful learner.

MOTIVATION

The first self-regulatory component we studied was motivation, and the key motivation concept is self-efficacy, which is the evaluation students make about their abilities and skills to successfully complete a task. The key question learners ask is: "Am I capable of succeeding at this task?" Students with high efficacy are more likely than their low-efficacy peers to choose difficult tasks, expend greater effort, persist longer, use more complex learning strategies, and experience less fear and anxiety regarding academic tasks. Setting goals is one way to enhance your self-efficacy. As you work on academic tasks, you should determine your progress by analyzing your performance according to your goals; as you see that you are making progress toward your goals, your self-efficacy should improve. Without goals, it is difficult to be motivated to achieve.

Learning to use the learning strategies you have been taught in this course is another way to enhance your self-efficacy because these strategies help you master the content in the course. As you begin to excel in your academic tasks, your self-efficacy beliefs change, and you become more willing to work harder and persist at new tasks. Thus, you become more motivated to learn. You see

TABLE 1
Examples of Academic Challenges

"I have a problem because I never or only sometimes ..." (Insert response [a]) or **"I have a problem because I usually ..."** (Insert response [b])

Self-Regulation Components	Academic Challenges	Chapter
Motivation	[a] choose to complete academic tasks	2
	[a] put forth the effort needed to do well on certain tasks	2
	[a] persist when tasks are difficult, boring, or unchallenging	2
	[a] set goals and develop plans to attain them	4
	[a] deal with my emotions	5
	[a] eliminate my fear of failure	2
	[b] experience anxiety when I study, attend class, or take exams	5
Methods of learning/monitoring performance	[a] take notes in class and remember the content	9
	[a] read my textbooks or articles	8
	[a] prepare for quizzes and exams	10
	[a] remember the information I studied	3
	[b] experience difficulty taking exams	11
Use of time	[a] have time to do the things I value	6
	[a] have time to complete my academic tasks as well as I would like	6
	[a] have time to review my work before handing it in	6
	[a] have time to test myself before quizzes and exams	6
	[b] miss important events such as classes, review sessions, appointments, and meetings	6
	[b] escape from academic events and tasks	2,5,6
Physical and social environment	[a] select or arrange the physical setting to make my learning more effective	7
	[a] seek assistance from peers, tutors, teaching assistants, and professors when I need help	7
	[a] seek help from non-social resources (e.g., study aids, the web, books) when I need it	7
	[b] have difficulty attending to or concentrating on academic tasks	7
	[b] encounter internal or external distractions that interrupt my studying	7

that motivation is not something beyond your control; it is not an innate trait that is part of your personality and that is unchangeable. You have learned in this book how to change your motivation by changing your beliefs and perceptions.

You have also learned that anxiety and fear of failure can have detrimental effects on your motivation to learn. Use the self-talk, breathing, meditation, and mindfulness strategies to reduce your anxiety. The reduction in anxiety will not occur unless you practice the strategies over and over again until they become a natural part of your behavior. Identify other strategies that help you reduce anxiety, such as listening to music or exercising. Finally, we want you to focus on strategies to help you reduce any concerns about fear of failure. Understanding the concepts and practicing the strategies in Chapter 2 will be very useful to you, especially if you come to believe that your self-worth is not dependent on your ability to perform, but more on your effort, learning strategies, and attitude.

In Chapter 5, we mentioned that emotions influence students' motivation, learning, and achievement. In addition, anxiety, fear, and boredom negatively impact your psychological and physical health, while enjoyment, hope, and pride impact positively on these factors. Fortunately, there is evidence to indicate that you can self-regulate or take charge of your emotions so you can respond more positively to the academic demands of college.

Becoming aware of your negative self-talk and disputing any irrational thinking patterns is a useful strategy to deal with negative events in your life because it helps to change your thinking. Once you change your thinking, you can change your emotions and behavior. One way to reduce boredom is to increase the value of the situation. This change is made through changing one's thinking about the task by considering ways in which the task can be made more interesting or useful.

METHODS OF LEARNING/MONITORING OF PERFORMANCE

One of the most important concepts discussed in the book was the mindset students have regarding their intelligence. Research evidence indicates that students who believe intelligence is malleable or changeable (i.e., can be developed), rather than fixed or unchangeable, are more likely to try harder, set higher goals, and use more advanced learning strategies. Again, we see that the way you think can influence your academic performance. The fact that your thoughts and beliefs influence motivation, emotions, and learning is an important theme that cuts across many chapters in the book. This fact should encourage you to consider your thoughts and beliefs as they relate to all aspects of your behavior.

Your study of the information-processing system indicated that without attention to tasks, information cannot get into long-term memory so you can store and retrieve it. In fact, lack of attention is one of the reasons why information doesn't even get into your working memory. This is why if you don't take good notes, you forget so much information before you leave the classroom. Remember also our discussion about the costs of multitasking, or really, task switching. Continuously switching between tasks such as studying and responding to texts results in an increase in the time you spend on tasks and a decrease in the quality of your work.

One of the reasons why students have difficulty with complex tasks is that they use inappropriate learning strategies. We described how learning strategies can be organized into three components—rehearsal, elaboration, and organizational. Rehearsal is used for learning rote or verbatim material. The problem is that too many students use rehearsal for learning complex material when they should be using elaboration and organizational strategies. The focus in the book on these latter strategies in Chapters 8 and 9 for learning from course materials and taking notes will help you store and retrieve information for exams. Changing headings into questions is another major learning strategy in the book. Remember, you are not studying effectively unless you generate and answer questions from your textbooks and notes. Keep practicing these strategies because they will pay off in the long run.

The use of elaboration and organizational learning strategies will help you monitor your performance because you should not have to wait for an instructor to grade your paper or exam to know how much information you attained. Constant monitoring of your learning should occur each time you read or take notes. In this way, you can make the necessary changes in your study strategies.

An important part of monitoring your learning is to develop a study plan before each major exam. Just like coaches need to develop a "game plan" for sports, a student should develop and implement a test plan for preparing for an exam. Students who develop test plans as a habit tell us it is one of the most beneficial strategies they learned in the course.

USE OF TIME

In Chapter 6 of the book, we reported a study where time management was a better predictor of grades in the senior year of college than SAT scores. This investigation illustrated the importance of time management. In the self-observation exercise (Exercise 6.1), you had an opportunity to assess how you use time. This information was followed by some time-management strategies for you to consider. We recognize the usefulness of social networking platforms, but we have become concerned about some of our students reporting excessive time texting, tweeting, snapchatting, or reviewing the social media pages of their friends. These activities can "eat up" several hours a week and can lead to reduced study and test preparation. Most of the major time wasters involve interesting activities that bring us considerable enjoyment but are often not really important and certainly not urgent. Remember Quadrant 4? We don't want you to omit these activities, but consider how you can put them in perspective as you determine how you will use your time. Take our suggestion and develop a time-management plan each week. Don't worry about the fact that you often need to change your plan. What is most important is that your plan will help you complete your required activities.

PHYSICAL AND SOCIAL ENVIRONMENT

The last component of self-regulation we will consider is your control of your physical and social environment. As we pointed out in the book, successful learners restructure their physical and social environment to improve their learning. The social environment deals with *where* you study and learn as well as *how* you use your resources or obtain assistance from others. In Chapter 7, you had an opportunity to assess the environment where you study. By now, you may have made many changes in the location of your study environment. The important point, however, is that you don't feel distracted and can attend to any task you may have to complete.

Asking for help and working cooperatively with your peers are also important aspects of self-regulated learning. In Chapter 7, we gave you suggestions for how to prepare and participate in a meeting with your instructor. We emphasized the importance of meeting personally or in small groups with your instructors. Learning how to do so can be one of the best strategies for improving your academic performance. Using the guidelines for participating in study groups can lead to the productive use of such learning.

It is now time for us to leave you. We hope that by reading this book and taking a learning strategies course, you now feel more confident about the challenges of college life. Continue to use the book as a reference as you proceed through your courses. We all need a refresher from time to time.

Best wishes as you move toward the attainment of your goals.

Glossary

Academic self-regulation: The strategies students use to control the factors influencing their learning.

Acronyms: Mnemonics that use the first letter in each word of a list to form a word (e.g., SMART goals).

Active listening: A type of communication in which the listener summarizes and paraphrases what he or she has heard from another individual so the individual feels that he or she has been understood.

Attention: A selective process that controls awareness of events in the environment.

Attribution: An individual's perception of the causes of his or her own success or failure.

Chunking: Grouping of data so that a greater amount of information may be retained in working memory.

Cognitive: Explanations of learning and motivation that focus on the role of the learner's mental processes.

Concentration: The process of continual refocusing on a perceived stimulus or message.

Diagrams: A visual description of the parts of something.

Diaphragmatic breathing: Deep breathing that is done either sitting or lying on the back by contracting the diaphragm so that in breathing, the stomach moves but the chest remains as still as possible.

Distributed practice: Learning is divided into short and frequent study sessions over a long period of time.

Elaboration strategies: Integration of meaningful knowledge into long-term memory through adding detail, summarizing, creating examples, and analogies.

Emotionality: The physiological and psychosomatic aspects of anxiety such as headaches and stomach distress.

Encoding: The process of transferring information from working memory to long-term memory.

Fixed mindset: An individual's belief that brain and intelligence cannot be developed and that success is dependent on the amount of intelligence one has to begin with.

Goal properties: The more specific, proximal, and difficult goals are, the more effective they are likely to be.

Growth mindset: An individual's belief that brain and intelligence can be developed and that success is dependent on the amount of effort applied.

Hierarchies: An organization strategy that places ideas into levels and groups.

Identity: A self-constructed image of who one is, what one values, and the related goals.

I-message:: Assertive statements that focus on the sender's needs and feelings, rather than the traits and behaviors of the receiver in order to raise the odds another person can hear you clearly.

Information processing system: : The cognitive structure through which information flows, is controlled, and is transformed during the process of learning.

Irrational thinking:: Belief that we have little ability to influence our feelings and that events directly cause our emotions and behavior.

Learning strategies:: Techniques or methods that students use to acquire information.

Long-term memory (LTM):: The part of the information processing system that holds information for long periods.

Maintenance rehearsal:: A strategy to keep information activated in the working memory by repeating the information mentally.

Massed practice: Learning is grouped into a few extended sessions over a short period of time.

Mastery goal: An orientation toward learning as much as possible for the purpose of self-improvement, irrespective of the performance of others.

Matrices: An organization that displays the comparative relations existing within topics and across topics.

Meaningful learning: A process of learning whereby the student attempts to make sense of the material so it will be stored in the long-term memory and retrieved when needed.

Meditation: A form of mental relaxation whereby individuals assume a comfortable position, close their eyes, focus on breathing, and attend to one sound or image at a time. There are many different forms of meditation.

Metacognition: Awareness and understanding of one's own thought processes.

Mindfulness: Awareness and acceptance of our thoughts, feelings, bodily sensations, and surrounding environment.

Mirror question: A question that reflects the information in notes.

Mnemonic: A memory technique that makes the task of remembering easier.

Multitasking: Performing two tasks that require conscious processing simultaneously, switching from one task to another, or performing the tasks in rapid succession.

Neuroplasticity: The ability of the brain to grow and change as a result of input from the environment.

Note making: The active and meaningful engagement with class notes by elaborative strategies such as creating mirror and summary questions.

Organizational strategies: Learning strategies that impose structure on material via hierarchical or other relationships among the material's parts.

Performance goal: An orientation toward learning in which outperforming others is a major concern.

Possible selves: Future-oriented images of self that individuals expect and hope to become as well as are afraid of becoming.

Progressive muscle relaxation: A systematic technique where muscles are tensed and relaxed in order to achieve a deep state of relaxation.

Rehearsal strategies: The process of repeating information over and over in working memory to retain it.

Retrieval: The process of remembering or finding previously stored information in the long-term memory.

Rote learning: A process of learning whereby the student learns through repetition without gaining a deep understanding of material.

Self-efficacy: The belief that one can successfully complete a specific task.

Self-plagiarism: Using any portion of previously submitted academic work as if it were new, without the instructor's permission.

Self-talk: The inner speech we use to make evaluative statements about our behavior.

Self-worth: The need for students to maintain a positive image of themselves and their ability.

Sequences: An organization strategy that shows the order of steps, events, stages, or phases.

Short-term sensory store (STSS): The part of the information processing system that briefly stores information from the senses.

SMART goals: An acronym identifying the criteria for setting goals—specific, measurable, action-oriented, realistic, and timely.

Social cognitive theory: Explanations of learning and motivation that explain learning and motivation as an interaction between cognitive, behavioral, and contextual factors.

Social loafing: The tendency of individual group members to reduce their work effort as groups increase in size.

Stereotype threat: The fear of doing something that would inadvertently confirm a stereotype. An example is an older person who takes an exam after being told that elderly individuals forget much of what they learn.

Summary question: A question that reflects the major theme or main ideas of the total lecture.

Task switching: The brain switching back and forth while performing two or more complex tasks.

Testing effect: The phenomenon that when information is retrieved from memory such as via self-testing and quizzes, one's memory of the retrieved information is strengthened.

Value orientation: The different reasons for engaging in tasks such as enjoyment, usefulness, importance, and cost-benefit analysis.

Working memory (WM): The part of the information-processing system in which the active processing of information takes place.

Worry: The cognitive aspect of anxiety such as negative beliefs.

Appendices

Appendix A provides an overview of effective strategies for writing research papers and preparing for and delivering individual and group projects. Appendices B and C are designed to help you plan, develop, and implement a self-regulation study so you can become a more successful learner. Appendix B provides you with the tools and assistance needed to apply the steps of the self-regulation process introduced in Chapter 1. Appendix C includes two self-regulation studies completed over a two- to three-week period by students in an educational psychology course on study strategies. Some of the material provided by students was slightly edited to reduce the length of the report. Therefore, as you read these studies, you will be told when additional information was provided by the students, but not reported here. The topics of the self-regulation studies are listed below:

> Self-regulation Study 1: Methods of learning (improving quiz scores)—written by Fernando Barba.
> Self-regulation Study 2: Motivation (reducing anxiety)—written by Catherine Dizon.

At the end of each case study, you will find a brief analysis of strengths and areas that need improvement. Remember, there is no one way to complete a self-regulation study. Be creative in developing your own instruments to assess your behavior and developing strategies for change.

Appendix A: Writing Research Papers and Making Individual or Group Presentations

Most undergraduate courses require writing a research paper and professors are increasingly including assignments such as individual or group presentations. This section reviews strategies of how to write a research paper, and how to plan and deliver an effective presentation. First, we will discuss two foundational skills for both assignments: locating credible resources and presenting them with academic integrity.

LOCATING CREDIBLE RESOURCES

You were likely introduced to credible versus not credible resources by the time you were in middle school. You learned that although turning to the internet for resources and references is very convenient, the problem is that anyone can publish anything they want and present it as "the truth." You also likely received the warning that Wikipedia does not count as a credible reference. You may have learned about primary sources such as materials produced in a period of interest in history (such as writing by Cicero in the first century BCE) and secondary sources, materials produced by experts after the time period being studied. Key to credibility of sources other than primary sources is the peer review process: the scrutiny and evaluation of work by experts in the same field. Table A.1 presents different sources in descending order of credibility. The first four sources qualify as scholarly evidence and the remaining five do not. In locating evidence for a research paper or presentation, you want to primarily use peer-reviewed journal articles and research reports as your sources, although a book from an academic publishing house and a doctoral dissertation also qualify as scholarly evidence. The other sources can be used to illustrate the general impact of an issue (such as a topic being debated in news articles and op-eds) but they are not scholarly evidence.

ENSURING ACADEMIC INTEGRITY

Institutions of higher education depend on the principle of academic integrity which at the core is the expectation that students submit original work as well as protect their own work from being misused by others. Table A.2 describes different types of academic dishonesty: plagiarism, cheating, unauthorized collaboration, and falsifying academic records.

As the table presents, plagiarism includes **self-plagiarism**. Please note that you may not take portions of academic work submitted in one class and submit it in another unless you ask for permission from both the original and

Self-Plagiarism: Using any portion of previously submitted academic work as if it were new, without the instructor's permission.

the other course's instructor. Possible consequences for plagiarism include earning an "F" in the assignment or exam, an "F" in the entire course, dismissal for an academic program, suspension or expulsion, and even revocation of admission or the degree.

In order to avoid plagiarism, you can present someone else's work by either paraphrasing or direct quoting. Generally, you will want to paraphrase more than using direct quotes. In order to paraphrase, use synonyms and change the arrangement of words and phrases. Table A.3 presents an example of paraphrasing with an embedded direct quote. Generally, you will want to limit quotes to

TABLE A.1
Determining Credibility of Sources

Source	Description
Qualify as Scholarly Evidence	
Peer-reviewed or refereed journal	This is the main source of evidence to make or support claims in the academic world. Articles are subjected to a blind review process in which other scholars anonymously provide judgment concerning the appropriateness of methodology and credibility of findings. To determine if a journal is peer reviewed, go to the journal website. If you are searching your college's electronic database, be sure to limit a database search to peer-reviewed journals only.
Major research report	Reports from major research bodies such as the World Bank, UNESCO, RAND, and ones referenced in this textbook, such as the American College Health Association, generally undergo an internal review and external peer review process before being disseminated. These reports result in findings that are well respected and credible.
Book from academic publishing house	Academic publishers have editorial boards that review content and often employ peer review processes involving the same rigor as the peer review process of journals. Academic books are regularly cited as support in academic writing. Examples of academic publishing houses are Cambridge and Oxford University Press, Springer Nature, Routledge and Elsevier.
Doctoral dissertation	Though the quality of dissertations ranges widely, dissertations represent documents that have undergone significant advisement and scrutiny by multiple scholars on the advising committee. Dissertations should be evaluated carefully but are a credible and often overlooked source of evidence.
Do Not Qualify as Scholarly Evidence	
Non-peer-reviewed books, reports, and articles	Many books and journals from trade publishing houses do not use peer review or blind review and publication decisions rest with the decision of an editor or editors. For these, credibility is usually assigned largely based on prestige of publisher and/or author. Examples of major trade book publishers are the Hachette Book Group, HarperCollins, Macmillan, Penguin Random House, and Simon and Schuster.
Newspaper article	A newspaper article involves some vetting by an editor and citation of sources according to journalistic practices, but is not peer reviewed by experts. A newspaper article generally does not qualify as evidence to support scholarly claims but may be used to raise awareness about a topic or illustrate impact or general understanding.
News and general interest periodicals/ magazines	News and general interest periodicals are generally a commercial enterprise to provide information or entertainment. They do not always cite sources and may or may not be authored by experts.
Newspaper editorial or op-ed	An editorial is an opinion article that communicates the opinion of a newspaper, magazine, or website's editorial board. An op-ed refers to "opposite the editorial page" or "opinion editorial" and is writing which expresses the opinion of an author usually not affiliated with the publication's editorial board. These pieces are meant to persuade or create interest by conveying a view or position by the editor(s) of a paper or by a guest author.
Self-published book, article, or blog	The emergence of self-publishing and online publishing means an ability to publish an article or book without any vetting process. Posting to a blog is one of the simplest forms of self-publishing with wide variance in quality and currently no standardized way to evaluate credibility.

Adapted From Filback and Robison (2014).

TABLE A.2
Types of Academic Dishonesty

Plagiarism and Self-plagiarism	Plagiarism:
	Representing another's material from any source as one's own
	Not correctly referencing the source when using another's words or ideas verbatim or in near-verbatim form
	Self-plagiarism:
	Using any portion of previously submitted academic work as if it were new, without the instructor's permission
Cheating	Use of unauthorized assistance such as paying someone else to write a research paper
	Allowing another student to copy work
	Possessing notes or other materials not explicitly allowed by the professor during an exam
	Talking with fellow students during exams
	Looking at another student's exam
	Continuing to write after the allotted time period
	Taking a test for someone else or permitting someone else to take a test for you
Unauthorized Collaboration	Working with others unless expressly permitted by the instructor
	Providing a copy of an exam or answer key to others
	Sharing with another a solution to homework or other assignments
Falsifying Academic Records	Attempting to change, alter, or being an accessory to changing a grade in a grade book, work submitted on a test or a final project, a "supplementary grade report," or other university academic records
	Misrepresentation of official records including but not limited to: academic transcripts; exam papers altered for re-grading; forged signatures; and letters of recommendation

Adapted from Academic Integrity, University of Southern California (2013)

TABLE A.3
Paraphrasing Original Material

Original	Paraphrasing (in APA style)
With the term multitasking, people mean the simultaneous and/or concurrent performance of two or more tasks requiring cognition or information processing (e.g., attending to the road while driving and simultaneously talking on a cell phone). The problem here is that human cognitive architecture and brain functioning only allows for switching between different tasks (i.e., performing a number of different tasks or partial tasks in quick succession) rather than the simultaneous performance of tasks, even though the performance seems subjectively to occur simultaneously. Kirschner, P. A., & van Merriënboer, J. J. G. (2013). Do learners really know best? Urban legends in education. *Educational Psychologist, 48*(3), 169–183.	Kirschner and van Merriënboer (2013) point out that there is a difference between multitasking and task switching. Individuals may perceive that they are multitasking while in reality, due to the limitations related to "human cognitive architecture" (p. 171), they are switching from one task to the other.

key terms and expressions used by the original author. Be sure to check your college's writing centers resources as well as web-based resources for additional information. Also, different styles such as the Modern Language Association (MLA), American Psychological Association (APA), and The Chicago Manual of Style (CMOS) have different approaches to indicate that you are presenting original work by someone else. Your professor will communicate which style of referencing is expected.

The skills of locating credible sources and presenting them with academic integrity are critical in producing research papers and individual or group presentations. We will next turn to discussing how to approach these two types of assignments.

WRITING A RESEARCH PAPER

The vast majority of courses require writing a research paper as this type of assignment develops written communication skills and the ability to support arguments, both critical for professional success. Before we discuss the specific strategies, we want to emphasize that general self-regulatory skills of time management and combatting procrastination tendencies (Chapter 6) are foundational to succeed in writing research papers. Generally, the syllabus presents a research paper as a course requirement at the beginning of the term. Often, the research paper is not due until the end of the course. Therefore, you may have the illusion that you have "all the time in the world." However, chances are that both researching and writing will require much more time that you think. In addition, events beyond your control such as getting sick may occur. Remember from Chapter 5 that cold/flu/sore throat rank as number five in impediments to academic performance! Begin the task of writing a research paper sooner rather than later. Use the principles of distributed versus massed study (Chapter 2), which enable you to create one or several drafts and receive feedback from your instructor before turning in your final paper. Also, review Chapter 10 for effective strategies of how to develop a study plan and modify them for writing a research paper.

Table A.4 presents the steps that you can adapt as a general approach to writing a research paper.

TABLE A.4
Steps of Writing a Research Paper

Focus on a Researchable Topic	Generally, it is effective to define the topic by looking at it as a question to be answered, a problem to be solved, or an argument to be made. Your decision as to the purpose of the paper will decide the type of research you will identify for your paper.
Locate Sources	Use the guidelines for credibility of sources presented in Table A.1 to identify relevant information. You want to use primary or peer-reviewed journal articles, textbooks, and research reports as your sources.
Organize, Analyze, and Synthesize Information	Via organizing, analyzing, and synthesizing information from the sources, identify main ideas with supporting sources.
Create a Thesis Statement	It is generally not possible to create a thesis statement before you have analyzed and synthesized information from the sources. An effective thesis statement generally answers the question you asked or presents possible solutions for the problem you posed to be solved.
Create an Outline	Adapt the structure presented in Chapter 11 for taking essay exams: an introduction, body, and conclusion. The body will be comprised of several paragraphs, each presenting a main idea with supporting and related sources. It is often best to outline the paragraphs of the body first and then create the introduction and conclusion.
Write the First Draft	Present the main ideas and supporting details, and organize your writing by paragraphs, each with one main idea and supporting details. Be sure to include transitional words. This is similar to organizing your response to an exam essay prompt presented in Chapter 11.
	Don't worry about the first draft not being in finalized language. Focus on getting your thoughts down without worrying about the exact words you are using. You will go back and choose the appropriate words when revising your draft.
Revise Your Draft	Focus on clear, appropriate, academic language. As required, include a title page, a table of contents, an abstract, and, of course, a reference section.

PLANNING AND DELIVERING AN EFFECTIVE INDIVIDUAL OR GROUP PRESENTATION

Higher education institutions are shifting from only instructor-centered presentations such as the traditional lecture format to including student individual or group presentations. These approaches prepare students for the professional skills related to oral communication and, in the cases of group presentations, collaborative work.

Both individual and group presentations require research, organization, and practice. In a group presentation, the benefit is that each individual's workload is decreased. However, group presentations require coordination between multiple students and can result in frustration. Remember the phenomenon of social loafing from Chapter 7 where some group members do all the work while other group members free ride and still get credit? By keeping your group to below five people if possible, utilizing effective communication, and solid planning, you can have a good experience delivering a group presentation.

The first step in group presentations is forming the group. Please review Table 7.3 for the initial steps in forming groups: exchanging names and contact information, discussing each member's interest in the topic, and reviewing the goal of collaborative efforts. As you start working on the presentation, there are certain common steps irrespective of the nature of the group's project. Most of the steps apply to creating an individual presentation as well. Table A.5 presents these steps in

TABLE A.5
Steps of Creating a Group Presentation

Divide the Work	Divide the presentation into parts (e.g., the different sections, the introduction, the conclusion).
	Decide on the order in which each part must be completed.
	Determine the timetable by working backward from when the presentation is due.
	Decide who is responsible for each part.
	Spell out the specifics of what each individual must produce. This includes the length of everyone's individual presentation and number of references, if any.
	Agree about steps to be taken if someone will not be able to meet a deadline.
	Decide about a regular schedule of meetings or at the minimum, check-ins.
	Decide whether it is more effective to meet in person or virtually.
Check in and Assess Progress	Review what each group member has accomplished.
	Provide feedback about each other's work in terms of whether the material is aligned with the plan and if not, what is missing or what must be omitted (feelings may be hurt, but it is best that material not needed or not directly related be omitted).
	Create new goals as needed. It is common to discover that modifications to the original plan are needed.
Plan the Presentation	When everyone's contributions are becoming finalized, make decisions about the oral presentation. Don't hurry this part, though, as the content of the presentation is critical and should be held as the priority.
	Decide on a presentation format. Will you use PowerPoint, Prezi, or other media? Will you include illustrative video clips? Whatever media you use, make sure that your choices are compatible with technology in the presentation room.
	Confirm whether the person who created the introduction will start the presentation.
	Decide on transitions from one presenter to the next (e.g., "As Shaun stated, ... I will next ..."). Transitions ensure a cohesive flow.
	Make decisions about physical arrangements for the presentation (e.g., will you all stand in front of the room? Will the presenter step forward?).
	Practice the presentation, including the introduction and conclusion, and transitions. Ensure everyone stays in their time limit.
	Support the group members' delivery skills. Ensure everyone knows to 1) print out the slides so they do not have to turn around to check the slides behind them; 2) connect with the audience by creating eye contact and projecting their voice to the back of the room; and 3) use body language or raise their voice to emphasize a key point.

a suggested order. You may change the order as necessary or even go back and forth between the steps in order to ensure a quality presentation. However, completing each step will help you create a strong presentation.

Whether you are creating a group or individual presentation, the next sections about creating effective slides and delivering an effective and engaging presentation apply.

CREATING EFFECTIVE SLIDES

Though the credibility of content is the foundation of an effective academic presentation, how you deliver it makes a difference in the success of communicating your work. Table A.6 presents tips on how to use visual elements to support your oral presentation as well as to avoid overloading your audience's working memory capacity (which as you recall from Chapter 3 is limited). A busy template, dazzling icons, and an abundance of text on a slide in addition to the orally delivered important information challenges our information processing capacity.

In summary, this section reviewed strategies for creating typical college assignments: research papers and individual or group presentation. We highlighted the importance of distinguishing credible from not credible resources and the role of peer review as a key determining factor of scholarly credibility. We emphasized the importance of ensuring academic integrity by paraphrasing original material and being clear with your audience when you are quoting the original directly. Finally, we reviewed general steps of writing a research paper and planning an individual or group presentation.

TABLE A.6
Creating Effective Slides

Aim for Simplicity	Choose a simple slide template.
	Be sure to use the same font throughout the presentation.
	Remove clutter such as unnecessary icons.
	Don't use cartoonish clip art.
	Keep plenty of empty space.
	Limit complicated transitions such as "Fly In" and "Float In"; opt for simple ones such as "Appear."
Limit Text	The slides are meant to highlight key points, not to be redundant with your oral presentation.
	Avoid complete sentences; opt for bullet points if you need to include text.

Appendix B: A Guide for Completing a Self-Regulation Study

You have been asked throughout this book to reflect on your academic behavior and determine what action you need to take to become a more successful learner. The four-step self-regulatory process was introduced in Chapter 1 to help address academic problems. The process includes self-observation and evaluation, goal setting and strategic planning, strategy implementation and monitoring, and strategic-outcome monitoring. The first Follow-Up Activities in Chapters 5 through 11 provide a series of questions for each of the steps to guide you in your self-study.

The purpose of this appendix is to provide tools and assistance to help you either (a) complete a follow-up study focused on the content in one of the chapters you have read or (b) design a study in an area of interest or concern. You will need to answer a series of questions to complete the four steps in the self-regulatory process. The information under the next four headings will help you answer these questions so you will be able to reduce or eliminate a problem to improve your academic performance. You can refer to Appendix C at any time to view examples of self-regulation studies that were completed by students in a similar class over a two- to three-week period.

SELF-OBSERVATION AND EVALUATION

The first step of a self-regulation study requires you to observe and evaluate your behavior to select an academic problem you want to solve. An academic problem is defined as any behavior, belief, or perception that has a detrimental impact on your academic performance and is preventing you from attaining your academic potential or goals.

You have learned that your ability to manage or control factors associated with your motivation, methods of learning, use of time, and physical and social environment will enhance your academic performance. These factors include your beliefs, perceptions, physiological responses (e.g., in the case of anxiety), feelings, and behaviors.

There are a number of ways you can determine what aspect of your behavior to study and modify. First, you may have come into this course with an understanding of some aspect of your academic behavior that needs to be modified. Second, you can take a diagnostic test such as the Learning and Study Strategies Inventory (LASSI; Weinstein et al., 1987) to identify your strengths and weaknesses. Your instructor may have used this instrument or some other study skills assessment in your course. Third, you can identify one of the self-regulation components—motivation, methods of learning, use of time, or physical and social environment—you are concerned about, and then complete the related self-observation exercises in this book. Table B.1 provides a list of these exercises according to the self-regulation component addressed.

By completing some or all of these exercises, you will learn about (a) behaviors that you never, sometimes, or always engage in that could benefit your academic performance, or (b) behaviors that you always engage in that have a detrimental effect on your performance.

Once you identify these problems, you will select one problem for your study that you *need* and *want* to solve. Notice that the terms *need* and *want* are included in this statement. Changing behavior is a difficult thing to do. It requires you to invest a significant amount of time and effort in the four-step self-regulation process. Therefore, it is important for you to take the time to select a problem that you need and want to change so that you will be committed to solving it. Table B.2 provides examples of academic problems by chapter that you may wish to consider for your study.

TABLE B.1
Self-Observation Exercises

Self-Regulation Components	Self-Observation Exercises	Chapter and Exercise #
Motivation	Analyzing my personal and sociocultural background	2.1
Analyzing classroom experiences	2.2	
Identifying your values	4.1	
Assessing emotions	Chapter and 5.1	
Assessing self-talk	Follow-up 5–4	
Exploring anxiety-producing situations in school	Follow-up 5–5	
Methods of learning	Assessing reading strategies	8.1
Analyzing note-taking strategies	9.1	
Assessing exam preparation	10.1	
Use of time	Assessing time wasters	6.1
Assessing use of time	6.2	
Identifying your escapist techniques	Follow-up 6–2	
Identifying your favorite procrastination beliefs	Follow-up 6–4	
Physical and social environment	Evaluating study environments	7.1

Once you select a problem, you will need to observe and evaluate your problem in the same manner as a doctor observes a patient to prescribe treatment. That is, you will need to start by providing information (e.g., diagnostic test scores, answers to self-observation exercises) that supports the fact that your problem exists, as well as information (e.g., grades) that demonstrates the type of impact it has had on your academic performance. Then you will need to gather information on the history of your academic problem (e.g., How long have you had the problem? Under what circumstances have you experienced it?). Finally, you will need to spend time collecting additional information (data) on your problem so you can discover and appropriately diagnose all of the internal factors, such as beliefs, perceptions, physiological responses (e.g., anxiety), and behaviors that are contributing to it. Like a doctor, you will be more likely to prescribe the appropriate treatment (i.e., strategies) if you take the time at the beginning of your study to collect data that will enable you to determine all of the factors that are contributing to your problem. If you choose to guess which factors are contributing to your problem, you will most likely have to prescribe several treatments (strategies) before you find one that will effectively reduce or eliminate your problem. As a result, you will save time by thoroughly investigating your problem at the start of your study.

There are two ways you can gather information (data) on the symptoms of your problem and the internal factors and behaviors that contribute to it. The first way is to look at documents to which you already have access. Table B.3 provides a list of documents that you may wish to consult. The second way is to set aside a period of time (preferably one to two weeks) to study your problem. During this time, you can collect documents listed in Table B.3. In addition, you can use instruments such as charts, journals, tally sheets, and checklists to collect data on the symptoms of your problem and the internal factors and behaviors that contribute to it. Each of these instruments is described in the following section.

CHARTS

Charts are tools you can use to diagnose the internal beliefs, perceptions, physiological responses, feelings, or behaviors that contribute to your academic problem. Charts include topics that are

TABLE B.2
Examples of Academic Problems

Self-Management	Academic Problems	Chapter Components
"I have a problem because I never, or only sometimes ..." (Insert response [a]) or "I have a problem because I usually ..." (Insert response [b])		
Motivation	[a] choose to complete academic tasks	2
	[a] put forth the effort needed to do well on certain academic tasks	2
	[a] persist when tasks are difficult, boring, or unchallenging	2
	[b] worry or experience anxiety as I study, attend class, or take exams	5
Methods of Learning	[a] take notes in class	9
	[b] experience difficulty with material delivered in class	9
	[a] read my textbooks or articles	8
	[a] prepare for quizzes and exams	10
	[a] remember the information I studied	3
	[b] have difficulty taking exams	11
Use of Time	[a] have time to do the things I value	6
	[a] have time to complete my academic tasks as well as I would like	6
	[a] have time to review my work before handing it in	6
	[a] have time to test myself before quizzes and exams	6
	[b] miss important events such as classes, review sessions, appointments, meetings	6
	[b] escape from academic events and tasks	2, 5, 6
Physical and Social Environment	[a] select or arrange the physical setting to make my learning more effective	7
	[a] seek assistance from peers, tutors, teaching assistants, and professors when I need help	7
	[a] seek help from non-social resources (e.g., study aids, the web, books) when I need it	7
	[b] have difficulty attending to or concentrating on academic tasks	7
	[b] encounter internal or external distractions that interrupt my studying	7

placed across the top row and details that are placed underneath each topic. For example, if your problem is that you never or only sometimes remember the information you study, you may wish to use a chart like the one below to record the strategies you use as you study. (Chart C.1.

The advantage of using this type of chart is that it will help you see the relationship between (a) environmental factors (i.e., where you studied, when you studied, and with whom you studied), (b) motivation (i.e., your interest level, confidence level, and goals), (c) learning strategies (e.g., rehearsal, elaboration, and organization), and (d) your performance outcomes. As a result, it should become easier for you to identify beliefs, perceptions, physiological responses, feelings, and behaviors you need to change.

There are several examples of charts that you may wish to use or model, including:

- A chart for analyzing efficacy scores (Chapter 2)
- A weekly priority task list (Chapter 6)
- A chart for becoming aware of misdirected attention (Chapter 7)

TABLE B.3
Documents

Self-Regulation Components	Documents
Motivation	Written goals
	Journals, video diaries (e.g., to evaluate self-efficacy, attributions, and self-talk)
Methods of Learning	Class notes
	Notes from readings
	Study plans
	Study aids (i.e., flashcards, outlines, and representations)
	Practice tests
Use of Time	Attendance sheets
	Course syllabi
	Semester calendars
	Weekly priority tasks lists
	Weekly schedules
Physical and Social	Notes from meetings with instructors, teaching assistants, tutors, and classmates
Environment	Non-social resources (i.e., articles, books, study guides)
Performance	Scores on assignments, quizzes, exams, papers, and presentations
All Components	The self-observation checklists in this book
	Results from any learning and study skills assessments

You may also find it is helpful to design your own chart(s) for your study. The following list provides a number of topics you may wish to include on a chart:

- Environmental factors (e.g., dates, times, locations, and people)
- Internal or personal factors—beliefs and perceptions (demonstrated by your self-efficacy, attributions, and self-talk), physiological responses (e.g., anxiety), and your mood (e.g., whether you are interested or bored)
- Behaviors—(a) motivation (e.g., goals, choices, levels of involvement [effort], and persistence); (b) methods of learning (e.g., use of rehearsal, elaboration, and organizational strategies); (c) use of time (e.g., planning, prioritizing, and scheduling; the times when tasks are assigned, started, and completed); and (d) physical and social environment (types of internal and external distractions, the amount of time spent attending to or concentrating on tasks) and the use of social resources

JOURNALS

Daily journals (or diaries), whether recorded in words or video, provide an effective means of collecting information about your internal beliefs, perceptions, and feelings. For example, the Follow-Up Activity in Chapter 5, titled "Assess Self-Talk," asks you to keep a journal to help you identify the type(s) of self-talk you exhibit. Journals may also help you to keep track of the strategies you use and the behaviors you exhibit throughout your study.

TALLY SHEETS

Tally sheets are tools you can use to count the number of times a particular belief, perception, physiological response, feeling, or behavior occurs within the time frame you establish for your study (Cartwright & Cartwright, 1984). You may design tally sheets a number of ways based on what you

CHART C.1
Class: Motivation and Learning Strategies from: 10/26 to 11/3

Date	Task	Strategy Use	Physical/Social Environment (including course procedures and requirements)	Motivation
10/26	Read Ch. 3	None	Roommate wanted to go out for pizza	Was not interested in the content
10/27	Study for quiz	Reread and underlined	Quiz this morning	Didn't feel like studying
10/27	Take quiz	Wrote answers	Sat next to a friend who felt confident before the quiz and completed the quiz early	Was anxious and didn't have enough time to complete my thoughts
10/28	Read Ch. 7	Underlined text, turned headings into questions, came up with a few examples from my own experience		Believed I could relate to this content and was confident about it
11/1	Read article	Turned headings into questions, underlined answers, and developed a matrix	Read article in library	Was disappointed in my last quiz score (+6/10), wanted to get at least a +8 on my quiz and believed the material was interesting
11/2	Study for quiz	Asked the questions I developed to test myself, reviewed the matrix	Discussed my thoughts about the article with a classmate	Answered all of the questions I asked myself and was confident after studying
11/3	Take quiz	Made a brief outline of each answer before starting	Compared my summary with a classmate's summary and saw that mine was more detailed	Was confident about the quiz because I was able to predict the questions and was able to finish early

would like to learn about your problem. For example, if your problem is that you always encounter distractions that interrupt your studying, you may find either of these tally sheets helpful.

The advantage of using these tally sheets is that they will enable you to determine the number of times you were distracted (i.e., 25 vs. 12) within the time frame you selected. The first tally sheet will help you learn where your distractions most frequently occur, whereas the second tally sheet will enable you to determine your *rate* of distraction. You can calculate this rate by dividing the number of minutes you spend studying by the number of distractions you encounter. For example, if you calculate the rate for each of the rows in the sample tally sheet, you will find that you were distracted once every 12 minutes in the evening, once every 15 minutes in the morning, and once every 20 minutes in the afternoon. Thus, the afternoon appears to be the best time for you to study.

The disadvantage of using the tally sheets is that they limit the amount of information you can gain from using them. For example, the tally sheets only provide you with information about the location where, or time periods when, the student experienced distractions. However, they do not provide you with information about the types of internal and external distractions experienced. Therefore, if you decide to use tally sheets in your study, your instructor will most likely require that you keep a journal that describes what you learn each day from your tally sheets (Chart C.2).

CHART C.2
From: 10/1 to: 10/5 Distractions during Studying

Location	Tally	Total
Room	ʼʼʼ |||	8
Library	||	2
Lounge	ʼʼʼ ʼʼʼ	10
Friend's Room	ʼʼʼ	5
Total		25

Distractions during Studying

Date	From	To	Task and Number of Distractions	Total Time	Distractions
10/1	7:30 p.m.	8:30 p.m.	ʼʼʼ	60 m	5
10/2	9:00 a.m.	9:45 a.m.	|||	45 m	3
10/2	1:00 p.m.	2:00 p.m.	||||	60 m	4
Total				165 m	12

Adapted from Alberto & Troutman (1986).

CHECKLISTS

Checklists are similar to tally sheets. The only difference is that checklists use checkmarks to monitor whether or not a particular behavior on a list has or has not occurred. For example, you may wish to use a checklist to keep track of such things as: your class attendance, the criterion for an assignment that you have met, the assignments listed on the course syllabus that you have finished, and the items on your weekly priority task list that you have completed.

Once you complete a thorough investigation of your problem using one or more of the previously described methods, you will need to provide a brief narrative description of what you learned from each document, chart, journal, tally sheet, or checklist you use (i.e., just like a doctor makes notes of what he or she learns in a patient's chart). For example, if you were to collect the data displayed in the first chart (Motivation and Learning Strategies class), you might describe the fact that you were not confident about your study techniques and received a low quiz grade when you (a) were not interested in the content, (b) used rehearsal strategies (e.g., underlining and rereading), or (c) were anxious during the exam. However, when you were confident and received a high quiz score, you (a) could relate to the material, (b) used elaboration and organization strategies (e.g., turned headings into questions, came up with your own examples, and developed a matrix), (c) studied at the library, (d) discussed your thoughts with a classmate, (e) tested yourself before the exam, and (f) made a brief outline before answering each question. This narrative description serves two purposes. First, it helps identify the changes you need to make to reduce or eliminate your problem. In addition, it helps you and your instructor keep track of your reasoning throughout the course of your study.

GOAL SETTING AND STRATEGIC PLANNING

By now, you should have established a SMART goal such as: "I want to obtain a 3.0 GPA this semester" or "I want to earn a B in my Psychology class this semester." Chapter 4 describes the steps you need to take to make sure you set a specific, measurable, action-oriented, realistic, and time-bound (SMART) goal (Smith, 1994). Once you establish a SMART long-term goal, you need to set a SMART intermediate goal related to your self-regulation problem. For example, if your problem is that "you only sometimes remember the information you studied in your biology course" and, as a result, have low quiz and exam scores (i.e., Cs or below), you may wish to set a SMART intermediate goal such as earning at least a B on the rest of your quizzes and exams this semester. Your long-term and intermediate goals will provide the direction for what you hope to accomplish in your self-study.

Once you establish your SMART long-term and intermediate goals, you will need to identify strategies to help you reduce or eliminate your problem and reach your goal(s). Table B.4 provides a list of the strategies found in each chapter. To reduce or eliminate your problem, you will need to select a strategy (or set of strategies) that you know you will feel comfortable using. For example, one solution (or strategy) may be sufficient for solving certain problems, whereas other problems may require the use of many strategies. For instance, if your problem is that you only sometimes remember the information you studied in your biology course, you may need to choose strategies to improve your motivation, time management, and social and physical environment in addition to your methods of learning. The strategies you choose should be based on the factors that you found were contributing to your problem in the self-observation and evaluation stage of your study.

Once you select the strategies you will use to reduce your problem and meet your intermediate goal, you will need to develop an action plan. This action plan should include the time frame for your study and should discuss (a) the strategies you plan to use, (b) when you plan to use each strategy, and (c) the method(s) you plan to use to record your progress. For example, if your intermediate goal is "to obtain at least a B on the rest of the quizzes in your biology course," you may develop a strategic action plan similar to the following.

As you develop your plan, ask yourself the following question: "Why should I use each of these strategies?" If you cannot justify your answer based on the information you learned from the self-observation and evaluation stage of your study, you need to find an alternative strategy (or set of strategies) to use. Please keep in mind that the number or type of strategies used to modify behavior will vary according to the nature of the problem. This means that you will not necessarily use strategies in all of the components of academic self-regulation. (Chart C.3)

STRATEGY IMPLEMENTATION AND MONITORING

Now is the time for you to try to reduce or eliminate your problem by implementing each of the strategies specified in your action plan. During this time, you will need to do three things. First, you will need to keep track of all of the strategies you use in an attempt to change your behavior, as well as the date and time when you use each strategy. This information will enable you to determine the extent to which you follow your strategic plan. Second, you will need to keep track of the methods you use to record your progress (e.g., documents, charts, journals, tally sheets, or checklists). Finally, you will need to evaluate your progress by asking the following questions:

- "Are the data collection methods I am using working?"
- "Are the strategies I am using working?"

To answer the first question, "Are the data collection methods I am using working?" you will need to check to see if (a) you have followed the data recording methods specified in your plan, (b) you are comfortable with these methods, and (c) you have enough data to objectively evaluate your progress. If you fail to meet any of these criteria, you will need to change your data collection methods.

To answer the second question, "Are the strategies I am using working?" you will need to see if (a) you are comfortable using these strategies and (b) you are meeting the criterion you set in both your SMART goal and strategic action plan. For example, if your intermediate SMART goal is to

TABLE B.4
Strategies to Solve Academic Problems

Components of Academic Behavior	Strategies	Chapter
Motivation		
Goal setting	Align values, goals, and daily tasks.	4
	Set long-term and short-term SMART goals.	4
Self-rewards	Arrange or imagine rewards for positive behaviors or successes, for example: "If I do well on my homework, I will treat myself to my favorite show."	5
	Arrange or imagine punishments for negative behaviors or failures, for example: "If I don't do well on my homework, I won't be able to watch my favorite show."	5
Self-talk	Use rational thinking and positive self-talk to combat irrational beliefs and perceptions; attribute successes and failure to effort.	2
Relaxation techniques	Use diaphragmatic breathing and progressive muscle relaxation.	5
	Use meditation.	5
Methods of Learning		
Elaborating and organizing	Use elaboration strategies such as:	
	Asking and answering questions as you read, take notes, and study;	3, 8, 9
	Paraphrasing and summarizing;	3
	Creating analogies; and	3
	Creating acronyms.	3
	Use organizational strategies such as:	
	Outlining; and	8
	Representations.	8
Reviewing records	Review class notes and handouts before and after each lecture.	10
	Review your course syllabus, class notes, handouts, course books, and previous quizzes and exams as you prepare for further testing.	10, 11
Planning	Determine how you will prepare for exams.	10
	Determine how to approach different types of exam questions.	11
Self-testing	Test yourself to see if you recall information.	10
Use of Time		
Planning	Make sure your daily tasks are aligned with your values and goals.	6
	Break down your tasks into smaller more manageable parts.	6
	Set goals for your daily tasks.	6
	Determine how you will eliminate your procrastination beliefs.	6
Scheduling	Maintain a monthly calendar.	6
	Maintain a weekly priority tasks list.	6
	Maintain a weekly schedule.	6
Physical and Social Environment		
Seeking social assistance	Seek help from peers, tutors, or instructors when you need it.	7
Seeking information	Use campus resources.	7
	Locate additional study aids and books in areas that are difficult for you.	7

obtain at least a B on the rest of your quizzes and exams in your biology course this semester, you will need to record and evaluate all of your weekly quiz scores. If you meet your goal and are comfortable with the strategies you are using, you do not need to modify your action plan. However, if you find that you are uncomfortable with the strategies or that the strategies you are using are not helping you meet your goal (e.g., you are not earning at least a B on your quizzes and exams), you will need to adjust your strategies in your strategic action plan. Once you evaluate the effectiveness

CHART C.3
An Example of a Strategic Action Plan
Timeline: From: February 1 to February 21

Self-regulatory strategies	When will I use the strategy?	What method will I use to record or indicate my progress?
Change headings to questions and answer questions	Each time I read	Markings in textbooks
Develop at least one representation per chapter	When I review chapter	Notes
Test myself on mirror and summary questions in notes	After each lecture	Notes
Complete study for each quiz two days before exam	For each quiz	Check off on weekly calendar
Attend office hours or get help from a classmate	Each time I have a question or do not get 80% on my practice quiz in my textbook	Practice quiz score and notes from meeting
Put a note on my door and put my cell phone on silent mode	Each time I study for a quiz	Develop a checklist for number of distractions per study session

of your data collection methods and strategies, you will need to ask: "What changes, if any, do I need to make?" You may wish to change (a) the instruments you use to record your data or (b) the strategies you use as you attempt to reduce or eliminate your problem. In addition, you may wish to change the time frame in which you plan to implement different strategies. During this strategy implementation and monitoring stage, it is extremely important for you to make a note of all the changes you make to your study along the way.

STRATEGIC-OUTCOME MONITORING

Strategic-outcome monitoring is the last step in the self-regulation process. At the end of the time frame specified in your strategic action plan, you will need to refer to your intermediate SMART goal to answer the following questions: "Did I attain each of the goals I set for myself?" and "How do I know?" In addition, you will need to ask yourself: "What did I learn from my self-study?" To answer this question, you will need to review every document, chart, journal, tally sheet, or checklist you collect and describe what each piece of evidence tells you. This evidence should help you determine which strategies were the most and least effective in helping you reduce or eliminate your problem. In addition, this information should help you determine if there are any changes you need to make to improve your academic performance in the future.

Once you complete all four steps of your self-regulation study, your instructor will most likely ask for you to write a report describing the process you used and the extent to which you were able to modify or change your behavior. You will find the questions in the Follow-Up Activities provide a structure for writing the paper. The following are the questions for a self-regulation study in time management.

Self-Observation and Evaluation.   How do I manage my time? Do I need to change the way I plan and manage my study schedule? If yes, what problem(s) do I encounter? What are the symptoms of my problem (i.e., when, where, and how often does my problem occur)? How much of an impact does this problem have on my academic performance? What factors (e.g., beliefs, perceptions, physiological responses, feelings, or behaviors) contribute to this problem? What do I need to change to reduce or eliminate my problem(s)?

Goal Setting and Strategic Planning.   What are my goals? What strategies will I use to improve my time management? When will I use these strategies? How will I record my progress?

Strategy Implementation and Monitoring.   What strategies did I use to improve my time management? When did I use these strategies? What method(s) did I use to record my progress (e.g., documents, charts, journals, tally sheets, and checklists)? When did I use these methods? How and when did I monitor my progress to determine if my new time-management plan was working? What changes, if any, did I make along the way?

Strategic-Outcome Monitoring.   Did I attain the goal(s) I set for myself? Have the modifications in my time management improved my academic performance and personal life? What strategies were the most and least effective? What additional changes, if any, do I need to make in the future?

Appendix C: Examples of Self-Regulation Studies

SELF-REGULATION STUDY #1: METHODS OF LEARNING (IMPROVING QUIZ SCORES)

Introduction

This semester I decided to take the initiative to set a goal that I am determined to accomplish—to earn a 3.0 grade point average. This goal should motivate me to do all of my work for my classes. At times, I believe that the motivation I had at the start of the semester diminished. I have found this to be especially true in my Policy Planning and Development class.

Self-Observation and Evaluation

I have elected to do my case study for my Policy Planning and Development class. In this class, I want to improve my quiz scores because they will heavily determine my grade at the end of the course. These quizzes are pop quizzes, and the element of surprise is what I find most disturbing because the quizzes consist of both the readings and the lectures. Thus, I must make sure I really learn the information so that I can recall it at any time.

So far I have taken four quizzes, and all of my scores have been relatively low. I have earned one F, one D, and two Cs. [Note: the student also provided documentation of these quiz scores.] The reason these scores are so low is because I have not kept up with the reading material and my attendance in class has been poor (see Attachment 1). [Note: the student also provided a copy of his syllabus, which indicated the readings he did and did not complete.]

Goal Setting and Strategic Planning

My goal for this self-regulation study is to improve my scores on the next two quizzes (i.e., Quiz 5 and 6) in my Policy Planning and Development Course. I will start by attaining at least a C on the next quiz. The strategies I plan to use to accomplish this goal are listed in the following chart:

Strategies	When	Method of Recording
Reading		
I will be on schedule for all of my readings	During the next week	I will highlight each reading I complete on my syllabus
I will turn headings into questions and answer these questions	Each time I read a chapter or article	Textbook
Class Notes		
I will attend all of my lectures and discussion sessions and use the note-taking strategy I learned in Chapter 9	Until the end of the semester	I will use a checklist to keep track of my attendance, and I will provide documentation of my note taking
Office Hours		
I will set up appointments with my professor and my teaching assistant	Before the next quizzes	I will provide my weekly schedule (noting the appointment times) as well as documentation of the notes I take at each appointment

To earn better quiz scores, I must start with the basics. I will catch up on all of my readings and ask myself questions on what I read. All of these assignments are marked on my syllabus. As I read each assignment, I will use the reading comprehension strategies in Chapter 8.

Then, when I finish each assignment, I will highlight it on my syllabus so that I will know I have read it. I also plan to attend all of my lectures and discussion sessions, because my professor often gives hints about the material that will be on our quizzes. At each class, I will take good notes during these lectures using the note-making strategy in Chapter 9. These notes should help me predict which questions will show up on the quizzes. Finally, I plan to set several appointments with my professor and teaching assistant. In these meetings, I will ask questions about the content I do not understand.

STRATEGY IMPLEMENTATION AND MONITORING

So far I have used all of the strategies listed in my plan, and my strategies seem to be working. On my fifth quiz (11/5), I earned a B, which exceeded my goal [note: the student also provided documentation of this score]. I feel I was able to earn a decent grade on this quiz because I followed the strategies set forth in my plan. I was able to catch up with the readings, and I have used the reading strategies I learned. [Note: the student provided documentation of the readings he completed using this strategy.]. I completed these readings in a tranquil and quiet environment. I also attended every lecture since the start of this study and took notes using the procedures in Chapter 9 (see Attachment 2). [Note: the student also provided documentation of the notes he took using this strategy.] I feel that the most positive step I made was that I scheduled an appointment with my teaching assistant. At this meeting, my teaching assistant gave me plenty of useful information (see Attachment 3). [Note: the student also provided documentation of his notes from this meeting.] Because of my success, I plan to continue to abide by my plan and hope to earn even higher grades.

STRATEGIC-OUTCOME MONITORING

Quiz 6 took place on November 19, and I earned an A. [Note: the student provided documentation of this score]. I must admit, I felt confident before taking the quiz—it was the first time I had used positive self-talk in this class. I followed all of the steps in my strategic plan, and my results were extremely satisfying. I read all of my reading materials, attended every lecture, and was able to set an appointment with my professor. The appointment was very helpful, so I plan to continue attending office hours.

Overall, my strategic plan had a positive impact on my quiz scores. I have been able to raise my grades significantly. Hopefully, I will continue to maintain this progress on the last two quizzes and final exam in this course.

ANALYSIS OF SELF-REGULATION STUDY #1

SELF-OBSERVATION AND EVALUATION

Strengths.   The student uses his course quiz grades to identify his problem—not performing as well as he would like to in his Policy Planning and Development class. In addition, he provides evidence of the symptoms of his problem (poor attendance and not keeping up with his reading assignments) by including an attendance chart and by checking off the assignments he has and has not completed on his syllabus.

Areas for Improvement.   The student could have improved his study by providing the reader with more information related to the history of his problem (e.g., when he first noticed the problem). In addition, he could have strengthened his study by exploring internal factors (e.g., beliefs, perceptions, physiological responses, and feelings) and other behaviors that may be contributing to his problem.

Evidence Sheet

Attachment 1: Class Attendance Before

9/3	9/8	9/10	9/15	9/17	9/22	9/24	9/29	10/1	10/6
X	X			X	X				X

10/8	10/13	10/15	10/20	10/22	10/27	10/29
X		X	X			X

Attachment 2: Class Attendance After

11/3	11/5	11/10	11/12	11/17	11/19	11/24
X	X	X	X	X	X	X

Attachment 3: Weekly Schedule

Monday, November 2

Tuesday, November 3
Election Day (US)
Wednesday, November 4
1. Study for English quiz
2. Wrote journal for educational psychology course
3. Meet with TA
4. Study for quiz

Thursday, November 5
1. Study for quiz PLDV
2. Work on portfolio for educational psychology course
3. Read for English
Friday, November 6

Saturday, November 7

Sunday, November 8

GOAL SETTING AND STRATEGIC PLANNING

Strengths.   The student develops a SMART goal to improve his scores on the next two quizzes in his Policy Planning and Development Course and to get at least a C on his next quiz. Further, he developed a detailed plan to help him reach his goals, which includes: using the reading comprehension and note-making strategies discussed in Chapters 8 and 9; setting up office hours with both his professor and teaching assistant; and studying in a quiet environment. One of the strengths of his plan is that he decided to use more than one method (e.g., his weekly schedule and notes) to record his use of strategies (i.e., attending office hour appointments). Moreover, by displaying this plan in a chart, the student makes it easy for the reader to follow both when and how he plans to implement each strategy.

Areas for Improvement.   Although the student specifies how he will record his use of learning strategies and how he will keep track of his office hour appointments, he does not specify how he will record where he studies. A chart or structured diary would have been an easy means for him to record information related to his physical environment.

STRATEGIC IMPLEMENTATION MONITORING

Strengths.   The student adhered to his plan and provided concrete evidence of the reading assignments he completed (e.g., by marking them off on his syllabus and documenting his use of reading comprehension strategies), his attendance at class lectures (e.g., through his attendance sheet and notes using the note-making strategy), and his office hour appointments (e.g., by providing his weekly calendar and meeting notes). To determine if his strategies were working, he looked at his fifth quiz score (a B−) and decided that because his score exceeded his goal of attaining at least a C, he would continue with his plan.

Areas for Improvement.   The student could have improved his study by providing the reader with information about his physical environment (e.g., did he study in a quiet place as he had planned?). In addition, in the next section of his paper, the student mentions that he decided to use self-talk midway through his study. He should have addressed this change in this section of the paper.

STRATEGIC-OUTCOME MONITORING

Strengths.   The student demonstrates that he met his goal of improving his scores on the next two quizzes in his Policy Planning and Development Course by providing the reader with documentation of his quiz scores both before his study (e.g., one F, one D, and two Cs) and after his study (e.g., a B and an A).

Areas for Improvement.   The student could have improved his study by discussing what he learned from his self-regulation study (e.g., what strategies were the most and least effective and what changes, if any, he would make in the future).

SELF-REGULATION STUDY #2: MOTIVATION (I.E., REDUCING ANXIETY)

SELF-OBSERVATION AND EVALUATION

Identifying my problem wasn't very difficult. I had an idea of what my problem was before I was given this assignment. I have realized it since the beginning of this class; however, I never took it into full consideration. I really began to notice my problem in the middle of this course when I completed the Follow-Up Activities in Chapter 5 (see Attachment 1). My answers to the first exercise, "Assessing Self-Talk," indicate that I am full of anxiety and negative self-talk, and my answers to the second exercise, "Exploring Anxiety-Producing Situations in School," display my high test anxiety. My problem with anxiety is also evident on the anxiety scale of the Learning and Study Skills Inventory. My score of 14 in anxiety and worry about school performance is ranked extremely high among other college students.

After identifying my problem, I carefully examined my behavior and the way I handle my learning skills. I found that I display many of the different types of negative self-talk. At times, I find myself catastrophizing and worrying about everything, feeling like I should be perfect at everything, and filtering by only seeing the bad. It sounds pretty crazy, but it's true. I display negative self-talk in many situations in my life where I undergo pressure and stress. For example, I talk negatively to myself when I prepare for tests, when assignments are due, or just when I'm stressed out with certain tasks and problems in my life. At times, my negative self-talk impacts my sense of self-worth, my self-efficacy, and even my performance (see Attachment 2). For example, in this course, my self-efficacy ratings are always lower than my quiz scores. In addition, my quiz scores in math (a course I am anxious about) are low. Although I am a hard worker who always persists and strives to do my best, I find that my best is never enough for me. I also find that my anxiety affects my self-esteem and views about myself. I seem to never be satisfied with what I accomplish.

I believe that my internal beliefs, perceptions, and behaviors contribute to my anxiety problem. My self-efficacy beliefs are mostly average or below average. This, in turn, causes me to start saying negative things about myself, which has an effect on my performance. I also use failure-avoiding techniques that build my anxiety. For example, I tend to put things off until the last minute, which makes me more stressed and prevents me from being satisfied with my level of performance. Now that I have recognized these factors, I have developed a plan that deals with all of this information.

GOAL SETTING AND STRATEGIC PLANNING

My goal for this study is to reduce my negative self-talk and procrastination so that I will feel less anxious and more confident in myself, and as a result improve my performance on the exams I take between November 16th and November 20th. To accomplish this goal, I have developed the following plan.

The first part of my plan entails making a weekly calendar and scheduling assignments early so I will complete them early—maybe even a week in advance. This should prevent me from procrastinating so I can reduce my stress and anxiety. The second part of my plan involves using more positive self-talk. I plan to speak to myself every day (mornings and sometimes evenings) for one week through a journal. During this time, I will assure myself that I can successfully accomplish each task I face. This should get me started using positive self-talk in my everyday life and should boost my confidence level. The third part of my plan involves using the meditation and relaxation techniques in this book each day to help reduce my anxiety and stress. This should help me deal with the physical aspect of my anxiety problem. The last part of my plan involves using the Universal Smart Test Taker Trick sheet that my English professor recently gave me. When I take writing exams, I become nervous and uptight. At times, my mind even goes blank. I feel this sheet will help reduce my anxiety as I prepare my next written exam (i.e., my Art of Asia paper).

Strategies	When	Method of Recording
Weekly Schedule		
Schedule tasks so they are done ahead of time (preferably one week in advance)	Make a weekly schedule at the beginning of the week	I will check off each task I complete on my schedule
Self-Talk		
Use positive self-talk to improve my confidence	Each day (mornings and sometimes evenings) I will speak to myself through a journal reflection	Daily journal reflections
Meditation and relaxation techniques	Each day I will use one of the meditation and relaxation techniques in this book	I will mark each time I practice these techniques and the results onto a weekly calendar
Universal Writing Tricks sheet	Before taking my writing exam	I will provide documentation of these procedures along with my daily journal reflections

STRATEGY IMPLEMENTATION AND MONITORING

I implemented all of the strategies as specified on my plan. I started by scheduling time on my weekly schedule so that I would have plenty of time to write my Art of Asia midterm paper and study for my math and educational psychology exams (see Attachment 3). I completed all of my daily tasks as planned, except for reviewing my readings for my educational psychology class on Sunday. Then, during my exam week, I used several meditation and relaxation techniques (see Attachment 4). Each day I described how these strategies made me feel prior to my exams. As you can see, I felt that these techniques really helped me ease my tension and test anxiety. I also used the Universal Writing Tricks sheet that was provided by my professor to help me write my Art of Asia midterm. [Note: the student provided a list of these strategies in her evidence section.] Finally, I used my self-talk reflection journal to record my self-talk each day throughout the week (see Attachment 5).

STRATEGIC-OUTCOME MONITORING

My plan was somewhat effective, but not as effective as I hoped it would be. On the one hand, I found that my weekly schedule helped me stay on task and prevented me from procrastinating. I began studying for my math and educational psychology tests, and writing my papers several days in advance (see Attachment 3). I feel that because I was able to stick to this schedule, I was able to reduce my anxiety. In addition, I feel that the meditation and relaxation techniques and universal writing tricks I implemented (see Attachment 4) effectively reduced my anxiety and stress levels. [Note: the student included the Universal Writing Trick form.] The grades I earned in my math and writing courses improved during this time (see Attachment 6). Furthermore, my self-efficacy ratings and quiz scores in my educational psychology course became more aligned after implementing these strategies (see Attachment 6). On the other hand, the one thing I am still struggling with is my negative self-talk and confidence level (see Attachment 6). My reflection journals demonstrate that although I am beginning to use positive self-talk, I still display a lot of self-doubt. I build a fear of failure, and this fear contributes to my anxiety.

CONCLUSION

I can't completely say that this case study eliminated my anxiety problem. I also can't say that all of the strategies I used were fully effective. I also can't say that I am a changed person. However, I do know that this case study helped me reduce my anxiety. It also helped me become more aware of my problem. Before this study, I never took notice of my problem. I never really understood how and why it was there.

This case study increased my knowledge of the problem I have within myself. It made me more determined to change my attitude. I used to be in complete fear of failure. I can't say that I am not in fear of failure anymore because I'd be lying. But now I can look at my mistakes as stepping-stones to succeed in life. I can also see my mistakes as a means to enhance my motivation and feel better about myself. As I completed this case study, I explored new ways to expand my learning capabilities. I also applied skills that I can use in the future. I found out that I am capable of changing my behavior to achieve my full potential not only for my education, but also for myself.

EVIDENCE

ATTACHMENT 1: CHAPTER 5 FOLLOW-UP ACTIVITIES 1 AND 2

Activity 1: Assess Self-Talk   During the next week, monitor your self-talk and evaluate how it affected your motivation and self-confidence. Consider all situations and tasks in which you engage—academic, athletic and recreational, social, occupational, and personal. Include in your report the following information: date, situation (e.g., academic), setting (describe where you were and what you were trying to accomplish), and report the self-talk as specifically as possible. Finally, discuss what strategies you used to deal with any negative self-talk.

Date: Wednesday 11/4
Setting: Computer lab: typing peer review rough draft for English due the next day
Self-talk: Anxiety and Worry—"How am I going to do this?" etc. Strategy: None

Date: Thursday 11/5
Setting: Dorm—studying for my math quiz
Self-talk: "I'll never pass this quiz."
Strategy: None

Date: Monday 11/9
Setting: Class during my Arts of Asia exam
Self-talk: Nervous worrier—although I studied well, I was very negative and I worried about my performance.
Strategy: None

Comments: I find myself full of anxiety and negative self-talk. I do not use positive self-talk.

Activity 2: Explore Anxiety-Producing Situations in School   The following is a list of items the student indicated she identified with:

a. Worry about performance
   I should have reviewed more. I'll never get through.
   My mind is blank, I'll never get the answer. I must really be stupid. I
   knew this stuff yesterday. What is wrong with me?
   I can't remember a thing. This always happens to me.
b. Worry about bodily reactions
   I'm sweating all over—it's really hot in here.
   My stomach is going crazy, churning and jumping all over.
   Here it comes—I'm getting really tense again. Normal people just
   don't get like this.
c. Worry about how others are doing
   I know everyone's doing better than I am. I must be the dumbest one in the group.
   I am going to be the last one done again. I must be really stupid. No
   one else seems to be having trouble. Am I the only one?
d. Worry about the possible negative consequences
   If I fail this test, I'll never get into the program.
   I'll never graduate.
   I'll think less of myself.
   I'll be embarrassed.

Effective strategies: Try to use positive self-talk to counter my negative statements.

ATTACHMENT 2: PREVIOUS PERFORMANCE EDUCATIONAL PSYCHOLOGY

Edpsych 110	1	2	3	4	5	6	7	8	9	Total
Quiz score	10	9	8	7	10	8	9	10	9	80
Efficacy score	8	6	5.5	6	6.5	7	8	8	6	61

Midterm #1: 83%

Math

Math	1	2	3	4
Quiz score	6	6	6	7

Attachment 3: Weekly Schedule

Week of 11/9–11/15

Mon. Nov. 9	Tues. Nov. 10	Wed. Nov. 11	Thurs. Nov. 12	Fri. Nov. 13	Sat. Nov. 14	Sun. Nov. 15
		Write rough draft for assign. #4 Finished at 4:30 p.m.	Writing 8 p.m. Revise rough draft Finished at 9:16 p.m.	2 p.m. write Arts of Asia rough draft Also typed final paper		1. Review math ch. 52. Review educ. psych. Did not complete

Mon. Nov. 16	Tues. Nov. 17	Wed. Nov. 18	Thurs. Nov. 19	Fri. Nov. 20
1. Revise Art of Asia rough draft Finished at 5:30 p.m. 2. Review Educ. Psych. Finished at 10:30 p.m.	Math quiz 5.3-.5	Writing assign. #4 due Review Educ. Psych. Finished at 11:30 p.m.	Exam 2. Educ. Psych.	Math test (5 & 6) Art of Asia paper due

Attachment 4: Chart of My Anxiety-Reducing Techniques

Date	Relaxation and Meditation	Result Techniques
Nov. 17 7:45	Before math quiz I used diaphragmatic breathing technique for 7 minutes (math quiz at 8:00 a.m.).	I feel that I had rhythm to perform better. It allowed me to open my feelings and calm down.
Nov. 18 9:30 a.m.	I meditated with soft, slow music to relax from my studies and work for 15 minutes.	I feel it eased my tension for my math quiz. I was able to calm down and felt less uptight and nervous.
Nov. 19 7:45 a.m.	I relaxed with soft slow music for 15 minutes (Edpsych 110 exam at 9 a.m.).	I relaxed and felt prepared for my test. It reduced my stress and nervousness. Beforehand I was afraid that I might forget the information I had learned. It made me less uptight and more energized to take the test.
Nov. 20 8:45 a.m.	I meditated to soft music (math exam).	It reduced the anxiety I had because of the overwhelming work I did in the past 2 weeks. I feel that it relaxed me for my math test.

Goal Setting and Strategic Planning

Strengths.   The student sets a goal to reduce her negative self-talk and procrastination so she will feel less anxious and more confident in herself and ultimately improve scores on the exams she takes between November 16 and 20. By listing her grades in her math and educational psychology courses, she made it possible to monitor her progress toward this goal. Further, her plan, which includes monitoring her self-talk through a self-reflection journal and monitoring her anxiety through a chart, made it possible for her to monitor her anxiety and confidence levels. The student selects a variety of strategies such as breaking tasks down into manageable parts, scheduling tasks ahead of time, and using positive self-talk, meditation and relaxation techniques, and techniques suggested by her professor to combat her problem. Her strategic-planning chart makes it easy for the reader to follow her use of each of these strategies.

Areas for Improvement.   The student could have improved her study by providing more information about the extent of her negative self-talk and procrastination prior to her study. This would have enabled her to determine if the strategies she implements reduce these behaviors. Likewise, she could have provided information regarding her anxiety and confidence levels both prior to and during her study. This information would have made it easier for her to assess whether or not she met her goal. Finally, although the student provided information about her previous academic performance in her educational psychology and math courses, she did not provide any information about her previous performance in her Art of Asia course. Thus, it is not possible to determine if she improved her performance in this class.

Strategic Implementation and Monitoring

Strengths.   The student implemented all of the strategies in her plan and provided the reader with evidence of the fact she scheduled tasks in advance and used both positive self-talk and relaxation and meditation techniques.

Areas for Improvement.   The student used her daily reflection journal to record her self-talk once or twice each day. In this journal, it is clear that the student encounters many negative beliefs and perceptions, yet does not challenge each negative statement she makes. She would have learned a lot more about herself if she had recorded each negative statement she made throughout the day, each positive counterstatement, and her perceptions of whether each counterstatement worked (e.g., on a chart). This information would have enabled her to determine which types of counterstatements are the most and least effective and adjust her behavior accordingly. In addition, although the student provided documentation of the Universal Writer Tricks form that she used to help her with her Art of Asia exam, she did not provide the reader with any evidence that she actually used these strategies.

Attachment 5: Self-Talk Reflection Journal

Mon. Nov. 16th   Today is the first day I implemented my plan. Today I had nothing due, but this week I have a load of assignments to turn in. Furthermore, I have two papers due, a quiz, and two tests. I've got to believe I can do all of this. I've done it before. It is 9:30 p.m. right now. I guess I can start studying. I can achieve … I can achieve … I'm trying to think positive. This is hard. I'm saying the words, but do I mean it? I've always been able to keep my head up before. Don't worry, this week will be fine! I know I can do it.

Tues. Nov. 17th   Well, I'm about to head to class. It's 7:45. I've got a quiz in this class. It's only two sections—I can handle it. I didn't study that hard, though, but I kind of know the material. I was worrying about my other assignments. Well, I know it will be easy and just right. Oh, it's 7:50 a.m. Got to go. I'll pass!

Well, I'm back now and its 3:30. I'm about to go to work. The quiz was okay—I think I did well. I was speaking to myself, trying to think positive. I guess I'll find out Thursday how I did and I'll record it in here. I won't be able to write in here tonight, so I guess this is it.

Wed. Nov. 18th   Well, today is my mom's and cousin's birthday. This should be a good day. I've got to think positive today. It's about 8:35 a.m. and I'm about to go to my 9 a.m. class right now. Today I will turn in my fourth writing assignment for my writing class. I worked hard on it all last week. I think I did pretty well. I always get good grades on my papers. It had better be good! Well, I'll be back later.

Hello, I'm back from the library and it's 11:30 p.m. I just finished reviewing for my educ. psych. 110 test. I feel pretty confident, but I'm worried that I'll forget some information. Do you think I'll forget? I studied pretty well. Well, I'm going to call my mom right now, and then sleep or maybe watch television?

Thurs. Nov. 19th   Gosh, I hate waking up early for this 8 a.m. class. Today I have my Edpsych 110 test at 9 a.m. Aaah! I studied, but I don't know. I'm afraid I'll fail. I know I can do it. I did well on Exam 1. Anyhow, I'm getting my math quiz back from Tuesday. That should be cool! Well, it's 7:15 a.m. right now and I'm hungry. I think I'll get some food downstairs—I might get a stomachache before the test. I hope I pass!

Well, I'm back from work. It's 3:30 p.m. I'm about to watch television right now. Then I'm going to study for my math test tomorrow. It's pretty easy, so I think I can do it. Well, I can't wait until this weekend, when I can relax. My friend is having a party that should be fun and I'm going home Friday afternoon—Yes! Gotta study. Bye.

Fri. Nov. 20th   It's 7:30 a.m. I woke up early to review for my math test. I'm really scared right now. I'm not very confident. I reviewed a little here and there. I know the material though. I also have a paper due for my Art of Asia class at 2 p.m. today. I finished it a while ago, so at least that stress is gone. I can't wait to go home this weekend. I will soon be able to see my friends again. I guess I'll leave for class now.

I'm back from my math test. It wasn't as hard as I thought it would be. I don't want to be too confident because it might turn out negative. I hope I did well. Well, I'm going to turn in my Art of Asia paper. Then I am going to go home … Yeah!

Attachment 6: Grades after Using My Strategies

Future educ. psych. quizzes

Quiz	7	8
Efficacy Score	7	8

Educ. psych. midterm: 94%
Math quiz: 10/10
Math exam: 90%
Art of Asia paper: 92%

ANALYSIS OF SELF-REGULATION STUDY #2

Self-Observation and Evaluation

Strengths.   The student does a good job identifying her anxiety problem and describing both internal factors (e.g., low confidence and low self-efficacy) and behaviors (e.g., negative self-talk) that contribute to her problem. Further, she provides the reader with evidence to support her self-evaluation: her scores on the Learning and Study Skills Inventory, answers to the Follow-Up Activities in Chapter 5, quiz and self-efficacy scores in this course, and her quiz scores in her math course that support her self-evaluation claims.

Areas for Improvement.   The student could have improved her study by completing a more thorough analysis of her self-talk by listing and classifying each negative statement she made. She mentions that her self-talk can be classified as catastrophizing, shoulds, and filtering but she does not support this claim with evidence. If she had classified each statement she made, she would have been better able to determine the type of positive self-talk she needs to counteract her beliefs and ultimately change her behavior. In the next section of her paper, the student mentions that her tendency to procrastinate contributes to her anxiety. Here she could have improved her study by providing the reader with information on how she uses her time, as well as the extent of her procrastination.

STRATEGIC-OUTCOME MONITORING

Strengths.   The student demonstrates that she met her goal by improving her performance in her math and educational psychology courses. In addition, she provides support for the fact that she felt more confident and less anxious through her self-reflection journal and relaxation and meditation chart. Thus, her conclusions are consistent with the evidence she provides.

Areas for Improvement.   The student could have strengthened her study by comparing both her use of negative self-talk and her tendency to procrastinate before and after her study. This information would have enabled her to determine if her strategies helped her accomplish her goal (i.e., to reduce these behaviors). In addition, the student could have improved her study by providing information on her previous performance in her Art of Asia class. This information would have enabled the reader to determine if the 92 percent score she earned was an improvement over the previous scores.

References

Adams, S. K., & Kisler, T. S. (2013). Sleep quality as a mediator between technology-related sleep quality, depression, and anxiety. *CyberPsychology, Behavior and Social Networking, 16*(1), 25–30.

Alberto, P. A., & Troutman, A. C. (1986). *Applied Behavior Analysis for Teachers* (2nd ed.). Columbus, OH: Merrill.

Allen, J., & Robbins, S. (2010). Effects of interest–major congruence, motivation, and academic performance on timely degree attainment. *Journal of Counseling Psychology, 57*(1), 23–35.

Alter, A. L., Aronson, J., Darley, J. M., Rodriguez, C., & Ruble, D. N. (2010). Rising to the threat: Reducing stereotype threat by reframing the threat as a challenge. *Journal of Experimental Social Psychology, 46*, 166–171.

American College Health Association. (2018). *American College Health Association-National College Health Assessment II: Undergraduate Student Reference Group Executive Summary*, Spring 2018. Hanover, MD. Retrieved from www.acha.org/documents/ncha/NCHA-II_Spring_2018_Undergraduate_Reference_Group_Executive_Summary.pdf

Ames, C., & Archer, J. (1988). Achievement goals in the classroom: Students' learning strategies and motivation processes. *Journal of Educational Psychology, 80*, 260–267.

Ames, R., & Lau, S. (1982). An attributional analysis of student help-seeking in an academic setting. *Journal of Educational Psychology, 74*, 414–423.

Anderson, L. E., & Carta-Falsa, J. (2002). Factors that make faculty and student relationships effective. *College Teaching, 50*(4), 134–138.

Armstrong, S. L., & Newman, M. (2011). Teaching textual conversations: Intertextuality in the college reading classroom. *Journal of College Reading and Learning, 41*(2), 6–21.

Aronson, J. (2002). Stereotype threat: Contending and coping with unnerving expectations. In J. Aronson (Ed.), *Improving Academic Achievement: Impact of Psychological Factors on Education* (pp. 279–301). San Diego, CA: Academic Press.

Baker, L. (1989). Metacognition, comprehension monitoring, and the adult reader. *Educational Psychology Review, 1*, 3–38.

Bandura, A. (1977). Self-efficacy: Towards a unifying theory of behavioral change. *Psychological Review, 84*(2), 191–215.

Bandura, A. (1982). Self-efficacy mechanism in human agency. *American Psychologist, 37*, 122–147.

Bandura, A. (2015). On deconstructing commentaries regarding alternative theories of self-regulation. *Journal of Management, 41*(4), 1025–1044.

Bandura, A. (2018). Toward a psychology of human agency: Pathways and reflections. *Perspectives on Psychological Science, 13*(2), 130–136.

Bargh, J. A. (2015). Automatic information processing: Implications for communication and affect. In L. Donohew, H. E. Sypher, & E. T.. Higgins (Eds), *Communication, Social Cognition, and Affect* (pp. 9–27). London, UK: Psychology Press.

Bargh, J. A., & Chartrand, T. L. (1999). The unbearable automaticity of being. *American Psychologist, 54*, 462–479.

Beck, A. T. (1976). *Cognitive Therapies and Emotional Disorders*. New York: New American Library.

Bembenutty, H. (2011). Introduction of learning in postsecondary education. *New Directions for Teaching and Learning, 125*, 3–8.

Benson, H. (1976). *The Relaxation Response*. New York: Avon.

Berger, N., & Archer, J. (2018). Qualitative insights into the relationship between socioeconomic status and students' academic achievement goals. *Social Psychology of Education, 21*, 787–803.

Bjork, R. A. (2015). Forgetting as a friend of learning. In D. S. Lindsday, C. M. Kelley, A. P. Yonelinas, & H. L. Roediger (Eds), *Remembering: Attributions, Processes and Control in Human Memory* (pp. 15–28). New York: Taylor & Francis.

Bliss, E. (1983). *Doing It Now*. New York: Bantam.

Bloomberg Radio (Producer). (2018, March 30). *Bloomberg Radio Interview with Serena Williams* (B. Ritholtz, interviewer) [Interview transcript]. Retrieved from https://ritholtz.com/2018/03/transcript-serena-williams/

Boroujeni, S. T., & Shanbazi, M. (2011). The effect of instructional and motivational self-talk on performance of basketball's motor skill. *Procedia Social and Behavioral Sciences, 15*, 3113–3117.

Bower, G. H., Clark, M. C., Lesgold, A., & Winzenz, D. (1969). Hierarchical retrieval schemas in recall of categorized word lists. *Journal of Verbal Learning and Verbal Behavior, 8*, 323–343.

Bowman, L. L., Levine, L. E., Waite, B. M., & Gendron, M. (2010). Can students really multitask? An experimental study in instant messaging while reading. *Computers and Education, 54*, 927–931.

Bransford, J. D. (1979). *Human Cognition: Learning, Understanding, and Remembering.* Belmont, CA: Wadsworth.

Bransford, J. D., & Johnson, M. K. (1972). Contextual prerequisites for understanding: Some investigations of comprehension and recall. *Journal of Verbal Learning and Verbal Behavior, 11*, 717–726.

Britton, B. K., & Tesser, A. (1991). Effects of time management practices on college grades. *Journal of Educational Psychology, 83*, 405–410.

Brown, A. L. (1978). Knowing when, where, and how to remember: A problem of meta-cognition. In R. Glaser (Ed.), *Advances in Instructional Psychology* (pp. 77–165). Hillsdale, NJ: Erlbaum.

Brown, D. (2017). An evidence-based analysis of learning practices: The need for pharmacy students to employ more effective study strategies. *Currents in Pharmacy Teaching and Learning, 9*(2), 163–170.

Brownlow, S., & Reasinger, R. D. (2000). Putting off until tomorrow what is better done today: Academic procrastination as a function of motivation toward college work. *Journal of Social Behavior and Personality, 15*(5), 15–34.

Bryson, C., & Hand, L. (2007). The role of engagement in inspiring teaching and learning. *Innovations in Education and Teaching International, 44*, 349–362.

Burka, J. B., & Yuen, L. M. (1983). *Procrastination: Why You Do It and What to Do about It.* Reading, MA: Addison-Wesley.

Byrnes, J. P. (2001). *Minds, Brains, and Learning: Understanding the Psychological and Educational Relevance of Neuroscientific Research.* New York: Guilford Press.

Campus Computing Project. (2018). The 2018 Campus computing survey. Retrieved from https://www.campuscomputing.net/content/2018/10/31/the-2018-campus-computing-survey

Carpenter, S. K., Cepeda, N. J., Rohrer, D., Kang, S. H. K., & Pashler, H. (2012). Using spacing to enhance diverse forms of learning: Review of recent research and implications for instruction. *Educational Psychological Review, 24*, 369–378.

Cartwright, C. A., & Cartwright, G. P. (1984). *Developing Observation Skills* (2nd ed.). New York: McGraw-Hill.

Castillo, L., Conoley, C. W., Choi-Pearson, C., Archuleta, D. J., & Phoummarth, M. J. (2006). University environment as a mediator of Latino ethnic identity and persistence attitudes. *Journal of Counseling Psychology, 53*, 267–271.

Cheever, N. A., Rosen, L. D., Carrier, M., & Chavez, A. (2014). Out of sight is not out of mind: The impact of restricting wireless mobile device use on anxiety levels among low, moderate and high users. *Computers in Human Behavior, 37*, 290–297.

Coffield, F., Moseley, D., Hall, E., & Ecclestone, K. (2004). *Learning Styles and Pedagogy in Post-16 Learning: A Systematic and Critical Review.* Norwich, UK: Learning and Skills Research Centre.

Cortina, J., Elder, J., & Gonnet, K. (1995). *Comprehending College Textbooks* (3rd ed.). New York: McGraw-Hill.

Covey, S. R. (1990). *The 7 Habits of Highly Effective People.* New York: Simon & Schuster.

Covington, M. V. (1992). *Making the Grade: A Self-Worth Perspective on Motivation and School Reform.* New York: Cambridge University Press.

Covington, M. V., & Omelich, C. (1979). Effort: The double-edged sword in school achievement. *Journal of Educational Psychology, 71*, 169–182.

Covington, M. V., & Roberts, B. (1994). Self-worth and college achievement: Motivational and personality correlates. In P. R. Pintrich, D. R. Brown, & C. E. Weinstein (Eds), *Student Motivation, Cognition, and Learning: Essays in Honor of Wilbert J. McKeachie* (pp. 157–187). Hillsdale, NJ: Erlbaum.

Covington, M. V., von Hoene, L. M., & Voge, D. J. (2017). *Life beyond Grades: Designing College Courses to Promote Intrinsic Motivation.* Cambridge, UK: Cambridge University Press.

Cowan, N. (2005). Working memory capacity: Essays in cognitive psychology. The magical number 4 in short-term memory: A reconsideration of mental storage capacity. *Behavioral Brain Science, 24*, 87–185. New York: Taylor & Francis.

Cox, R. D. (2009). *The College Fear Factor: How Students and Professors Misunderstand One Another.* Cambridge, MA: Harvard University Press.

Crede, M., Roch, S. G., & Kieszczynka, U. R. (2010). Class attendance in college: A meta-analytic review of the relationship of class attendance with grades and student characteristics. *Review of Educational Research, 80*, 272–295.

Dahlstrom, E., & Bichsel, J. (2014). *ECAR Study of Undergraduate Students and Information Technology, 2014 Research Report*. Louisville, CO: ECAR. Retrieved from www.educause.edu/ecar. Accessed on February 17, 2016.

Daniel, D. B., & Woody, W. D. (2013). E-textbooks at what cost? Performance and use of electronic v. print texts. *Computers and Education, 62*, 18–23.

Daschmann, E. C., Goetz, T., & Stupnisky, R. H. (2011). Testing the predictors of boredom at school: Development and validation of the precursors to boredom scales. *British Journal of Educational Psychology, 81*(3), 421–440.

Davis, R. A. (1986). *Oceanography: An Introduction to the Marine Environment*. Dubuque, IA: Brown.

Dembo, M. H. (1994). *Applying Educational Psychology in the Classroom* (5th ed.). White Plains, NY: Longman.

Dieckmeyer, D., & Dembo, M. (2007). *Opening Pandora's Box: A Multicase Study of the Motivations of Developmental Reading Students in Community College*. Paper presented at the annual meeting of the American Educational Research Association, Chicago, IL.

Dole, J., Duffy, G., Roehler, L., & Person, P. D. (1991). Moving from the old to the new: Research on reading comprehension instruction. *Review of Educational Research, 61*, 239–264.

Douce, L. A., & Keeling, R. P. (2014). *A Strategic Primer on College Student Mental Health*. Retrieved from www.apa.org/pubs/newsletters/access/2014/10-14/college-mental-health.pdf. Accessed on November 17, 2015. Washington, DC: American Council on Education.

Duckworth, A. L., & Seligman, M. E. P. (2005). Self-discipline outdoes IQ in predicting academic performance of adolescents. *Psychological Science, 16*(12), 939–944.

Dunlosky, J., Rawson, K. A., Marsh, E. J., Nathan, M. J., & Willingham, D. T. (2013). Improving students' learning with effective learning techniques: Promising directions from cognitive and educational psychology. *Psychological Science, 14*(1), 4–58.

Dweck, C. S. (2006). *Mindset: The New Psychology of Success*. New York: Ballentine Books.

EAB. (2016). *How Late Is Too Late? Myths and Facts about the Consequences of Switching College Majors*. Washington, DC: Student Success Collaborative.

Eagan, K., Stolzenberg, E. B., Ramirez, J. J., Aragon, M. C., Suchard, M. R., & Hurtado, S. (2014). *The American freshman: National Norms Fall 2014*. Los Angeles, CA: Higher Education Research Institute, UCLA.

Eccles, J. A. (2007). Motivational perspective on school achievement: Taking responsibility for learning and teaching. In R. J. Sternberg, & R. F. Subotnik (Eds), *Optimizing Student Success in Schools with the New Three Rs* (pp. 199–202). Charlotte, NC: Information Age.

Eggen, P., & Kauchak, D. (1997). *Educational Psychology: Windows on Classrooms* (3rd ed.). Columbus, OH: Merrill.

El-Hindi, A. E. (2003). Connecting reading and writing: College learners' metacognitive awareness. In N. A. Stahl, & H. Boylan (Eds), *Teaching Developmental Reading: Historical, Theoretical, and Practical Background Readings* (pp. 350–362). Boston, MA: Bedford/St. Martin's.

Elliot, A. J., & Church, M. A. (1997). A hierarchical model of approach and avoidance achievement motivation. *Journal of Personality and Social Psychology, 72*, 218–232.

Ellis, A. (1998). How rational emotive behavior therapy belongs in the constructivist camp. In M. F. Hoyt (Ed.), *The Handbook of Constructive Therapies: Innovative Approaches from Leading Practitioners* (pp. 83–99). San Francisco, CA: Jossey-Bass.

Ellis, A., & Knaus, W. J. (1977). *Overcoming Procrastination*. New York: New American Library.

Engle, J., & Tinto, V. (2008). *Moving beyond Success: College for Low-Income, First-Generation Students*. Washington, DC: The Pell Institute.

Erikson, E. (1968). *Identity, Youth, and Crisis*. New York: Norton.

Ferrari, J. R. (2001). Getting things done on time: Conquering procrastination. In C. R. Snyder (Ed.), *Coping with Stress: Effective People and Processes* (pp. 30–46). New York: Oxford University Press.

Ferrari, J. R., Johnson, J. L., & McCown, W. G. (1995). *Procrastination and Task Avoidance: Theory, Research, and Treatment*. New York: Plenum.

Filback, R., & Robison, M. (2014). *Determining Credibility of Sources* [Class handout]. Los Angeles, CA: Rossier School of Education, University of Southern California.

Flavell, J. H. (1976). Metacognitive aspects of problem solving. In L. B. Resnick (Ed.), *The Nature of Intelligence* (pp. 231–235). Hillsdale, NJ: Erlbaum.

Flett, G. L., Hewitt, P. L., & Martin, T. R. (1995). Dimensions of perfectionism and procrastination. In J. R. Ferrari, J. L. Johnson, & W. G. McCown (Eds), *Procrastination and Task Avoidance: Theory, Research, and Treatment* (pp. 113–136). New York: Plenum.

Foner, E. (2017). *Give Me Liberty! An American History, Volume 2* (5th ed.) New York: Norton & Company, pp. 574–575.

Frender, G. (1990). *Learning to Learn*. Nashville, TN: Incentive.

Gagné, E. D. (1985). *The Cognitive Psychology of School Learning*. Boston, MA: Little Brown.

Gagné, E. D., Yekovich, C. W., & Yekovich, C. W. (1997). *The Cognitive Psychology of School Learning* (2nd ed.). New York: HarperCollins.

Gallwey, W. T. (1974). *The Inner Game of Tennis*. New York: Random House.

Garcia, T. (1995). The role of motivational strategies in self-regulated learning. *New Directions in Teaching and Learning, 63*, 29–42.

Garfield, H. Z. (1984). *Peak Performance*. New York: Warner.

Gaskins, I., & Elliot, T. (1991). *Implementing Cognitive Strategy Instruction across the School*. Cambridge, MA: Brookline.

Gillen-O'Neel, C., Huynh, V. W., & Fuligni, A. J. (2013). To study or to sleep? The academic costs of extra studying at the expense of sleep. *Child Development, 84*(1), 133–142.

Glaser, R. (1996). Changing the agency for learning: Acquiring expert performance. In K. Ericsson (Ed.), *The Road to Excellence: The Acquisition of Expert Performance in the Arts and Sciences, Sports and Games* (pp. 303–312). Mahwah, NJ: Lawrence Erlbaum Associates.

Goetz, E. T., Alexander, P. A., & Ash, M. J. (1992). *Educational Psychology: A Classroom Perspective*. New York: Macmillan.

Gollwitzer, P. (1999). Implementation intentions: Strong effects of simple plans. *American Psychologist, 54*(7), 493–503.

Gordon, T. (2001). *Leader Effectiveness Training: Proven Skills for Leading Today's Business into Tomorrow*. Berkeley, CA: Berkeley Publishing Group.

Hall, K. G., Domingues, D. A., & Cavazos, R. (1994). Contextual interference effects with skilled baseball players. *Perceptual and Motor Skills, 78*(3), 835–841.

Halpern, D. F. (1996). *Thought and Knowledge: Introduction to Critical Thinking* (3rd ed.). Mahwah, NJ: Lawrence Erlbaum Associates.

Hanson, T. L., Drumheller, K., Mallard, J., McKee, C., & Schlegel, P. (2011). Cell phones, text messaging, and Facebook: Competing time demands of today's college students. *College Teaching, 59*(1), 23–30.

Harackiewicz, J. M., Barron, K. E., Carter, S. M., Lehto, A. T., & Elliot, A. J. (1997). Predictors and consequences of achievement goals in the college classroom: Maintaining interest and making the grade. *Journal of Educational Psychology, 73*, 1284–1295.

Hardy, J., Gammage, K. L., & Hall, C. R. (2001). A descriptive study of athlete self-talk. *Sport Psychologist, 15*, 3006–3318.

Hartman, M., & Prichard, J. (2018). Calculating the contribution of sleep problems to undergraduates' academic success *Sleep Health, 4*(5), 463–471.

Hattie, J. A. C., & Donoghue, G. M. (2015). *Learning Strategies: A Synthesis and Conceptual Model*. Science of Learning Centre, University of Melbourne. Retrieved from www.nature.com/articles/npjscilearn 201613

Heiman, M., & Slomianko, J. (1993). *Success in College and beyond*. Cambridge, MA: Learning to Learn.

Hock, F. M., Deshler, D., & Schumaker, J. B. (2006). Enhancing student motivation through the pursuit of possible selves. In C. Dunkel, & J. Kerpelman (Eds), *Possible Selves: Theory, Research and Applications* (pp. 205–220.) New York: Nova Science Publishers.

Holt, J. (1982). *How Children Fail* (rev. ed.). New York: Delta.

Hopko, D. R., Ashcraft, M. H., Gute, J., Ruggierto, K. J., & Lewis, C. (1998). Mathematics anxiety and working memory: Support for the existence of a deficient inhibition mechanism. *Journal of Anxiety Disorders, 12*, 343–355.

Hunt, M. G., Marx, R., Lipson, C., & Young, J. (2018). No more FOMO: Limiting social media decreases loneliness and depression. *Journal of Social and Clinical Psychology, 37*(10), 751–768.

Husmann, P. R., & O'Loughlin, V. D. (2018). Another nail in the coffin for learning styles? Disparities among undergraduate anatomy students' study strategies, class performance, and reported VARK learning styles. *Journal of Social and Clinical Psychology, 37*, 751–768.

Isaacson, R. M. (2002, April). *Shocking College Students into Self-Regulation: When Hand-Holding and Jump-Starting Isn't Working*. Paper presented at the annual meeting of the American Educational Research Association, New Orleans, CA.

Jacobson, E. (1938). *Progressive Relaxation*. Chicago, IL: University of Chicago Press.

Jefferson County Schools. (1982). *Senior High Study Skills Booklet*. Jefferson County, Colorado, CO: Jefferson County Schools.

Jehangir, R. R. (2010). *Higher Education and First-Generation Students: Cultivating Community, Voice, and Place for the New Majority*. New York: Palgrave Macmillan.

Johnson, D. W. (2003). *Reaching Out: Interpersonal Effectiveness and Self-Actualization* (8th ed.). Boston, MA: Allyn & Bacon.

Johnson, D. W., Johnson, R. T., and Smith, K. A. (2013). *Cooperative Learning: Improving University Instruction by Basing Practice on Validated Theory*. Retrieved from http://personal.cege.umn.edu/~smith/docs/Johnson-Johnson-Smith-Cooperative_Learning-JECT-Small_Group_Learning-draft.pdf

Kanfer, R., & Heggestad, E. D. (1997). Motivational traits and skills: A person-centered approach to work motivation. *Research in Organizational Behavior, 19*, 1–56.

Karabenick, S. A., & Dembo, M. H. (2011). Understanding and facilitating self-regulated help seeking. *New Directions for Teaching and Learning, 126*, 33–43.

Karabenick, S. A., & Knapp, J. R. (1991). Relationship of academic help-seeking to the use of learning strategies and other instrumental achievement behavior in college students. *Journal of Educational Psychology, 83(2)*, 221–230.

Karabenick, S. A., & Newman, R. S. (Eds). (2011). *Help Seeking in Academic Settings: Goals, Groups, and Contexts*. New York: Routledge.

Kiewra, K. A. (2004). *Learn How to Study and Soar to Success*. Upper Saddle River, NJ: Pearson Education.

Kiewra, K. A., & DuBois, N. F. (1998). *Learning to Learn*. Boston, MA: Allyn & Bacon.

Kirschner, P. A., & De Bruyckere, P. (2017). The myths of the digital native and the multitasker. *Teaching and Teacher Education, 67*, 135–142.

Kirschner, P. A, & van Merriënboer, J. J. G. (2013). Do learners really know best? Urban legends in education. *Educational Psychologist, 48(3)*, 169–183.

Klassen, R. B., Krawchuk, L. L., & Rajani, S. (2008). Academic procrastination of undergraduates: Low self-efficacy to self-regulate predicts higher levels of procrastination. *Contemporary Educational Psychology, 33*, 915–931.

Kong, Y., Seo, Y. S., & Zhai, L. (2018). Comparison of reading performance on screen and on paper: A meta-analysis. *Computers and Education, 123*, 138–149.

Kornell, N., Castel, A. D., Eich, T. S., & Bjork, R. A. (2010). Spacing as the friend of both memory and induction in young and older adults. *Psychology and Aging, 25(2)*, 498–503.

Kross, E., et al. (2014). Self-talk as a regulatory mechanism: How you do it matters. *Journal of Personality and Social Psychology, 106(2)*, 304–324.

Larson, R., & Richard, M. (1991). Boredom in the middle school years: Blaming schools versus students. *American Journal of Education, 99*, 418–443.

Latané, B., Williams, K., & Harkins, S. (1979). Many hands make light the work: The causes and consequences of social loafing. *Journal of Personality and Social Psychology, 37*, 822–832.

Lavoie, J. A. A., & Pychyl, T. A. (2001). Cyberslacking and the procrastination superhighway: A web-based survey of online procrastination, attitudes and emotion. *Social Science Computer Review, 19*, 431–444.

Levine, L. E., Waite, B. M., & Bowman, L. L. (2007). Electronic media use and distractibility for academic reading in college youth. *CyberPsychology & Behavior, 10(4)*, 560–566.

Levy, B. (1996). Improving memory in old age through implicit self-stereotyping. *Journal of Personality and Social Psychology, 71*, 1092–1107.

Lewis, N. A., Jr., & Oyserman, D. (2015). When does the future begin? Time metrics matter, connecting present and future selves. *Psychological Science, 26(6)*, 816–825.

Light, R. J. (2001). *Making the Most of College: Students Speak Their Minds*. Cambridge, MA: Harvard University Press.

Locke, E. A., & Latham, G. P. (1990). *A Theory of Goal Setting and Task Performance*. Englewood Cliffs, NJ: Prentice Hall.

Locke, E. A., & Latham, G. P. (2002). Building a practically useful theory of goal setting and task motivation: A 35-year odyssey. *American Psychologist, 57*, 705–717.

Locke, E. A., & Latham, G. P. (2013). *New Developments in Goal Setting and Task Performance*. New York: Routledge.

Lund, H. G., Reider, B. D., Whiting, A. B., & Prichard, J. R. (2010). Sleep patterns and predictors of disturbed sleep in a large population of college students. *Journal of Adolescent Health, 46*, 124–132.

MacCann, C., Fogarty, G. J., & Roberts, R. D. (2012). Strategies for success in education: Time management is more important for part-time than full-time community college students. *Learning and Individual Differences, 22*, 618–623.

McCombs, B., & Encinias, P. (1987). Goal Setting. Coping Strategies Program. Unpublished manuscript, University of Colorado at Denver, CO.

McKay, M., Davis, M., & Fanning, P. (1997). *Thought and Feelings: Taking Control of Your Moods and Your Life*. Oakland, CA: New Harbinger.

McWhorter, K. T. (2010). *Study and Critical Thinking Skills in College* (7th ed.). Boston, MA: Longman.

Markus, H., & Nurius, P. (1986). Possible selves. *American Psychologist, 41*, 954–969.

Marshall, C. (2014). *Cat videos on YouTube: 2 million uploads, 25 billion views*. ReelSEO. Retrieved from www.reelseo.com/2-million-cat-videos-youtube/

Martin, A. (2010). *Building Classroom Success: Eliminating Academic Fear and Failure*. New York: Continuum International Publishing Group.

Martin, M. M., Cayanus, J. L., Weber, K., & Goodboy, A. K. (2009), College students' stress and its impact on their motivation and communication with their instructors. In D. H. Elsworth (Ed.), *Motivation in Education* (pp. 91–111). New York: Nova.

Mayer, R. E. (2008). *Learning and Instruction* (2nd ed.). Upper Saddle River, NJ: Pearson.

Mearns, K., Meyer, J., & Bharadwaj, A. (2007). *Student Engagement in Human Biology Practical Sessions*. Refereed paper presented at the Teaching and Learning Form, Curtin University of Technology. Retrieved from http//otl.curtin.edu.au/tlf/tlf2007/refereed/mearns.html

Merrell, K. W. (2001). *Helping Students Overcome Depression and Anxiety*. New York: Guilford.

Mihajlov, M., & Vejmelka, L. (2017). Internet addiction: A review of the first twenty years. *Psychiatria Danubina, 29*, 260–272.

Miller, G. A. (1956). The magical number seven, plus or minus two: Some limits on our capacity to process information. *Psychological Review, 63*, 81–97.

Morales, E. (2010). *How Protective Factors Mitigate Risk and Facilitate Academic Resilience among Poor Minority College Students*. New York: Nova Science Publishers.

Mrazek, M. D., Franklin, M. S., Phillips, D. T., Baird, B., & Schooler, J. W. (2013). Mindfulness training improves working memory capacity and GRE performance while reducing mind wandering. *Psychological Science, 24*(5), 776–781.

Mueller, P. A., & Oppenheimer, D. M. (2016). Technology and note-taking in the classroom, boardroom, hospital room, and courtroom. *Trends in Neuroscience and Education, 5*, 139–145.

Mullen, A. L. (2010). *Degrees of Inequality: Culture, Class, and Gender in American Higher Education*. Baltimore, MD: John Hopkins University Press.

Nett, U. E., Goetz, T., & Daniels, L. M. (2010). What to do when feeling bored? Students' strategies for coping with boredom. *Learning and Individual Differences, 20*, 626–638.

Newman, E. (1996). *No More Test Anxiety*. Los Angeles, CA: Learning Skills Publications.

Newman, R. S. (1991). Goals and self-regulated learning: What motivates children to seek academic help. In M. L. Maehr & P. L. Pintrich (Eds), *Advances in Motivation and Achievement* (Vol. 7, pp. 151–183). Greenwich, CT: JAI.

Newman, R. S., & Schwager, M. T. (1992). Student perceptions and academic help-seeking. In D. H. Schunk & M. T. Meece (Eds), *Student Perceptions in the Classroom* (pp. 123–146). Hillsdale, NJ: Lawrence Erlbaum Associates.

Oliver, E. J., Markland, D., Hardy, J., & Petherick, C. M. (2009). The effects of autonomy-supportive and controlling environments on self-talk. *Motivation and Emotion, 32*, 200–212.

Ormrod, J. E. (2015). *Human Learning* (7th ed.). Englewood Cliffs, NJ: Prentice Hall.

Ottens, A. J. (1991). *Coping with Academic Anxiety* (2nd ed.). New York: Rosen.

Oyserman, D., Bybee D., & Terry, K. (2006). Possible selves and academic outcomes: How and when possible selves impel action? *Journal of Personality and Social Psychology, 91*(1), 188–204.

Oyserman, D., Bybee, D., Terry, K., & Hart-Johnson, T. (2004). Possible selves as roadmaps. *Journal of Research in Personality, 38*, 130–149.

Oyserman, D., Destin, M., & Novin, S. (2015). The context-sensitive future self: Possible selves motivate in context, not otherwise. *Self and Identity, 14*(2), 173–188.

Oyserman, D., & Markus, H. (1990). Possible selves and delinquency. *Journal of Personality and Social Psychology, 59*, 112–125.

Pashler, H., McDaniel, M., Rohrer, D., & Bjork, R. (2009). Learning styles: Concepts and evidence. *Psychological Science in the Public Interest, 9*(3), 103–119.

Pauk, W. (1993). *How to Study in College*. Boston, MA: Houghton-Mifflin.

Pekrun, R., Elliott, A. J., & Maier, M. A. (2006). Achievement goals and discrete achievement emotions: A theoretical model and prospective test. *Journal of Educational Psychology, 98*(3), 583–597.

Pekrun, R., Goetz, T., Daniels, L. M., & Stupnisky, R. H. (2010). Boredom in achievement settings: Exploring control-value antecedents and performance outcomes of a neglected emotion. *Journal of Educational Psychology, 102,* 531–549.

Pekrun, R., Perry, R. P., & Linnenbrink-Garcia, L. (2014). Control-value theory of achievement emotions. In Pekrun, R., & Linnenbrink-Garcia. L. (Eds), *International Handbook of Emotions in Education.* New York: Routledge.

Peurifoy, R. Z. (1995). *Anxiety, Phobias, and Panic.* New York: Warner.

Pintrich, P. R. (1994). Student motivation in the college classroom. In K. W. Prichard, & R. M. Sawyer (Eds), *Handbook of College Teaching: Theory and Applications* (pp. 23–43). Westport, CT: Greenwood.

Poli, R. (2017). Internet addiction update: Diagnostic criteria, assessment and prevalence. *Neuropsychiatry, 7,* 4–8.

Pope, R. L., & Reynolds, A. L. (2017). Multidimensional identity model revisited: Implications for student affairs. *New Directions in Student Services, 157,* 15–24.

Prochaska, J. O., & Prochaska, J. M. (1999). Why don't continents move? Why don't people change? *Journal of Psychotherapy Integration, 9,* 83–102.

Ramirez, G., & Beilock, S. L. (2011). Writing about test worries boosts exam performance in the classroom. *Science, 331,* 211–213.

Reeve, J. (1996). *Motivating Others: Nurturing Inner Motivational Resources.* Boston, MA: Allyn & Bacon.

Reeve, J. (2015). *Understanding Motivation and Emotion* (6th ed.). Hoboken, NJ: John Wiley and Sons.

Richardson, R. C., & Skinner, E. F. (1992). Helping first-generation minority students achieve degrees. In L. S. Zwerling & H. B. London (Eds), *First Generation College Student: Confronting the Cultural Issues* (pp. 29–43). San Francisco, CA: Jossey-Bass.

Richland, L. E., Kornell, N., & Kao, L. S. (2009). The pretesting effect: Do unsuccessful retrieval attempts enhance learning? *Journal of Experimental Psychology, 15*(3), 243–257.

Robertson, A. K. (1994). *Listen for Success: A Guide for Effective Listening.* Burr Bridge, IL: Irwin Professional.

Roediger, H. L., II, & Butler, A. C. (2011). The critical role of retrieval practice in long-term retention. *Trends in Cognitive Sciences, 15,* 20–27.

Roediger, H. L., & Pyc, M. A. (2012). Inexpensive techniques to improve education: Applying cognitive psychology to enhance educational practice. *Journal of Applied Research in Memory and Cognition, 1,* 242–248.

Rohrer, D., & Taylor, K. (2007). The shuffling of mathematics problems improves learning. *Instructional Science, 35*(6), 481–498.

Rowland, C. A. (2014). The effect of testing versus restudy on retention: A meta-analytic review of the testing effect. *Psychological Bulletin, 140*(6), 1432–1463.

Rubinstein, J. S., Meyer, D. E., & Evans, J. E. (2001). Executive control of cognitive processes in task switching. *Journal of Experimental Psychology: Human Perception and Performance, 27*(4), 763–797.

Sabini, U. (1995). *Social Psychology* (2nd ed.). New York: Norton.

Sana, F., Weston, T., & Cepeda, N. J. (2013). Laptop multitasking hinders classroom learning for both users and nearby peers. *Computers and Education, 62,* 24–31.

Schacter, D. L. (2001). *The Seven Sins of Memory: How the Mind Forgets and Remembers.* Boston, MA: Houghton Mifflin.

Schraw, G., & Dennison, R. S. (1994). Assessing metacognitive awareness. *Contemporary Educational Psychology, 19,* 460–475.

Schunk, D. H. (1982). Verbal self-regulation as a facilitator of children's achievement and self-efficacy. *Human Learning, 1,* 265–277.

Schunk, D. H. (1989). Self-efficacy and cognitive skill learning. In C. Ames & R. Ames (Eds), *Research on Motivation in Education: Goals and Cognition* (Vol. 3, pp. 13–44). San Diego, CA: Academic Press.

Schunk, D. H. (1991). Goal setting and self-evaluation: A social cognitive perspective on self-regulation. In M. L. Maehr, & P. R. Pintrich (Eds), *Advances in Motivation and Achievement* (Vol. 7, pp. 85–113). Greenwich, CT: JAI.

Seaman, J. E., Allen, I. E., & Seaman, J. (2018). *Grade Increase: Tracking Distance Education in the United States.* Babson Survey Research Group. Retrieved December 12, 2018 from https://files.eric.ed.gov/full text/ED580852.pdf

Shin, R. Q., Welch, J. C., Kaya, A. E., Yeung, J. G., Obana, C., Sharma, R., Vernay, C. N., & Yee, S. (2017). The intersectionality framework and identity intersections. *Journal of Counseling Psychology and the Counseling Psychologist: A Content Analysis Journal of Counseling Psychology, 64*(5), 458–474.

Simon, S. B., Howe, L. W., & Kirschenbaum, H. (1995). *Values Clarification. A Handbook of Practical Strategies for Teachers and Students.* New York: Hart.

Skinner, M. E. (2004). College students with learning disabilities speak out: What it takes to be successful in postsecondary education. *Journal of Postsecondary Education and Disability, 17*(2), 91–104.

Smith, H. (1994). *The 10 Natural Laws of Successful Time and Life Management.* New York: Warner.

Smith, M. S., Glenberg, A., & Bjork, R. A. (1978). Environmental context and human memory. *Memory & Cognition, 6*(4), 342–353.

Smith, R. M. (1982). *Learning How to Learn: Applied Theory for Adults.* New York: Cambridge University Press.

Spencer, S. J., Steele, C. M., & Quinn, D. M. (1999). Stereotype threat and women's math performance. *Journal of Experimental Social Psychology, 35,* 4–28.

Steel, P. (2007). The nature of procrastination: A meta-analytic and theoretical review of quintessential self-regulatory failure. *Psychological Bulletin, 133*(1), 65–94.

Steel, P., & Ferrari, J. (2013). Sex, education and procrastination: An epidemiological study of procrastinators' characteristics from a global sample. *European Journal of Personality, 27*(1), 51–58.

Steele, C. M. (1999, August). *Thin Ice: "Stereotype Threat" and Black College Students.* Retrieved from The Atlantic Monthly online www.theatlantic.com/issues/99aug/9908stereotype.htm

Steele, C. M., & Aronson, J. (1995). Stereotype threat and the intellectual test performance of African-Americans. *Journal of Personality and Social Psychology, 69,* 797–811.

Steele, C. M., Spencer, S. J., Hummel, M., Carter, K., Harber, K., Schoem, D., & Nisbett, R. (1997). *African-American College Achievement: A "Wise" Intervention.* Unpublished manuscript, Stanford University, CA.

Stepich, D. A., & Newby, T. J. (1988). Analogical instruction within the information processing paradigm: Effective means to facilitate learning. *Instructional Science, 17,* 129–144.

Tandoc, E. C., Ferrucci, P., & Duffy, M. (2015). Facebook use, envy, and depression among college students: Is facebooking depressing? *Computers in Human Behavior, 43,* 139–146.

Tindell, D. R., & Bohlander, R. W. (2012). The use and abuse of cell phones and text messaging in the classroom: A survey of college students. *College Teaching, 60*(1), 1–9.

Titsworth, S. B., & Kiewra, K. A. (2004). Spoken organizational lecture cues and student notetaking as facilitators of student learning. *Contemporary Educational Psychology, 29,* 447–461.

Travis, F., Haaga, D. A. F., Hagelin, J., Tanner, M., Nidich, S., Gaylord-King, C., Grosswalk, S., Rainforth, M., & Schneider, R. H. (2009). Effects of transcendental meditation practice on brain functioning and stress reactivity in college students. *International Journal of Psychophysiology, 71,* 170–176.

Twenge, J. M., Martin, G. N., & Campbell, W. K. (2018). Decreases in psychological well-being among American adolescents after 2012 and links to screen time during the rise of smartphone technology. *Emotion, 18*(6), 765–780.

University of Southern California. (2013). *Academic Integrity.* Retrieved December 13, 2018 from https://sjacs.usc.edu/files/2015/11/Academic-Integrity-sheet-2013.pdf

US Department of Education, National Center for Education Statistics (NCES). (2018). *The Condition of Education 2018. Undergraduate Retention and Graduation Rates.* Retrieved from https://nces.ed.gov/programs/coe/indicator_ctr.asp

Van Blerkom, D. L. (1994). *College Study Skills: Becoming a Strategic Learner.* Belmont, CA: Wadsworth.

Van Blerkom, D. L. (2012). *College Study Skills: Becoming a Strategic Learner* (7th ed.). Boston, MA: Wadsworth.

Vasts, R., Haith, M. M., & Miller, S. A. (1992). *Child Psychology: The Modern Science.* New York: Wiley.

Wang, W. (2001). Internet dependency and psychosocial maturity among college students. *International Journal of Human-Computer Studies, 55,* 919–938.

Weiner, B. (1986). *An Attributional Theory of Motivation and Emotion.* New York: Springer-Verlag.

Weiner, B. (2018). The legacy of an attribution approach to motivation and emotion: A no-crisis zone. *Motivation Science, 4*(1), 4–14.

Weinstein, C. E., Acee, T. W., & Jung, J. (2011). Self-regulation and learning strategies. *New Directions for Teaching and Learning, 126,* 45–53.

Weinstein, C. E., Schulte, A. C., & Palmer, D. R. (1987). *LASSI: Learning and Study Strategies Inventory.* Clearwater, FL: H&H.

Weinstein, C. L., & Mayer, R. E. (1986). The teaching of learning strategies. In M. Wittrock (Ed.), *Handbook of Research on Teaching* (3rd ed., pp. 315–327). New York: Macmillan.

Weir, K. (2017, March). Seven ways to overhaul your smartphone use. *Monitor on Psychology, 48*(3), 48.

West, C., & Sadoski, M. (2011). Do study strategies predict academic performance in medical school? *Medical Education*, *45*(7), 696–703.

Wieber, F., von Suchodoletz, A., Heikamp, T., Trommsdorff, G., & Gollwitzer, P. M. (2011). If-then planning helps school-aged children to ignore attractive distractions. *Social Psychology*, *42*(1), 39–47.

Willingham, D. T., Hughes, E. M., & Dobolyi, D. G. (2015). The scientific status of learning styles. *Teaching of Psychology*, *42*(3), 266–271.

Wolff, F. I., & Marsnik, N. C. (1992). *Perceptive Listening* (2nd ed.). Fort Worth, TX: Harcourt Brace.

Wolters, C. A. (1998). Self-regulated learning and college students' regulation of motivation. *Journal of Educational Psychology*, *90*, 224–235.

Woo, E. (2018). The neuroscience of education. *Rossier Magazine*, Spring-Summer, 5–7.

Xue, G., Dong, Q., Chen, C., Lu, Z., Mumford, J. A., & Poldrack, R. A. (2010). Greater neural pattern similarity across repetitions is associated with better memory. *Science*, *97*, 330.

Youngs, B. B. (1985). *Stress in Children: How to Recognize, Avoid, and Overcome It.* New York: Arbor House.

Zeidner, M. (2007). Test anxiety in educational contexts: Concepts, findings, and future directions. In P. A. Schutz & R. Pekrun (Eds), *Emotion in Education* (pp. 165–184). San Diego, CA: Elsevier.

Zeidner, M., & Matthews, G. (2011). *Anxiety 101*. New York: Springer.

Zhao, C., & Kuh, G. (2004). Adding value: Learning communities and student engagement. *Research in Higher Education*, *45*, 115–118.

Zimmerman, B. J. (1989). *Self-Regulated Learning and Academic Achievement: Theory, Research, and Practice*. New York: Springer-Verlag.

Zimmerman, B. J. (1998). Academic studying and the development of personal skill: A self-regulatory perspective. *Educational Psychologist*, *33*(2/3), 73–86.

Zimmerman, B. J. (2011). Motivational sources and outcomes of self-regulated learning and performance. In B. J. Zimmerman & D. H. Schunk (Eds), *Handbook of Self-Regulation of Learning and Performance* (pp. 49–64). New York: Taylor Francis.

Zimmerman, B. J. (2015). *Self-Regulated Learning: Theories, Measures, and Outcomes. International Encyclopedia of the Social & Behavioral Sciences*. Elsevier. Retrieved from www.sciencedirect.com/ science/article/pii/B9780080970868260601

Zimmerman, B. J., Bonner, S., & Kovach, R. (1996). *Developing Self-Regulated Learners: Beyond Achievement to Self-Efficacy*. Washington, DC: American Psychological Association.

Zimmerman, B. J., & Kitsantas, A. (1997). Developmental phases in self-regulation: Shifting from process to outcome goals. *Journal of Educational Psychology*, *89*, 29–36.

Zimmerman, B. J., & Kitsantas, A. (1999). Acquiring writing revision skill: Shifting from process to outcome self-regulatory goals. *Journal of Educational Psychology*, *91*(2), 241–250.

Zimmerman, B. J., & Martinez-Pons, M. (1986). Development of a structured interview for assessing student use of self-regulated learning strategies. *American Educational Research Journal*, *23*, 614–628.

Zimmerman, B. J., & Martinez-Pons, M. (1988). Construct validation of a strategy model of student self-regulation. *Journal of Educational Psychology*, *80*, 284–290.

Zimmerman, B. J., & Risemberg, R. (1997). Self-regulatory dimensions of academic learning and motivation. In G. D. Phye (Ed.), *Handbook of Academic Learning: Construction of Knowledge* (pp. 105–125). San Diego, CA: Academic Press.

Zimmerman, B. J., & Schunk, D. H. (2008). Motivation: An essential dimension of self-regulated learning. In D. H. Schunk, & B. J. Zimmerman (Eds), *Motivation and Self-Regulated Learning: Theory, Research, and Applications* (pp. 1–36). Mahwah, NJ: Erlbaum.

Zimmerman, B. J., Schunk, D. H., & DiBenedetto, M. K. (2015). A personal agency view of self-regulated learning: The role of goal setting. In F. Guay, H. Marsh, D. M. McInerney, & R. G. Craven (Eds), *International Advances in Self Research. Self-Concept, Motivation and Identity: Underpinning Success with Research and Practice* (pp. 83–114). Charlotte, NC: IAP Information Age Publishing.

Name Index

Subject Index

Lightning Source UK Ltd.
Milton Keynes UK
UKHW030618111122
411890UK00025B/432